Belay Seyoum

Export-Import Theory, Practices, and Procedures

Pre-publication
REVIEW

"**I**f there ever was a hand-holding guide for taking exporters and/or importers through all the necessary steps of the processes involved, this is it. Everything from how to obtain an ATA carnet to a detailed guide on the various available kinds of letters of credit is included. A number of off-text highlight boxes, examples, and other learning devices are effectively used. For example, customs valuation, which can be a bedeviling exercise, is fully explained and illustrated with two examples and appropriate off-text material. The end-of-chapter material is also very useful in and of itself. This includes the chapter summaries, a list of references for further reading, and a list of relevant World Wide Web resources that will be as highly useful to the time-pressured executive as to the researcher.

Overall, I found this book to be both informative and effective. Readers in the export and/or import business, and those who help to train them in everything from college to seminar settings, will find it a highly useful addition to their library."

Nicolas Papadopoulos, DBA
Professor of Marketing
and International Business
and Director, International
Business Study Group,
School of Business, Carleton University,
Ottawa, Canada

Export-Import Theory, Practices, and Procedures

INTERNATIONAL BUSINESS PRESS
Erdener Kaynak, PhD
Executive Editor

New, Recent, and Forthcoming Titles:

How to Manage for International Competitiveness edited by Abbas J. Ali

International Business Expansion into Less-Developed Countries: The International Finance Corporation and Its Operations by James C. Baker

Product-Country Images: Impact and Role in International Marketing edited by Nicolas Papadopoulos and Louise A. Heslop

The Global Business: Four Key Marketing Strategies edited by Erdener Kaynak

Multinational Strategic Alliances edited by Refik Culpan

Market Evolution in Developing Countries: The Unfolding of the Indian Market by Subhash C. Jain

A Guide to Successful Business Relations with the Chinese: Opening the Great Wall's Gate by Huang Quanyu, Richard Andrulis, and Chen Tong

Industrial Products: A Guide to the International Marketing Economics Model by Hans Jansson

Euromarketing: Effective Strategies for International Trade and Export edited by Salah S. Hassan and Erdener Kaynak

How to Utilize New Information Technology in the Global Marketplace: A Basic Guide edited by Fahri Karakaya and Erdener Kaynak

International Negotiating: A Primer for American Business Professionals by Michael Kublin

The Eight Core Values of the Japanese Businessman: Toward an Understanding of Japanese Management by Yasutaka Sai

Implementation of Total Quality Management: A Comprehensive Training Program by Rolf E. Rogers

An International Accounting Practice Set: The Karissa Jean's Simulation by David R. Peterson and Nancy Schendel

Privatization and Entrepreneurship: The Managerial Challenge in Central and Eastern Europe by Arieh Ullmann and Alfred Lewis

U.S. Trade, Foreign Direct Investments, and Global Competitiveness by Rolf Hackmann

Business Decision Making in China by Huang Quanyu, Joseph Leonard, and Chen Tong

International Management Leadership: The Primary Competitive Advantage by Raimo W. Nurmi and John R. Darling

The Trans-Oceanic Marketing Channel: A New Tool for Understanding Tropical Africa's Export Agriculture by H. Laurens van der Laan

Handbook of Cross-Cultural Marketing by Paul A. Herbig

Guide to Software Export: A Handbook for International Software Sales by Roger Philips

Executive Development and Organizational Learning for Global Business edited by J. Bernard Keys and Robert M. Fulmer

Contextual Management: A Global Perspective by Raghbir (Raj) S. Basi

Japan and China: The Meeting of Asia's Economic Giants by Kazua John Fukuda

Export Savvy: From Basics to Strategy by Zak Karamally

Strategic Networks: The Art of Japanese Interfirm Cooperation by Frank-Jürgen Richter

Export-Import Theory, Practices, and Procedures by Belay Seyoum

Globalization of Business: Practice and Theory by Abbas J. Ali

Internationalization of Companies from Developing Countries by John Kuada and Olav Jull Sørensen

Export-Import Theory, Practices, and Procedures

Belay Seyoum

International Business Press®
An Imprint of The Haworth Press, Inc.
New York • London • Oxford

Published by

International Business Press®, an imprint of The Haworth Press, Inc., 10 Alice Street, Binghamton, NY 13904-1580

Cover design by Jennifer M. Gaska.

The Library of Congress has cataloged the hardcover edition of this book as:

Seyoum, Belay, 1956
    Export-import theory, practices, and procedures / Belay Seyoum.
       p.   cm.
    Includes bibliographical references and index.
    ISBN 0-7890-0567-0 (hardcover : alk. paper)
     1. Exports. 2. Imports. 3. Export marketing. 4. International trade. I. Title.
HF1414.4.S49 2000
382—dc21
                                                            99-36499
                                                               CIP

ISBN 0-7890-0568-9 (pbk.)

CONTENTS

ABOUT THE AUTHOR

Belay Seyoum is Associate Professor of International Business Studies at Nova Southeastern University in Fort Lauderdale, Florida, where he teaches a variety of courses in international business and economics. Prior to coming to Nova Southeastern, Dr. Seyoum taught international business at Concordia University and McGill University in Montreal, Canada. Dr. Seyoum has published two books as well as numerous articles in the area of international trade in several prestigious academic journals such as the *Journal of World Trade,* the *International Trade Journal,* the *Columbia Journal of World Business,* and the *Journal of Global Business.*

Preface

This book resulted from the author's realization of the inadequacy of existing books to serve the needs of the academic/professional audience. Most of the books published in this area lack substance and provide only soft coverage of international trade operations. Another problem is that they hardly discuss theoretical issues such as the role of exports/imports in the global economy or pertinent regulatory and policy issues. Current books are almost exclusively devoted to export activities and provide only cursory treatment of import processes. Furthermore, most offer no discussion of current research information in the area.

STRENGTHS AND FEATURES OF THIS BOOK

1. *Conceptual and theoretical approach:* The book develops a conceptual/theoretical framework to explain international trade operations. Important scholarly studies are adequately treated in each chapter. Sufficient attention is also given to important legal and policy issues affecting export/import trade.
2. *Depth and breadth:* The book provides a comprehensive and analytical treatment of pertinent topics in the area. In addition to exports, the book provides an in-depth examination of import trade. Adequate coverage is also given to emerging areas such as intellectual property, countertrade, the role of logistics and transportation, regional trade arrangements, and so forth. There is no book on the market that comes close in terms of scholarly substance.
3. *Presentation:* The book is written in a pedagogically sound manner by including end-of-chapter summaries, references, World Wide Web sources, as well as learning aids such as vignettes, figures, and tables.

ACKNOWLEDGMENTS

I would like to acknowledge the assistance of my brother, Gizachew Seyoum, for his help with preparing the vignettes as well as for his valuable comments. I also thank Lia Hemphill for proofreading several chapters of the manuscript and for her feedback.

Writing a book is a major undertaking. However, the reward comes not only from its publication but from its useful contribution to those in the field (students, professors, professionals, researchers, etc.), not only in understanding international trade policies and practices, but also in encouraging additional research and dialogue.

Introduction

A Brief History of International Trade

ANCIENT PERIOD

- International trade based on the free exchange of goods started as early as 2500 B.C. Archaeological discoveries indicate that the Sumerians of Northern Mesopotamia enjoyed great prosperity based on trade by sea in textiles and metals. The Greeks profited by the exchange of olive oil and wine for grain and metal somewhere before 2000 B.C.
- By around 340 B.C., many devices of modern commerce had made their appearance in Greece and its distant settlements: banking and credit, insurance, trade treaties, and special diplomatic and other privileges.
- With the decline of Greece, Rome became powerful and began to expand to the East. In the first century A.D., the Romans traded with the Chinese along the silk road and developed many trade routes and complex trading patterns by sea. However, the absence of peace made traveling unsafe and discouraged the movement of goods, resulting in the loss of distant markets.
- By the time of the breakup of the Roman Empire in the fifth century, the papacy (papal supremacy) had emerged as a strong institution in a new and unstable world. The church's support (sponsorship) for the crusades (eleventh century) revived international trade in the West through the latter's discovery and introduction of new ideas, customs, and products from the East. New products such as carpets, furniture, sugar, and spices brought from Egypt, Syria, India, and China stimulated the markets and the growing commercial life of the West. This helped Italian cities such as Venice and Genoa to prosper and to replace Constantinople as the leading center of international commerce. Letters of credit and bills of exchange and insurance of goods in transit were extensively used to accommodate the growing commercial and financial needs of merchants and travelers.

- By the end of the fifteenth century, the center of international commerce had moved from the Mediterranean to Western Europe. Spain, Portugal, and later Holland became the focal points of international commercial activity. The more developed areas of Europe were changing from a subsistence economy to one relying heavily on imports paid by money or letters of credit.

COLONIAL PERIOD (1500-1900)

- With the discovery of America in 1492, and sea routes to India in 1498, trade flourished and luxury goods and food products such as sugar, tobacco, and coffee became readily available in the markets of Europe.
- The principal motivations behind global expansion (colonization) in the fifteenth century had been to enhance national economic power (mercantilist policy) by exploiting the colonies for the exclusive benefit of the mother country. Colonies were regarded as outposts of the home economy that would reduce trade dependence on rival nations and augment national treasure through exports as well as discoveries of precious metals. This first phase of colonization, which lasted until the advent of the Industrial Revolution in England (1750), was characterized by the following general elements with respect to commerce:
  1. All commerce between the colonies and the mother country was a national monopoly, meaning all merchandise exports/imports had to be carried by ships of the mother country and pass through specified ports.
  2. Little encouragement was provided toward the development or diversification of indigenous exports. For example, in 1600, precious metals constituted 90 percent of colonial exports to Spain. In the mid-1650s, British imports from its colonies were mainly concentrated in three primary products: sugar, tobacco, and furs. To protect domestic producers, competing colonial exports were restricted or subject to special duties. The patterns of economic relations were fashioned on the basis of dissimilarity, that is, noncompetitiveness of colonial and metropolitan production.
  3. Certain enumerated products could only be exported to the mother country or another colony. The policy ensured a supply of strategic foodstuffs and raw materials.
  4. Private companies in the metropolis received a charter from the government that granted them (i.e., the companies) a monopoly

of trade in the colonies. In most cases, the charter also granted complete local administrative authority, ranging from the making of laws and administration of justice to imposition of taxes. Examples of this include the British East India Company (1600), the Dutch West India Company (1621), and Hudson's Bay Company (1670).

- The second historical phase of overseas expansion (1765-1900) was dictated more by commercial considerations than by mere territorial gains. Britain emerged as the dominant colonial power and by 1815 had transformed its empire into a worldwide business concern. By the 1860s, the Industrial Revolution had transformed the social and economic structure of England, and mass production dictated an expansion of the market for goods on an international scale. The political economy of mercantilism that had proliferated over the preceding century was gradually replaced by that of free trade. By 1860, Britain had unilaterally repealed the Corn Laws, abolished the Navigation Act restrictions (foreign ships were permitted to take colonial goods anywhere), as well as the commercial monopolies given to particular companies. Preferential duties on empire goods were gradually abolished. In trade, as in foreign policy, Britain led the free trade ideology based on non-discrimination. At the time, Britain was most likely to benefit from free trade because of its industrial and commercial lead over other nations.

1900 TO THE PRESENT

- The major characteristics of economic relations from 1900 until the outbreak of World War I were the further development of trade and the emergence of a world economy. These were also the result of the international migration of people and capital from Europe, particularly Britain, since the 1850s, to other countries such as the United States, Australia, Argentina, Brazil, and Canada. This pattern of world economy provided the industrial economies with new sources of food and raw materials and new markets for exports of manufactures. For example, by 1913, Brazil was the source of two-thirds of German coffee imports, whereas North Africa supplied over half of French imports of wine. However, much of the import trade in Europe was subject to trade restrictions, such as tariffs, to secure home markets for local producers. Even within Britain, there were mounting pressures for the abolition of free trade.

- The post-World War I recovery was further delayed by the disruption of trading links, as new nations were created and borders were re-drawn. State intervention and restrictive economic policies had been consolidated in Europe and other countries by the end of the war. The U.S. government introduced the Fordney-McCumber Tariff in 1922, which imposed high tariffs on agricultural imports, and later the Smoot-Hawley Tariff in 1930, which provoked widespread retal-iation. Britain imposed high duties on various industrial products, such as precision instruments and synthetic organic chemicals, to en-courage domestic production under the Safeguarding of Industries Act, 1921. The volume of world trade in manufactures fell by 35 per-cent between 1929 and 1932, and prices also fell by a similar amount. The volume of trade in primary products fell by 15 percent, but prices fell by about 50 percent. To alleviate the worst effects of the Depression, countries resorted to more protectionism. This wave of protectionism produced a massive contraction of international trade and further aggravated the Depression. Many of the barriers placed on trade included tariffs and quotas, a variety of price mainte-nance schemes, as well as arbitrary currency manipulation and for-eign exchange controls and management.
- To avoid a repetition of the economic situation of the previous two decades, Allied countries met even before the war to discuss the in-ternational financial arrangements that should govern trade and capi-tal movements in the postwar world. In 1944, they established the International Monetary Fund (IMF) and the International Bank for Reconstruction and Development (IBRD). The IMF was to be con-cerned with facilitating the growth and expansion of global trade through the system of fixed exchange rates, while IBRD was estab-lished to promote long-term investment. This was followed by an agreement (the General Agreement on Tariffs and Trade, or the GATT) in 1948 to permit the free flow of goods among nations.

SECTION I:
OVERVIEW
OF INTERNATIONAL TRADE

Chapter 1

Growth and Direction
of International Trade

International trade is the exchange of goods and services across national boundaries. It is the most traditional form of international business activity and has played a major role in shaping world history. It is also the first type of foreign business operation undertaken by most companies because importing or exporting requires the least commitment of, and risk to, company's resources. For example, a company could produce for export by using its excess production capacity. This is an inexpensive way of testing a product's acceptance in the market before investing in local production facilities. A company could also use intermediaries, who will take on import-export functions for a fee, thus eliminating the need to commit additional resources to hire personnel or maintain a department to carry out foreign sales or purchases (Daniels and Radebaugh, 1994).

International trade in services has grown over the past decade at an annual rate of about 16 percent compared to that of about 7 percent for merchandise trade. Trade in services constitutes between 20 to 25 percent of overall world trade today (U.S. Department of Commerce, 1990). In some countries, such as Panama and the Netherlands, services account for about 40 percent or more of total merchandise trade. Typical service exports include transportation, tourism, banking, advertising, and construction, retailing, and mass communication.

IMPORTANCE OF INTERNATIONAL TRADE
TO THE GLOBAL ECONOMY

International trade allows manufacturers and distributors to seek out products, services, and components produced in foreign countries. Companies acquire them because of cost advantages or to learn about advanced technical methods used abroad, for example, methods that help reduce the

7

cost of production, lower prices, and, in turn, induce more consumption, thus producing increased profit (Asheghian and Ibrahimi, 1990). Trade also enables firms to acquire resources that are not available at home. Besides providing consumers with a variety of goods and services, international trade increases incomes and employment. In 1990, the number of U.S. jobs supported by merchandise exports to all foreign markets reached 7.2 million. U.S. merchandise exports to all foreign markets contributed to 25 percent of the growth in U.S. civilian jobs between 1986 and 1990 (Davis, 1992). It is estimated that each billion dollars of merchandise exports supports about 25,000 jobs. Even though imports are associated with loss of jobs due to plant closings or production cutbacks of domestic industries, the export job generation effect is about 7.5 percent larger than the import job loss effect (Belous and Wyckoff, 1987). Most occupations show a net job gain from an equal amount of exports and imports, except for blue-collar occupations, which are shrinking in most developed countries due to increasing pressure from low-wage imports.

Exports create high-wage employment. In a study of recent wage statistics, the U.S. Trade Representative's Office found that U.S. workers employed in export-related jobs earn 17 percent more than the average worker in the United States. Export-related wages are higher for manufacturing and service sector jobs. Although service-related jobs generally pay less than manufacturing jobs, service jobs in the export sector were found to pay more, on average, than manufacturing jobs in the overall economy (U.S. Department of Commerce, 1994).

DETERMINANTS OF TRADE

Why do some countries export or import more than others? Several studies have been conducted to establish major factors that influence exports. The trade and exchange rate regime (import tariffs, quotes, exchange rates), presence of an entrepreneurial class, efficiency-enhancing government policy, as well as secure access to transport and marketing services are considered to be important influential factors of export behavior (Kaynak and Kothavi, 1984). A study on the nature, composition, and determinants of Singapore's technology exports suggests that the country's open trade and investment regime and its development-oriented economic policy have been the key factors in enhancing the country's exports. Singapore's economy has shown continued and remarkable growth in exports for over thirty years with only two brief and mild recessions in the mid-1970s and mid-1980s. Its total trade as a proportion of gross domestic product (GDP) remains one of the highest in the world—over 250 percent (Fong and Hill, 1991).

Much of the research literature on imports underlines the importance of high per capita incomes, price of imports, and the exchange rate in determining import levels (Lutz, 1994). For developing countries, however, determinants of import demand also include factors such as government restrictions on imports and availability of foreign exchange. A recent study examining the factors influencing import demand in Pakistan from 1959 to 1986 found that the policies of devaluation and raising tariffs were not significant in reducing imports except in the case of imports of machinery and equipment (Sarmand, 1989).

VOLUME AND DIRECTION OF TRADE

The growth in the volume of world merchandise trade has always exceeded the growth of output (1870 to 1997), except for the period 1913 to 1950, which was marked by global political and economic instability (World Bank, 1999). Since 1950, while world economic output has shown steady growth, world exports have increased at an average annual rate of more than ten times the estimated rate for the previous period (Rostow, 1978). The volume of world trade in 1997 more than tripled the 1970 figure, approaching $7 trillion (U.S.).* The dollar value of total world trade in 1997 was greater than the gross national product (GNP) of every nation in the world, except the United States. Another measure of the significance of world trade is that one-fourth of everything grown or made in the world is now exported.

Since 1970, the average annual growth in world merchandise exports is estimated at about 12 percent. The rapid increase in the growth of world trade after World War II can be traced to increased consumption of goods and services as more people joined the middle class in many countries of the world. Trade liberalization, both at the regional and international levels, has created a global environment that is conducive to the growth and expansion of world trade. New technologies such as computers, telecommunications, and other media also assisted in the physical integration of world markets.

Small countries tend to be more dependent on international trade than larger ones because they are less able to produce all that they need. Larger countries (in terms of population) import fewer manufactured goods on a

---

*Dollar amounts are in U.S. dollars throughout the text, unless otherwise noted.

per capita basis because such countries tend to have a diversified economy that enables them to produce enough to meet most of their own needs. This view can be exemplified by comparing the United States, Japan, India, and China, which have low import propensities, to such countries as Belgium or the Netherlands.

Merchandise trade currently accounts for about four-fifths of world trade. The top seven exporters accounted for just over one-half of world merchandise exports (United States, Germany, Japan, France, United Kingdom, Italy, Canada). Merchandise trade includes three major sectors: agriculture, mining, and manufacturing. Trade in manufactured goods has been the most dynamic component of world merchandise trade. Commercial service exports exceeded $1.2 trillion in 1995 (World Bank, 1999), but growth for the last few years has lagged behind the growth of merchandise trade.

Industrial market economies account for the largest part of world trade. Trade among these countries is estimated to be greater than 67 percent of global trade. In view of their role in world trade, Western countries also account for major shares of trade with developing countries and an increasing share of trade with East European countries.

IMPORTANT DEVELOPMENTS IN TRADE

- In 1994, the World Trade Organization (WTO) was established, replacing the General Agreement on Tariffs and Trade (GATT) under the Final Act of the Uruguay Round. As of the enforcement date of the WTO agreement, member countries of the GATT became original members of the WTO. WTO became the principal agency of the United Nations (UN) with responsibility for international trade.
- The Final Act of the Uruguay Round was signed (1994) by 124 governments, providing for a global reduction in trade barriers, establishment of a multilateral framework of discipline for trade in services, and protection of trade-related intellectual property rights. The agreement also strengthened existing multilateral rules in agriculture, textiles, and clothing and provided for a more effective and reliable dispute settlement mechanism.
- There has been a steady growth in the role of developing countries in world trade. In 1993, developing countries accounted for over one-third of the world's top twenty-five exporters and importers. Since the 1980s, a number of newly industrializing countries (NICs), particularly the four in the Pacific Rim (Hong Kong, Singapore, South Korea, and Taiwan) have greatly increased their roles in world trade.

Another important development has been the opening up of China and Eastern Europe for trade and investment.

- There has been a marked increase in the establishment of common markets and free-trade areas, thus further increasing economic linkages among nations through trade, investment, and the operation of multinational companies. The most notable examples are the Canada/U.S. Free Trade Agreement (FTA), the North American Free Trade Agreement (NAFTA), the Asian Free Trade Area (AFTA), and the Preferential Trade Area for Eastern and Southern American Common Market (MERCOSUR).
- Export trade is no longer limited to big multinational firms. Small and medium-sized businesses are increasing their share of exports and already account for almost one-fourth of all exporters in the United States. In addition, such firms represent the largest pool of potential exporters and can play a significant role in improving the U.S. balance of trade, while enhancing their competitiveness and increasing their profits. These firms also have the advantage of developing much more flexible structures than the big multinational firms.
- Given the dynamic role of services in today's economy, trade in services has shown continued growth in most countries. Even though services trade takes place mainly among developed nations, some developing countries have established strong service sectors that are competitive on a global scale in areas such as engineering, construction, tourism, or finance. The liberalization of services trade (under NAFTA, European Economic Community [EEC], and WTO), in tandem with the advent of communication and information technology, will inevitably induce an upsurge in services trade. Among the developed countries, the United States has had a healthy surplus in service trade for some years. In 1995, U.S. service exports exceeded imports by $68 billion, offsetting 35 percent of the deficit in merchandise trade. A few developing nations, such as Egypt, India, and Pakistan, also have a surplus in their service accounts, largely resulting from tourism and workers' remittances.

CHAPTER SUMMARY

Major Benefits of International Trade

To acquire a variety of goods and services, to reduce cost of production, to increase incomes and employment, to learn about advanced technical methods used abroad, and to secure raw materials.

Determinants of Trade

Major Determinants of Exports

Presence of an entrepreneurial class; access to transportation, marketing, and other services; exchange rates; and government trade and exchange rate policies.

Major Determinants of Imports

Per capita income, price of imports, exchange rates, government trade and exchange rate policies, and availability of foreign exchange.

Volume of Trade

1. World trade approached $7 trillion in 1997 and was more than triple what it was in 1970.
2. Services trade accounts for 20 to 25 percent of total trade.
3. Since 1970, average annual growth in world merchandise exports is estimated at about 12 percent.
4. The industrial market economies account for 67 percent of global trade.

Major Developments in Trade

1. The establishment of the World Trade Organization (WTO) as a permanent trade organization.
2. The introduction of rules under the WTO to govern trade in services, trade-related intellectual property, and investment measures.
3. The marked increase in the establishment of regional trading arrangements such as NAFTA, MERCOSUR, and so on.
4. Growing role of developing countries in world trade.
5. Increasing participation of small and medium-sized businesses in export trade.
6. The dynamic role of services in today's economy and continued growth in trade in services.

Chapter 2

International and Regional Agreements Affecting Trade

THE GATT AND WTO

The General Agreement on Tariffs and Trade (GATT) was established in 1945 as a provisional agreement pending the creation of an International Trade Organization (ITO). The ITO draft charter, which was the result of trade negotiations at the Havana Conference of 1948, however, never came into being due to the failure of the U.S. Congress to approve it. Other countries also declined to proceed with the ITO without the participation of the United States. Thus, the GATT continued to fill the vacuum as a de facto trade organization, with codes of conduct for international trade, but with almost no basic constitution designed to regulate its international activities and procedures. Since the GATT, in theory, was not an "organization," participating nations were called "contracting parties" and not members (Jackson, 1992; Hoekman and Kostecki, 1995).

Since its inception, the GATT has used certain policies to reduce trade barriers between contracting parties (CPs):

- *Nondiscrimination:* All CPs must be treated in the same way with respect to import-export duties and charges. According to the most-favored nation treatment, each contracting party (CP) must grant to every other CP the most-favorable-tariff treatment that it grants to any country with respect to import and export of products. Certain exceptions, however, are allowed, such as free-trade areas, customs unions, or other preferential arrangements in favor of developing nations. Once imports have cleared customs, a CP is required to treat foreign imports the same way as it treats similar domestic products (the national treatment standard).
- *Trade liberalization:* The GATT has been an important forum for trade negotiations. It has sponsored periodic conferences among CPs

to reduce trade barriers (see International Perspective 2.1). The most recent was the Uruguay Round (1986-1994) that gave rise to the establishment of a permanent trade organization (World Trade Organization, or WTO).

- *Settlement of trade disputes:* The GATT has played an important role in resolving trade disputes between CPs. In certain cases in which a party did not follow the GATT's recommendations, it ruled for trade retaliation that is proportional to the loss or damage sustained. It is fair to state that the existence of the GATT has been a deterrent to trade wars between nations.
- *Trade in goods:* The GATT rules apply to all products both imported and exported, although most of the rules are relevant to imports. It was designed primarily to regulate tariffs and related barriers to imports such as quotas, internal taxes, discriminatory regulations, subsidies, dumping, discriminatory customs procedures, and other nontariff barriers. The Uruguay Round (1994) resulted in a new general agreement on trade in services, trade-related aspects of intellectual property (TRIPs), and trade-related investment measures (TRIMs). Thus, CPs have gone beyond the original purpose of the GATT to achieve unrestricted trade in goods, to reduce barriers to trade in services, investment, and to protect intellectual property (Collins and Bosworth, 1995).

The Uruguay Round and WTO

In 1982, the United States initiated a proposal to launch a new round of GATT talks. The major reasons behind the U.S. initiative were (1) to counter domestic pressures for protectionism precipitated by the strong dollar and rising trade deficit, (2) to improve market access for U.S. products by reducing existing tariff and nontariff barriers to trade, (3) to reverse the erosion of confidence in the multilateral trading system, (4) to extend GATT coverage to important areas such as services, intellectual property, and investment, and (5) to bring developing nations more effectively into the international trading system.

Despite the initial reluctance of many developing nations, the effort culminated in the conclusion of a successful trade negotiation (the Uruguay Round) in 1994. The results of the Uruguay Round are summarized as follows.

Trade Liberalization

Significant progress was made toward reducing trade barriers in the areas of agriculture and textiles, which had long been resistant to reform. Tariff

---

International Perspective

2.1

GATT NEGOTIATIONS (1947-1994)

GATT Round	Explanation
Geneva (1947)	23 countries participated in establishing the GATT in 1947. Average tariff cut of 35 percent on trade estimated at $10 billion.
Annecy, France (1949)	33 countries participated in tariff reductions.
Torquay, UK (1951)	34 countries participated in tariff reductions.
Geneva (1956)	22 countries participated in tariff reductions on trade estimated at $2.5 billion.
Dillon (1960-1961)	45 countries participated in tariff reductions on trade estimated at $5 billion.
Kennedy (1962-1967)	48 countries participated in tariff reductions on trade estimated at $40 billion.
Tokyo (1973-1979)	99 countries participated in reductions of tariff and non-tariff barriers on trade valued at $155 billion.
Uruguay (1986-1994)	Broadening of the GATT to include services, intellectual property, and investment. It also resulted in the establishment of WTO. 124 countries participated in reductions of tariff and nontariff barriers on trade valued at $300 billion.

---

reductions of about 40 percent were achieved. The new agreement also opened access to a broad range of government contracts (Government Procurement Agreement).

Trade Rules

The Uruguay Round added new rules relating to unfair trade practices (dumping, subsidies) and the use of import safeguards.

New Issues

The agreement broadened the coverage of the GATT to include areas such as trade in services (GATS), trade-related aspects of intellectual property (TRIPs), and trade-related investment measures (TRIMs). The GATS established rules to liberalize trade in services that is estimated to be almost $1 trillion (Schott and Buurman, 1994). The TRIPs agreement established new trade disciplines with regard to the protection and enforcement of intellectual property rights. TRIMs provided for the elimination of trade-distorting investment requirements such as local content, limitation of ownership, or exports of certain shares of domestic production.

Institutional Reforms

In the area of institutional reform, the Uruguay Round strengthened the multilateral dispute settlement mechanism and established a new and permanent international institution, the World Trade Organization, responsible for governing the conduct of trade relations among its members. The new dispute settlement procedure instituted an appeals procedure, expedited decision making, and encouraged compliance with GATT decisions. Members of WTO are required to comply with the GATT rules as well as various agreements (Rounds) negotiated under GATT auspices.

The reduction of trade barriers under the Uruguay Round is expected to increase global output by about $500 billion by the year 2000. For the United States, liberalization of trade in services is likely to increase its service exports, meaning U.S. service exports will not only continue to expand but may equal U.S. merchandise trade in less than a decade.

THE NORTH AMERICAN FREE TRADE AGREEMENT

The North American Free Trade Agreement (NAFTA) established a free-trade area between Canada, the United States, and Mexico. The agreement came into effect on January 1, 1994, after a difficult ratification by the U.S. Congress and approval by the Canadian and Mexican legislatures. NAFTA gave rise to the largest free-trade zone in the world—360 million people and a joint gross domestic product exceeding $6 trillion and constitutes the most comprehensive free-trade pact ever negotiated among regional trading partners. It is also the first reciprocal free-trade pact between a developing nation and industrial countries. Canada and the United States agreed to suspend the operation of the Canada/U.S. Free Trade Agreement as long as both countries are parties to NAFTA, and to establish certain transitional arrangements.

Negotiating Objectives

The United States

Since World War II, the United States has advocated trade liberalization and the elimination, on a reciprocal and nondiscriminatory basis, of measures that restrict commercial transactions across national boundaries. To achieve this, it had relied on the General Agreement on Tariffs and Trade, now the World Trade Organization, and had demonstrated its commitment through its active participation in the successive rounds of trade negotiations under the GATT framework. However, the GATT process has been slow and ineffective in liberalizing trade, in general, and in certain sectors such as agriculture, in particular. The regional approach was thus considered an attractive alternative to the multilateral framework for achieving rapid progress in trade liberalization. Second, the proliferation of regional common markets and the continued expansion of the European Community are considered to be important factors influencing the United States to enter into a regional free-trade agreement, as a response to the prevailing trend in international economic relations. Third, it was logical to embark on a free-trade arrangement with Canada and Mexico not only due to their geographical proximity but also because they are the most important trading partners to the United States. The United States is the destination for over 80 percent of Canadian and Mexican exports. Both countries also import about one-third of U.S. exports. The United States is also the largest investor in both countries. It was in the interest of the United States to maintain and expand existing trade and investment opportunities through a regional trade arrangement.

Canada

NAFTA permits Canadian firms to achieve economies of scale by operating larger and more specialized plants. It also provides secure access to a large consumer market. Even though tariff rates between the United States and Canada have declined over time, there has been an increase in protectionist sentiment and use of aggressive trade remedies to protect domestic industries in the United States. These measures create uncertainty for producers with respect to investment in new facilities. NAFTA reduces this uncertainty because it provides rules and procedures for the application of trade remedies and the resolution of disputes.

Mexico

NAFTA provides secure access to the U.S. and Canadian markets for Mexican goods and services. Its low labor costs and access to the U.S.

market attract foreign direct investment to Mexico (Echeverri-Carroll, 1995). In view of the adverse impact of its import substitution policy in the 1980s and the debt crisis, trade liberalization is considered to be an effective means of fostering domestic reform and of achieving sustainable growth. Ostry briefly describes Mexico's objectives:

> So NAFTA is a means of consolidating an export-led growth path both by improving secure access to the U.S. market and encouraging a return of flight capital as well as new investment. (quoted in Randall, Konrad, and Silverman, 1992, pp. 27-28)

Overview of NAFTA

Market Access for Goods

NAFTA incorporates the basic national treatment obligation of the GATT. This means that goods imported from any member country will not be subject to discrimination in favor of domestic products. It provides for a gradual elimination of tariffs over fifteen years for trade between Mexico and Canada as well as between Mexico and the United States, except for certain agricultural products. Under the Canada-U.S. Free Trade Agreement, tariffs between the two countries were eliminated in January 1998.

By January of 1998, tariffs had been phased out for about 65 percent of all U.S. exports to Mexico. For certain import-sensitive sectors in which quotas are imposed, the agreement provides for replacement with a sliding tariff quota over ten or fifteen years. NAFTA also provides for a gradual elimination of nontariff barriers such as customs user fees, import licenses, export taxes, and duty drawbacks on NAFTA-made goods. Since NAFTA would gradually phase out tariffs within the free-trade area, such drawbacks would no longer be necessary. To qualify for preferential market access, however, goods must be wholly or substantially made or produced within the member countries. For example, farm goods wholly grown or substantially processed within the NAFTA region would qualify for NAFTA treatment.

Services

The agreement governs financial, telecommunications, trucking, and rail services. With respect to financial services, NAFTA commits each party to treat service providers such as banks and insurance companies from other NAFTA parties no less favorably than it treats its own service providers in similar circumstances. It also commits members to gradually phase out, during the transition period, limits on equity ownership by foreign individuals or corporations and on market share by foreign financial institutions. Mexico is allowed to set temporary capital limits for banks, securities firms, and insurance companies during the transition period. The agreement allows members to take prudent measures to protect the integrity of the financial system or consumers of financial services. It includes a freeze on restrictions governing cross-border trade in financial services and also provides for consultations and a dispute settlement mechanism.

NAFTA commits members to impose no conditions on access to, or use of, public telecommunication networks (i.e., reasonable and nondiscriminatory terms) unless they are necessary to safeguard the public service responsibilities of the network operators or the technical integrity of the networks. It also imposes an obligation to prevent anticompetitive conduct by monopolies in basic services.

The agreement would also (1) remove most limitations on cross-border trucking and rail by the year 2000, and liberalize Mexican investment restrictions in these sectors, and (2) preserve existing cabotage laws, that is, laws that allow a truck to carry goods to and from a given destination but not to make additional stops unless the vehicle and cargo are registered in the country.

Investment

Investment includes majority-controlled or minority interests, portfolio investments, and investments in real property from member countries. All three countries agree to (1) provide national treatment to investors from member countries, a treatment that is not less favorable than that given to an investor from a non-NAFTA country, (2) prohibit the imposition and enforcement of certain performance requirements in connection with the conduct or operation of investments, such as export requirements or domestic content, (3) severely restrict or prohibit investment in their most strategic industries, such as energy (Mexico), cultural industries (Canada), nuclear energy (all three countires), and broadcasting (all three countries). Both Canada and Mexico reserve the right to screen potential investors in certain cases. The parties also agree to subject disputes raised by foreign investors to international arbitration.

Intellectual Property

NAFTA mandates minimum standards for the protection of intellectual property rights (IPRs) in member countries and requires each country to extend national treatment to IPRs owned by nationals of other countries. The scope of IPR protection includes patents, trademarks, trade secrets, copyright, and industrial designs. It also extends to semiconductors, sound recordings, and satellite broadcast signals. Patents are to be provided for products or processes that are new, useful, and nonobvious. They are valid for twenty years from the date of filing or seventeen years from the date of grant. The agreement permits the use of compulsory licensing (i.e., a requirement to grant licenses to local companies or individuals if the patent is not used in the country) in limited circumstances. NAFTA protects registered trademarks for a term of no less than seven years, renewable indefinitely. It harmonizes members' laws on trademark protection and enforcement. The agreement prohibits "trademark linking" requirements in which foreign owners of trademarks are to use their mark in conjunction with a mark owned by a national of that country. NAFTA requires adequate protection for trade secrets and does not limit the duration of protection. Copyright protection is extended to computer software and provides owners of computer programs and sound recordings with "rental rights" (i.e., the right to authorize or prohibit the rental of programs or recordings). It ensures protection of copyright for a minimum period of fifty years and gives effect to the 1971 Berne Convention on artistic and literary works.

Government Procurement

Purchase of goods and services by government entities in member countries is estimated at about $1 trillion. NAFTA extends the national treatment standard (equal treatment to all member country providers) for all goods and services procured by federal government entities unless specifically exempted. Procurement contracts must, however, meet certain minimum value thresholds: $50,000 for contract of goods and/or services and $6.5 million for construction contracts procured by federal government entities. For government enterprises, the threshold is $250,000 for contract of goods and/or services and $8 million for construction services. For U.S. and Canadian entities, the free-trade agreement (Canada-U.S.) maintains the threshold at $25,000 for goods contracts. It provides tendering procedures and bid-challenging mechanisms to seek a review of any aspect of the procurement process by an independent authority.

Safeguards

If a surge in imports causes serious injury to domestic producers, a member country is allowed to take emergency action temporarily, that is, up to four years, to protect the industry. A request for emergency action is usually initiated by a domestic industry. A number of factors are considered by the investigating tribunal in arriving at a decision on injury: the level of increase in imports; market share of the imports; changes in sales, production, profits, employment, and other pertinent variables.

Technical and Other Standards

NAFTA requires a member to provide sixty days notice before adopting new standards, allowing for comments before implementation. It prohibits members from using standards as a disguised restriction to trade. Working groups are established to adopt or harmonize technical and other standards pertaining to specific sectors.

Other Areas

The agreement (1) requires members to create and maintain rules against anticompetitive business practices, (2) allows for temporary entry of businesspersons and certain professionals who are citizens of another member country—NAFTA does not create a common market for the movement of labor—(3) establishes institutions such as the Free Trade Commission (FTC) to supervise the implementation of the agreement and resolve disputes, and (4) creates a secretariat, composed of national offices in each country, to support the commission. The agreement also allows any country or group of countries to join NAFTA, subject to approval by each member country and on such terms as agreed upon by the Free Trade Commission.

Dispute Settlement

Disputes arising over the implementation of the agreement may be resolved through (1) consultations, (2) mediation, conciliation, or other means of dispute resolution that might facilitate an amicable resolution, or (3) a panel of nongovernment experts. If the decision is made by a binding panel (binding dispute settlement), the parties are required to comply within thirty days or else compensation/retaliation measures may result. If the decision is reached by a nonbinding panel, parties shall comply or agree on another solution within thirty days or else compensation/retaliation measures may result. Panel reports are not automatically enforceable in domestic law.

There are separate dispute settlement mechanisms for certain specialized areas such as financial services, investment, environment, standards, private commercial disputes, as well as dumping and subsidies.

Preliminary Assessment of NAFTA

The full impact of NAFTA can only be determined in the long term, after the necessary economic adjustments have taken place. Although a short-term assessment of such a comprehensive agreement is often inadequate and sometimes misleading, a cursory discussion is presented on economic conditions since NAFTA.

Overall Increase in Trade Between Members

U.S. exports to Mexico rose by 36.3 percent and exports to Canada rose by 33.4 percent between 1993 and 1996. During the same period, exports by Mexico and Canada to the United States rose by 82.7 percent and 41.1 percent, respectively.

Increase in the U.S. Trade Deficit

The U.S. merchandise trade deficit with Canada and Mexico has quadrupled since NAFTA. By 1996, U.S. exports to Canada and Mexico had grown to $190 billion, while imports increased to $229 billion, resulting in a trade deficit of $39 billion. The trade deficit with Mexico is mainly attributed to the 1994-1995 peso crisis, devaluation, and recession in Mexico, which reduced Mexico's ability to purchase U.S. goods, while making Mexican goods cheaper in the U.S. market. Most of Mexico's export trade is in the auto and auto parts, apparel, and furniture sectors. The growing trade deficit with Canada is largely due to the appreciation of the U.S. dollar. The U.S. dollar has appreciated by about 20 percent against the Canadian dollar since 1991.

NAFTA's Impact on Jobs Is Uncertain

There is no conclusive evidence on NAFTA's effect on jobs. There are certain indications, however, that NAFTA may have had a negligible effect on jobs. The U.S. Department of Labor has certified that 107,632 workers have lost their jobs, as of February 1997, due to production shifted to Mexico or Canada. Most of the job dislocations appear to be concentrated in the apparel and electronic industries. The Economic Policy Institute, for example, estimated net job losses due to NAFTA at 425,000 in its first three years.

Substantial Increase in Foreign Investment in Mexico

Foreign direct investment in Mexico almost doubled between 1994 and 1996 compared to the period 1991 to 1994. NAFTA appears to be the incentive that attracted U.S. and non-NAFTA investment to Mexico.

THE EUROPEAN ECONOMIC COMMUNITY

The European Economic Community (EEC) is the oldest and most significant economic integration scheme, involving fifteen West European countries: Austria, Belgium, Denmark, Finland, France, Germany, Greece, Ireland, Italy, Luxembourg, The Netherlands, Portugal, Spain, Sweden, and the United Kingdom. (See International Perspective 2.2 for the stages of economic integration.) Established under the Treaty of Rome in 1957, the EEC has an aggregate population of about 370 million and a total economic output (GDP) of $7.2 trillion (1998) and involves the largest transfer of national sovereignty to a common institution. In certain designated areas, for example, international agreements can only be made by the community on behalf of member states. In the next decade, Hungary, Poland, the Czech Republic, and Slovakia possibly will join as full members of the EEC (Kaufmann, 1993).

The pursuit of such integration was partly influenced by the need to create a lasting peace in Europe as well as to establish a stronger Europe that could compete against the United States and Japan. Since the countries were not large enough to compete in global markets, they had to unite to exploit economies of large-scale production. (International Perspective 2.3 describes the institutions governing the European Union.)

The objectives of the EEC are stated as follows:

- To create free trade among member states and provide uniform customs duties for goods imported from outside the EEC (common external tariff).
- To abolish restrictions on the free movement of all factors of production, that is, labor, services, and capital. Member states are required to extend the national treatment standard to goods, services, capital, etc., from other member countries with respect to taxation and other matters (nondiscrimination).
- To establish a common transport, agricultural, and competition policy. (To contrast with NAFTA, see Table 2.1.)

A number of the objectives set out in the Treaty of Rome were successfully accomplished. The Common Agricultural Policy (CAP) was established

---

International Perspective

2.2

STAGES OF ECONOMIC INTEGRATION

Preferential Trade Arrangements: Agreement among participating nations to lower trade barriers. Example: British Commonwealth preference scheme, 1934.

Free-Trade Area: All barriers are removed on trade among members but each nation retains its own barriers on trade with nonmembers. Example: The European Free Trade Area (EFTA) formed in 1960 by Austria, Denmark, Norway, Portugal, the United Kingdom, Sweden, and Switzerland.

Customs Union: In addition to an agreement to lower or remove trade barriers, members establish a common system of tariffs against nonmembers (common external tariff). Example: The European Common Market.

Common Market: A common market includes all the elements of a customs union and allows free movement of labor and capital among member nations. Example: The European Common Market achieved common-market status in 1970.

Economic Union: Economic union goes beyond a common market and requires members to harmonize and/or unify monetary and fiscal policies of member states. Example: Benelux, which includes Belgium, The Netherlands, and Luxembourg, formed in the 1920s, and also is part of the EEC.

TABLE 2.1. NAFTA and EEC: Major Differences

NAFTA	EEC
NAFTA does not provide for a common external tariff.	EEC has a common external tariff.
NAFTA has no provision for economic assistance or economic/monetary union.	EEC provides for economic assistance to members and an economic/monetary union.
NAFTA does not provide for free movement of labor.	EEC allows for free movement of labor.

International Perspective

2.3

INSTITUTIONS OF THE EUROPEAN UNION

The European Council: Composed of representatives (Ministers) of member states, the council sets out the general direction of the union. The council approves legislation and international agreements, acting on a proposal from the commission and after consulting the European Parliament.

The European Commission: Members of the commission are chosen by the mutual agreement of national governments and serve four-year terms. They neither represent nor take orders from member states. The commission initiates policies and ensures members' compliance with the treaty.

The European Parliament: Composed of 626 representatives directly elected, the European Parliament supervises the commission, adopts the community budget, and influences the legislative process. Any agreement concerning international cooperation must be reviewed and accepted by the parliament before it is concluded. The parliament, however, does not have express legislative powers.

The Court of Justice: Settles disputes arising from the treaty, that is, interprets and applies the EEC treaty. The judges are appointed by mutual agreement of member states and serve six-year terms. The court ensures uniform interpretation and application of community law, evaluates legality of legislation adopted by the council and the commission, and provides rulings on community law when requested by national courts in member states.

---

in 1962 to maintain common prices for agricultural products throughout the community and to stabilize farm incomes. Tariffs among member nations were eliminated and a common external tariff established in 1968. However, efforts to achieve the other objectives, such as a single internal market (elimination of nontariff barriers), free movement of services or capital, and so forth, have been slow and difficult. Coordinated or common policies in certain areas, such as transport, simply did not exist (Archer and Butler, 1992).

The European Commission presented a proposal in 1985 to remove existing barriers to the establishment of a genuine common market. The proposal, which was adopted, titled the Single European Act (SEA), constitutes a major revision to the Treaty of Rome. The Single European Act set the following objectives for members:

- To complete the single market by removing all remaining barriers to trade through elimination of customs controls at borders, harmonization of technical standards, liberalization of public procurement, provision of services, removal of obstacles to the free movement of workers, and so on. In short, efforts involved the removal of physical, technical, and fiscal (different excise and value-added taxes) barriers to trade.
- To encourage monetary cooperation leading to a single European currency. The Maastricht Treaty of 1991 further reinforced this and defined plans for achieving economic and monetary union.
- To establish cooperation on research and development (R&D) and create a common standard on environmental policy.
- To harmonize working conditions across the community and improve dialogue between management and labor.

SEA established a concrete plan and timetable to complete the internal market by 1992. It is fair to state that most of the objectives set out under the act were accomplished in 1999: border checks are largely eliminated, free movement of workers has been achieved through mutual recognition of qualifications from any accredited institution within the EEC, free movement of capital (banking, insurance, and investment services) has been made possible, with certain limitations, and the single currency was introduced in January 1999 (Breitfelder, 1998). Certain nontariff barriers remain and, hopefully, will in time be abolished. (See Table 2.2 for other regional trade agreements.)

In spite of these accomplishments, economic performance in most member countries leaves a lot to be desired. Unemployment rates have been high; rates of economic growth (GDP) have been quite low for the last two decades (except for Ireland and the United Kingdom).

A legitimate fear of non-EEC exporters is whether national trade barriers will be replaced by community barriers. It is plausible to contend that the EEC is unlikely to become any more protectionist than at present, given the realities of economic interdependence and possible retaliation by other countries (El-Agraa, 1997).

CHAPTER SUMMARY

The GATT/WTO

The principal objectives of the GATT are nondiscrimination, trade liberalization, and settlement of trade disputes among members.

TABLE 2.2. Other Major Regional Trade Agreements

The European Free Trade Association (EFTA), 1960	*Members:* Iceland, Liechtenstein, Norway, Switzerland *Objectives:* Removal of customs barriers and differing technical standards. Free trade with EEC strictly limited to commercial matters.
The Preferential Area for Eastern and Southern American Common Market (MERCOSUR), 1991	*Members:* Argentina, Brazil, Paraguay, Uruguay. Chile and Bolivia joined as associate members. *Objectives:* Free trade and industrial cooperation.
The Central American Common Market (CACM), 1960	*Members:* Costa Rica, El Salvador, Guatemala, Honduras, Nicaragua *Objectives:* Free trade and a common external tariff.
The Andean Pact, 1969	*Members:* Bolivia, Colombia, Chile, Ecuador, Peru, Venezuela *Objectives:* Free trade and industrial development.
The Association of Southeast Asian Nations (ASEAN), 1967	*Members:* Indonesia, Malaysia, the Philippines, Singapore, Thailand *Objectives:* Reduction of trade barriers, industrial cooperation.
The Caribbean Common Market (CARICOM), 1973	*Members:* Antigua and Barbuda, the Bahamas, Barbados, Belize, Dominica, Grenada, Guyana, Jamaica, Montserrat, St. Kitts and Nevis, St. Lucia, St. Vincent and the Grenadines, Trinidad and Tobago, Suriname. *Objectives:* Political unity, economic cooperation.
The Southern African Customs Union (SACU), 1969	*Members:* Botswana, Lesotho, Namibia, South Africa, Swaziland *Objectives:* Free movement of goods, common external tariff.
The Economic Community of West African States (ECOWAS), 1974	*Members:* Benin, Burkina Faso, Cape Verde, Côte d'Ivoire, The Gambia, Ghana, Guinea, Guinea-Bissau, Liberia, Mali, Mauritania, Niger, Nigeria, Senegal, Sierra Leone, Togo *Objectives:* Economic and monetary union.

The Uruguay Round of the GATT and the Birth of WTO

Important results of the Uruguay Round trade negotiations (1986-1994) include reductions in tariffs; adoption of new trade rules on unfair trade practices; GATT coverage extended to trade in services, intellectual property, and trade-related investment measures; the birth of WTO.

The North American Free Trade Agreement (NAFTA)

Scope of coverage: market access for goods, services, investment, protection of intellectual property, government procurement, safeguards, standards, dispute settlement.

NAFTA: Preliminary Assessment

Increases in overall trade among members, increase in the U.S. trade deficit on merchandise trade with members, and a sharp rise in foreign investment in Mexico.

The European Economic Community (EEC)

Major Objectives of the EEC

To create free trade and a common external tariff among members, to abolish restrictions on the free movement of all factors of production, to establish common policies in the areas of transport, agriculture, competition etc.

Institutions of the EEC

The European Council, the European Commission, the European Parliament, the Court of Justice.

Other Regional Trade Agreements

The European Free Trade Association (EFTA), Preferential Trade Area for Eastern and Southern American Common Market (MERCOSUR), The Central American Common Market (CACM), The Andean Pact, The Association of Southeast Asian Nations (ASEAN), The Caribbean Common Market (CARICOM), The Southern African Customs Union (SACU), The Economic Community of West African States (ECOWAS).

SECTION II:
EXPORT MARKETING AND STRATEGY

Chapter 3

Setting Up the Business

Whether it is a new or existing export-import business, its legal form, or structure, will determine how the business is to be conducted, its tax liability, and other important considerations. Each form of business organization has its own advantages and disadvantages, and the entrepreneur has to select the one that best fulfills the goals of the entrepreneur and the business (for questions to consider before starting a business, see International Perspective 3.1).

Selection of an appropriate business organization is a task that requires accounting and legal expertise and should be done with the advice of a competent attorney or accountant.

OWNERSHIP STRUCTURE

In this section, we examine different forms of business organizations: sole proprietorships, partnerships, corporations, and limited-liability companies.

Sole Proprietorships

A sole proprietorship is a firm owned and operated by one individual. No separate legal entity exists. There is one principal in the business who has total control over all export-import operations and who can make decisions without consulting anyone. The major advantages of sole proprietorships are as follows:

1. They are easy to organize and simple to control. Establishing an export-import business as a sole proprietorship is simple and inexpensive and requires little or no government approval. At the state level, registration of the business name is required, while at the federal level, sole proprietors need to keep accurate accounting re-

31

cords and attach a profit or loss statement for the business when
filing individual tax returns (Schedule C, IRS Form 4010). They
must operate on a calendar year and can use the cash or accrual
method of accounting.

2. They are more flexible to manage than partnerships or corporations.
The owner makes all operational and management decisions concerning the business. The owner can remove money or other assets
of the business without legal or tax consequences. He/she can also
easily transfer or terminate the business.

3. Sole proprietorships are subject to minimal governmental regulations compared to other business concerns.

4. The owner of a sole proprietorship is taxed as an individual, at a rate
lower than the corporate income tax rate. Losses from the export-
import business can be applied by the owner to offset taxable income
from other sources. Sole proprietors are also allowed to establish
tax-exempt retirement accounts (Harper, 1991).

The major disadvantage of running an export-import concern as a sole
proprietorship is the risk of unlimited liability. The owner is personally
responsible for the debts and other liabilities of the business. Insurance can
be bought to protect against these liabilities; however, if insurance protec-

---

International Perspective

3.1

**ESTABLISHING AN APPROPRIATE BUSINESS ORGANIZATION:
SOME CONSIDERATIONS**

- Does the entrepreneur intend to be the sole owner of the export-import
  business? If not, how many people will have an ownership interest?
- Does the entrepreneur need additional capital and/or expertise?
- What legal form provides the greatest flexibility for management?
- What legal form affords the most advantageous tax treatment for the
  business concern and individual entrepreneurs?
- Which legal structure is easy and less expensive to establish and subject
  to a low degree of government regulation?
- How important is it to limit personal liability of owners?
- Which legal structure is the most appropriate in light of the goals and
  objectives of the export-import business?

tion is not sufficient to cover legal liability for defective products or debts, etc. judgment creditors' next recourse is the personal assets of the owner. Another disadvantage is that the proprietor's access to capital is limited to personal funds plus any loans that can be obtained. In addition, very few individuals have all the necessary skills to run an export/import business, and the owner may lack certain skills. The business may also terminate upon the death or disability of the owner.

Partnerships

A partnership is an association of two or more persons to carry on as co-owners of a business for profit. "Persons" is broadly interpreted to include corporations, partnerships, or other associations. "Co-ownership" refers to a sharing of ownership of the business and is determined by two major factors: share of the business profits and management responsibility. The sharing of profits creates a rebuttable presumption that a partnership exists. The presumption about the existence of a partnership is disproved if profits are shared as payment of a debt, wages to an employee, interest on a loan, or rent to a landlord.

> *Example:* Suppose Gardinia Export Company owes Kimko Realty $10,000 in rent. Gardinia promises to pay Kimko 20 percent of its business profits until the rent is fully paid. Kimko Realty is sharing profits from the business but is not presumed to be a partner in the export business.

Although a written agreement is not required, it is advisable for partners to have some form of written contract that establishes the rights and obligations of the parties. Since partnerships dissolve upon the death of any partner who owns more than a 10 percent interest, the agreement should ascertain the rights of the deceased partner's spouse and that of surviving partners in a way that is least disruptive of the partnership.

A partnership is a legal entity only for limited purposes, such as the capacity to sue or be sued, to collect judgments, to have title of ownership of partnership property, or to have all accounting procedures in the name of the partnership. Federal courts recognize partnerships as legal entities in such matters as lawsuits in federal courts (when a federal question is involved), bankruptcy proceedings, and the filing of informational tax returns (the profit and loss statement that each partner reports on individual returns). The partnership, however, has no tax liability. A partner's profit or loss from the partnership is included in that partner's income tax return and taxed as income to the individual partner (Cooke, 1995).

Partners are personally liable for the debts of the partnership. However, in some states, the judgment creditor (the plaintiff in whose favor a judgment is entered by a court) must exhaust the remedies against partnership property before proceeding to execute against the individual property of the partners.

What are the duties and powers of partners? The fiduciary duty that partners owe the partnership and the other partners is a relationship of trust and loyalty. Each partner is a general agent of the partnership in any business transaction within the scope of the partnership agreement. For example, when a partner in an import business contracts to import merchandise, both the partner and the partnership share liability unless the seller knows that the partner has no such authority. In the latter case, the partner who signed the contract will be personally liable but not the partnership. A partner's action can bind the partnership to third parties if his/her action is consistent with the scope of authority, that is, expressed or implied authority provided in the partnership agreement (Cheeseman, 1997a).

Limited Partnerships

A limited partnership is a special form of partnership that consists of at least one general (investor and manager) partner and one or more limited (investor) partners. The general partner is given the right to manage the partnership and is personally liable for the debts and obligations of the limited partnership. The limited partner, however, does not participate in management and is liable only to the extent of his/her capital contribution. Any person can be a general or limited partner, and this includes individuals, partnerships, or corporations. Limited partners have no right to bind the partnership in any contract and owe no fiduciary duty to that partnership or the other partners due to the limited nature of their interest in the partnership.

Whereas a general partnership may be formed with little or no formality, the creation of a limited partnership is based on compliance with certain statutory requirements. The certificate of limited partnership must be executed and signed by the parties. It should include certain specific information and be filed with the secretary of state and the appropriate county to be legal and binding. The limited partnership is taxed in exactly the same way as a general partnership. A limited partner's losses from an export-import business could be used to offset income generated only by other passive activities, that is, investments in other limited partnerships (passive loss rules). They cannot be used against salaries, dividends, interest, or other income from portfolio investments. Both types of partnership can be useful in international trade. They bring complementary assets needed to distribute and/or commercialize the product or service. The combination of skills by different partners usually increases the speed with which the product/service enters a market and generally contributes to the success of the business. Limited partners may also be useful when capital is needed by exporters or importers to prepare a marketing plan, expand channels of distribution, increase the scope and volume of goods or services traded, and so on. However, potential exists for conflict among partners unless a partnership agreement eliminates or mitigates any sources of conflict. If limited partners become involved in marketing or other management decisions of the export/import firm, they are considered general partners and, hence, assume unlimited risk for the debts of the partnership (Anderson and Dunkelberg, 1993).

Corporations

A corporation is a legal entity separate from the people who own or operate it and created pursuant to the laws of the state in which the business is incorporated. Many export-import companies prefer this form of business organization due to the advantage of limited liability of shareholders. This means that shareholders are liable only to the extent of their investments. These companies could be sued for any harm or damage they cause in the distribution of the product, and that incorporation limits the liability of such companies to the assets of the business. Other advantages of incorporation are *free transferability of shares, perpetual existence, and ability to raise additional capital by selling shares in the corporation.* However, most of these companies are closely held corporations, that is, shares are owned by few shareholders who are often family members, relatives, or friends and not traded on national stock exchanges.

Export-import corporations as legal entities have certain rights and obligations: they can sue or be sued in their own names, enter into or enforce contracts, own or transfer property. They are also responsible for violations of the law. Criminal liability includes loss of the right to do business with the government, a fine, or any other sanction.

If an export-import company that is incorporated in one state conducts intrastate business (transacts local business in another state), such as selling merchandise or services in another state, it is required to file and qualify as a "foreign corporation" to do business in the other state. Conducting intrastate business usually includes maintaining an office to conduct such business. Using independent contractors for sales, soliciting orders to be accepted outside the state, or conducting isolated business transactions do not require qualification to do business in another state. The qualification procedure entails filing certain information with the

secretary of state, payment of the required fees, and appointing a registered agent that is empowered to accept service of process on behalf of the
corporation.

The process of forming a corporation (incorporating) can be expensive
and time-consuming. A corporation comes into existence when a certificate of incorporation, signed by one or more persons, is filed with the
secretary of state. The corporation code in every state describes the types
of information to be included in the articles of incorporation. Generally,
they include such provisions as the purpose for which the corporation is
organized, its duration, and powers of the corporation.

Many businesses incorporate their companies in the state of Delaware
even when it is not the state in which the corporation does most of its
business. This is because Delaware has laws that are very favorable to
businesses' internal operations and management. It is even more ideal for
those companies that plan to operate with little or no surpluses or that have
a large number of inaccessible shareholders, making obtaining their consent difficult when needed (Friedman, 1993).

One of the main disadvantages of a corporation as a form of business
organization is that its profits are subject to double taxation. Tax is imposed by federal and state governments on profits earned by the company,
and, later, those profits are taxed as income when distributed to shareholders. Companies often avoid this by increasing salaries and bonuses for
their owners and reporting substantially reduced profits. In this way, the
income will be subject to tax when the owners or shareholders receive it
rather than at the corporate level *and* the individual level.

It is important that export-import companies maintain a separate identity from that of their owners. This includes having a separate bank account, keeping export/distributor contracts in the name of the company,
holding stockholders meetings, and so on. In circumstances in which
corporations are formed without sufficient capital or there is a nonsepara-
tion of corporate and personal affairs, courts have disregarded the corporate entity. The implication of this is that shareholders may be found
personally liable for the debts and obligations of the company. The corporate entity is also disregarded in cases in which the corporation is primarily
used to defraud others and for similar illegitimate purposes, such as money
laundering, trade in narcotics, or funneling money to corrupt officials
(bribery).

Directors and officers of export-import companies owe a duty of trust
and loyalty to the corporation and its shareholders. Directors and officers
must act within their scope of authority (duty of obedience) and exercise
honest and prudent business judgment (duty of care) in the conduct of the

affairs of the corporation. In the absence of these, they could be held personally liable for any resultant damages to the corporation or its shareholders. Breach of duty of obedience and care by directors and officers of an export-import company could include one or more of the following:

- *Investment of profits:* Investment of profits from export-import operations in a way that is not provided in the articles of incorporation or corporate bylaw.
- *Corporate decisions:* Making export-import decisions without being adequately informed, in bad faith, and at variance with the goals and objectives of the company.

S Corporations

The Subchapter S Revision Act of 1982 divides corporations into two categories: S corporations and all other corporations, that is, C corporations. If an export company elects to be an S corporation, it has the best advantages of a corporation and a partnership. Similar to a corporation, it offers the benefits of limited liability but still permits the owner to pay taxes as an individual, thereby avoiding double taxation. One advantage of paying taxes at the level of the individual shareholder is that export-import companies' losses could be used to offset shareholders' taxable income from other sources. It is also beneficial when the corporation makes a profit and when a shareholder falls within a lower-income tax bracket than the corporation. However, the corporation's election to be taxed as an S corporation is based on the following preconditions:

1. *Domestic entity:* The corporation must be a domestic entity, that is, it must be incorporated in the United States.
2. *No membership in an affiliated group:* The corporation cannot be a member of an affiliated group (not part of another organization).
3. *Number of shareholders:* The corporation can have no more than thirty-five shareholders.
4. *Shareholders:* Shareholders must be individuals or estates. Corporations and partnerships cannot be shareholders. Shareholders must also be citizens or residents of the United States.
5. *Classes of stock:* The corporation cannot have more than one class of stock.
6. *Corporate income:* No more than 20 percent of the corporation's income can be from passive investment income (dividends, interest, royalties, rents, annuities, etc.).

Failure to maintain any one of these conditions will lead to cancellation of the S corporation status. Another election after cancellation of status cannot be made for five years.

Limited-Liability Companies

This form of business organization combines the best of all the other forms. It has the advantages of limited liability and no restrictions on the number of owners or their nationalities (as in the case of S corporations). It is taxed as a partnership, and, unlike limited partnerships, it does not grant limited liability on the condition that the members refrain from active participation in the management of the company. To be taxed as a partnership, a limited-liability company (LLC) can possess any of the following attributes: two or more persons as associates, objectives to carry on business and divide gains, limited liability, centralized management, and continuity and free transferability of interests (Cheeseman, 1997b). Such a company can be formed by two or more persons (natural or legal) and its articles of incorporation filed with the appropriate state agency. LLCs provide the advantage of limited liability, management structure (participation in management without being subject to personal liability), and partnership tax status. It has become a popular form of business for subsidiaries of foreign corporations as well as small-scale and medium-sized businesses (August, 1997).

BUSINESS OR TRADE NAME

A sole proprietorship or partnership that is engaged in export-import business can operate under the name of the sole proprietor or one or more of the partners. There are no registration requirements with any government agency. However, if the sole proprietorship or partnership operates under a fictitious name, it must file a fictitious business name statement with the appropriate government agency. Most states also require publication of the trade name in a local newspaper serving the area where the business is located.

> *Example:* Suppose John Rifkin wants to operate an export-import business (sole proprietorship) under the name "Global." This is commonly stated as, "John Rifkin doing business as Global."

Corporations are required to register their business name with the state. It is important to obtain permission to use a trade name before incorporation. This is intended to ensure that (1) the trade name does not imply a purpose inconsistent with that stated in the articles of incorporation and (2) the trade name is not deceptively similar to registered and reserved names of other companies incorporated to do business in the state. The secretary of state or other designated agency will do a search before authorizing the party to use the name (Cheeseman, 1997a).

Unlike the effect of corporate name registration, registration of fictitious names does not prevent the use of the same name by others. This is because most states do not have a central registry of fictitious business names and because registration of such names is simply intended to indicate the person doing business under the trade name. To avoid registration of a similar trade name, it is advisable to check records of counties as well as local telephone directories for existing fictitious business names (McGrath, Elias, and Shena, 1996).

Another important issue is the potential problems that ensue when such names are used as trademarks to identify goods or services. Suppose John Rifkin intends to use the trade name "Global" to market his perfume imports. It is important to ensure that the same or similar name is not being used or registered with the U.S. Patent and Trademarks Office by another party prior to Rifkin's use of "Global" as a mark. The basic principles also apply in the case of corporations. If Rifkin used "Global" as a trademark in connection with his trade or business for some time, he acquires exclusive use of the mark regardless of the previous registration of the same or similar mark by others. Once a trader acquires a reputation in respect to his mark, then it becomes part of his goodwill, which is regarded by law as personal property that may be sold or licensed.

BANK ACCOUNTS, PERMITS, AND LICENSES

An export-import firm must open a bank account with an international bank that can accommodate specialized transactions, such as letters of credit, foreign exchange payments, forfeiting, and so forth. Some international banks have subsidiaries in importing countries that can verify the creditworthiness of foreign buyers (Barnes, 1997). Sole proprietors and partnerships can open a bank account by submitting an affidavit of the fictitious business name statement to the bank with the initial deposit. In the case of a corporation, banks often require articles of incorporation, an affidavit that the company exists, and its tax identification number. It is important to check with the city or county to determine if permits or business licenses are required.

LOCATION AND USE OF PROFESSIONAL SERVICES

When the export-import business is small, it is economical to use one's home as an office during the early phase of operations. Besides saving money and travel time, using a portion of a home for business provides opportunities for deduction of expenses related to the business. All of the direct expenses for the business part of the home, for example, painting or repairs are deductible expenses. The business use of a home may, however, provide the wrong impression to credit-rating agencies or clients who may decide to pay an impromptu visit. Another problem with using one's home is that it may violate a city's bylaws prohibiting the conduct of any trade or business in an area that is zoned strictly for residential purposes. Home owner's insurance coverage may not cover business equipment, merchandise, or supplies. It may be advisable to rent from a company with extra space or to rent an office with basic services.

The use of professional services (use of attorneys, accountants, consultants) is important not only during the early stages of the business but throughout its operation as an informal source of guidance on liability, expansion, taxes, and related matters. If the entrepreneur does not have sufficient resources to pay for such services, many professionals are willing to reduce rates, defer billing or make other arrangements.

ORGANIZING FOR EXPORT: INDUSTRY APPROACH

The Small Business Administration (SBA) states that, besides multinational firms such as General Motors or IBM, many small-scale industries export their output (Delphos, 1990). For many of these companies, a number of organizational issues need to be addressed to achieve an optimal allocation of resources. Some of the issues include (1) the level at which export decisions should be made, (2) the need for a separate export department, and (3) if the decision is made to establish a separate department, its organization within the overall structure of the firm, including coordination and control of several activities. Such organizational issues involve three related areas:

1. *Subdivision of line operations based on certain fundamental competencies:* This relates to functional (production, finance, etc.), product, and geographical variables. A firm's organizational structure is often designed to fit its corporate strategy, which is, in turn, responsive to environmental realities (Albaum et al., 1994).

2. *Centralization or decentralization of export tasks and functions:* Centralization is generally advantageous for firms with highly standardized products, product usage, buying behavior, and distribution outlets. Advantages from centralization also tend to accrue to firms (a) with few customers and large multinational competitors and (b) with high R&D to sales ratio and rapid technological changes.
3. *Coordination and control:* Coordination and control of various activities among the various units of the organization is determined by the information-sharing needs of central management and foreign units.

Organizational Structures

An international company can organize its export-import department along functional, product, market, or geographical lines.

Some firms organize their international division at headquarters based on functional areas. Under this arrangement, functional staff located at the head office (marketing, financing, etc.) serve all regions in their specialties. Such a structure is easy to supervise and provides access to specialized skills. However, it could lead to coordination problems among various units as well as duplication of tasks and resources. It is generally suitable for companies that produce standardized products during the early stages of international operations.

Organization of export operations along product lines is suitable for firms with diversified product lines and extensive R&D activities. Under this structure, product division managers become responsible for the production and marketing of their respective product lines throughout the world. Even though this structure poses limited coordination problems and promotes cost efficiency in existing markets, it leads to duplication of resources and facilities in various countries and inconsistencies in divisional activities and procedures.

Organization along geographical lines is essentially based on the division of foreign markets into regions that are, in turn, subdivided into areas/subsidiaries. The regions are self-contained and obtain the necessary resources for marketing and research. This structure is suitable for firms with homogenous products that need efficient distribution and product lines that have similar technologies and common end-use markets (Albaum et al., 1994). It allows firms to respond to the changing demands of the market. This organizational approach makes coordination of tasks difficult when new and diverse products are involved. It also leads to duplication of certain tasks at the regional level. Certain companies adopt a mixed structure to manage international marketing activities. This structure combines two or more competencies on a worldwide basis. This approach is described as follows:

> Instead of designating international boundaries, geographical area divisions or product divisions as profit centers, they are all responsible for profitability. National organizations are responsible for country profits, geographical area divisions for a group of national markets and product divisions for worldwide product profitability. (Albaum et al., 1994, pp. 469-470)

A separate export department within a firm may become necessary as overseas sales volume increases. However, the provision of additional resources for a separate department is not warranted at the early phase of market entry, since such activities can often be handled by domestic marketing units.

GENERAL PRINCIPLES OF TAXATION

The United States levies taxes on the worldwide income of its citizens, residents, or business entities. The United States, the Netherlands, and Germany are some of the few countries that impose taxes on the basis of worldwide income; most other countries tax income only if it is earned within their territorial borders. For U.S. tax purposes, an individual is considered a U.S. resident if the person (1) has been issued a resident alien card, (2) has a "substantial presence" in the United States, for example, a foreign individual present in the United States for as least 183 days out of a three-year period ending in the current year (a weighed average), or (3) has made a first election to be treated as a U.S. resident for tax purposes.

A company incorporated in the United States is subject to tax on its worldwide income, as in the case of U.S. citizens and residents. A partnership is not treated as a separate legal entity, and, hence, it does not pay taxes. Such income is taxed in the hands of the individual partners, whether natural or legal entities.

Example 1

Suppose Joan, a U.S. citizen, has an export-import business as a sole proprietor and also works as manager in a fast-food restaurant. The profit from the business is added to her employment income. If the business operates at a loss, the loss will be subtracted from her employment or other income, thus reducing the tax payable.

Example 1A: Joan's Income Tax Liability As Sole Proprietor

	Year 1	Year 2
Joan's salary	30,000	31,500
Export-import profit (loss)	12,000	(8,500)
Total income	42,000	23,000
Personal exemption	(2,500)	(2,500)
Itemized deduction	(10,000)	(10,000)
Taxable income	29,500	10,500

Example 1B: Joan's Income Tax Liability Under a Corporation

Taxable income of export-import company	48,000
Less corporate income tax (15%)	(7,200)
Distributed divided to Joan	40,800
Divided tax on Joan's individual tax return	(11,887)
Total corporate and individual income tax	19,087

As illustrated in example 1B, a corporation's income is subject to double taxation, first at the corporate level and then on the individual income tax return. Such incidences of double taxation are often reduced when deductions and other allowances are applied against taxable income. If earnings are left in the business, the tax rate may be lower than what would be paid by a sole proprietor. If the export-import business is incorporated as an S corporation, earnings are taxed only once at the owner's individual tax rate. Payment of Social Security tax is also avoided by withdrawing profits as dividends.

TAXATION OF EXPORT-IMPORT TRANSACTIONS

Taxation of U.S. Resident Aliens or Citizens

U.S. citizens and resident aliens are taxed on their worldwide income. In general, the same rules apply irrespective of whether the income is earned in the United States or abroad. Foreign tax credits are allowed against U.S. tax liability to mitigate the effects of taxes by a foreign country on foreign income. This also avoids double taxation of income earned by a U.S. citizen or resident, first in the foreign country where the income is earned (foreign source income) and then in the United States. Such benefits are available mainly to offset income taxes paid or accrued to a foreign country and may not exceed the total U.S. tax due on such income.

Example

Nicole, who is a U.S. resident, has a green card. She exports appliances (washers, dryers, stoves, etc.) to Venezuela and occasionally receives service fees for handling the maintenance and repairs at the clients' locations in Caracas and Valencia. Last year, she received $9,000 in export revenues (taxable income) and $3,500 in service fees (taxable income). No foreign tax was imposed on Nicole's export receipt of $9,000. However, she paid $2,200 in taxes to Venezuela on the service fees. Nicole also received $15,000 from her part-time teaching job at a community school (taxable income). Assume a 30 percent U.S. tax rate:

Source of Income	Taxable Income	Tax Liability
Venezuela	9,000	2,700
Venezuela	3,500	2,200
United States	15,000	4,500
Total Income	**27,500**	**9,400**

$$\text{Foreign tax limit} = \text{U.S. tax liability} \times \frac{\text{Taxable income from all foreign sources}}{\text{Total taxable worldwide income}}$$

The credit is the lesser of creditable taxes paid ($2,200) or accrued to all foreign countries (and U.S. possessions) or the overall foreign tax credit limitation ($3,750). The foreign tax credit limitation = 30 percent (27,500) × 12,500/27,500 = 3,750.

If the foreign tax credit limitation is lower than the foreign tax owed, (i.e., suppose the foreign tax was greater than $3,750), the excess amount can be carried back two years and forward five years to a tax year in which the taxpayer has an excess foreign credit limitation.

Taxation of Nonresident Aliens

A nonresident alien is an individual who is neither a citizen nor a resident of the United States. A nonresident alien is subject to U.S. income tax only on income from sources within the United States.

Taxation of Foreign Corporations

A foreign export-import corporation is subject to tax only on income derived from U.S. sources or effectively connected with a trade or business conducted in the United States. Even though sales revenues by foreign exporters are not generally subject to U.S. tax, income derived from services such as engineering, computers and so forth, and investments in the United States is subject to U.S. tax.

Taxation of Foreign Branches

An export-import firm may enter a foreign market by establishing a branch in a foreign country. Branches are often used to retain exclusive control of overseas operations or to deduct losses on initial overseas activities. However, they can be incorporated abroad when such operations become profitable to enable the firm to defer any U.S. income taxes owed on profits until they are remitted to the United States. A branch is not a separate corporation; it is considered an extension of the domestic corporation. One of the major disadvantages of operating a branch is that it exposes the domestic firm to liability in a foreign country. Foreign branch taxes are paid when they are earned (not when remitted to the United States, as in the case of a foreign corporation), and losses are reported when incurred. Foreign taxes paid or accrued on branch profits are eligible for foreign tax credits.

Taxation of Foreign Subsidiaries and Branches

An export-import firm can enter a foreign market by establishing a separate corporation (subsidiary) to conduct business. The parent corporation and subsidiary are separate legal entities and their individual liabilities are limited to the capital investment of each respective firm. Foreign taxes are paid when the subsidiary receives the income, but U.S. taxes are paid when distributed to shareholders as a dividend. Foreign taxes paid (a ratable share) are eligible for a tax credit at the time of distribution of dividend to the U.S. taxpayer. A U.S. shareholder (parent firm) can also claim a proportional share of a dividends-received deduction.

Example

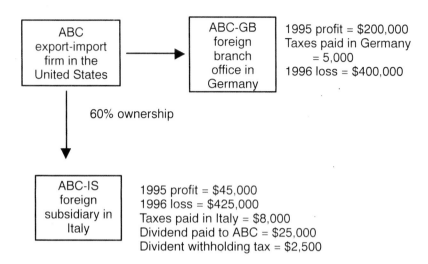

1. The 1995 profit ($200,000) of the German branch is taxable to ABC export-import firm in 1995. Remittance of reported earnings to the United States is not required for tax purposes. However, 1995 profits earned by the Italian subsidiary are subject to tax in the United States only when remitted, that is, taxes could be deferred until remitted to the U.S. parent.
2. The 1996 losses by ABC-GB can be used to offset ABC's 1996 taxable income from its U.S. operations. However, ABC-IS's losses cannot be used to reduce ABC's 1996 taxable income. The $425,000 loss incurred can only be used to reduce profits earned in other years and distributed as dividends to ABC company.
3. Taxes paid by ABC-GB to Germany can be claimed to offset ABC's U.S. taxes due on its profits. In the case of ABC-IS's taxes paid on profits to Italy, ABC can claim a foreign tax credit for the taxes withheld on its dividend receipts for the given year. This does not reduce all or most of the foreign taxes incurred or paid on the subsidiary's profits, since it is limited only to taxes withheld from a foreign subsidiary's dividend remittances. The introduction of the "deemed paid foreign tax credit" was intended to remedy this inequity. Under this method, the U.S. shareholder (ABC) will be deemed to have paid a portion of ABC-IS's foreign taxes, corresponding to the proportion of dividends received and not on any withholding taxes on the dividends distributed.

However, the deemed paid foreign tax credit is available to U.S. companies that own at least 10 percent of the foreign subsidiary's voting stock at the time of distribution and is based only on actual dividends paid. It is also limited only to corporate U.S. shareholders.

Deemed paid tax credit (DPTC) is calculated as follows:

$$\text{DPTC} = \frac{\text{Dividends paid to U.S. corporate shareholder from post-1986 undistributed earnings}}{\text{Accumulated post-1986 undistributed earnings}} \times \begin{array}{c} \text{Post-1986} \\ \text{creditable} \\ \text{taxes paid or} \\ \text{accrued by} \\ \text{foreign} \\ \text{subsidiary} \end{array}$$

$$\text{DPTC} = \frac{\$25,000}{\$45,000} \times 8,000 = \$4,444$$

ABC's U.S. Tax Liability:

Dividend	$25,000
DPTC	$4,444
Gross income	29,444
Corporate tax (35%)	$10,305
Gross U.S. tax liability	$10,305
Less DPTC	($4,444)
Less dividend tax withheld	$2,500
Net ABC tax liability	$3,361

Taxation of Controlled Foreign Corporations

A controlled foreign corporation (CFC) is a foreign corporation in which U.S. shareholders own more than 50 percent of its voting stock or more than 50 percent of the value of its outstanding stock in any of the foreign corporation's tax years. Rules governing CFCs are concerned with preventing U.S. businesspersons from escaping high marginal tax rates in the United States by operating through controlled corporations in a foreign country that imposes little or no tax. The parent company could sell goods or services to a foreign subsidiary and manipulate prices so that most of the profits are allocated to the subsidiary in a country that imposes little or no tax, thus avoiding U.S. and foreign taxes. The CFC could also be used as a base company to make sales outside its country of incorporation or as a holding company to accumulate passive investment income such as interest, dividends, rent, and royalties.

U.S. shareholders must report their share of CFC's subpart F income each year. Subpart F income includes foreign base company income (foreign base sales, services, shipping, and personal holding company income), CFC's income from insurance of U.S. and foreign risks, boycott-related income and bribes, and other illegal payments.

A U.S. shareholder is subject to tax on the subpart F income only when the foreign corporation is a CFC for at least thirty days during its tax year. A U.S. shareholder of a CFC must then include his/her pro rata share of the subpart F income as a deemed dividend that is distributed on the last day of the CFC's tax year or the last day on which the CFC status is retained (McDaniel and Ault, 1981; Ogley, 1995).

Example

Manaco Corporation located in Hong Kong is a CFC owned by XYZ Company of San Diego, California. Manaco Corporation buys computer parts from XYZ Company and sells about 80 percent of the parts in other Asian countries. The remainder is sold to retailers in Hong Kong. Profits earned from sales in foreign countries are foreign base sales income, that is, subpart F income, and taxable to XYZ Company during the current year. Sales to foreign countries of goods manufactured by Manaco in Hong Kong would not constitute foreign base sales income.

Taxation of Foreign Sales Corporations

Foreign Sales Corporations (FSCs) and Domestic Sales Corporations (DISCs) are discussed in Chapter 15.

Deductions and Allowances

Export-import businesses may deduct ordinary and necessary expenses. Ordinary and necessary expenses are defined by the Internal Revenue Service as follows:

An ordinary expense is one that is common and accepted in your type of business, trade, or profession. A necessary expense is one that is helpful and appropriate for your trade, business, or profession. An expense does not have to be indispensable to be considered necessary. (Internal Revenue Service, 1996a, p. 6)

When one starts the export-import business, all costs are treated as capital expenses. These expenses are part of the investment in the business and generally include

1. the cost of getting started in the business before beginning export-import operations, such as market research, expenses for advertising, travel, utilities, repairs, employees' wages, salaries, and fees for executives and consultants; and
2. business assets, such as building, furniture, trucks, etc., and the costs of making any improvements to such assets, for example, a new roof, new floor, and so on. The cost of the improvement is added to the base value of the improved property.

The cost of specific assets can be recovered through depreciation deductions. Other start-up costs can be recovered through amortization; that is, costs are deducted in equal amounts over sixty months or more. Organizational costs for a partnership (expenses for setting up the partnership) or corporation (costs of incorporation, legal and accounting fees, etc.) can be amortized over sixty months and must be claimed on the first business tax return (Siegal, Ford, and Bornstein, 1993).

Once the business has started operations, standard business deductions are applied against gross income. Standard business deductions include the following:

1. *General and administrative expenses:* Office expenses such as telephones, utilities, rent, legal and accounting expenses, salaries, professional services, dues, and so forth. These also include interest payments on debt related to the business, taxes (real estate and excise taxes, estate and employment taxes), insurance, and amortization of capital assets.
2. *Personal and business expenses:* If an expense is incurred partly for business and partly for personal purposes, only the part used for business is deductible. If the export-import business is conducted from one's home, part of the expense of maintaining the home could be claimed as a business expense. Such expenses include mortgage interest, insurance, utilities, and repairs. To successfully claim such limited deductions, part of the home must be used exclusively and regularly as the principal place of business for the export-import

operation or as a place to meet customers or clients. Similarly, automobile expenses to conduct the business are deductible. If the car is used for both business and family transportation, only the miles driven for the business are deductible as business expenses. Automobile-related deductions also include depreciation on the car; expenses for gas, oil, tires, and repairs; and insurance and registration fees (Internal Revenue Service, 1996b).

3. *Entertainment, travel, and related business expenses:* Expenses incurred entertaining clients for promotion, travel expenses (the cost of air, bus, taxi fares), as well as other related expenses (dry cleaning, tips, subscriptions to relevant publications, convention expenses) are tax deductible (Internal Revenue Service, 1996c).

If deductions from the export-import business are more than the income for the year, the net operating loss can be used to lower taxes in other years (Internal Revenue Service, 1996c). All of these expenses have to be specifically allocated and apportioned between foreign and domestic source income.

Tax Treaties

Income tax treaties are entered into by countries to reduce the burden of double taxation on the same activity and to exchange information to prevent tax evasion. Tax treaty partners generally agree on rules about the types of income that a country can tax and the provision of a tax credit for any taxes paid to one country against any taxes owed in another country.

CHAPTER SUMMARY

Ownership Structure

The forms of business organizations are sole proprietorship, partnership, and corporation.

Business or Trade Name

Corporations are required to register their trade name with the state. Sole proprietorships and partnerships are required to register with the appropriate government agency if they operate under a fictitious name.

Bank Accounts, Permits, and Licenses

1. Opening a bank account: It is advisable to open an account with an international bank.

2. An export/import firm can be operated from a home during the early phase of the business. All direct expenses related to the business are tax deductible.
3. The use of professional services is important as a source of guidance on liability, taxes, expansion, and related matters.
4. Permits and licenses: It is important to check with the city or county to determine if permits or business licenses are required.

Organizational Issues

The level at which export decisions should be made, the need for a separate export department, coordination and control of various activities, organizational structure of the export-import department.

Common Organizational Structures

Organization along functional lines, organization along geographical lines, organization based on product or market.

Taxation of Export-Import Business

Deductions and allowances: organizational costs, general and administrative expenses, personal and business expenses, entertainment, travel, and related business expenses.

Chapter 4

Planning and Preparations
for Export

ASSESSING AND SELECTING THE PRODUCT

Although the basic functions of exporting and domestic selling are the same, international markets differ widely because of great variations in certain uncontrollable environmental forces. These include currency exchange controls/risks, taxation, tariffs, and inflation, which happen to originate outside the business enterprise. Such variations require managers who are aware of global threats and opportunities.

If a company already manufactures a product or service, it is reasonable to assume that its product or service is what will be exported. However, companies must first determine the export potential of a product or service before they invest their resources into the business of foreign trade. To establish the export potential of a product, firms must consider the following factors: *the success of the product in domestic markets, participation in overseas trade shows, advertising, and market data.*

If a product is successful in the domestic market, there is a good chance that it will be successful in markets abroad. However, a careful analysis of a product's overseas market potential is needed. One could start by assessing the demand for similar products domestically and abroad, as well as determining the need for certain adaptations or improvements. Trade statistics provide a preliminary indication of markets for a particular product in most countries. For products or services that are not new, low-cost market research is often available that can help determine market potential. Products that are less sophisticated and that have a declining demand in developed countries' markets often encounter a healthy demand in developing nations because the goods are less expensive and easy to handle (Weiss, 1987).

Participation in overseas trade shows is a good way to test the export potential of products or services. For example, by participating in a major bicycle trade show in Germany, Sun Metal Products, Incorporated, of

Warsaw, Indiana, which manufactures wire spoke wheels and alloy and steel rims for bicycles, made sales to eleven different European markets in 1991. Since then, Sun Metal's participation in other trade shows has led to increased sales in the Far East (U.S. Department of Commerce, 1992). Advertising in foreign media also helps in determining the export potential of a product or service. Life Corporation of Milwaukee, Wisconsin, advertised in the U.S. Department of Commerce's catalog to test the export appeal of its emergency oxygen packs, and over 40 percent of the firm's products now go to foreign countries. Market data may not be available for new or unique products or services. However, if an assessment of the actual and potential uses of the product or service indicates that it satisfies certain basic needs in the marketplace, initial sales can be made to establish demand as well as to determine potential improvements.

To achieve success, there must be a strong and lasting management commitment to the export business. The long-term commitment is necessary to ensure the recovery of high market entry costs related to product modification, legal representation, advertising, as well as the development of an agent/distributor network (see Table 4.1).

Companies already operating in the domestic market need to consider the development of export markets through the allocation of financial and personnel resources or through the use of outside experts. In the absence of sufficient knowledge about exporting, it is often advisable for companies to hire consultants who would be engaged in the establishment of the department and the training of personnel.

An individual entrepreneur, acting as a middleman between the manufacturer and the importer, can pick any product or service. The following are two approaches to selecting a product or service.

Systematic Approach

The systematic approach involves selection of a product or service based on overall market demand. An individual entrepreneur often selects a product line or service based on demand and growth trends by observing trade flows. A variety of statistical sources provide data (for products and services) pertaining to major export markets, projected total demand, and U.S. exports in each market, along with the rank of the countries based on the projected import value. This process of collecting and analyzing information will enable the potential exporter to draw conclusions on the best line of products or services as well as promising markets. It is, however, important to select products or services based on familiarity and skill. A computer technician is in a more advantageous position to export computers, computer parts, software, and computer services than a graphic designer because of

TABLE 4.1. The Export Decision: Management Issues

Experience
- With what countries is trade being conducted?
- Which product lines are most in demand, and who are the buyers or likely buyers?
- What is the trend in sales?
- Who are the main domestic and international competitors?
- What lessons have been learned from past experience?

Management and personnel
- Who will be responsible for the export department's organization and staff?
- How much management time should or could be allocated?
- What organizational structure is suitable?

Production capacity
- What is the firm's production capacity?
- What is the effect of exports on domestic sales, production capacity, and cost?
- Is a minimum order quantity required?
- What are the design and packaging requirements for exports?

Financial capacity
- What amount of capital is tied up in exports?
- What level of export department operating costs can be supported?
- What are the initial expenses of export efforts to be allocated?
- When should the export effort pay for itself?

Source: U.S. Department of Commerce, 1990, p. 3.

the former's prior knowledge about the product/service. This individual is more likely to be familiar with product- and/or service-specific issues such as quality, technical specifications, adaptability to overseas requirements, and maintenance or after-sales service.

Other important factors to consider in product/service selection include proximity of the producer or manufacturer to one's home or office in order to maintain close personal contact and to closely monitor/discuss product quality, production delays, order processing, and other pertinent matters. Once a potential product (service) for export has been identified, the individual must undertake market research to select the most promising markets based on import value and growth trends. Both in the case of manufacturing companies and individuals, one must consider if a given product has export potential before substantial time, effort, and capital are invested (Ball and McCulloch, 1996).

Reactive Approach

The reactive approach involves selecting a product based on immediate market need. Even though it is quite common to select the product and identify possible markets, certain exporters initially identify the consumer need and then select a product or service to satisfy the given market demand. A plethora of publications advertise products/services (exporters can also advertise) that are needed in foreign countries by public- or private-sector importers. The first step would be to contact potential importers to indicate one's interest in supplying the product and to obtain other useful information. Once there is a reasonable basis to proceed (based on the importer's response), potential suppliers of the product/service can be identified from the various directories of manufactures. In the United States, for example, the *Thomas Register of American Manufacturers* (1998) is considered to be the comprehensive source of U.S. manufacturers.

In both cases (systematic or reactive), selection of the manufacturer depends on a number of factors, including price, quality, proximity to home or office, as well as the manufacturer's commitment to export sales. There must be a long-term commitment from management to encourage the development of export markets, and this cannot be motivated by occasional needs to dispose of surplus merchandise. It is also important to consider the existence of export restrictions that limit the sale of these products to specific countries and their implications for sales and profits (other factors to consider are presented in International Perspective 4.1). Manufacturers may also impose certain restrictions when they have an agent/distributor or a subsidiary producing the goods in the market.

The reactive approach to selecting a product has certain disadvantages for the individual entrepreneur who acts as an intermediary between the manufacturer and importer:

1. *Lack of focus on a given product or market:* Chasing product orders in different markets impedes the development of a systematic export strategy. This approach ignores the idea of niche exporting, which is critical to the success of any export-import enterprise. It leads to exports of unfamiliar products and/or sales to difficult markets, which hampers the long-term growth and profitability of export businesses.
2. *Absence of a long-term relationship with the importer:* Selling different products to different markets impedes the development of a long-term relationship with importers. It also creates suspicion on the part of importing firms about the long-term reliability and commitment of the firm to exporting.

International Perspective

4.1

IMPORTANT FACTORS TO CONSIDER
IN SELECTING THE EXPORT PRODUCT

Shifting spending patterns: A basic determinant of how much a consumer buys of a product is the person's taste, his or her preference, as well as the price of the product (relative to the price of other products). Another major influence is the consumer's income. If the consumer's income increases, demand for most goods will rise. However, the demand for goods that people regard as necessities, such as fuel, tobacco, bread, or meat, tends to decline and exporters of such products are not likely to greatly benefit from rising consumer incomes in other countries. The demand for luxuries, such as new cars or expensive food, expands even more rapidly. Therefore, exporters should generally put more emphasis on goods that consumers regard as "luxuries" due to shifting spending patterns in response to rising incomes.

Products to be excluded from the list: Individuals starting an export-import trade should initially work with small to medium-sized manufacturers because large companies, such as IBM, have their own export departments or overseas subsidiaries that produce the goods in those markets. Products that compete with such large companies should not be considered at this stage. It is also important to avoid products/services that require too many export/licensing requirements as a condition of executing an international business transaction. Also, the fashion-oriented market is too volatile and unpredictable to warrant a full commitment until a later stage. This also extends to multimillion-dollar contracts for overseas government projects as well as sophisticated products that often require the development of training facilities and a network of technicians for after-sales service.

Emphasis on quality and niche marketing: Several studies on export-import trade indicate that firms which have shown a sustained increase in their sales and overall profits have often emphasized quality and concentrated on niches. In this age of diversity, marketers are being awakened to the erosion of the mass market. Traditional marketing methods are no longer as effective as they used to be, and a new emphasis on quality and niche marketing is proving successful. In the past, for example, Zimbabwe's clothing manufacturers relied on the domestic market for a substantial part of their sales. However, in little more than a year, the domestic marketplace has changed beyond recognition. With declining wages and real per capita incomes, the clothing industry is exploiting market niches. By adding value and exporting to nontraditional markets in Europe, the country generated foreign exchange revenues of over $2.3 billion in 1998 and expects to double its sales in the next few years. It is thus important to stay focused on a small number of target markets.

INTERNATIONAL MARKET RESEARCH

International market research deals with how business organizations engaged in international trade make decisions that lead to the allocation of resources in markets with the greatest potential for sales (Ball and McCulloch, 1996). This process of market screening helps to maximize sales and profits by identifying and selecting the most desirable markets.

Why Conduct International Market Research?

International market research is needed because export/investment decisions are often made without a careful and objective assessment of foreign markets and with a limited appreciation for different environments abroad. This is often a result of the perception that other markets are an extension of the domestic market and that methods/practices that work at home also work abroad. The cost of conducting international research is seen as prohibitively high, and managers make export decisions based on short-term and changing market needs (reactive approach). Firms that do international market research tend to outperform those which do not. A study of Fortune 500 firms in 1993 found that 60 percent of the respondents had advanced market-screening systems (Subramanian, Fernandes, and Harper, 1993).

The purpose of international marketing research is to (1) identify, evaluate, and compare the size and potential of various markets and select the most desirable market(s) for a given product or service and (2) reassess market changes that may require a change in a company's strategy. A firm may research a market by using either primary or secondary data sources.

Primary research (using primary data) is conducted by collecting data directly from the foreign marketplace through interviews, focus groups, observation, surveys, and experimentation with representatives and/or potential buyers. It attempts to answer certain questions about specific markets, such as sales potential or pricing. Primary research has the advantage of being tailored to the company's market and therefore provides specific information. However, collection of such data is often expensive and time-consuming.

Secondary market research is based on data previously collected and assembled for a certain project other than the one at hand. Such information can often be found inside the company or in the library, or it can be purchased from public or private organizations that specialize in providing information, such as overseas market studies, country market surveys, export statistics profiles, foreign trade reports, or competitive assessments of specific industries. Although such data are readily available and inexpensive, certain limitations apply to using secondary sources:

1. The information often does not meet one's specific needs. Because these materials are collected by others for their own purposes, they may be too broad or too narrow in terms of their coverage to be of much value for the research at hand. Also, such information is often out of date

2. There could be differences in definition of terms or units of measure that make it difficult to categorize or compare the research data.

3. It is difficult to assess the accuracy of the information because little is known about the research design or techniques used to gather the data.

INTERNATIONAL MARKET ASSESSMENT

International market assessment is a form of environmental scanning that permits a firm to select a small number of desirable markets on the basis of broad variables. Companies must determine where to sell their products or services because they seldom have enough resources to take advantage of all opportunities. Not using scanning techniques may create the tendency to overlook growing markets. For example, European companies have often neglected the fastest growing markets in Southeast Asia while expanding their traditional markets in North America. Assessment of foreign markets involves subjecting countries to a series of environmental analyses, with a view to selecting a handful of desirable markets for exports. In the early stages of assessment, secondary data are used to establish market size, level of trade, as well as investment and other economic and financial information.

Preliminary Screening (Basic Need and Potential)

The first step in market assessment is the process of establishing whether a basic need for the company's products or services exists in foreign markets. Basic need potential is often determined by environmental conditions such as climate, topography, or natural resources. In situations in which it is difficult to determine potential need, firms can resort to foreign trade and investment data to establish whether the product and/or service has been previously imported, its volume, its dollar value, and the exporting countries.

After establishing basic need potential, it is important to determine whether the need for the product or service has been satisfied. Needs may be met by local production or imports. If there are plans for local production by competitors, imports may cease or be subject to high tariffs or other barriers. Market opportunities still exist for competitive firms if a growing demand for the product cannot be fully met by local production insofar as governments do not apply trade restrictions in favor of local producers or imports from certain countries. If the research indicates that market opportunities exist, it is pertinent to consider the market's overall buying power by examining country-specific factors such as population, gross domestic product, per capita income, distribution of wealth, exports, and imports. While considering these factors, one should note that (1) per capita income might not be a good measure of buying power unless the country has a large middle class and no profound regional disparities, and (2) imports do not always indicate market potential. Availability of foreign currency as well as change in duties and trade policies should be monitored to ensure that they are conducive to the growth of imports in the country.

Second Screening (Financial and Economic Conditions)

Secondary screening involves financial and economic conditions such as trends in inflation, interest rates, exchange rate stability, and availability of credit and financing. Countries with high inflation rates (as well as controlled and low interest rates) should be carefully considered because they may limit the volume of imports by restricting the availability of foreign exchange. There is also a need to verify the availability of commercial banks that can finance overseas transactions and handle collections, payments, and money transfers.

Economic data are also used to measure certain indicators such as market size (relative size of each market as percentage of total world market), market intensity (degree of purchasing power), and growth of the market (annual increase in sales). Countries with advanced economies, such as the United States or Germany, account for a large percentage of the world market for automobiles, computers, and TVs. Their high per capita incomes reflect the attractiveness of the market and the degree of purchasing power. Such information will help in selecting countries with rapidly growing markets and high concentrations of purchasing power.

Third Screening (Political and Legal Forces)

It is important to assess the type of government (democratic/nondemocratic) and its stability. Countries with democratic governments tend to be politically stable and to favor open trade policies and are less likely to resort to measures that restrict imports or impede companies' abilities to take certain actions. Political instability may also lead to damage to property and/or disruption of supplies or sales. It could be as a result of wars, insurrections, takeover of property, and/or change of rules. Consideration should also be given to legal forces in these countries that affect export/ import operations. These include the following:

- *Entry barriers:* Product restrictions, high import tariffs, restrictive quotas, import licenses, special taxes on imports, product labeling, and other restrictive trade laws.
- *Limits on profit remittances and/or ownership:* Imposition of strict limits on capital outflows in foreign currencies, restrictions on or delays in remittance of profits, and ownership requirements to establish a business. In Indonesia, for example, foreign firms and joint ventures with a majority foreign share are not allowed to distribute products in the domestic market unless the foreign company manufactures the product. (Even then, such products can be sold only at the wholesale level.) (U.S. Trade Representative [USTR], 1997)
- *Taxes, price controls, and protection of intellectual property rights:* The existence of high taxes, price controls, and lack of adequate protection for intellectual property rights should be considered.

Fourth Screening (Sociocultural Forces)

This involves consideration of sociocultural forces such as customs, religion, and values that may have an adverse effect on the purchase or consumption of certain products. Examples include sales of pork and its derivatives and alcohol in Muslim countries.

Fifth Screening (Competitive Forces)

It is important to appraise the level and quality of competition in potential markets. The exporter has to identify companies competing in the markets, the level of their technology, the quality and price of their products and/or services, their estimated market shares, as well as other pertinent matters.

Final Selection (Field Trip)

This stage involves a visit to the markets that appear to be promising in light of the market assessment technique. Such visits could be in the form of trade missions (a group of business and government officials that visit a market in search of business opportunities) or trade fairs (a public display of products and services by firms of several countries to prospective customers). The purpose of such visit is to

- corroborate the facts gathered during the various stages of market assessment, and
- supplement currently available information by doing research in the local market, including face-to-face interviews with potential consumers, distributors, agents, and government officials.

This will facilitate final selection of the most desirable markets as well as the development of a marketing plan—product modification, pricing, promotion, and distribution.

DEVELOPING AN INTERNATIONAL BUSINESS PLAN

A business plan involves a process in which an entity puts together a given set of resources (people, capital, materials) to achieve defined goals and objectives over a specific period of time. In addition to providing the direction necessary for success, a sound business plan should be flexible to take advantage of new opportunities or to allow adjustments when certain assumptions or conditions change. This plan should be reviewed and progress assessed (perhaps once every three or four months) to ensure that implementation is consistent with overall goals and objectives laid out in the business plan.

Developing a business plan is an important factor for success, regardless of the size, type, or time of establishment of the business. Even though some export-import companies start a business plan after they have reached a certain stage, planning is needed at all stages of business development from inception to maturity (Williams and Manzo, 1983). It is a road map to one's targeted destination. By allowing for critical evaluation of different alternatives, a business plan forces entrepreneurs to set realistic goals, predict resource allocation, and project future earnings. Such a practice assists in avoiding costly mistakes and enhances the decision-making abilities of businesses (Silvester, 1995). A written business plan is the basis upon which other parties (e.g., bankers, potential partners, etc.) assess the overall business concern. It is used for obtaining bank financing, seeking investment funds, obtaining large contracts to supply governments or companies, or arranging strategic alliances to conduct joint marketing and other activities.

The structure of a typical business plan includes the following components (see Figure 4.1): executive summary description, the industry and company, target market, present and future competition, marketing plan and sales strategy, management and organization, long-term development and exit plan, as well as the financial plan (Cohen, 1995). Some plans also include critical risks/problems and community benefits.

EXPORT COUNSELING AND ASSISTANCE

A number of assistance sources are available to exporters.

The U.S. Department of Commerce

Through the local district office, the exporter has access to all assistance available through the International Trade Administration (ITA) and to trade information gathered overseas by the U.S. and foreign commercial services. The commercial services located in Export Assistance Centers throughout the United States and in more than seventy countries abroad provide export counseling and advice, information on markets abroad, international contacts, and advocacy services.

U.S. Export Assistance Centers (EACs)

EACs are intended to deliver a comprehensive array of export counseling and trade finance services to U.S. firms. They integrate the export marketing know-how of the Department of Commerce with the trade finance expertise of the Small Business Administration and Export-Import Bank. EAC trade specialists help U.S. firms enter new markets and increase market share by identifying the best markets for their products; developing an effective marketing strategy; advising on distribution channels, market entry, promotion, and export procedures; and assisting with trade finance. They are generally located with state promotion agencies, local chambers of commerce, and other local export promotion organizations.

Small Business Administration (SBA)

The SBA provides free export counseling services to potential and current small business exporters (through its field offices) throughout the

FIGURE 4.1. Structure of an International Business Plan

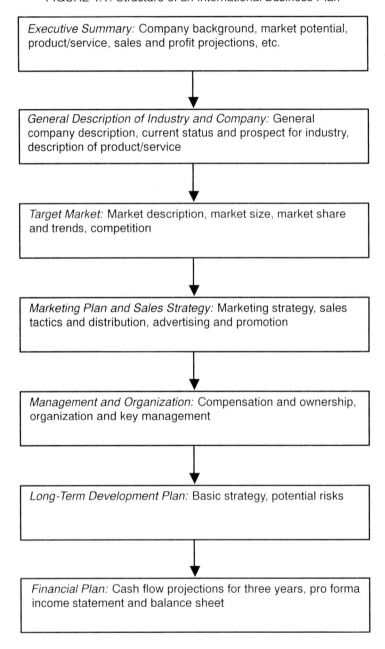

Executive Summary: Company background, market potential, product/service, sales and profit projections, etc.

General Description of Industry and Company: General company description, current status and prospect for industry, description of product/service

Target Market: Market description, market size, market share and trends, competition

Marketing Plan and Sales Strategy: Marketing strategy, sales tactics and distribution, advertising and promotion

Management and Organization: Compensation and ownership, organization and key management

Long-Term Development Plan: Basic strategy, potential risks

Financial Plan: Cash flow projections for three years, pro forma income statement and balance sheet

United States. Members of the Service Corps of Retired Executives (SCORE) and the Active Corps of Executives (ACE), with years of practical experience in international trade, assist small firms in evaluating export potential, developing and implementing export marketing plans, identifying problem areas, and so forth. Additional export counseling and assistance is offered through Small Business Development Centers (SBDCs) that are located within some colleges and universities. The centers are intended to offer technical help to exporters by providing, for example, an export marketing feasibility study and an analysis for the client firms. There is also an initial legal assistance program for small exporters on the legal aspects of exporting.

U.S. Department of Agriculture

The U.S. Department of Agriculture (USDA) provides a wide variety of programs to promote U.S. agricultural exports. Some of the trade assistance programs include promotion of U.S. farm exports in foreign markets, services of commodity and marketing specialists, trade fairs, and information services.

State Government and City Agencies

Many states, cities, and counties have special programs to assist their own exporters. Such programs generally include export education, marketing assistance, trade missions, and trade shows.

Private Sources of Export Assistance

Commercial banks, trading companies, trade clubs, chambers of commerce and trade associations, and trade consultants provide various forms of export assistance (see Table 4.2).

OVERSEAS TRAVEL AND PROMOTION

Once market research is conducted and the target countries are selected, the next step is to visit the countries to locate and cultivate new customers or to develop and maintain relationships with foreign distributors. As we enter the twenty-first century, the world has become one market, and this has naturally given rise to more intercultural encounters. The exporter has to be aware of certain important factors before embarking on a trip, not only to avoid embarrassment, but also to be able to conclude a successful business arrangement.

TABLE 4.2. Private Sources of Export Assistance

Private Sources	Services
Commercial banks	Advice on export regulations, exchange of currencies, financing exports, collections, credit information and assistance
Trading companies	Market research and promotion, shipping and documentation, financing sales, facilitating prompt payment, appointing overseas distributors, etc.
World trade clubs	Education programs on international trade and organization of promotional events
Chambers of commerce and trade associations	Chambers of commerce provide the following services: export seminars, trade promotion, contacts with foreign companies and distributors, issuance of certificates of origin, transportation routing and consolidating shipments. U.S. chambers of commerce abroad are also valuable sources of marketing information. Trade associations provide information on market demand and trends and other information on pertinent trade issues through newsletters.
Trade consultants	Advice on all aspects of exporting, ranging from domestic/foreign regulations to market research and risk analysis

Planning and Preparing for the Trip

Making Prior Arrangements

The most important meetings should be confirmed before leaving the United States. One should avoid traveling during national holidays or political elections in the host countries. Contacts can be made with the Department of Commerce country desk officers in Washington, DC, and/

or U.S. embassies abroad to obtain current and reliable information about the target countries.

Acquiring Basic Knowledge of the Host Country

Exporters should know some basic facts about the history, culture, and customs of the host countries. Several books and magazines cover business manners, customs, dietary practices, humor, and acceptable dress in various countries. It is essential to exercise flexibility and cultural sensitivity when doing business abroad. The exporter should also obtain prior information on such important areas as weather conditions, health care, exchanging currency, and visa requirements. Various travel publications provide such information.

Obtaining the ATA Carnet

For exporters who take product samples, duties and burdensome customs formalities can be avoided by obtaining the ATA (Admission Temporaire) carnet. The United States is a member of the ATA carnet system, which permits U.S. commercial and professional travelers to take material to member countries of the ATA carnet system for a temporary period of time without paying duty. An exporter should check whether a host country is a member of the ATA convention. The U.S. Council for International Business handles applications for carnets. A bond, a letter of credit, or a cash equivalent (as guarantee for 40 percent of the value) will, however, be required to cover outstanding duties in case the samples are not returned to the United States (Tuller, 1994; U.S. Department of Commerce, 1998).

Business Negotiations

Negotiations should be entered into with sufficient planning and preparation. The exporter should establish the line or boundary below which he/she is not willing to concede. It is also advisable to draft the agreements, since it will enable the exporter to include terms and conditions with important implications into the contract.

Documentation

The exporter should document the various meetings at the end of the day to avoid confusing one market with another. It also provides a record for company files. Once the trip is over and the exporter returns home, there should be an immediate follow-up, with a letter confirming the commitments and the timetable for implementation of these commitments.

Overseas Promotion

Overseas promotion of exports is often designed to open new markets, maintain and increase existing market share, and obtain market intelligence. Such efforts must meet strategic marketing goals and achieve the greatest impact at the lowest possible cost. Effective promotion should go beyond enabling the potential buyer to receive the desired information. It must be strong enough to motivate him/her to react positively. This requires the conveying of a message that does not offend cultural sensibilities and one that is uniquely designed for each market. The exporter can choose one or a combination of promotional tools: direct mail, advertising, trade fairs/missions, and publicity. The choice will depend on the target audience, company objectives, the product or service exported, the availability of internal resources, as well as the availability of the tool in a particular market (Czinkota, Ronkainen, and Moffett, 1996). Exporters may use the same promotional strategy in different foreign markets if the target markets vary little with respect to product use and consumer attitudes. In some cases, the product and/or promotional strategy must be adapted to foreign market conditions. For example, Tang sold in Latin America is especially sweet and promoted as a drink for mealtime. In the United States, people drink it in the morning and the product is promoted as a breakfast drink (Ball and McCulloch, 1996).

In certain developing countries where the rate of illiteracy is high, advertising in periodicals does not reach a broad audience. However, if the product or service marketed is intended for a small part of the population, such as the middle/high-income consumers, using periodicals could be an effective way of reaching the target market. For products that are intended for a broader audience, such as soap or cooking oil, radios or billboards could be an effective way of reaching many consumers in these countries.

It is often stated that adapting a product to local conditions and accentuating the local nature of a certain aspect of the product in the promotional material tend to create a favorable image among the public and stimulate product sales. This means that exporters should consider ways and means of localizing a certain part of their activity, such as product adaptation, to local conditions or assembly of parts, in the host countries. Such activities not only increase product sales but also create employment opportunities in the local economy. For less sophisticated products, a firm could export the necessary ingredients or components into a host country, preferably into a free-trade zone, and use local labor to produce or assemble the final product. In addition to being a good promotional tool for the product, such localization will enhance the competitiveness of the product by reducing cost.

Advertising

Advertising is any paid form of nonpersonal presentation and promotion of ideas, goods, or services by an identified sponsor. Typically, no one vehicle reaches an entire target audience, and, hence, exporters must evaluate the many alternatives so as to meet their desired objectives. One or a combination of vehicles can be used (magazines, newspapers, TV, radio, direct mail, billboards) to carry the advertisements to target audiences. Exporters should be aware of regulations in various countries that govern advertising. In some European countries, for example, television stations allow only a certain percentage (12 to 18 percent) of advertising per hour. In many developed countries, the advertising of tobacco and alcoholic beverages is heavily regulated. In some Latin American countries, such as Peru, commercial advertising on national television should be domestically produced. The advertising process involves (1) budgeting—how much it will cost and how much the exporter can afford, (2) determining the most effective and least expensive media to reach the potential customer, and (3) preparing the appropriate advertising package that emphasizes the important, but minimal, number of points.

Small exporters often use direct mail (correspondence and brochures) to reach their overseas customers. In Southeast Asian markets, direct mail is the most effective way of promoting the sale of industrial goods. Brochures have to be translated into the local language and accurate mailing lists have to be obtained. Mailing lists can be purchased from private firms—most libraries have various resources, such as trade publications and journals of various trade associations, from which a list of potential overseas customers can be obtained. In addition, such lists are available from the directory and catalog of trade shows and other government publications, such as *Foreign Trades Index*, the *Export Contact List Service*, and the *World Traders Data Reports* (WTDR).

The exporter can use one or a combination of the following media to advertise the product or service.

Foreign media. A product can be advertised in an overseas retailer's or distributor's catalog or trade publication. Cooperative advertising, that is, a group advertising program, can be arranged by business associations and local chambers of commerce. Cooperative advertising is more effective for noncompeting and/or complementary products. The advantage of such advertising is that it reduces expenses, especially for small exporters, and also enables exporters to combine advertising budgets to reach a larger audience than is normally possible individually.

Government-supported advertising. There are many government-supported (federal and state) promotional programs for U.S. exporting firms that facilitate the marketing of U.S. products overseas. Commercial News U.S.A. (CNUSA), for example, is a Department of Commerce advertising program designed to assist overseas buyers in finding U.S. products or services. It is an export catalog/magazine that promotes U.S. exports to more than 150 countries at a fraction of the cost of any other advertising.

Commercial publications. Many U.S. trade publications are widely read in numerous parts of the world. Advertising in such journals or magazines will enable the exporter to reach a broader market. Some of these publications include *Showcase U.S.A., Export,* and *Automobile and Truck International.*

Tuller describes the reasons why certain overseas promotional tools, such as advertising, fail to deliver:

> (a) the expected results were ill defined, (b) the time frame within which results could be expected was too short, (c) advertisements were inappropriately presented, (d) the wrong media was used. (Tuller, 1994, p. 225)

Personal Selling

Personal selling is often used during the first stages of internationalization. It is also used for the marketing of industrial, especially high-priced, goods. Personal selling entails oral presentations by sales personnel of the organization or agents to prospective overseas purchasers. Salespeople also collect information on competitive products, prices, services, and delivery problems that assist exporters in improving quality and service. In short, such media are used in cases in which advertising does not provide an effective line with target markets, the price is subject to negotiation, and the product/service needs customer application assistance.

Sales Promotion

Sales promotion refers to marketing activity other than advertising, personal selling, or publicity. It includes trade shows, trade fairs, demonstrations, and other nonrecurring selling efforts not in the ordinary routine (Asheghian and Ibrahimi, 1990). Trade shows are events at which firms display their products in exhibits at a central location and invite dealers or customers to visit the exhibits. It is estimated that over 2,000 trade shows take place in about eighty countries every year. They are a cost-effective way of reaching a large number of customers who might otherwise be difficult to reach. Adding to their benefit, from a cost and efficiency standpoint, is that trade shows help exporters to contact and evaluate potential agents and distributors. Trade Association data indicate that 54 percent of all qualified leads developed by U.S. exporters selling industrial products at trade shows were closed by a fax, letter, or phone call (Vanderleest, 1994).

Trade fairs can be organized by certain industries, trade associations or chambers of commerce. For example, the Hanover trade fair in Germany organizes regional and national fairs and exhibitions in various product sectors targeted at specialized audiences as well as the general public. Every year, it organizes approximately fifty trade fairs and exhibitions that attract about 28,000 exhibitors and 2.5 million visitors from over 100 countries around the world. The Seoul International Gift and Accessories show is one of the largest trade fairs for gift and fashion accessories in Asia. It attracts about 32,000 local and overseas visitors, resulting in about $15 million in sales.

Trade shows are also supported or organized by governments to promote exports. In the United States, the Department of Commerce (DOC) organizes various export promotion events, such as exhibitions, seminars, trade missions, and other customized promotions for individual U.S. companies. Under the International Buyer Program, the DOC selects twenty-four leading U.S. trade exhibitions each year in industries with high export potential. DOC offices abroad recruit foreign buyers and distributors to attend these shows, while program staff help exhibiting firms make contact with international visitors at the show to achieve direct export sales and/or international representation. The DOC, through the certified trade fair program, supports private-sector organized shows. Exhibitors use U.S. pavilions to create enhanced visibility and also receive the support of commercial services from U.S. embassies and consulates. The DOC and state agencies also jointly organize U.S. company catalogs/product literature to present to potential customers abroad and send the trade leads directly to participating U.S. firms. Many developed countries have similar programs to promote the sale of their products abroad.

Trade missions are another export sales promotion tool. Under a trade mission, a group of business people and/or government officials visits foreign markets in search of business opportunities. Missions typically target specific industries in selected countries. Events are also organized by private organizations or government agencies so that foreign buyer groups can come to the United States to meet individually with U.S. companies, exporters, or relevant trade associations. At these events, foreign businesses buy U.S. products, negotiate distributor agreements, find joint venture partners, or learn about current industry trends.

Publicity

Publicity is communicating with an audience through personal or nonpersonal media that are not explicitly paid for delivering the messages. This is done by planting commercially significant news about the exporter and/or products in a published medium or obtaining favorable presentation on the local media without sponsoring it. A carefully managed advertising and public relations program is essential to the long-term success of an export firm. The public relations (publicity) program could include charitable donations to schools, hospitals, and other social causes; sponsorship of youth athletic teams; participation in local parades, as well as inviting the media to cover special events sponsored or supported by the export company.

CHAPTER SUMMARY

Assessing and Selecting the Product

To establish market potential for a product/service, it is important to consider (a) success of the product in the domestic market, (b) participation in overseas trade shows, (c) advertising in foreign media, and (d) market data.

Approaches to selecting a product for export:

1. Systematic approach: product selection based on overall market demand.
2. Reactive approach: selection of a product based on immediate (short-term) market need.

International Market Research (IMR)

IMR helps business organizations in making business decisions that lead to the proper allocation of resources in markets with the greatest potential for sales. It involves five steps.

International Perspective

4.2

A TYPICAL EXPORT TRANSACTION

Step 1—The exporter establishes initial contact by responding to an overseas buyer's advertisement (ad) for a product that she or he can supply. Such ads are available in various trade publications. The exporter's letter briefly introduces the company and requests more information on the product needed as well as bank and trade references.

Step 2—The prospective buyer responds to the exporter's letter or fax by specifying the type and quantity of product needed, with a sample where appropriate. The potential importer also sends his/her trade references.

Step 3—The exporter checks with the consulate of the importer's country to determine (a) whether the product can be legally imported and any restrictions that may apply and (b) any requirements that need to be met. The consulate may indicate that a certificate of origin is needed to clear shipment at the foreign port. The exporter also verifies the buyer's bank and trade references through its bank and other U.S. government agencies, such as the Department of Commerce.

Step 4—The exporter (if an agent) contacts manufacturers of the product to (a) establish if the given product is available for export to the country in question and (b) obtain and compare price lists, catalogs, and samples.

Step 5—The exporter selects the product from responses submitted by manufacturers based on quality, cost, and delivery time. The sample selected is sent by airmail to the overseas customer to determine if the product is acceptable to the latter. In the meantime, the exporter prepares and sends a price quotation suggesting the mode of transportation and letter of credit terms. The price quotation should include commission and markup.

Step 6—The exporter obtains a positive response from the overseas customer and is requested to send a pro forma invoice to enable the latter to obtain an import and foreign exchange permit. The exporter sends the pro forma invoice.

Step 7—The overseas customer receives the pro forma invoice, opens a confirmed irrevocable letter of credit for the benefit of the exporter, and sends an order to the latter to ship the merchandise.

Step 8—The exporter verifies with its bank about the validity of the letter of credit and finds that it meets the agreed conditions in the export contract and that it will be honored by the bank if the exporter meets the terms. The exporter ships the merchandise and submits the required documents (such as bill of lading, commercial invoice, consular invoice, certificate of origin, packing list, etc.) to the bank with a request for payment. The exporter is paid, the merchandise is on transit, and the transaction is completed.

International Perspective

4.3

**THE TWELVE MOST COMMON MISTAKES
OF POTENTIAL EXPORTERS**

- Failure to obtain qualified export counseling and to develop a master international marketing plan before starting an export business
- Insufficient commitment by top management to overcome the initial difficulties and financial requirements of exporting
- Insufficient care in selecting overseas distributors
- Chasing orders from around the world instead of establishing a basis for profitable operations and orderly growth
- Neglecting export business when the U.S. market booms
- Failure to treat international distributors on an equal basis with domestic counterparts
- Assuming that a given market technique and product will automatically be successful in all countries
- Unwillingness to modify products to meet regulations or cultural preferences of other countries
- Failure to print service, sale, and warranty messages in locally understood languages
- Failure to consider licensing or joint venture agreements
- Failure to provide readily available servicing for the product

---

Source: U.S. Department of Commerce, 1990, p. 85.

Developing an Export-Import Business Plan

Typical structure of a business plan: executive summary, general description of industry and company, target market, marketing plan and sales strategy, management and organization, long-term development plan, financial plan.

Sources of Export Counseling

Public Sources

U.S. Department of Commerce, U.S. Export Assistance Centers, and The Small Business Administration.

Private Sources

Commercial banks, trading companies, world trade clubs, chambers of commerce and trade associations, trade consultants.

Business Travel and Promotion Abroad

Planning and Preparing for the Trip

Making prior arrangements, acquiring basic knowledge of host country, using the ATA carnet, preparing for business negotiations, documentation.

Overseas Promotion

Advertising, personal selling, sales promotion, and publicity.

Chapter 5

Export Channels of Distribution

DISTRIBUTION CHANNEL SELECTION

Export firms can be involved in two principal channels of distribution when marketing abroad.

Indirect Channels

With indirect channels, the firm exports through an independent local middleman that assumes responsibility for moving the product overseas. Indirect exporting entails reliance on another firm to act as a sales intermediary and to assume responsibility for marketing and shipping the product overseas. The manufacturer incurs no start-up cost, and this method provides small firms with little experience in foreign trade access to overseas markets without their direct involvement. However, using indirect channels has certain disadvantages: (1) the manufacturer loses control over the marketing of its product overseas, and (2) the manufacturer's success totally depends on the initiative and efforts of the chosen intermediary. The latter could give low priority to, or even discontinue, marketing the firm's products in cases in which the competitor's product provides a better sales or profit potential. A typical example of a firm involved in indirect exporting is International Trade and Marketing Corporation of Washington, DC. The company has exclusive agreements with ten U.S. suppliers of orthopedic equipment and supplies. It purchases 90 percent of the goods it handles for resale to overseas customers.

Direct Channels

With direct channels, the firm sells directly to foreign distributors, retailers, or trading companies. Direct sales can also be made through agents located in a foreign country. Direct exporting can be expensive and time-consuming. However, it offers manufacturers opportunities to learn about their markets and customers in order to forge better relationships with their trading partners. It also allows firms greater control over various activities. Systems Center, Incorporated, of Reston, Virginia, which makes computer software for mainframe computers, attributes much of its export success to its international network of sales agents (U.S. Department of Commerce, 1992). The decision to market products directly or to use the services of an intermediary is based on several important factors; these are detailed in the following material.

International Marketing Objectives of the Firm

The marketing objectives of the firm with respect to sales, market share, profitability, and level of financial commitment will often determine channel choice.

Manufacturer's Resources and Experience

A direct channel structure may be neither feasible nor desirable in light of a firm's limited resources and/or commitment. Small to medium-sized firms appear to use indirect channels due to their limited resources and small export volumes, whereas large firms use similar channels because of trade barriers in the host country that may restrict or prohibit direct forms of ownership (Kogut, 1986). Firms tend to use independent intermediaries during the early phases of their internationalization efforts compared to those with greater experience.

Availability and Capability of Intermediary

Every country has certain distribution patterns that have evolved over the years and are complemented by supportive institutions. Firms that have used specific types of distribution channels in certain countries may find it difficult to use similar channels in other countries. This occurs in cases in which distributors have exclusive arrangements with other suppliers/competitors or when such channels do not exist.

Customer and Product Characteristics

If the number of consumers is large and concentrated in major population centers, the company may opt for direct or multiple channels of distribution. In Japan, for example, over half of the population lives in the Tokyo-Nagoya-Osaka market area (Cateora, 1996). Another factor is that customers may also have developed a habit of buying from a particular channel and reluctant to change in the short term.

Direct exporting is often preferable if customers are geographically homogeneous, have similar buying habits, and are limited in number, which allows for direct customer contact and greater control (Seifert and Ford, 1989). The choice of channel structure is primarily dictated by market considerations. However, in certain situations, the nature of the product determines channel choice. In a study on export channels of distribution in the United States, 52.7 percent of the respondents indicated that the distribution was primarily dictated by the market, while 15.5 percent stated that the choice was dictated by the nature of the product exported (Ibid.). For example, industrial equipment of considerable size and value that requires more after-sales service is usually exported to the user or through the use of other direct channels. Direct channels are also frequently used for products of a perishable nature or of high unit value (since it will bring more profit) or for products that are custom-made or highly differentiated. Smaller equipment, industrial supplies, and consumer goods, on the other hand, tend to have longer channels. In Canada, for example, consumer goods are purchased by importing wholesalers, department stores, mail-order houses, chain stores, and single-line retailers.

Marketing Environment

The use of direct channels is more likely in countries that are more similar in culture to the exporter's home country. For example, U.S. sales to Canada are characterized by short (direct) marketing channels compared to the indirect channels used in Japan and Southeast Asia. In certain cases, firms have limited options in the selection of appropriate channels for their products. In the lumber industry, the use of export intermediaries is the norm in many countries. In Finland, over 90 percent of distribution of nondurable consumer goods is handled by four wholesale chains. Exporters have to use these distribution channels to gain significant penetration of the market (Czinkota, Ronkainen, and Moffett, 1998). Legislation in certain countries requires that foreign firms be represented by local firms that are wholly owned by nationals of the country. Under the foreign investment legislation of Vietnam, for example, foreign companies are not allowed to engage directly in trade in Vietnam other than the direct marketing of goods they have manufactured there. Exporters must market their goods indirectly by appointing a local agent or distributor. Some studies support the use of direct/integrated channels when there is a high degree of environmental uncertainty. The establishment of integrated channels is intended to place the firm closer to the market so as to react and adapt to unforeseen circumstances (Klein, Frazier, and Roth, 1990; Chan, 1992).

Control and Coverage

A direct or integrated channel affords the manufacturer more control over its distribution and its link to the end user. However, it is not a practical option for firms that do not have adequate foreign market knowledge or the necessary financial, operational, and strategic capabilities.

Firms that use indirect channels are still able to exercise control mechanisms to coordinate and influence foreign intermediary actions. Two types of controls are available for the manufacturer/exporter: process controls and output controls. Under process controls, the manufacturer's intervention is intended to influence the means intermediaries use to achieve desirable ends (selling technique, servicing procedure, promotion, etc.). Output controls are used to influence indirectly the ends achieved by the distributor. The latter includes monitoring sales volume, profits, and other performance-based indicators (Bello and Gilliland, 1997). It is important to note the following salient points with respect to manufacturers' coordination and control of independent foreign intermediaries:

- Manufacturers must rely on both unilateral and bilateral (collaboration) control mechanisms to organize and manage their export relationships with independent foreign intermediaries.
- The use of output controls tends to have a positive impact on foreign intermediaries' overall performance. Process controls, however, do not appear to account for performance benefits largely due to manufacturers' inadequate knowledge of foreign marketing procedures.
- Firms that export highly technical and sophisticated products tend to exercise high levels of control (process and output controls) over foreign intermediaries to protect their proprietary rights (trade secrets/ know-how) as well as to address unique customer needs.

In terms of coverage, firms that use longer channels tend to use different intermediaries (intensive coverage). However, recent studies show a positive relationship between channel directness and intensive coverage. This means that firms employing direct methods to reach their overseas customers tend to use a large number of different types of channel intermediaries.

Types of Intermediaries

One of the distinguishing features of direct and indirect channel alternatives is the location of the second channel. If the second channel is located in the producer's country, it is considered an indirect channel, whereas if it is located in the buyer's country, it is assumed to be a direct channel. This means that agents, distributors, or other middlemen could be in either category depending on whether they are located in the buyer's or seller's country. Channel alternatives are also defined on the basis of ownership of the distribution channel: a direct channel is one owned and managed by the company, as opposed to one in which distribution is handled by outside agents and middlemen. A firm's channel structure is also defined in terms of the percentage of equity held in the distribution organization: majority ownership (greater than 50 percent) is treated as a direct or integrated channel, while less than majority ownership is considered an indirect channel. The first definition of channel alternatives is used in this chapter.

INDIRECT CHANNELS

Several intermediaries are associated with indirect channels, and each type offers distinct advantages. Indirect channels are classified here on the basis of their functions.

Exporters That Sell on Behalf of the Manufacturer

Manufacturer's Export Agents (MEAs)

Manufacturer's export agents usually represent various manufacturers of related and noncompeting products. They may also operate on an exclusive basis. It is an ideal channel to use especially in cases involving a widespread or thin overseas market. It is also used when the product is new and demand conditions are uncertain. The usual roles of the MEA are as follows:

- Handle direct marketing, promotion, shipping, and sometimes financing of merchandise. The agent does not offer all services.
- Take possession but not title to the goods. The MEA works for commission; risk of loss remains with the manufacturer.
- Represent the manufacturer on a continuous or permanent basis as defined in the contract.

Export Management Companies (EMCs)

EMCs act as the export department for one or several manufacturers of noncompetitive products. Over 2,000 EMCs in the United States provide extensive services for manufacturers that include, but are not limited to, market analyses, shipping, documentation, promotion, financial and legal services, purchase for resale, and agency services (locating and arranging sale).

Most EMCs are small and usually specialize by product, foreign market, or both. Some are capable of performing only limited functions, such as strategic planning or promotion. EMCs solicit and carry on business in their own name or in the name of the manufacturer for a commission, salary, or retainer plus commission. Occasionally, they purchase products by direct payment or financing for resale to their own customers. The following are some of the disadvantages of using EMCs:

- Manufacturers may lose control over foreign sales. To retain sufficient control, manufacturers should ask for regular reports on marketing efforts, promotion, sales, and so forth. This right to review marketing plans and efforts should be included in the agreement.
- EMCs that work on commission may lose interest if sales do not come immediately. They may be less interested in new or unknown products and may not provide sufficient attention to small clients.
- Exporters may not learn international business since EMCs do most of the work related to exports.

Despite these disadvantages, EMCs have marketing and distribution contacts overseas and provide the benefit of economies of scale. EMCs obtain low freight rates by consolidating shipments of several principals. By providing a range of services, they also help manufacturers to concentrate on other areas. For example, Overseas Operations, Incorporated (an EMC), of Redondo Beach, California, handles builders' hardware, housing accessories, and computer software and accessories on a worldwide basis. The company represents several U.S. manufacturers on an exclusive basis and manages all aspects of each sale. The products are shipped directly from the manufacturers, and the company buys products as orders are obtained, making its profit on the markup (Barovick and Anderson, 1992).

International Trading Companies (ITCs)

Trading companies are the most traditional and dominant intermediary in many countries. In Japan, they date back to the nineteenth century and in Western countries, their origins can be traced back to colonial times. They are also prevalent in many less developed countries. They are demand driven; that is, they identify the needs of overseas customers and often act as independent distributors linking buyers and sellers to arrange transactions. They buy and sell goods as merchants taking title to the merchandise. Some work on a commission. They may also handle goods on consignment.

Example. Ultramedic International, a trading company based in New Hyde Park, New York, specializes in medical equipment and supplies, filling orders or sourcing for customers in Latin American markets. Overseas agents provide the company with the necessary information to submit bids or pursue business and it acts as liaison between foreign manufacturers and its customers. The company makes a profit by buying products from manufacturers at a 15 to 40 percent discount. The firm maintains a warehouse where all export packing and shipping is handled. Ultramedic represents many product lines and has several agents or distributors in each country (Barovick and Anderson, 1992).

Trading companies offer services to manufacturers similar to those provided by EMCs. However, there are some differences between the two channels:

- Trading companies offer more services and have more diverse product lines than export management companies. Trading companies are also larger and better financed than EMCs.
- Trading companies are not exclusively restricted to export-import activities. Some are also engaged in production, resource development, and commercial banking. Korean trading companies such as Daewoo and Hyundai, for example, are heavily involved in manufacturing. Some trading companies, such as Mitsubishi (Japan) and Cobec (Brazil), are affiliated with banks and engaged in extension of traditional banking into commercial fields (Meloan and Graham, 1995).

The disadvantages of ITCs are similar to the ones mentioned for EMCs. (International Perspective 5.2 presents a summary of the advantages and disadvantages of indirect channels.)

Exporters That Buy for Their Overseas Customers

Export Commission Agents (ECAs)

Export commission agents represent foreign buyers such as import firms and large industrial users and seek to obtain products that match the

---

International Perspective

5.1

EXPORT TRADING COMPANIES IN GLOBAL MARKETS

Trading companies have been the most traditional channels for international commercial activity. Trading companies supported by governments, such as the English East India Company (1600), The Dutch East India Company (1602), and The French Compagnie des Indes Orientales (1664), were established and enjoyed not only exclusive trading rights but also military protection in exchange for tax payments. Today, trading companies also perform the important functions of exporting, importing, investing, and countertrading. In Japan, for example, the Sogo Shosha, which includes the top nine trading companies, such as Mitsubishi and Mitsui, conducts about two-thirds of the country's imports and a half of its exports. In Korea, trading companies similar in scope to the Sogo Shosha (Daewoo, Hyundai, Samsung) are responsible for a substantial part of the country's exports and imports. In addition to trade, trading companies in these countries are involved in megaprojects, participate in joint ventures, and act as financial deal makers. The success of these conglomerates is due to (1) extensive market infor-

mation that allows for product or area diversification, (2) economies of scale that allow them to obtain preferential freight rates, etc., and (3) preferential access to capital markets that makes it easy to undertake large or risky transactions.

In view of the success of these trading companies, Brazil, Turkey, and the United States have enacted domestic legislation that allows the establishment of trading companies. The Brazilian Decree (No. 1298) of 1972, for example, sets up conditions for the registration of new enterprises with the government and allows local producers to export by selling to a trading company without losing their export incentives. In the United States, the Export Trading Company Act of 1982 allows businesses to join together to export goods and services or to assist unrelated companies to export their products without fear of violating antitrust legislation. Bank participation in trading companies was permitted to enable better access to capital. The legality of any action can be ascertained by precertification of planned activities with the U.S. Department of Commerce.

---

buyers' preferences and requirements. They reside and conduct business in the exporter's country and are paid a commission by their foreign clients. In certain cases, ECAs may be foreign government agencies or quasi-government firms empowered to locate and purchase desired goods. They could operate from a permanent office location in supplier countries or undertake foreign government purchasing missions when the need arises.

International Perspective

5.2
INDIRECT CHANNEL STRUCTURES

ADVANTAGES

- Little or no investment or marketing experience needed. Suitable for firms with limited resources or experience.

- Helps increase overall sales and cash flow.

- Good way to test-market products, develop goodwill, and allow clients to become familiar with a firm's trade name or trademark before making a substantial commitment.

DISADVANTAGES

- Firm's profit margin may be dwindled due to commissions and other payments to foreign intermediaries.

- Limited contact/feedback from end users.

- Loss of control over marketing and pricing; firm totally dependent on the marketing initiative and effort of foreign intermediary; product may be priced too high or too low.

- Foreign intermediary may not provide product support or may damage market potential.

- Limited opportunity to learn international business know-how and develop marketing contacts; creates difficulty in taking over the business after the relationship has ended.

Another variation of the ECA is the resident buyer. The major factor that distinguishes the resident buyer from other ECAs is that, in the case of the former, a long-term relationship is established in which the resident buyer not only undertakes the purchasing function for the overseas principal at the best possible price but also ensures timely delivery of merchandise and facilitates the principal's visits to suppliers and vendors (Onkvisit and Shaw, 1997).

Exporters That Buy and Sell for Their Own Accounts

Export Merchants (EMs)

Export merchants purchase products directly from manufacturers, pack and mark them according to their own specifications, and resell to their overseas customers. They take title to the goods and sell under their own names and, hence, assume all risks associated with ownership. Export merchants generally handle undifferentiated products or products for which brands are not important.

When export merchants, after receiving an order, place an order with the manufacturer to deliver the goods directly to the overseas customer, they are called export drop shippers. In this case, the manufacturer is paid by the drop shipper who, in turn, is paid by the overseas buyer. Such intermediaries are commonly used to export bulky (high-freight), low-unit-value products such as construction materials, coal, lumber, and so forth.

Another variation of export merchant is the export distributor (located in the exporter's country). Export distributors have exclusive rights to sell manufacturers' products in overseas markets. They represent several manufacturers and act as EMCs.

The disadvantage of export merchants as export intermediaries relates to lack of control over marketing, promotion, or pricing.

Cooperative Exporters (CEs)

These are manufacturers or service firms that sell the products of other companies in foreign markets along with their own (Ball and McCulloch, 1996). This generally occurs when a company has a contract with an overseas buyer to provide a wide range of products or services. Often, the company may not have all the products required under the contract and turns to other companies to provide the remaining products. The company (providing the remaining products) could sell its products without incurring export marketing or distribution costs. This channel is often used to export products that are complementary to that of the exporting firm. A good example of this is the case of a heavy equipment manufacturer that wants to fill the demand of its overseas customers for water drilling equipment. The heavy equipment company exports the drilling equipment along with its product to its customers (Sletten, 1994).

Webb-Pomerene Associations (WPAs)

These are organizations of firms in the same industry (export cartels) for the sole purpose of marketing their products overseas. They are exempted from antitrust laws under the U.S. Export Trade Act of 1918 and permitted to set prices, allocate orders, sell products, negotiate and consolidate freight, as well as arrange shipment. There are WPAs in various areas, such as pulp, movies, sulphur, and so on. WPAs are not permitted for services and the arrangement is not suitable for differentiated products because a common association label often replaces individual product brands. In addition to member firms' loss of individual identity, WPAs are vulnerable to lack of group cohesion, similar to other cartels, which undermines their effectiveness. Under the Export Trade Act, the only requirement to operate as a WPA is that the association must file with the Federal Trade Commission within thirty days after formation.

DIRECT CHANNELS

A company could use different avenues to sell its product overseas employing the direct channel structure. Direct exporting provides more control over the export process, potentially higher profits, and a closer relationship to the overseas buyer and the marketplace. However, the firm needs to devote more time, personnel, and other corporate resources that are needed than in the case of indirect exporting (Anonymous, 1987).

Direct Marketing from the Home Country

A firm may sell directly to a foreign retailer or end user, and this is often accomplished through catalog sales or traveling sales representatives who are domestic employees of the exporting firm. Such marketing channels are a viable alternative for many companies that sell books, magazines, housewares, cosmetics, travel, and financial services. Foreign end users include foreign governments and institutions, such as banks, schools, hospitals, or businesses. Buyers can be identified at trade shows, through international publications, and so on. If products are specifically designed for each customer, company representatives are more effective than agents or distributors. The growing use of the Internet is also likely to dramatically increase the sale of products and/or services directly to the retailer or end user. For example, Amazon.com has become one of the largest bookstores in the United States, with over 2.5 million titles. Direct marketing is also used when the manufacturer or retailer desires to increase its revenues and profits while providing its products or services at a lower cost. The firm could also provide better product support services and further enhance its image and reputation.

A major problem with direct sales to consumers results from duty and clearance problems. A country's import regulations may prohibit or limit the direct purchase of merchandise from overseas. Thus, it is important to evaluate a country's trade regulations before orders are processed and effected.

Marketing Through Overseas Agents and Distributors

Overseas Agents

Overseas agents are independent sales representatives of various non-competing suppliers. They are residents of the country or region where the product is sold and usually work on a commission basis, pay their own expenses, and assume no financial risk or responsibility. Agents rarely take delivery of, and never take title to, goods and are authorized to solicit purchases within their marketing territory and to advise firms on orders placed by prospective purchasers. The prices to be charged are agreed upon between the exporters and the overseas customers. Overseas agents usually do not provide product support services to customers. Agency agreements must be drafted carefully so as to clearly indicate that the agents are not employees of the exporting companies because of potential legal and financial implications, such as payment of benefits upon termination. In some countries, agents are required to register with the government as commercial agents.

Overseas agents are used when firms intend to (1) sell products to small markets that do not attract distributor interest, (2) market to distinct individual customers (custom-made for individuals or projects), (3) sell heavy equipment, machinery, or other big-ticket items that cannot be easily stocked, or (4) solicit public or private bids. Firms deal directly with the customers (after agents inform the firms of the orders) with respect to price, delivery, sales service, and warranty bonds. Given their limited role, agents are not required to have extensive training or to make a substantial financial commitment. They are valuable for their personal contacts and intelligence and help reach markets that would otherwise be inaccessible. The major disadvantages of using agents are (1) legal and financial problems in the event of termination (local laws in many countries discriminate against alien firms [principals] in their contractual relationships with local agents), (2) firms assume the attendant risks and responsibilities, ranging from pricing and delivery to sales services, including collections, and (3) agents have limited training and knowledge about the product and this may adversely impact product sales.

Overseas Distributors

These are independent merchants that import products for resale and are compensated by the markup they charge their customers. Overseas distributors take delivery of and title to the goods and have contractual arrangements with the exporters as well as the customers. No contractual relationships exist between the exporters and the customers and the distributors may not legally obligate exporters to third parties. Distributors may be given exclusive representation for a certain territory, often in return for agreeing not to handle competing merchandise. Certain countries require the registration and approval of distributors (and agents) as well as the representation agreement.

Distributors, unlike agents, take possession of goods and also provide the necessary pre- and postsales services. They carry inventory and spare parts and maintain adequate facilities and personnel for normal service operations. They are responsible for advertising and promotion. Some of the disadvantages of using distributors are (1) loss of control over marketing and pricing (they may price the product too high or too low), (2) limited access to or feedback from customers, (3) limited opportunity to learn international business know-how and about developments in foreign markets, and (4) dealer protection legislation in many countries that may make it difficult and expensive to terminate relationships with distributors (Anonymous, 1996).

LOCATING, CONTACTING, AND EVALUATING AGENTS AND DISTRIBUTORS

Once the firm has identified markets in which to use agents and distributors, it could locate these intermediaries by using various sources: government trade offices (the Department of Commerce in the United States), chambers of commerce, trade shows, international banks and other firms, trade and professional associations, and advertisements in foreign trade publications. After identifying potential agents and distributors in each desired market, the firm should write directly to each, indicating its interest in appointing a representative and including a brochure describing the firm's history, resources, product line, personnel, and other pertinent information.

Evaluation and selection of potential representatives (agents or distributors) is often based on some of the following factors: local reputation and overall background, experience with a similar product or industry and adequate knowledge of the market, commitment not to represent competing

```
┌─────────────────────────────────────────────────┐
│              ┌──────────────────────────┐        │
│              │  International Perspective │       │
│              └──────────────────────────┘        │
│                                                   │
│                        5.3                        │
│           THE JAPANESE DISTRIBUTION SYSTEM        │
```

Distribution channels in Japan are very different from our own; they are as inefficient as they are complex. The system is characterized by multiple layers of wholesalers who have developed close, personal relationships with other wholesalers, manufacturers, importers, and retailers. Moreover, these intimate relationships often serve as an informal barrier to U.S. companies wishing to sell directly to end-users or retailers.

Many American exporters find retailers/end-users unwilling to disrupt their longstanding, personal relationships with Japanese suppliers even when the U.S. company can offer a product of superior or equal quality at a cheaper price. Many Japanese retailers/end users are unwilling to make the switch to an "unreliable" foreign supplier. They fear a lack of commitment on the part of the foreign supplier will lead to problems. This system, although inefficient, does offer some important ad-

vantages for the participants. First, these close business relationships make it far easier for retailers/distributors to suggest product modifications and improvements. Second, this system encourages the sharing of information on product trends, innovations, competition, and overall market opportunities. Third, it contributes to a more cooperative business relationship.

The number of retail outlets in Japan is nearly the same as in the United States, despite the fact that the population of Japan is roughly half that of the United States and Japan is slightly smaller in geographical size than California. Distribution channels vary considerably from industry to industry and product to product, with particular differences between consumer and industrial goods. A foreign firm must understand existing distribution channels in order to utilize them or develop an innovative approach.

Sources: Kennedy, 1993, pp. 20-22; Czinkota and Woronoff, 1997, pp. 8-13.

brands, genuine interest, and ability to devote sufficient time and effort to the product line. In the case of distributors, it is also important to evaluate sales organization; financial, marketing, and promotion capability; installation and after-sales service; timely payments; and similar characteristics. Once the firm has selected an agent or distributor based on the aforementioned criteria, the next step will be to negotiate a formal agreement. Foreign representatives are also interested in firms that are committed to the market and willing to provide the necessary product support and training. They also want to protect their territory from sales by third parties or the firm itself.

CONTRACTS WITH FOREIGN AGENTS AND DISTRIBUTORS (REPRESENTATIVES)

It is estimated that about 50 percent of global trade is handled through overseas agents and distributors. Laws governing agents and distributors are complex and vary from country to country. In certain countries, protective legislation favors local representatives with respect to such matters as market exclusivity and duration or termination of contracts. In the event of termination without good cause, for example, a Belgian distributor is entitled to an indemnity.

Similar laws exist in France, Germany, and other countries. In Germany, maximum compensation payable to agents usually equals one year's gross commissions based on an average over the previous five years or the period of existence of the agency, whichever is shorter. In countries such as Egypt, Indonesia, Japan, and South Korea, representation agreements must be formally registered with, and their contents must be approved by, the appropriate authority. In many Latin American countries, local law governs service contracts if the services are to be performed in local jurisdictions and any representative agreement that is not in conformity with local law will be invalid and unenforceable. Thus, it is important that in the negotiation and drafting of such agreements, sufficient attention is given to the impact of local laws and other pertinent issues.

MAJOR CLAUSES IN REPRESENTATION AGREEMENTS

Definition of Territory

The contract should define the geographical scope of the territory to be represented by the agent or distributor and whether the representative has sole marketing rights. In exclusive contracts, the agreement has to clearly specify whether the firm reserves the right to sell certain product lines to a specific class of buyers, such as governments or quasi-government agencies. If agreements do not explicitly state that they are exclusive, they will often be deemed exclusive if no other representatives have been appointed within a reasonable time. The contract should also state whether the representative could appoint subagents or subdistributors and the latter's status in relation to the firm. It is also important to explicitly state the intention of the parties not to create an employer-employee relationship due to financial and tax implications.

Definition of Product

The contract should identify those products or product lines covered by the agreement as well as the procedures for the addition of successive products. It should also provide for the alteration or deletion of certain product lines based on the exporter's continued production, the representative's performance, or other events.

Representative's Rights and Obligations

The agreement should state that the representative will do its best to promote and market the product and to cooperate to attain the objectives of the exporting firm. It should also include (1) the representative's commitment to periodically inform the exporter of all pertinent information related to market conditions and its activities; (2) the parties' agreement to provide due protection to each other's confidential information as defined in the contract, which often includes seller's patents, trade secrets, and know-how, as well as the representative's marketing information, including customer lists; (3) a provision as to whose responsibility it is to arrange for all the necessary approvals, licenses, and other requirements for the entry and sale of goods in the foreign country; and (4) the right of the representative to carry noncompetitive and complementary products.

An agency agreement should state the nature and scope of an agent's authority to bind the exporter (which is often denied) as well as the agent's discretion with respect to pricing. All sales of products are to be in accordance with the price list and discount structure as established in the contract. The parties could also agree on mechanisms to implement changes in prices and terms. It is also important to stipulate the amount of compensation (commission) when it accrues to the account of the agent, and the time of payment. Most agreements state that all commissions shall not become due and payable until full settlement has been received by the firm. The agent could also be given the responsibility for collection with respect to sales it initiated.

Distributor agreements should state clearly that the overseas distributor acts as a buyer and not as an agent of the seller. The agreement could require the distributor to maintain adequate inventories, facilities, and competent personnel. The exporter could sometimes stipulate that orders representing a minimum value or quantity shall be placed within a fixed time. The agreement also defines the advertising and promotion responsibilities of the distributor, including an undertaking to advertise in certain magazines or journals a minimum number of times a year at its own expense, for example:

> The distributor agrees during the lifetime of this contract to provide and pay for not less than seven full-page advertisements per year, appearing at regular monthly intervals in the national journals or magazines of the industry circulating generally throughout the territory.

Exporter's Rights and Obligations

In agency contracts, the exporter is often required to provide the agent with its price schedules, catalogs, and brochures describing the company, its product, and other pertinent features. In distributor contracts, the exporter is required to provide the distributor and his/her personnel with training and technical assistance as is reasonably required in order to service, maintain, and repair products. In both agency and distributor agreements, the exporter should only warrant that the product complies with the specified standards of quality and also state the party that will be responsible for warranty service. The exporter is also required to provide sufficient supplies of the product and new developments in products, as well as marketing and sales plans.

Definition of Price

In agency agreements, all sales of products are made in accordance with the price list and discount structure agreed upon between the parties. However, the seller reserves the right to change prices at any time, usually upon a thirty- or sixty-days prior notice.

Distributor agreements also contain provisions relating to the price to be charged by the seller upon purchase of goods by the distributor. Any discounts available are also stated. In the case of products that are affected by inflation, the parties could set a definite price ruling on a specific date, such as the date of the sales contract or shipment. The parties could also agree that the exporter charge the distributor the best price it provides other customers at the time of sale (the most-favored-customer price) except for those products supplied to a holding company, subsidiary, or other associated companies of the supplier. The distributor agreement should also stipulate the terms of shipment, such as FOB (free on board) or CIF (cost, insurance, and freight), as well as the method of payment (open account, letter of credit, etc.), for example:

The prices specified are in U.S. dollars, exclusive of taxes and governmental charges, freight, insurance, and other transportation charges. Payment shall be on consignment. The product will be shipped FOB (Miami) to the buyer's address in Colombia.

Renewal or Termination of Contract

In many countries, issues relating to appointment, renewal, or termination of representatives are largely determined by local law. Many foreign representation agreements provide for a short trial period followed by a longer-term appointment if the representative's performance proves satisfactory. It is important to state the duration of appointment and the basis for renewal or termination. Any renewal or termination requires an act of notification to the representative.

In certain countries, the longer the period the representative has been appointed, the more difficult and expensive it is to terminate the contract. Representative agreements are terminated when one of the parties is guilty of nonperformance or of not performing to the satisfaction of the other party, for example:

> In the event that either party should breach any term or condition of this agreement or fail to perform any of its obligations or undertakings, the other party may notify the defaulting party of such default, and if such default is not rectified within sixty days, the party giving notice shall have the right, at its election, to terminate the agreement.

The previous clause is often used to terminate nonperforming representatives. It is, however, important to set certain targets and objective performance criteria against which the representative's performance will be measured: sales volume, inventory turnover rates, advertising, market share, and so on. It is also advisable to include other causes of termination, such as the following:

Right to Terminate Without Cause

A significant number of contracts allow for termination of the contract by either party with no prerequisite of action or omission by the other party upon giving advance notice, for example:

> Either party shall have the right to terminate the agreement at any time by giving not less than 180 days prior written notice of termination to the other party.

Force Majeure

Most contracts state the occurrence of specific events beyond the control of the parties as a basis for termination of the contract. The enumerated actions or events fall into four major categories: (1) acts of God, (2) wars and civil disorder, (3) acts of government, such as exchange controls, host government requirements, and so on, and (4) other acts beyond the parties' control.

Other Causes of Termination

Some contracts provide for termination of the contract in cases such as bankruptcy or liquidation of either party, assignment of contractual rights or duties, change of ownership or management, and nonexclusivity, or the firm's decision to establish its own sales office or assembly operations.

In most countries, the exporter can terminate a representative in accordance with the contractual terms and without payment of indemnity. In situations lacking reasonable grounds for termination, courts impose a liability for unjust termination that is often based on the volume of sales and goodwill developed by the representative, duration of the contract, and so forth. A typical formula is to award a one year's profit or commission to the distributor or agent based on an average over the previous five years or the duration of the contract, whichever is shorter. It may also include cost of termination of the representative's personnel.

Applicable Law and Dispute Settlement

The parties are at liberty to agree between themselves as to what rules should govern their contract. Most contracts state the applicable law to be that of the manufacturer's home state. This indicates the strong bargaining position of exporters and the latter's clear preference to be governed by laws about which they are well informed, including how the contract will function and its repercussions on the whole commercial and legal situation of the parties. In cases with no express or implied choice of law, courts have to decide what law should govern the parties' contract based on the terms and nature of the contract. Many factors are used to settle this issue in the absence of an express choice of law, including the place of contract, the place of performance, the location of the subject matter of the contract, as well as the place of incorporation and place of business of the parties. The contract should also provide for a forum (court) to settle the dispute relating to the validity, interpretation, and performance of the agreement.

Many representative contracts also provide that any dispute between the parties shall be submitted to arbitration for final settlement in accordance with the rules of the International Chamber of Commerce.

MAINTAINING AND MOTIVATING OVERSEAS REPRESENTATIVES

Agents and distributors can be motivated in many ways to do the best possible job of marketing and promoting the firm's product. This could be accomplished by, for example, developing good communications through regular visits from the home office, the organization of conferences, or providing inexpensive free trips for representatives during a given period. It is also important to inform representatives of the companies' goals and principles and to keep them abreast of new developments in the product line, supplies, promotion strategies, and to assist in training and market development. Firms could also motivate representatives through provision of better credit terms or price adjustments based on sales volume or other performance-based criteria.

CHAPTER SUMMARY

Export Channels of Distribution

Channels of distribution used to market products abroad:

1. Indirect channels: exports through independent parties acting as sales intermediaries
2. Direct channels: direct sales to foreign distributors, retailers, or trading companies

Determinants of Channel Selection to Market Products Abroad

1. International marketing objectives of the firm
2. Manufacturer's resources and experience
3. Availability and capability of intermediary
4. Customer and product characteristics

5. Marketing environment
6. Control and coverage

Indirect Channels

Types of indirect channels:

1. Exporters that sell on behalf of the manufacturer: manufacturers' export agents, export management companies, international trading companies
2. Exporters that buy for their overseas customers: export commission agents
3. Exports that buy and sell for their own account: export merchants, cooperative exporters, Webb-Pomerene associations

Direct Channels

Types of direct channels:

1. Direct marketing from the home country
2. Marketing through overseas agents and distributors: overseas agents, overseas distributors

Major Clauses in Representation Agreements

1. Definition of territory and product
2. Representative's rights and obligations
3. Exporter's rights and obligations
4. Definition of price
5. Renewal or termination of contract

Chapter 6

International Logistics and Transportation

Logistics is a total systems approach to management of the distribution process that includes the cost-effective flow and storage of materials or products and related information from point of origin to point of use or consumption.

There are two categories of business logistics:

1. *Materials management:* In the context of export-import trade, logistics applies to the timely movement or flow of materials/products from the sources of supply to the point of manufacture, assembly, or distribution (inbound materials). This includes the acquisition of products, transportation, inventory management, storage, and the handling of materials for production, assembly, or distribution. For example, products can be assembled in Canada for distribution in Canada and the United States.
2. *Physical distribution:* The second phase relates to the movement of the firm's product to consumers (outbound materials). It includes outbound transportation, inventory management, and proper packaging to reduce damage during transit and storage.

Materials management primarily deals with inbound flow, whereas physical distribution is concerned with the outbound flow of materials or products (Guelzo, 1986). Both inbound and outbound activities are interdependent and influence the company's objective of reducing cost while conforming to customer needs. The interdependence of such activities can be illustrated by the example of U.S. flower imports from Latin America. Atlantic Bouquet, a U.S. company, purchases most of its flowers from its sister company that has flower farms in Latin America. Continental Air freights the flowers from company-owned farms in Latin America to a warehouse in Miami before they are moved nationwide by air or truck for distances of less than 300 miles. A proper management of the logistics system, that is, the unique combination of packaging, handling, storage, and transportation, will ensure that the product is imported and made available to the customer at the right time and place and in the right condition.

The interdependence of functional activities has been articulated through various new approaches or concepts:

1. *The systems approach:* The systems concept is based on the premise that the flow of materials within and outside the firm should be considered only in the context of their interaction (Czinkota et al., 1998). This approach puts more emphasis on maximizing the benefits of the corporate system as a whole as opposed to that of individual units.
2. *Total cost approach:* This is a logistics concept based on evaluation of the total cost implications of various activities.
3. *The opportunity cost approach:* This approach considers the trade-off in undertaking certain logistic decisions. For example, the benefits and costs of sourcing components abroad versus buying from domestic sources. Additional costs associated with transportation, increases in safety stock inventory, warehousing costs, and so forth, are examined to ensure that the total opportunity cost of outsourcing abroad is not greater than other available options.

What is the importance of logistics to international trade? One of the major contributions of logistics to international trade is in the area of efficient allocation of resources. International logistics allows countries to export products in which they have a competitive advantage and import products that are either unavailable at home or produced at a lower cost overseas, thus allowing for efficient allocation of resources. For example, natural resource advantages and low-cost labor has enabled Colombia to export flowers to the United States and to import technology. Colombian flower exports have driven less efficient U.S. producers out of their own markets and forced the Dutch out of the rose and carnation markets in the United States (Thuermer, 1998). Such advantages from international trade cannot be realized without a well-managed logistics system. To the extent that logistics facilitates international trade, it contributes to the expansion of economic growth and employment. As import firms expand their ability to procure needed raw materials or components for their customers, international logistics management becomes a critical source of competitive advantage for both the firms and the customers. Such material procurement and sourcing decisions include the number and location of warehouses, levels of inventory to maintain, as well as selection of the appropriate transportation mode and carrier (Christopher, 1992). The development of advanced logistics systems and capabilities has also increased the efficient production, transportation, and distribution of products. For example, by outsourcing logistics to third-party operators, pharmaceutical and health care companies can reduce costs associated with inventory, overhead, labor, and warehousing. The use of various transportation modes facilitates rapid and consistent delivery service to consumers, which in turn reduces the need for safety stock inventory. Transportation cost is also reduced through shipment consolidation and special contracts with carriers for large shipments without adversely affecting delivery time. In short, a well-managed international logistics system can result in optimal inventory levels and optimal production capacity (in multiplant operations), thereby maximizing the use of working capital. All this helps to strengthen the competitive position of domestic companies in global trade.

EXTERNAL INFLUENCES ON LOGISTICS DECISIONS

A number of external factors influence international logistics decisions.

Regulations

Governments in many countries encourage their domestic carriers to handle their exports or imports since the provision of such transportation services contributes to the nation's balance of payments. This can be illustrated by U.S.-China trade, which is mostly transported by Chinese vessels. This occurs because the Chinese Foreign Trade Agency insists, whenever possible, on terms that allow it to control most of the transportation and thus use its state-run transport companies (Davies, 1987).

International logistics activity in the form of overseas transportation, handling of shipment, and distribution management also creates jobs. Besides the need to earn or save foreign currency and the creation of employment opportunities, governments support their national carriers to ensure national shipping capacity during war or other emergencies. Governments also control or limit the export and import of certain commodities through a host of devices, such as export controls, import tariffs, and nontariff barriers, for example, quotas or cumbersome import clearance procedures. There are also bilateral negotiations between countries on airline routes and the provision of various services, such as insurance. All this has an influence on international logistics and transportation. The process of privatization and deregulation in transportation and communications has reduced shipping costs and increased productivity. This has also increased the possibilities for different prices and services, thus underscoring the need to integrate marketing and logistics functions.

Competition

The proliferation of new products and services and short product life cycles creates pressures on firms to reexamine their logistics systems. This often requires the need to reduce inventory, lower overall costs, and develop appropriate logistics networks and delivery systems to retain and enhance their customer base. Crucial to the success of any logistics system is also a holistic examination of the relationship among transportation, warehousing, and inventory costs in order to adapt to the changing competitive environment. Such a reexamination of its various logistics functions resulted in a substantial reduction in inventory costs and delivery time for Cisco Systems of San Jose, California, in 1997. The company ships routers to Europe and needed to let customers know when orders would arrive and to be able to reroute an order to fill urgent requests. It hired UPS Worldwide Logistics to handle the various logistics functions. Using its expertise, UPS can now track Cisco's routers from San Jose, California, to European customers in under four days as opposed to three weeks. In cases in which UPS's planes or trucks cannot offer the quickest route, it subcontracts the job to other carriers such as KLM or Danzas, a European trucking firm. This resulted in more savings in inventories (Woolley, 1997).

Technology

Technology improvements, added to the deregulation of transportation and communications, have transformed the logistics industry. They have helped to increase logistics options, improve performance, and decrease costs. The use of communications technology has now integrated marketing and distribution activities with overseas customers, enabling the latter to know the date of shipment, the location of the cargo on transit, and the expected date of arrival. Importers have achieved total visibility of goods in transit and can make adjustments when a shipment is running late. Such tracking and tracing of cargo has the added advantage of synchronizing promotions and long-term inventory decisions for customers. Federal Express has recently developed a user-friendly software that tracks and traces shipments, eliminates the preparation of airway bills by hand, and allows printing on bar-coded shipping documents. Rates can be computed by plotting both origin and destination points. Vastera, Incorporated, a Dulles,

Virginia-based software firm, has also developed a multilingual logistics software package that handles multitask functions such as regulatory compliance and tariff information, documentation, shipment tracking, and letter of credit and duty drawback support (Fabey, 1997).

TYPICAL LOGISTICS PROBLEMS AND SOLUTIONS

Each export-import firm must use a logistics system that best fits its product line and chosen competitive strategy (see Table 6.1 for differences between domestic and international logistics).

Example 1

Arturo Imports, Incorporated, a Boca Raton, Florida-based firm, specializes in the importation of gift articles from South America and the Caribbean. It sells its products through company-owned retail stores in thirty U.S. states. The company has distribution centers in twenty locations all over the country and spends over $650,000 a year in warehousing costs. Over the last few years, it has come under increasing attack from competitors and has lost about 20 percent of its market share. Its profits also declined by over 15 percent in 1995 alone. The firm hired a consultant to advise it on how to reverse the situation. Based on the advice it received, Arturo Imports consolidated its operations in six distribution centers; reduced dead, obsolete, and slow-moving stock; and decreased the likelihood of stock-out (an item

TABLE 6.1. Differences Between Domestic and International Logistics

Domestic Logistics	International Logistics
• Domestic currency used	• Different currency and exchange rates
• One national regulation on customs procedures, documentation, packaging, and labeling requirements	• Different national regulations and many intermediaries participating in the distribution channel (customs brokers, forwarders, banks, etc.)
• Most goods transported by truck or rail	• Most goods transported by air or sea
• Generally, short distances, short lead times, and small inventory levels	• Long distances, longer lead times, and the need for higher inventory levels

that is out of stock) for products customers want to buy. It centralized its purchasing functions and switched to an intermodal air and truck (from ocean and rail) combination to ensure rapid delivery. The company began to see its market share and profit margin grow six months after implementing its new logistics systems.

Example 2

A U.S.-owned export firm in Bangor, Maine, serves a narrow product line in eastern Canada from two distribution centers located in Montreal and Toronto. The company began to reexamine its logistical infrastructure in response to its loss of profits and market share to competitors. It increased the number of branch warehouses and level of fast-moving inventory while reducing the market area served by each warehouse. It also extended its product line. In spite of the additional expenses incurred, the company began to see a marked increase in its profits and sales volume.

THE INTERNATIONAL LOGISTICS PROCESS

In export-import transactions, the following steps represent the approximate order of physical movement and distribution of goods to a foreign buyer.

Step 1

As a result of previous correspondence between the prospective seller and buyer, the prospective customer (buyer) places an order to purchase the desired merchandise, including such essential items as terms of sale, payment method, and other conditions. The parties must ensure that there are no restrictions on the export or import of the merchandise in question. The prospective exporter confirms receipt of the order and commits to fill the order based on the given terms and conditions. The seller's acceptance without modification of the terms creates a binding contract. In the event of any modification by the prospective seller, a binding contract is created only upon acceptance of the proposed modification by the prospective customer. A pro forma invoice is then prepared by the exporter, stipulating the essential terms and conditions of sale, and when accepted by the overseas customer, it may also serve as a contract. The prospective exporter must meet packaging, labeling, and other documentary requirements. In cases in which the exporter has inventory in different locations or countries, a determination has to be made as to which goods should be supplied on the basis of proximity to customer, tariff benefits, and so on. The exporter prepares the order for transportation. The order is then picked, packed, and labeled.

Step 2

A freight forwarder arranges for goods to be picked up and delivered to a carrier. The freight forwarder selects the transportation mode (airline, ship, truck, etc.), the carrier, as well as books the necessary space for the cargo. Such decisions will influence packing and documentation requirements. The forwarder confirms booking with the supplier, who will in turn confirm with the overseas customer. If the consignee is different from the buyer, the forwarder notifies the consignee.

Step 3

The carrier loads the cargo and the merchandise is transported to the customer. Unless otherwise stipulated in the contract, the buyer is responsible for the cost of preshipment inspection. Many developing countries have adopted this practice primarily to conserve foreign currency earnings and to control illegal flights of currency through transfer pricing, that is, overinvoicing of imports and underinvoicing of exports. Preshipment inspection also ensures that the shipment conforms to the contract of sale. However, it is costly and time-consuming for exporters and delays the physical movement and distribution of merchandise. Appropriate precautions should be taken to detect and control possible diversion of merchandise into the gray market. Export products may be sold below domestic prices if domestic advertising or R&D is not allocated to the export price. Such export products, if diverted to the domestic market, could potentially undermine the exporter's market position. Some of the warning signs of potential diversion include offers of cash payment when the terms of sale would normally call for financing, little or no background in the particular business, vague delivery dates, or shipping instructions to domestic warehouses. After the merchandise is transported, the forwarder sends the necessary documentation, that is, the commercial invoice, customs invoice, packing list, bill of lading or air waybill, and certificate of origin, to the customs broker who clears goods for the overseas customer at the port of destination.

Step 4

The customs broker submits documents to customs to obtain release of the merchandise. In some countries, assessed taxes and duties have to be paid before release of the merchandise. Customs may also physically examine the merchandise. Penalties may be imposed if any serious errors or problems are found in the documentation or with the imported merchandise. The customs broker informs the forwarder of the release of the merchandise.

Step 5

If the terms of sale provide for the seller to obtain release of merchandise from customs and deliver to the consignee, the forwarder picks up the merchandise from customs and arranges for delivery to the consignee. This step depends on the terms of sale. The consignee signs the bill of lading or air waybill, noting any irregularities, and accepts the merchandise.

International Perspective

6.1

EXPORT-IMPORT LOGISTICS IN THE EEC

The establishment of a single European internal market has important implications for logistics. With the removal of trade and other barriers among member nations, export-import firms could consider the possibility of centralizing stock in one or two locations to optimize their operations. This will lower inventory carrying cost while ensuring availability of fast-moving items. Certain functions, such as order handling and local delivery operations, can still be left under local responsibility. The Europe-wide distribution centers will, however, handle stocking, consolidation, and material processing functions. The centers can be selected on the basis of geographical proximity to consumers, multimodal facility for maximum distribution efficiency, warehouse space, and average turnaround for cargo. Other factors to consider also include safety of shipment, availability of skilled manpower, bonded warehouses, and other incentives, as well as the presence of efficient service providers. Many firms, for example, are considering France as a good location. The recently built all-cargo airport (Europort Vatry), ninety-three miles east of Paris, is an ideal distribution point for goods throughout the EEC. Seventy-five percent of the European population is within a 280-mile radius. The airport has an efficient multimodal facility: an airport complex for wide-bodied jets, a road transport center connecting with Europe's main highways, a rail freight terminal, and a logistics and business service area. Average turnaround for cargo at the airport is within twelve hours, compared to about thirty-six hours in most cargo airports.

LOGISTICS FUNCTIONS

Labeling

Importers are required to comply with domestic labeling laws. Even though an imported product may comply with the labeling requirements of the country where it was manufactured, it may not comply with the labeling laws of the importing country. Labeling requirements are imposed in many countries to ensure proper handling (e.g., Do Not Roll; Keep Frozen) or to identify shipments (e.g., Live Animals). Exporters need to be aware of certain labeling requirements to avoid unnecessary delays in shipping. The cartons or containers to be shipped must be labeled with the following: *shipper's mark, or purchase order number, country of origin, weight in both pounds and kilograms, the number of packages, handling instructions, final destination and port of entry, and whether the package contains hazardous material.* Markings should appear on three faces of the container. It is also advisable to repeat the instructions in the language of the importing country.

Under the U.S. Clean Air Act (amended in 1990), all products containing ozone-depleting substances are required to be labeled. More detailed and specific regulations can be obtained from freight forwarders, since they keep track of changing labeling laws in various countries.

Packing

The rigors of long-distance transportation of goods require protection of merchandise from possible breakage, moisture, or pilferage. This means that goods in transit must be packed not only to allow the overseas customer to take delivery of the merchandise but also to ensure its arrival in a safe and sound condition. Consumers in many countries often prefer packaging with recyclable or biodegradable containers due to environmental concerns. For example, about 70 percent of packaging material used in any of the federal states in Germany must be recycled or reused. Packaging cost has an influence on product design. In certain cases, it is considered less costly to ship disassembled parts or dense cargo to save shipping cost.

Merchandise should be packed in strong containers, adequately sealed, and filled, with the weight evenly distributed. Goods should be packed on pallets if possible, to ensure greater ease in handling, and should be made of moisture-resistant material. Packing must be done in a manner that will ensure safe arrival of the merchandise and facilitate its handling in transit and at its destination. (See International Perspective 6.2 for an example of product packing tips.)

International Perspective

6.2

PACKING HANDICRAFT EXPORTS: IMPORTANT POINTERS

Prior to packing: Dusting, cleaning, removing fingerprints, and drying items.

Major problems to consider in packaging: Tarnishing, corrosion, staining, decay, breakage, and moisture.

Preventing moisture: Using a drying agent (silica gel) to reduce humidity, reducing surface area of package, drying items, and packing materials in packages with moisture-tight seals.

Preventing damage: Cushioning fragile or high-cost handicrafts. Handicrafts exported in large quantities should be palletized when possible.

Heavy items: For heavy handicrafts, wooden boxes are recommended.

Small items: Bulk packaging with separators to protect individual items.

Outer packaging: Corrugated fiberboard and wooden boxes are recommended.

Insufficient packing not only results in delays in the delivery of goods but will also entitle the customer to reject the goods or claim damages. Export products must be packed to comply with the laws of the importing country. For example, Australia and New Zealand prohibit the use of straw or rice husk as packaging materials. The United Nations has adopted standards for packaging hazardous materials and provides for training of personnel, use of internationally accepted standards, and certain other conditions. Freight forwarders and marine insurance companies can advise on packaging.

Traffic Management

Traffic management is the control and management of transportation services. Such functions include selection of mode of transportation carriers, consolidation of small cargo, documentation, and filing of loss and damage claims. The international logistics manager's selection of a given mode of transportation depends on a number of factors. First, for products that are perishable, such as cut flowers, delivery speed is of the essence. Speed may also be required in cases involving important delivery dates or deadlines. In such cases, airfreight becomes the only viable mode of transport to successfully deliver the product to the overseas customer on time. Airfreight is also more reliable than other modes of transport that have more cumbersome unloading operations, which could expose the cargo to loss or damage. Second, the selection of transportation mode is influenced by cost considerations. Since airfreight is more expensive than other modes of transport, the international logistics manager has to determine whether such high costs are justified. Export firms tend to transport compact products or high-priced items by air because such products are more appropriate for airfreight or because the price justifies the cost. Third, government pressures could be imposed on exporters to transport by national carriers, even when other more economical alternatives exist. The choice of airport or port may be another important decision to be made. Such choices may be influenced by the desire to consolidate cargo or the presence of adjoining highways (to the port) on which weight limits are not rigorously enforced (Guelzo, 1986).

Inventory and Storage

The proper management of an export-import firm's inventory is a critical logistics function. The costs associated with holding inventories can easily account for 25 percent or more of the value of the inventories themselves and could potentially create liquidity problems for many firms. In addition to this are the cost of storage, interest paid on borrowed money, and the risks of deterioration and obsolescence. It is important to establish certain guidelines with respect to such issues as maximum holding period, time of shipment of inventories to the supplier, and other related factors. Acceptable levels of inventory can still be maintained to serve overseas customers on time without unduly increasing costs and creating storage problems. To reduce warehousing costs, it may be necessary to store inventory in distribution centers based on customer needs. Inventories that are slow moving (no activity for six to twelve months) can be shipped from the exporter or manufacturer. Appropriate inventory planning and control will reduce the number of storage facilities as well as carrying and freight costs.

In certain situations, accumulating inventories may have its own benefits. In countries that have certain macroeconomic problems, inventory may be a good edge against inflation and devaluation of currency.

TRANSPORTATION

Three modes of transportation are available for exporting products overseas: air, water (ocean and inland), and land (rail and truck). Whereas inland water, rail, and truck are suitable for domestic transportation and movement of goods between neighboring countries (the United States to Canada, France to Germany, etc.), air and ocean transport are appropriate for long-distance transportation between countries that do not share a common boundary.

Export-import firms may use a combination of these methods to deliver merchandise in a timely and cost-efficient manner. The exporter should consider market location (geographical proximity), speed (e.g., airfreight for perishables or products in urgent demand, etc.), and cost when determining the mode of transportation. Even though air carriers are more expensive, their cost may be offset by reduced packing, documentation, and inventory requirements. It is important to establish with the importer the destination of the goods, since the latter may wish the goods to be shipped into a free-trade zone that allows for exemption of import duties while the goods are in the zone.

Air Transportation

Airfreight is the least utilized mode of transportation for cargo and accounts for less than 1 percent of total international freight movement (see Table 6.2 for advantages and disadvantages of this transportation type). However, it is the fastest growing mode and not just confined to the movement of high-value products. A 1996 study by McDonnell Douglas forecast that oversized freight business would increase tenfold to $1.5 billion per year by 2010. A similar study by Boeing also found that about 4.5 million tons of heavy, outsized freight worldwide could be transported by air (Anonymous, 1998a). A number of factors are likely to contribute to such growth in airfreight:

1. In view of the heavy infrastructure investment being made in many developing countries, the potential need exists for imports of heavy equipment and services. It is estimated that such imports could amount to about $17.8 billion in surface transport, sea, and airport projects in South America alone. Certain types of equipment exports to these countries, such as bulldozers, buses, or oil-drilling equipment, often do not fit in a standard ocean container (Anonymous, 1998a; Reyes and Gilles, 1998).
2. Since many of these projects are built from supplies shipped to the sites on a just-in-time basis, delays in delivering cargo can lead to heavy financial losses or penalties for the suppliers. Such needs cannot be accommodated by using the traditional modes of carriage for heavy freight. Airfreight becomes the only viable means of moving such cargo to ensure timely delivery.
3. Technological changes over the last two decades have significantly altered the size and design of aircraft to handle heavy cargo. For

example, the recent version of the Boeing 747 can carry more freight (even with passengers) than all-cargo versions of the previous generation of jets. The all-cargo plane has a weight capacity of about 122 tons (Anonymous, 1998a; Reyes and Gilles, 1998). Furthermore, improvements in terminal facilities in many countries have also contributed to increased speed and better handling and storage of shipments at airports, thus minimizing loss or damage to merchandise.

4. Integrators and forwarders have also played a role. The development of air carriers that provide integrated services (DHL, UPS) has increased the amount of air cargo. For example, UPS Sonic Air Service offers a guaranteed door-to-door service to most international destinations, regardless of size or weight limitations, within twenty-four hours. In addition, the role of forwarders as consolidators of small shipments makes it easier for shippers to send their merchandise by air without being subject to the minimum charge for small shipments. The forwarder consolidates various small shipments and tenders them to the airline in volume in exchange for a bill of lading furnished as the shipper of the cargo. The role of a forwarder is similar to that of a non-vessel-operating carrier in ocean freight.

TABLE 6.2. Advantages and Disadvantages of Air Transportation

Advantages	Disadvantages
• Faster delivery of perishable commodities, production parts, etc. • Shipments do not require heavy packing (standard domestic packing is sufficient). • Reduces inventory and storage costs. • Reduces insurance cost and documentation. • Achieves savings in total transportation cost and provides reliability of service.	• Generally expensive for high-bulk freight. Value must be high enough to justify higher freight cost. • Inefficient for shorter distances, which are handled faster by trucks. Only the express air services, such as UPS or DHL, have equally competitive services. • Shipping containers must be small enough to fit into an air carrier. • Not suitable for products that are sensitive to low pressures and variations in temperature.

Air Cargo Rates

Determinants of air cargo rates. Distance to the point of destination as well as weight and size of the shipment are important determinants of air cargo rates. The identity of the product (commodity description) and the provision of any special services also influence freight rates. If a product is classified under a general cargo category (products shipped frequently), a lower rate applies.

Products can also be classified under a special unit load (for shipments in approved containers) or a commodity rate (negotiated rates for merchandise not classified as general cargo). Special services such as charter flight or immediate transportation could substantially increase the freight rate.

Rate setting. The International Air Transport Association (IATA) is the forum in which fares and rates are negotiated among member airlines. Over the last few years, such fares and rates have been set by the marketplace, and tariff conference proposals have tended to become reference points. IATA's cargo service conferences also promote among members the negotiation of certain standards and procedures for cargo handling, documentation and procedures, shipment of dangerous goods, etc.

International air express services (the integrators). The big carriers are under increasing competitive pressure from the integrated air service providers such as Federal Express or UPS. While the traditional carriers provide airport-to-airport service, the integrators have the added advantage of furnishing direct delivery services to customers, including customs clearance and payment of import duties at foreign destinations. Even though the strength of integrators had been in the transportation of smaller packages, they are now offering services geared to heavyweight cargo.

Ocean Freight

Ocean shipping is the least expensive and the dominant mode of transportation in foreign trade. It is especially suitable for moving bulk freight such as commodities and other raw materials. Today, almost all ocean freight travels by containers, which results in minimal handling at ports. If a full-container-load cargo is to be shipped, a freight forwarder arranges for the container to be delivered to the shipper's premises. Once the container is fully loaded, it is moved by truck to a port to be loaded onto a vessel. Less-than-container-load freight is usually delivered at the port for consolidation with other shipments.

Types of Ocean Carriers

The following are the three major types of ocean carriers. (See also International Perspective 6.3.)

Private fleets. These are large fleets of specialized ships owned and managed by merchants and manufacturers to carry their own goods. Apart

================== **International Perspective** ==================

6.3

TYPES OF OCEAN CARGO/VESSELS

Types of Ocean Cargo

Containerized: Cargo loaded at a facility away from the pier or at a warehouse into a metal container usually 20 to 40 feet long, 8 feet high, and 8 feet wide. The container is then delivered to a pier and loaded onto a "containership" for transportation. Some cargo cannot be containerized, e.g., automobiles, live animals, bulk products.

Bulk: Cargo that is loaded and carried in bulk, without mark or count, in a loose unpackaged form, having homogenous characteristics. To be loaded on a containership, bulk cargo would be put in containers first. It could also be stowed in bulk instead of being loaded into containers. Example: coal, iron ore, raw sugar, etc.

Break-Bulk: Packaged cargo that is loaded and unloaded on a piece-by-piece basis, i.e., by number or count. This can be containerized or prepared in groups of packages covered by shrink wrap for shipment. Example: coffee, rubber, steel, etc.

Neo-Bulk: Certain types of cargo that are often moved by specialized vessels. Example: Autos, logs.

Types of Ocean Vessels

Tankers: Vessels designed to carry liquid cargo, such as oil, in large tanks. They can be modified to carry other types of cargo, such as grain or coffee.

Bulk Carriers: Vessels that carry a variety of bulk cargo.

Neo-Bulk Carriers: Vessels designed to carry specific types of cargo.

General Cargo Vessels: These include (1) containerships: vessels that . carry only containerized cargo, (2) roll-on and roll-off (RO/RO) vessels: vessels that allow rolling cargo such as tractors, cars to be driven aboard the vessel, and (3) LASH (lighter aboard ship) vessels: vessels that can carry very large containers, such as barges. It enables cargo to be loaded on barges in shallow waters and then loaded on board a vessel.

Barges: Unmanned vessels generally used for oversized cargo and towed by a tugboat.

Combination Carriers: Vessels that carry passengers and cargo, oil and dry bulk, or containers and bulk cargo. Other combinations are also possible.

from its cost advantages, ownership of a private fleet ensures the availability of carriage that meets the firm's special needs. Such ships can occasionally be leased to other firms at times of limited activity. Some firms in certain industries, such as oil, sugar, or lumber, own their own fleets.

Tramps (chartered or leased vessels): Tramps are vessels leased to transport, usually, large quantities of bulk cargo (oil, coal, grain, sugar, etc.) that fill the entire ship (vessel). Chartered vessels do not operate on a regular route or schedule. Charter arrangement can be made on the basis of a trip or voyage between origin and destination or for an agreed time period, usually several months to a year. The vessel could be leased with or without a crew (bare-boat charter). The major factors for the continued existence of tramp shipping are that (1) it provides indispensable ocean transportation at the lowest possible cost, and (2) it is adaptable to the changing and/or unanticipated requirements for transportation. When charter rates are low, commodity traders tend to move materials in advance of actual delivery time to take advantage of low transportation costs (Wood et al., 1995). The just-in-time system that delivers products when they are needed is not often feasible in cases in which transport and distribution could be impeded by severe winter weather. A commodity trader's decision to purchase and export a product is influenced by the spread between the export and purchase price, the charter rate, and any warehousing or storage cost. This means that an exporter can purchase and export a product even before delivery time if the charter rate and storage cost are substantially less than the spread to allow for a reasonable profit margin.

Conference lines. A shipping conference line is a voluntary association of ocean carriers operating on a particular trade route between two or more countries. Shipping conferences date back to the nineteenth century when such associations were established for trade between England and its colonies. One of the distinguishing features of a liner service is that sailings are regular and repeated from and to designated ports on a trade route, at intervals established in response to the quantity of cargo generated along that route. Even though the sailing schedule is related to the amount of business available, it is general practice to dispatch at least one ship each month (Kendall, 1983). The purpose of a shipping conference is the self-regulation of price competition, primarily through the establishment of uniform freight rates and terms and conditions of service among the member shipping lines. In spite of its cartel-like structure, it is considered to be a necessary evil to ensure the stability and growth of international trade by setting rate levels that are more stable and predictable and by reducing predatory price competition.

Conference agreements become effective between carriers unless rejected, the forty-fifth day after filing with the Federal Maritime Commission (FMC), or the thirtieth day after publication of notice of filing in the Federal Register, whichever day was later.

Conferences serving U.S. ports must be "open," that is, they must admit any common carrier willing to serve the particular trade or route under reasonable and equal terms and conditions. This is generally intended to preclude conferences from using membership limitations as a means of discriminating against other U.S. carriers. Conferences are also allowed to form an exclusive patronage contract with a shipper, allowing the latter to obtain lower rates by committing all or a fixed portion of its cargo to conference members. Vessels engaged in liner service may be owned or leased. Conferences compete with independent lines, chartered vessels, and each other, although the same carrier could belong to several conferences.

> *Example:* An exporter in Taiwan intends to arrange for shipment of its textiles by a conference carrier to New York. A case for a lower (tariff) rate for large shipments can be made to a conference rate-making committee that consists of member lines. If the conference elects to reject the application for a lower rate, several options are available to the exporter: (1) the exporter may request a member of the conference to establish the rate independently of the conference, (2) the product could be shipped through nonconference carriers (independent or other conference lines) that offer a reasonably low tariff, (3) the product could be shipped through other ports using other conference carriers, or (4) the shipper could consider non-vessel-operating common carriers (NVOCC) or tramp vessels, depending on the amount of cargo. NVOCCs take possession of smaller shipments from several shippers and consolidate them into full-container loads for shipment by an ocean carrier. NVOCCs charge their own tariff rates and obtain a bill of lading as the shipper of the consolidated merchandise.

Land Transport and Intermodal Service

. Land transportation carriers (trucks, trains) are mainly used to transport exports to neighboring countries as well as to move goods to and from an airport or seaport. A substantial volume of U.S. exports to Canada and Mexico is moved by rail and/or trucks. Compared to rail transport, trucking has the advantage of flexibility, faster service, lower transportation costs, and less likelihood of damage to merchandise on transit. Rail transport has its own unique advantages: capacity to handle bulk cargo, free storage in transit, as well as absorption of loading, unloading, wharfage, and lighter charges. With the proliferation of free-trade agreements in various regions, there is likely to be a marked growth in the role of land carriers in transporting exports among countries that are in the same geographical area. For example, in eastern and southern Africa, an agreement that allows movement of land carriers across countries would make trucks and trains the dominant mode of transportation for exports. This is because land transport already accounts for over 80 percent of the region's freight movements and with a regional arrangement, these transportation services could easily be extended to neighboring countries with limited capital investment.

The use of land transportation is considered economically justifiable for large flows of cargo over distances greater than 500 kilometers (310 miles). A recent Swedish study on intermodal techniques (rail/truck) in transportation found that improving the competitiveness of intermodal transport for short-distance trips requires the operation of "corridor trains" that make short stops every 100 or 200 kilometers along a route (Anonymous, 1998b). Intermodal transport is not just limited to moving goods between rail and truck; it is also used for any service that requires more than one means of transportation (e.g., rail and ocean, truck and ocean) under one bill of lading. Such arrangements, ideally, must seek the fastest and least costly transportation for the shipper. The essence of intermodal contract is an agreement between different types of carriers (steamship lines, railroads, trucking firms, airlines, etc.) to achieve certain well-defined and carefully described functions. The advantages of such a mode of transport is simplicity for the shipper and consignee (one bill of lading and no other arrangements necessary), reduced damage because of fewer handlings, and reduced pilferage due to limited exposure of cargo. Such services are already offered by the integrators in the airline industry.

Examples of Intermodal Service

A truck will move merchandise from the exporter's warehouse outside New York City to a railroad yard some fifty miles away. The railroad will take the container to a New York port where it will be placed aboard a ship to Rotterdam, Holland. The whole movement would be covered by a single contract of carriage issued by the trucker as the initiating carrier.

Fresh oranges that arrive by sea from Chile to Miami, Florida, are then distributed to a network of inland points by air and then delivered door to door to customers by truck.

The Role of Freight Forwarders in Transportation

A freight forwarder is the party that facilitates the movement of cargo to the overseas destination on behalf of shippers and processes the documentation or performs activities related to those shipments. Freight-forwarding activity dates back to the thirteenth century when traders employed middlemen, or "frachtors," to cart and forward merchandise throughout Europe. The frachtor's responsibility later extended to provision of long-distance overseas transportation and storage services, issuance of bills of lading, and collection of freight, duties, and payment from consignees (Murr, 1979).

In the United States, the forwarding industry developed in the latter part of the nineteenth century. It started in New York, where the bulk of U.S. export trade was handled, to provide various transportation services to shippers. Ullman succinctly points out the changing role of the ocean freight forwarder in the United States:

> Many forwarding concerns originally started as freight brokers, but with the continuing increase in manufactured shipments, the forwarding work took precedence over the broker activity. Today, some forwarders handle ship loads of large parcels either on a common carrier or tramp vessels as brokers, but for the most part, forwarders deal with individual shipments varying in size or containers. (Ullman, 1995, p. 130)

Role and Function of Freight Forwarders

The freight forwarder (1) advises the exporter on the most economical choice of transportation and the best way to pack and ship the cargo to minimize cost and prevent damage, and (2) books for air, ocean, or land transportation (or intermodal movement of cargo) and arranges for pickup, transportation, and delivery of the goods. The forwarder also ensures that the goods are properly packed and labeled and documentation requirements are met so the cargo is cleared at the port of destination. When a letter of credit is used, the forwarder ensures that it is strictly complied with to enable the exporter to receive payment. Thus, the advantage of a forwarder goes far beyond moving freight. Forwarders help shippers and consignees by tracking and tracing cargo. They can also negotiate better rates with carriers because they can purchase space on airlines or ships at wholesale prices. The wide array of services they provide also helps shippers save time and money.

Freight forwarders are a significant part of U.S. commerce and facilitate the growth and expansion of international trade. A U.S. Senate report on the industry describes freight forwarding as follows:

> a highly important segment of the economy of the United States in that its functioning makes possible participation in the nation's foreign commerce by many industries and businesses whose lack of familiarity with the complexities and formalities of exporting procedures might hinder or even preclude such participation if forwarding services were not freely available. (Ullman, 1995, p. 133)

Today, it is generally estimated that over 90 percent of export firms use the services of an international freight forwarder. Most of the forwarding activity is still concentrated in ocean shipping, although some diversification into air and land transportation has occurred.

A forwarder is distinguishable from a non-vessel-operating common carrier (NVOCC). NVOCCs are international ocean carriers that do not operate their own vessels. They fulfill the role of the shipper with respect to carriers and that of a carrier with respect to shippers. Typical NVOCCs will guarantee a steamship line a certain amount of freight per week or month and purchase the necessary space on a wholesale basis for shipment of cargo to and from a given port. They publish their own tariffs and receive and consolidate cargo of different shippers for transportation to the same port. They issue bills of lading to acknowledge receipt of cargoes for shipment. Unlike NVOCCs, freight forwarders do not publish their own tariff and consolidate small shipments. Forwarders use the services of NVOCCs and facilitate the movement of cargo without operating as carriers. NVOCCs are often owned by freight forwarders or large transportation companies.

A forwarder also differs from a customs broker in that the latter deals with the clearing of imports through customs, whereas a forwarder facilitates the transportation of exports. The broker is licensed by the Treasury Department; while the forwarder is licensed by the Federal Maritime Commission (FMC).

Licensing Requirements

To be eligible for an ocean freight forwarder's license, the applicant must demonstrate to the FMC that (1) he or she has a minimum of three years' experience in ocean freight forwarding duties in the United States and the necessary character to render such services, and (2) the individual has obtained and filed a valid surety bond with the FMC. A shipper whose primary business is the sale of merchandise can perform forwarding services without a license to move its own shipments. In such a case, the shipper is not entitled to receive compensation from the carrier for its services. A license is not required for an individual employee or unincorporated branch office of a licensed ocean freight forwarder. A common carrier or agent thereof may also perform forwarding services without a license with respect to cargo carried under such carrier's own bill of lading (FMC, 1984).

Other Obligations and Responsibilities

- A description of the freight forwarder as consignee on an inland transport bill of lading (i.e., truck or rail) may subject the forwarder to liability for freight charges to the airport or seaport. This can be avoided by clearly indicating on the forwarder's delivery instructions that the forwarder is acting merely as an agent and does not have any ownership interest in the merchandise.
- The forwarder is liable to the shipper for its own negligence in selecting the carrier, handling documentation, directing cargo, and classifying shipments. The forwarder, for example, must not totally rely on the shipper's instructions with respect to the classification of a shipment. The forwarder must take reasonable measures to ensure that the classification is proper and consistent with the description on the commercial invoice, bill of lading, and other documents.
- In cases in which the forwarder acts as an NVOCC, liability is that of a common carrier for loss or damage to cargo.
- The forwarder's liability is limited to the lesser of $50.00 per shipment or the fee charged for its services. Any claims by the exporter against the forwarder must be presented within ninety days from the date of exportation.
- Each freight forwarder is required to maintain current and accurate records for five years. The records should include general financial data, types of services, receipts, and expenses.
- Forwarders are prohibited from providing any rebates to shippers or sharing any compensation or forwarding fees with shippers, consignees, or sellers. NVOCCs can receive compensation from carriers only when they act as mere forwarders, that is, when they do not issue bills of lading or otherwise undertake carriers' responsibilities.

CHAPTER SUMMARY

Logistics

The process of planning, implementing, and controlling the flow and storage of materials from the point of origin to the point of consumption

Two Categories of Logistics

1. Materials management: the timely movement of materials from sources of supply to point of manufacture, assembly, or distribution
2. Physicial distribution: movement of a firm's products to consumers

Logistics Concepts

1. The systems approach: emphasis on maximizing benefits of the corporate system as a whole as opposed to that of individual units
2. The total cost approach
3. The opportunity cost approach

Importance of Logistics to International Trade

1. Efficient allocation of resources
2. Expansion of economic growth and employment

External Influences on Logistics Decisions

1. Regulations: export controls, tariffs, nontariff barriers, privatization and deregulation of transportation and communications
2. Competition: competitive pressures on firms to examine logistics systems to reduce costs, etc.
3. Technology: new technologies now enable importers to know the date of shipment, location of cargo on transit, and expected date of arrival. It also handles other logistics functions.

Logistics Functions

Labeling, packing, traffic management, inventory, and storage

Air Transportation

Reasons for the Growth of Airfreight

Growing demand for imports of heavy equipment and services in many developing countries; the need for timely delivery of imports; technological changes; the role of integrators and forwarders

Determinants of Air Cargo Rates

Distance, weight and size of cargo, commodity description, special services

Ocean Freight

Types of ocean carriers: private fleet, tramps, conference lines

Land Transport

1. Rail transport: handles bulk cargo; absorbs loading, unloading, and other charges
2. Trucking: compared to rail transport, trucking has the advantage of flexibility, faster service, and lower transportation costs

Freight Forwarders

A freight forwarder facilitates the movement of cargo to the overseas destination on behalf of shippers and processes the documentation or performs activities related to those developments.

Role and function of a freight forwarder:

1. Advises shipper on the most economical choice of transportation.
2. Books space and arranges for pickup, transportation, and delivery of goods.

Licensing requirements: To be eligible for a license as a freight forwarder, the applicant must demonstrate to the FMC that he or she has

1. a minimum of three years' experience in ocean freight forwarding duties in the United States;
2. the necessary character to render such services; and
3. a valid surety bond filed with the FMC.

SECTION III:
EXECUTING THE TRANSACTIONS

Chapter 7

Pricing in International Trade

Price is an important factor in determining a firm's ability to compete in world markets. For many companies, pricing policies and procedures are secret information and not easily available to outsiders. Export prices should be high enough to make a reasonable profit and yet low enough to be competitive in the market. Products rarely sell on one factor alone, and the exporter should be competitive on nonprice factors of different kinds. Sources of nonprice competition include reliable delivery, short delivery time, product reliability, product quality, as well as any other feature considered unique by customers. This form of product differentiation based on specific characteristics of a product or service gives firms a competitive advantage (Dussauge, Hart, and Ramanantsoa, 1987). Apple Computer increased its market share in Japan not only by slashing prices but also by broadening distribution outlets and through the addition of Japanese software packages.

The crucial element in determining price relates to the value consumers place on the product. Value results from consumers' perceptions of the total satisfaction provided by the product (Hiam anad Schewe, 1992). Companies can charge high prices and manage to remain competitive if the price charged is lower than, or in alignment with, the perceived value of the product or service. In competitive markets, high prices represent an indication of the social desirability of producing the product or service. They may also be justified in export markets if the sale also involves transfers of technology or training.

Pricing in world markets is often used as an instrument of accomplishing the firm's marketing objectives. The firm could use price to achieve certain levels of market share, profits, or returns on investments or to reach some other specific goal. The following policies for pricing and markups generally apply to both domestic and export markets:

- High markups are common in industries with relatively few competitors. Markups are also higher in industries in which companies produce differentiated products rather than homogeneous ones. The high markups could be taken as rent arising from market power. For example, in the chemical industry, the biggest profits lie in specialty chemicals designed and produced for particular industrial uses (Reich, 1991). High markups may also be due to R&D expenditures and costs of increasing the skills of the workforce.

• Export prices tend to be relatively low in sectors in which there is increased competition. Changes in competitors' prices or the state of demand are more likely to trigger a reduction in export prices. Markups are relatively low for textiles, food, electric machinery, and motor vehicles; they remain high in industries such as medicines, computers, industrial chemicals, and television and communications equipment (Martens, Scarpetta, and Pilat, 1996). The low markups for the former are due to the fragmented and nondifferentiated nature of these industries, which makes it difficult to exercise market power.

A company needs to develop a workable guideline with respect to pricing of its product or service in export markets. Its pricing policy should be firm enough to achieve the targeted level of profits or sales, while maintaining some flexibility to accommodate the overall marketing objectives of the firm. Flexibility is seen as an absolute necessity for optimizing profits, and a firm may use all pricing methods according to the type of product being sold, the class and type of customer, and the competitive situation in the marketplace. Mismanagement of export pricing could often lead to pressures for price reductions or the development of parallel markets. Parallel, or gray, markets are created when the product is purchased at a low price in one market and sold in other markets enjoying higher prices. For example, Eastman Kodak prices its films higher in Japan than in other countries. An importer in Japan can purchase the product at a discount in a foreign country and sell it in the Japanese market at a price lower than that charged by authorized Kodak dealers. Appropriate pricing and control systems of quality and distribution outlets are important in reducing such incidences of parallel markets.

DETERMINANTS OF EXPORT PRICES

A number of variables influence the level of export prices. Some of these are internal to the firm; others are factors that are external to the firm. A major internal variable is the cost that is to be included in the export price. The typical costs associated with exports include market research, credit checks, business travel, product modification, special packaging, consultants, freight forwarders, and commissions (Anonymous, 1993). An additional cost is the chosen system of distribution. The long distribution channels in many countries are often responsible for price escalation. The use of manufacturers' representatives offers greater price control to the exporter. Another internal variable is the degree of product differentiation, that is, the extent of a product's perceived uniqueness or continuance of service. Generally, the higher the product differentiation a firm enjoys, the more independent it can be in its price-setting activities.

The external forces that influence export pricing include the following:

- *Supply and demand:* The pricing decisions for exports are subject to the influence of the supply of raw materials, parts, and other inputs. In a competitive economy, any increase in demand is followed by a higher price, and the higher price should, in turn, moderate demand. It is often stated that exports of manufactured goods exhibit the same price characteristic as primary products, their prices varying with the state of world demand and supply (Silberston, 1970). The classical supply-and-demand approach—whereby price acts as an allocating device in the economy and supply equals demand at an equilibrium price—is largely based on certain assumptions: perfect buyer information, substitutability of competing goods, and marginal cost pricing. The classical assumption that reducing prices increases demand ignores the interpretation of price changes by buyers. Studies have shown that consumers perceive price as an indicator of quality and may interpret lower product prices as a sign of poor quality (Piercy, 1982). If a product has a prestigious image, price can be increased without necessarily reducing demand.
- *Location and environment of the foreign market:* Climatic conditions often require product modification in different markets, and this is reflected in the price of the export product. Goods that deteriorate in high-humidity conditions require special, more expensive packaging. For example, engines that are to be exported to countries in the tropics require extra cooling capacity.

  Economic policies such as exchange rates, price controls, and tariffs also influence export pricing. Exchange rate depreciation (a drop in the value of a currency) improves price competitiveness, thus leading to increased export volumes and market shares. For example, in 1984 to 1985, when the dollar had appreciated to roughly double its 1980 value against the German mark, luxury German cars were selling for lower prices in the United States than in Germany. In export markets where buyers are used to negotiating prices, a flexible price is preferable over one that uniformly applies to all buyers.

- *Government regulations in the home country:* Different regulations in the home country have a bearing on export pricing. For example, U.S. government action to reduce the impact of its antitrust laws on competition abroad has enhanced the price competitiveness of American companies.

PRICING IN EXPORT MARKETS

The export price decision is distinct from the domestic price decision in the home market. The export decision has to consider variations in market conditions, existence of cartels or trade associations, as well as the existence of different channels of distribution. The presence of different environmental variables in export markets militates against the adoption of a single export-pricing policy (ethnocentric pricing) around the world. Another factor against uniform pricing is that different markets may be at different stages in the life cycle of a product at any given time.

It is customary to charge a high price during the introduction and growth stages of a product and to progressively reduce the price as the product matures. Other pricing alternatives include (1) polycentric pricing, which is pricing sensitive to local conditions, and (2) geocentric pricing, whereby a firm strikes an intermediate position. There are four approaches to export pricing.

Cost-Based Pricing

The most common pricing approach used by exporters is one that is based on full-cost-oriented pricing. Under this procedure, a markup rate on full cost is determined and then added to the product's cost to establish the price. The markup rate could be based on the desired target rate of return on investment.

The Marginal Approach to Pricing

Marginal pricing is more common in exporting than in domestic markets. It is often employed by businesses that have unused capacity or to gain market share. In this case, the price does not cover the product's total cost, but instead includes only the marginal (variable) cost of producing the product to be sold in the export market. This will result in the sale of a product at a lower price in the export market than at home and often leads to charges of dumping by competitors.

Skimming versus Penetration Pricing

Skimming, or charging a premium price for a product, is common in industries that have few competitors or in which the companies produce differentiated products. Such products are directed to the high-income, price-inelastic segment of the market.

Penetration-pricing policy is based on charging lower prices for exports to stimulate market growth. Increasing market share and maximizing revenues could generate high profits.

Demand-Based Pricing

Under this method, export prices are based on what consumers or industrial buyers are willing to pay for the product or service. When prices are set by demand, market surveys will help supply the data to identify the level of demand. The level of demand generally establishes the range of prices that will be acceptable to customers. Companies often test-market a product at various prices and settle on a price that results in the greatest sales.

A firm does not have to sell a product at or below market price to be competitive in export markets. A superior or unique product can command a higher price. Cartier watches and Levi's jeans are examples of products that, despite their high prices, generate enormous sales worldwide due to their reputation. These are products for which consumers feel a strong demand and for which there are few, or no, substitutes (products with inelastic demand). In cases in which demand for the product is elastic, consumers are sensitive to changes in price. For example, rebates and other discount schemes often revive lagging export sales in the auto industry (which is characterized by elastic demand). In April 1997, Toyota launched a special sales campaign in Tokyo to give away money (about one million yen to 100 customers) to some of the customers of the competitor car it sells in Japan on behalf of General Motors.

Competitive Pricing

Competitive pressures are important in setting prices in export markets. In this case, export prices are established by maintaining the same price level as the competition, reducing prices or increasing the price with some level of product improvement. However, price-cutting is generally a more effective strategy for small competitors than for dominant firms. An important factor in establishing a pricing strategy is also a projection of likely responses of existing and potential competitors (Oster, 1990).

TERMS OF SALE

Despite wide differences among national laws, there is a high degree of uniformity in contract practices for the export and import of goods. The universality of trade practices, including terms of sale, is due to the development of the law merchant by international mercantile custom. The law merchant refers to the body of commercial law that developed in Europe during the medieval period for merchants and their merchandise (Brinton et al., 1984).

Trade terms are intended to define the method of delivery of the goods sold and the attendant responsibilities of the parties. Such terms also help the seller in the calculation of the purchase price (Anonymous, 1993). A seller quoting the term of sale as FOB, for example, will evidently charge a lower price than if quoting CIF because the latter includes not only the cost of goods but also expenses incurred by the seller for insurance and freight to ship the goods to the port of destination. The national laws of each country often determine the rights and duties of parties with respect to terms of sale. In the United States, the Revised American Foreign Trade Definitions (1941) and The Uniform Commercial Code govern terms of sale. Since 1980, the sponsors of the Revised American Foreign Trade Definitions recommend the use of Incoterms. Parties to terms of sale could also agree to be governed by Incoterms, published by the International Chamber of Commerce in 1953 (latest revision, 1990), which now enjoys almost universal acceptance (Herman, 1989). The Uniform Commercial Code and Incoterms complement each other in many areas. Trade terms are not understood in the same manner in every country, and it is important to explicitly state the law that governs the contract. For example, a contract should state "FOB New York (Incoterms)" or "CIF Liverpool (Uniform Commercial Code)."

CIF (Cost, Insurance, and Freight) (Named Port of Destination)

The CIF contract places upon the seller the obligation to arrange for shipment of the goods. The seller has to ship goods described under the contract to the delivery destination and arrange for insurance to be available for the benefit of the buyer (International Chamber of Commerce, 1990). The cost of freight is either borne by the seller or paid by the buyer upon arrival of the merchandise. The seller has to tender the documents, such as invoice, bill of lading, and policy of insurance, to the buyer so that the latter can obtain the goods upon delivery or recover damages for any loss. The buyer must accept the documents tendered by the seller when they are in conformity with the contract of sale and pay the purchase price

(Ibid.). Import duties, consular fees, and charges to procure a certificate of origin as well as import licenses are the responsibility of the buyer. Export licenses have to be obtained by the seller. The CIF contract may provide certain advantages to the overseas customer because the seller often possesses the expert knowledge and experience to make favorable arrangements with respect to freight, insurance, and other charges. This could be reflected in terms of reduced import prices for the overseas customer. The following are central elements of CIF contracts.

Transfer of Risk and Title

Under a CIF contract, risk passes to the buyer on delivery, that is, when the goods are put on board the ship at the port of departure. Title to the goods passes when the bill of lading, which certifies ownership, is delivered to the buyer. Such passage of the title is, however, conditional. The condition is that ownership of the goods may revest in the seller if, upon examination, the buyer finds them to be not in conformity with the contract. The reversionary interest is valid insofar as the buyer does not do anything inconsistent with this condition, such as, for example, selling to third parties.

Rejection of Documents versus Rejection of Goods

When proper shipping documents in conformity with the contract are tendered, the buyer must accept them and pay the purchase price. As stated previously, the goods can be rejected if they are found not to be in conformity with the contract. It may also happen that the documents are not in accordance with the contract of sale (for example, discrepancies exist between the documents and the letter of credit/or contract of sale) but the goods are. In this case, the buyer could accept the goods but reject the documents and claim damages for a breach of a condition relating to the documents. Thus, under a CIF contract, the right to reject the documents is separate and distinct from the right to reject the goods.

Payment has to be made against documents. Tender of the goods cannot be an alternative to tender of the documents in CIF contracts. The buyer's acceptance of conforming documents does not impair subsequent rejection of the goods and recovery of the purchase price if, upon arrival, the goods are not in accordance with the terms of sale.

Loss of Goods

If the goods shipped under a CIF contract are destroyed or lost during transit, the seller is entitled to claim the purchase price against presentation of proper shipping documents to the buyer. Since insurance is taken for the benefit of the buyer, the buyer can claim against the insurer insofar as the risk is covered by the policy. If the loss is due to some misconduct on the part of the carrier that is not covered by the policy, the buyer could recover from the carrier.

Variants of CIF

C & F. Cost and Freight (named port of destination). This differs from a CIF contract in that the buyer is to arrange for insurance. This contract is used when the buyer can obtain insurance at a lower cost or the buyer's government insists on the use of a local insurance company to conserve foreign exchange.

CIFC. This includes cost, insurance, freight, and commission charged by the exporter.

CIFE. This stands for cost, insurance, freight, and exchange to cover for currency fluctuations.

CIFI. This includes cost, insurance, freight, and interest to cover for delays in payment of the purchase price.

FOB (Free on Board) (Named Port of Shipment)

The central feature of FOB contracts is the notion that the seller undertakes to place the goods on board the ship designated by the buyer. This includes responsibility for all charges incurred, up to and including delivery of the goods over the ship's rail (International Chamber of Commerce, 1990). The buyer has to nominate a suitable ship and inform the seller of its name, loading point, and the required delivery time (Ibid.). If the ship that was originally nominated is unable or unavailable to receive the cargo at the agreed time of loading, the buyer has to nominate a substitute ship and pay for all additional charges. Once the seller delivers the goods on board the ship, the buyer is responsible for all subsequent charges, such as freight, marine insurance, unloading charges, import duties, and other expenses due on arrival at the port of destination. Unless otherwise stated in the contract of sale, it is customary in FOB contracts for the seller to procure the export license because the latter is more familiar with licensing practices and procedures in the exporting country.

Passage of Risk and Title

In FOB contracts, transfer of risk and property occurs upon the seller's delivery of the goods on board the vessel. The seller's responsibility for loss or damage to the goods terminates on delivery to the carrier. The ship's rail is thus considered the dividing line between the seller's and buyer's responsibility in terms of passage of property and transfer of risk.

Variants of FOB

FOB with additional services. Under this method, the seller arranges for shipping and insurance at the risk and expense of the buyer. The seller nominates a suitable ship, enters into a contract with the carrier, puts the goods on board the vessel, and sends the bill of lading and other documents to the buyer.

FOB, buyer contracting with carrier. In this case, the buyer nominates the carrier and enters into a contract with the latter. Upon delivery of the goods, the bill of lading goes directly to the buyer and does not pass through the seller.

FOB airport. With this contract, the seller is responsible for delivering the goods into the charge of the air carrier or its agent, which is often the air carrier's transit shade at the airport. The seller must also contract at the buyer's expense for the carriage of goods.

FAS (Free Alongside Ship) (Named Port of Shipment)

This term requires the seller to deliver the goods to a named port alongside a vessel to be designated by the buyer (International Chamber of Commerce, 1990). "Alongside the vessel" has been understood to mean that the goods should be within reach of a ship's lifting tackle. The risks and title to the goods pass to the buyer upon the seller's delivery alongside the ship (Ibid.). This implies that all charges and risks for the goods from the time they are effectively delivered alongside the vessel are borne by the buyer. The buyer must also pay all costs and charges incurred in obtaining any export license, clean document in proof of delivery (this is to certify that the goods have been delivered in apparent good order and condition), and certificate of origin. In all FAS contracts, there is an implied duty on the part of the seller to cooperate in arranging a loading and shipping schedule and to render, at the buyer's request, and expense every assistance in obtaining necessary documents, even though the buyer's obligation ends when the cargo is delivered alongside the vessel.

Ex Works, Ex Warehouse, or Ex Store

Under this term, the seller agrees to place the goods at the disposal of the buyer at the time and place designated for delivery. The seller bears all risk and expenses until the goods are delivered to the buyer. The term denotes that the overseas buyer or the buyer's agent must collect the goods at the seller's works, warehouse, or store (International Chamber of Commerce, 1990). The purchase price becomes payable at the time of delivery. The buyer bears all risks and charges related to the goods from the time they are delivered, such as payment of customs duties, taxes, and procurement of appropriate documents needed for exportation. Transfer of risk and property occurs at the time of delivery at the seller's place of business.

This term of sale is similar to a domestic sales transaction, although the product is destined for export.

FOR or FOT (Named Port of Shipment)

Under the term FOR (free on rail) or FOT (free on truck), the seller bears responsibility for all charges, up to and including loading of the goods on the railway wagon (International Chamber of Commerce, 1990). The term "truck" conveys the same meaning as a railway wagon. It is the buyer's duty to arrange for the rail transportation. The seller is required, at the buyer's expense, to provide the buyer with the necessary documents, such as export permits and certificate of origin, to enable exportation of the goods (Ibid.). The buyer must pay the purchase price upon delivery of the goods into the custody of the railway. Transfer of risk and property pass at the point of delivery.

Ex Quay (Named Port of Destination)

Ex quay contracts denote that the seller accepts responsibility beyond the requirements of a typical CIF contract. The seller's obligation extends to delivery of the goods at the quay at the port of destination. This includes unloading charges, import duties, lighterage, porterage, and dock dues (International Chamber of Commerce, 1990). Transfer of risk and property to the buyer occurs at the place of delivery. Exporters are often reluctant to sell goods under this term because they either do not have an agent in the buyer's country and/or are unfamiliar with the local business customs and regulations.

Delivery at Frontier (Named Place of Delivery)

This term is used when both the exporter and importer share land frontiers where air or sea carriage is not used. A seller and an overseas buyer could agree to have the seller deliver the goods at the named frontier against payment of the purchase price. The parties should agree on which party assumes responsibility for insurance.

Ex Ship (Named Ship and Named Port of Arrival)

Under this term, the seller is required to arrange for shipment to the port of destination and for delivery of the goods to the buyer. The buyer makes payment upon delivery and physical possession of the goods. The major differences between this and a CIF contract are as follows:

1. In an ex ship contract, delivery is effected upon unloading and physical transfer of the goods to the buyer. In CIF contracts, delivery is effected upon loading the goods on board the vessel.
2. In an ex ship contract, property passes upon physical delivery to, and possession of the goods by, the buyer. In CIF contracts, property passes upon delivery of the documents to the buyer.
3. In an ex ship contract, the buyer is under no obligation to pay the purchase price if the goods are lost in transit. In CIF contracts, the buyer is required to pay against documents. However, the loss of goods gives the buyer the right to seek recovery from the carrier or the insurance company, depending on the circumstances.

Container Trade Terms

These are trade terms that can be used for all modes of transportation, even though they are more suitable for container and other modes of multimodal transport. The terms include free carrier (named point of delivery to carrier), freight/carriage and insurance paid to (named point of destination), and freight/carriage paid to (named point of destination).

Free Carrier

The term free carrier (named point of delivery to carrier) is quite similar to the FOB contract, except that the seller is required to deliver the goods into the custody of the carrier. The buyer bears all risks for the goods from the time they are delivered into the charge of the carrier named by the buyer. Unlike the common FOB term, the seller is not responsible for placing the goods on board the carrier (plane, truck) nominated by the buyer.

Delivery Duty Paid (Named Point of Destination)

Exporter is responsible for all costs, risks, and duties until the goods are delivered into the possession of the buyer in the latter's country. However, the parties can agree for delivery to a foreign inland delivery of merchandise, that is, before payment of customs duties (delivery duty unpaid).

Freight/Carriage and Insurance Paid To (Named Point of Destination)

This is similar to a CIF contract. However, the quotation can apply to any form of carriage, and the transfer of risk takes place when the goods have been delivered into the custody of the carrier.

Freight/Carriage Paid To (Named Point of Destination)

This is similar to "freight/carriage and insurance paid to," except the seller is not required to cover for insurance. (For responsibilities of parties, see Table 7.1.)

Preparing the Price Quotation

Once the overseas customer agrees to buy merchandise based on the information provided by the seller, the buyer requests a pro forma invoice. The pro forma invoice specifies the kind, quantity, and value of the goods. This invoice is useful to the buyer when applying for a letter of credit or foreign currency payment. The profit or markup should be included in the initial ex factory price (see Table 7.2).

TABLE 7.1. Responsibilities of Parties: INCOTERMS, 1990

Responsibility	Ex W	Free carrier	FAS	FOB	CIF	DAF	DES	DEQ	DDU	CPT	CIP
Export Packing	SR	SR	SR	SR	SR	SR	SR	SR	SR	SR	SR
Loading/ carriage to port of exit	BR	SR	SR	SR	SR	SR	SR	SR	SR	SR	SR
Commercial invoice	SR	SR	SR	SR	SR	SR	SR	SR	SR	SR	SR
Shipment inspection	BR	BR	BR	BR	BR	BR	BR	BR	BR	BR	BR
Certificate of origin	SR	SR	SR	SR	SR	SR	SR	SR	SR	SR	SR
Export License	BR	SR	SR	SR	SR	SR	SR	SR	SR	SR	SR

Loading on board carrier	BR	BR	BR	SR	SR	SR	SR	SR	SR	SR	SR
Ocean freight/ airfreight	BR	BR	BR	BR	SR	SR	SR	SR	SR	SR	SR
Transfer of risk on ocean transport	BR	BR	BR	BR	BR	SR	BR	SR	SR	BR	BR
Marine insurance	BR	BR	BR	BR	SR	SR		SR		BR	SR
Import (customs) clearance	BR	BR	BR	BR	BR	BR	BR	SR	BR	SR	BR
Foreign delivery expenses	BR	BR	BR	BR	BR	BR	BR	BR	SR	BR	BR

Abbreviations:

BR = Buyer	SR = Seller
Ex W = Ex Works	FAS = Free Alongside Ship
FOB = Free on Board	CIF = Cost, Insurance, Freight
DAF = Delivery at Frontier	DES = Delivered Ex Ship
DEQ = Delivered Ex Quay Duty Paid	DDU = Delivered Duty Unpaid
CPT = Carriage Paid To	CIP = Carriage, Insurance Paid To

TABLE 7.2. Price Determination Worksheet

Price (or cost) per unit _____ × _____ units = total	+
Profit (or mark up)	+
Commissions	+
Financing costs	+
EX FACTORY	=
Crating/containerization charges (if done at factory)	+
Labeling and marking costs (if done at factory)	+
Drayage charges (usually associated with movement of containers from railroad ramp to plant and back to ramp)	+
Loading charges, if applicable	+
Demurrage and detention charges, if applicable	+
Other charges (specify)	+

TABLE 7.2 *(continued)*

FREE ON BOARD (FOB) **TRUCK OR RAILCAR AT POINT OF ORIGIN**	=
Inland freight charges (including fuel surcharges)	+
Unloading charges at port facilities	+
Drayage to packer (crater/containerizer), if applicable	+
Containerization/crating charges (if done at port)	+
Labeling and marking (if done at port)	+
Freight forwarding and documentation charges (including charges associated with consular fees, export license, postage, telex, and telephone/telegram use, etc.)	+
Drayage to warehouse and unloading, if applicable	+
Warehousing charges, if applicable	+
Loading and drayage to pier from packer or warehouse, if applicable	+
Wharfage charges	+
Terminal notification charges	+
Demurrage/detention at port	+
FREE ALONGSIDE VESSEL AT PORT OF _____	=
Vessel loading charges	+
Heavy lift or extra-length charges, if applicable	+
Other charges (specify)	+
FREE ON BOARD VESSEL AT PORT OF _____	=
Ocean freight charges	+
Bunker or other surcharges, if applicable	+
COST AND FREIGHT TO _____	=
Insurance	+
COST, INSURANCE, AND FREIGHT TO _____	=

CHAPTER SUMMARY

Sources of Export Competitiveness

Price and nonprice factors such as reliable delivery, short delivery time, product reliability, product quality, design flexibility, support services, financial services

Export Pricing Objectives

Market share, profits, a targeted level of return on investment

Pricing and Markup Policy

1. High markups are common in industries with relatively few competitors and which produce differentiated products.
2. Low markups are common in sectors of increased competition.

Determinants of Export Prices

Internal Variables

Cost of production, cost of market research, business travel, product modification and packing, consultants, freight forwarders, and level of product differentiation

External Variables

Supply and demand, location and environment of foreign market, and home country regulations

Approaches to Export Pricing

1. Cost-based pricing: export price is based on full cost and markup or full cost plus a desired amount of return on investment.
2. Marginal pricing: export price is based on the variable cost of producing the product.
3. Skimming versus penetration pricing: price skimming is charging a premium price for a product; penetration pricing is based on charging lower prices for exports to increase market share.

4. Demand-based pricing: export price is based on what the market could bear.
5. Competitive pricing: export prices are based on competitive pressures in the market.

Sea and Inland Waterway Transport (Terms of Sale)

1. FAS, free alongside ship (named port of shipment): requires the seller to deliver goods to a named port alongside a vessel to be designated by the buyer. Seller's responsibilities end upon delivery alongside the vessel.
2. FOB, free on board (named port of shipment): seller is obliged to deliver the goods on board a vessel to be designated by the buyer.
3. CIF cost, insurance, freight (named port of destination): this term requires the seller to arrange for carriage by sea and pay freight insurance to a port of destination. Seller's obligations are complete when the documents are tendered to the buyer. Cost and freight (port of destination) is the same as CIF terms, except the seller does not arrange for insurance. See Variants of CIF.
4. Ex ship (named port of destination): this term requires the seller to deliver goods to a buyer at an agreed port of arrival.
5. Ex quay (named port of destination): seller is required to deliver goods at the quay at the port of destination.

Air and Rail Transport (Terms of Sale)

1. FOR or FOT, free on rail or truck (named point of shipment): seller is to load the goods on the railway wagon or truck.
2. Free carrier (named point of delivery to carrier): seller required to deliver the goods into the custody of the carrier.
3. Delivery at frontier (named place of delivery): seller delivers goods to buyer at the named frontier.

Any Mode of Transport (Terms of Sale)

1. Ex works (named point of shipment): seller to place the goods at the seller's works, warehouse, or store so that the buyer will take delivery of the goods.
2. Free carrier (see number 2 under air and rail transport).
3. Freight/carriage, insurance paid to (named point of destination): similar to a CIF term, except goods are to be delivered into the custody of the carrier.

4. Delivery at frontier (see number 3 under air and rail transport).
5. Delivered duty paid or unpaid (named place of destination)

In 4 and 5, seller pays all costs to place goods at disposal of buyer. Project/installation contracts whereby seller's agents or employees receive the goods at the port of arrival.

Chapter 8

Export Sales Contracts

HARMONIZATION OF CONTRACT LAW

Export sales contracts are central to international commercial transactions and around them revolves a series of connected, but distinct, relationships, including cargo insurance, transportation, and payment arrangements. The rules and practices governing such contracts vary from one export transaction to another, based on the agreement of the parties as well as the legal system. National legal systems on contracts may differ, but the basic principles of contracts, such as good faith and consideration, are generally recognized and accepted in many countries. There is also a movement toward convergence among the world's different legal systems in the area of international commercial law (DiMatteo, 1997; Lubman, 1988). Today, it is almost difficult to identify any examples of substantial divergence that produce important and predictable differences in the outcomes of commercial disputes (Rosett, 1982). Certain differences in theory or approach are often offset by the countervailing force of international usage or custom, which brings about a predictable and harmonious outcome in commercial dispute resolution. It is pertinent to identify the motives behind this move toward harmonization of international contract law:

- *Increase in trade and other economic relations between nations*
- *The growth of international customary law:* Commercial custom and usage have often been used in the drafting and interpretation of commercial law. Today, certain customs and practices, derived from merchants in Europe, regarding documentary drafts, letters of credit, and so forth, are universally accepted and form the basis for domestic and international commercial law.
- *The adoption of international conventions and rules:* There have been several attempts at unification of international contract law.

The most recent attempt at progressive harmonization of the law of international trade is one undertaken by the United Nations Commission on International Trade Law (UNCITRAL). UNCITRAL produced a set of uniform rules on international trade that are a product of different national legal systems, including the Convention for International Sale of Goods (CISG). The CISG Convention, which entered into force on January 1, 1988, governs the formation of international sales contracts and the rights and obligations of parties under these contracts. Many important trading nations, such as France, Germany, Italy, the Netherlands, Singapore, and the United States, have signed or ratified the convention. The CISG applies to contracts for the commercial sale of goods between parties whose "places of business" are in different nations that have agreed to abide by the convention. "Place of business" is often interpreted to mean the country that has the closest relationship to the contract and is closest to where it will be performed, for example, the place where the contract is to be signed or the goods delivered. Parties to a sales contract are at liberty to specify the application of a law of some third country that recognizes the convention in the event of a dispute. The CISG does not apply to certain types of contracts, such as sales of consumer goods, securities, labor services, electricity, ships, vessels, and aircrafts, or to the supply of goods for manufacture if the buyer provides a substantial part of the material needed for such manufacture. The CISG is intended to supersede the two Hague conventions (UNIDROIT rules) on international sales.

The International Chamber of Commerce (ICC) has also published several valuable documents on international trade. The Uniform Rules for Contract Guarantees (1978) deals with the issue of performance and bank guarantees supporting obligations arising in international contracts. The ICC also has rules on adaptation of long-term contracts to changing economic and political circumstances.

Standard contract forms are often used in certain types of international commercial transactions, such as trade in commodities or in capital goods. These contracts are prepared by trade associations, such as the Cocoa Association of London, the Refined Sugar Association, or certain agencies of the United Nations (model contracts for the supply of plant, equipment, and machinery for export or for the export of durable consumer goods and engineering articles).

International Perspective

8.1

TENDERING FOR EXPORT CONTRACTS

In many countries, government purchases over a certain size are required to be awarded under tender. Purchase of goods under tender is common in cases involving goods and services purchased in large volumes and the likelihood of price competition. Tenders are also offered in the case of contracts for purchase or installation of complex projects that involve the purchase of goods and services. Tenders provide the purchaser the unique advantage of selecting the best supplier from among a large pool of bidders in terms of quality, price, and other factors, allowing the purchaser to avoid charges of patronage and favoritism.

The tendering process begins with a purchaser of goods and services inviting potential suppliers for submission of tenders (bids). However, with important projects, bidders are prequalified before submitting tenders to ensure that they satisfy the basic criteria that are critical for awarding the contract: necessary technical qualifications and compliance with local laws in submitting the bid. The invitation to submit bids (for prequalification or final selection) is usually announced in newspapers, and this guarantees a fair, competitive, and transparent tendering process and affords some protection against corruption and nepotism by civil servants.

The invitation to submit tenders is announced in the newspapers to the public or to selected bidders who are prequalified. This stage in the tendering process is often called a request for proposal (RFP). At this stage, potential bidders are invited to submit tenders with certain conditions (e.g., technical specifications, commercial terms, etc.) that are to be included in the proposal. Suppliers may be requested to submit bid bonds to ensure that a supplier will not decline to sign the contract when the bid is accepted.

Once a proposal is accepted, the successful supplier is awarded the contract. In most cases, however, the award is just a first step prior to negotiation of the contract. In the event of failure to conclude the final contract, the customer would have to negotiate with the second bidder on the list.

PERTINENT CLAUSES IN EXPORT CONTRACTS

An export contract is an agreement between a seller and an overseas customer for the performance, financing, and other aspects of an export transaction. An export transaction is not just limited to the sale of final products in overseas markets but extends to supply contracts for manufacture or production of the product within a given time period. Parties should have a well-drafted and clear contract that properly defines their responsibilities and provides for any possible contingencies. This is critical in minimizing potential conflicts and allowing for a successful conclusion of the transaction.

Although many export contracts are concluded between the seller and an overseas buyer (the main contract), the buyer may also enter into a contract with an independent consultant for technical assistance and with a lender for financing in the case of complex projects. The exporter as prime contractor may enter into joint venture agreements with other firms, such as subcontractors or suppliers, to bid on and perform on a project. Parties could also establish a partnership, corporation, or a consortium in order to bid on and undertake different aspects of the transaction while assuming joint responsibility for the overall project. Such collaboration is common when one firm lacks the financial or technical resources to perform the contract.

It is relevant to state briefly how these joint venture arrangements differ from one another. Members may form a partnership for the purpose of undertaking the export contract. Each of the members remains responsible for the entire transaction even though the parties may be carrying out different portions of the export transaction. Parties could also establish a new corporation to act as exporters or prime contractors. In the case of a consortium, each partner of the venture has a separate contract with the customer for performance of a portion of the work and, hence, is not responsible to the other members.

Scope of Work Including Services

The goods to be sold should be clearly spelled out in the contract. There is also a need to include the scope of work to be performed by the exporter, such as installation, training, and other services. The scope of work to be performed is usually contained in the technical specification, which should be incorporated into the main contract (by listing it with the other documents intended to form the contract). It is also important to specify whether the agreed price covers certain services, such as packaging, special handling, or insurance. Any contribution by the overseas customer should be explicitly stated as to the consequences of the failure to perform those services to enable the exporter to complete the transaction on time. Such contributions could include provision of office space and other support services, such as secretarial and translation, government licenses, permits, and personnel necessary for the performance of the contract.

Price and Delivery Terms

The total price could be stated at the time of the contract, with a price escalation clause that provides for increases in the price if certain events occur. Such provisions are commonly used with goods that are to be manufactured by the exporter over a certain period of time and when inflation is expected to affect material and labor costs. Such a clause also extends to increases in costs arising from delays caused by the overseas customer. It is important to draft the contract with a clear understanding between the parties as to whether such a clause applies when there is an excusable delay. In many contracts, the price escalation clause is in force in cases of excusable delay in performance by the exporter.

The contract should also specify the currency in which payment is to be made. Foreign exchange fluctuations could adversely affect a firm's profit. In addition, government exchange controls in the buyer's country may totally or partially prevent the exporter from receiving payment for goods and services. Hence, it is important to provide the necessary protection against such contingencies. The following contract provisions would be helpful to the exporter.

Shifting the Risk to the Overseas Customer

An exporter may shift the risk by providing in the contract that payment is to be made in the exporter's country and currency. This ensures protection against currency fluctuations and exchange controls.

Payment in Importer's Currency

Even though the seller will generally prefer payment in U.S. dollars, such a requirement may be difficult to comply with if U.S. dollars are not readily available in the buyer's country. The exporter may have to accept payment in the importer's currency. In such a situation, the exporter could fix the exchange rate in the invoice and would thus be compensated in the event of devaluation. Suppose Smith, Incorporated, of California exports computers to Colombia; the price could be stated as follows: "300 million Colombian pesos at the exchange rate of $1=1,000 pesos. The importer will compensate the exporter for any devaluations in the peso from the rate designated in the contract."

Another method of protection against fluctuations in the importer's currency is to add a risk premium on the price at the time of the contract. Yet another method is to establish an escrow account in a third country in an acceptable (more stable) currency from which payments would be made under the contract.

The contract should clearly indicate the delivery term (e.g., FOB, New York, or CIF, London) since there are different implications in terms of risk of loss, insurance, ownership, and tax liability. The seller would ideally prefer to be paid cash in advance (before delivery of goods or transfer of title) in its own currency or by using a confirmed irrevocable letter of credit. The buyer would often desire payment in its own currency on open account or consignment. Hence, the provision to be included in the contract has to accommodate the competing interests of both parties.

Delivery, Delay, and Penalties

The most common type of clause included in export contracts is one that provides for a fixed or approximate delivery date and that stipulates the circumstances under which the seller will be excused for delay in performance and even for complete inability to perform. Most contracts state that either party has the right to cancel the contract for any delay or default in performance if it is caused by conditions beyond its control, including, but not limited to, acts of God and government restrictions, and that neither of the parties shall be liable for damages (force majeure clause). The force majeure clause may also cover a number of specified events, including the inability of the exporter to obtain the necessary labor, material, information, or other support from the buyer to effect delivery. It should also include certain warranty obligations, such as delays in manufacture of replacement components. It is important to state that the force majeure (excusable delay) clause will apply even though any of the causes existed at the time of bidding, were present prior to signing the contract, or occured after the seller's performance of its obligations was delayed for other causes. Some force majeure clauses provide for the temporary suspension of the contract until the causes for the nonperformance are removed; others state that the agreement will be terminated at the option of either of the parties if performance remains impossible for some stated period.

Contracts often provide for damages if the delay is caused by one of the parties. In the event that the delay is caused by the exporter (i.e., unexcused delay), some contracts specify that the importer will be entitled to recover liquidated damages (even in the absence of actual damages), whereas others provide that payment would be limited to damages actually incurred by the buyer. (See International Perspective 8.2.)

The converse of the seller's obligation to deliver is the buyer's obligation to accept delivery as stipulated in the contract. If delay in delivery is caused by the buyer, most contracts provide that the seller will be entitled to direct damages incurred during the delay, such as warehousing costs, salaries and wages for personnel kept idle, or loss of profit. Some contracts even provide for payment of indirect (consequential) damages, such as loss of productivity or loss of future profits due to delays caused by the buyer. Both parties can possibly eliminate or reduce potential risks of excusable delay by inserting (1) a best-efforts clause, without expressly providing for consequences in the event of delay, or (2) an overall limitation of liability clause. In cases in which the contract does not expressly impose the previous obligation on the customer, the customer remains responsible for delays caused personally or by someone for whom the customer is responsible. In most legal systems a party has an implied duty to cooperate in the performance of the work by the other party or to not interfere with the performance of the other party.

Quality, Performance, and Liability Limitations

Most contracts state that the seller warrants to the buyer that the goods manufactured by the seller will be free from defects in material, workmanship, and title and will be of the kind and quality described in the contract. It is not uncommon to find deficiencies in performance, even when the exporter provides a product with state-of-the-art design, material, and workmanship. Hence, it is advisable to use certain approaches to limit risk exposure:

- Specify in the contract the performance standards that are to be met, and provide warranties for those which can be objectively tested, such as machine efficiency, for a specified period, usually a year.
- Stipulate the kinds of damages that may be suffered by the buyer for which the seller is not responsible, such as loss of profit for machine downtime, extra costs of acquiring substitute services, as well as other damages that are incidental or consequential.
- Limit the liability, especially in exports of machinery and equipment, to a specific amount expressed either in reference to the total contract price or as a certain sum of money. This limit should cover all liability or liabilities arising from product quality or performance.
- Carefully evaluate the cost implications of an extended warranty or an evergreen warranty provision before agreeing to include it in the contract. An evergreen warranty is automatically renewed each time a failure protected under the warranty provision is corrected.

Taxes and Duties

In the United States, Canada, and other developed countries, an exporter will not be subject to any taxes (i.e., when products are exported to these countries) if business is not performed through an agent, a branch, or a subsidiary. However, when the price includes a breakdown for installation and other services to be performed in the importing country, such income could be taxable as earnings from services. In some cases, it may be advisable to reserve the right to perform these services through a local affiliate to restrict exposure to foreign taxes. It is thus important to consider the tax and customs duty implications of one's pricing and other export decisions relating to shipment of components or assembly of (final) products. It is also helpful to evaluate the impact of tax treaties with importing countries.

Guarantees and Bonds

It is quite common for overseas importers to require some form of guarantee or bond against the exporter's default. Public agencies in many countries are often prohibited from entering into major contracts without some form of bank guarantee or bond. Guarantees are more commonly used than bonds in most international contracts. These are separate contracts and independent of the export agreement.

Bid guarantees or bonds are often provided at the first stage of the contract from all bidders (potential exporters) to provide security to the overseas customer. Then, performance guarantees or bonds are provided by the successful bidder(s) to protect the overseas customer against damages resulting from failure of the seller to comply with the export contract. Last, payment guarantees or bonds are provided so the importer can secure a refund of the advance payment in case of the exporter's default.

In the case of a bank guarantee, a standby letter of credit is issued by a bank, under which payment is made to the importer on demand upon failure of the exporter to perform its obligation under the export contract. Most importers favor a contract provision that allows them to obtain payment from the bank by simply submitting a letter that the exporter has defaulted and demanding payment. However, it may be advisable to stipulate in the standby credit that the amount of the credit becomes payable to the importer only upon the finding by a court or arbitration tribunal that the supplier of goods or services is in default of the contract.

A bank guarantee (standby credit) and a bond are similar in that both instruments are a form of security provided by a third party (a bank in the case of a guarantee; a surety company in the case of a bond) to the importer against the exporter's default. Both instruments are only issued if the exporter has a good credit standing, and they both specify the amount payable in the event of default, the period within which such claims can be made, as well as the fee charged for such services.

In export trade, there is a tendency to make standby credits payable on the submission of a letter by the importer that simply alleges default by the exporter and demands payment. This is not usually the case with bonds, which are payable only when the importer has shown that the exporter is in default under the export contract. Bonds also usually require that the importer has met its obligations under the contract before realizing any benefits from the bond. In short, the surety company will conduct an investigation on the conduct of the parties before making a decision about payment. Second, the bank in the case of a standby letter of credit does not have the option of performing the contract (e.g., completing delivery of goods not made by exporter, paying losses incurred by exporter, etc.), as in the case of a surety company. The bank guarantor is required to pay the full amount of the standby credit without regard to the actual damages suffered. Under a bond, the surety is obliged to make good on only the actual damages suffered by the overseas buyer. In both cases, the exporter has to reimburse the bank or the surety company for any payments made under the guarantee or bond, respectively. In view of the widespread use of guarantees (standby credits) in international trade and the possibility of abuse, many countries provide their exporters an insurance program that protects them against wrongful drawing on the credit. In 1978, the International Chamber of Commerce adopted the "Uniform Rules for Contract Guarantees," which deals with guarantees, bonds, and other undertakings given on behalf of the seller and applies only if the guarantee or bond explicitly states the intentions of the parties to be governed by these rules. In view of the limited acceptance of the Uniform Rules for Contract Guarantees, the ICC adopted, in 1992, the "Uniform Rules for Demand Guarantees," which attempts to standardize existing guarantee practice. As in the case of contract guarantees, the parties have to state their intention to be subject to these rules.

Applicable Law and Dispute Settlement

The fundamental principle of international contract law is that of freedom of contract. This means that the parties are at liberty to agree between themselves as to what rules should govern their contract. Most contracts state the applicable law to be that of the exporter's country. This indicates the strong bargaining position of exporters and their clear preference to be governed by laws about which they are well informed. It may be possible to arrange a split jurisdiction, whereby the portion of the contract to be performed in the customer's country will be interpreted under the importer's laws and the portion to be performed in the exporter's country will be governed by the laws of that country.

International Perspective

8.2

ACCEPTANCE OF STANDARD INTERNATIONAL CONTRACTS

In 1982, a buyer in Indonesia contracted to buy from a seller in England 400,000 metric tons of white sugar (C&F, Indonesian port for delivery in 1983/1984). The contract provided for payment under an irrevocable letter of credit against shipping documents in London. The contract was to be governed by English law and provided for arbitration of disputes in London under the Rules of the Refined Sugar Association. It was also expressly stated in the contract that the buyer was to be totally responsible for obtaining the necessary license and that failure to obtain the license was not to be considered sufficient ground for invoking force majeure.

As sugar prices collapsed during 1982/1983, the buyer declined to open a letter of credit in order to pay the seller in London. In June 1984, the seller commenced arbitration proceedings in London, as provided in the contract, claiming damages for breach of contract. The buyer initiated two lawsuits against the seller in London, seeking the court to declare the contracts to be illegal since the Indonesian government declined to buy the sugar and refused to provide an import license. The seller was awarded $27 million in damages to be paid in three installments. The buyer paid the first installment and brought a lawsuit against the seller in Indonesia, seeking a court order declaring the contract illegal because it violated a decree stating that only the government agency could import sugar into Indonesia. The Indonesian court held that the contract violated the decree (local law) and was therefore illegal. The court ignored the following:

1. The contracts provided only for shipment to an Indonesian port, not importation into Indonesia, and the risk of not being able to import was expressly assumed in the contract by the buyer.
2. Under English law, delivery of shipping documents does not require that the goods be imported into the country of destination.

Source: Adapted from Hornick, 1990, pp. 8-10.

In cases where there is no express or implied choice of law, it may be the role of the courts to decide what law should govern the contract based on the terms and nature of the contract. The factors to be considered often include the place of negotiation of the contract, the place of performance, location of the subject matter, place of business, and other pertinent matters.

For several reasons, a large and growing number of parties to export contracts provide for arbitration to settle disputes arising under their contracts. Despite the wide use of arbitration clauses, the superiority of arbitration over judicial dispute resolution is not quite clear-cut, and parties considering arbitration should also be aware of the disadvantages in this choice, such as lack of mandatory enforcement mechanisms and difficulty obtaining recognition and enforcement of the award, which requires a separate action of law. It is also stated in some contracts that the parties agree to abide by the award and that the award is binding and final and enforceable in a court of competent jurisdiction.

CHAPTER SUMMARY

Export Contract

An export contract is an agreement between a seller and an overseas customer for the performance, financing, and other aspects of an export transaction. It also includes supply contracts for the manufacture of a product within a given period.

Factors Behind the Move Toward Harmonization of International Contract/Commercial Law

1. Increases in global trade and economic relations between nations
2. The growth of international customary law
3. The adoption of international conventions and rules

   - The Vienna Convention on international sale of goods
   - The ICC rules on contract agreements
   - Standard contracts developed by trade associations

Major Clauses in Export Contracts

- Scope of work
- Price and delivery terms
- Quality, performance, and liability
- Taxes and duties
- Guarantees and bonds
- Applicable law and dispute settlement

Chapter 9

Documentation, Risk, and Insurance

DOCUMENTATION IN EXPORT-IMPORT TRADE

A number of documents are used in export-import trade. The completion and submission of required documents is critical to the successful shipment, transportation, and discharge of cargo at the port of destination. The documents used depend on the requirements of both the exporting and importing countries. Much of the documentation is routine for freight forwarders or customs brokers acting on the firm's behalf, but the exporter is ultimately responsible for the accuracy of the documentation. Information on documentation requirements in importing countries can be obtained from overseas customers, foreign government embassies and consulates, as well as various export reference books, such as the *Export Shipping Manual* and *Air Cargo Tariff Guide*. In the United States and other developed countries, government departments have specialists on individual foreign countries and can advise on country conditions and documentation requirements.

Air Waybill

The air waybill is a contract of carriage between the shipper and air carrier. It is issued by the air carrier and serves as a receipt for the shipper. When the shipper gives the cargo to a freight consolidator or forwarder for transportation, the air waybill is obtained from the consolidator or forwarder. Air waybills are nonnegotiable and cannot be issued as a collection instrument. Air waybills are not particular to a given airline and can be from any other airline that participates in the carriage (Wood et al., 1995).

Bill of Exchange (Draft)

A bill of exchange is an unconditional written order by one party (the drawer) that orders a second party (the debtor or drawee) to pay a certain sum of money to the drawer (creditor) or designated third party. For example, Hernandez Export, Incorporated, of Lawton, Oklahoma, sends an importer in Uzbekistan a draft for $30,000 after having shipped a truckload of autoparts. The company's draft orders the overseas buyer in Uzbekistan to pay $30,000 to its agent, Expotech, in Uzbekistan. In this scenario, Hernandez, Incorporated, is the drawer, the importer is the drawee, and Expotech is the payee. In many cases, the drawee is the overseas buyer and the drawer/payee is the exporter. When a draft is payable at a designated future date, it is a time draft. If it is payable on sight, it is a demand or sight draft.

Bill of Lading (B/L)

A bill of lading is a contract of carriage between the shipper and the steamship company (carrier). It certifies ownership and receipt of goods by the carrier for shipment. It is issued by the carrier to the shipper. A straight bill of lading is issued when the consignment is made directly to the overseas customer. Such a bill of lading is not negotiable. An order bill of lading is negotiable, that is, it can be bought, sold, or traded. In cases in which the exporter is not certain about payment, the exporter can consign the bill of lading to the order of the shipper and endorse it to the buyer on payment of the purchase price. When payment is not a problem, the bill of lading can be endorsed to the consignee (Zodl, 1995; Wells and Dulat, 1996).

Inland Bill of Lading

An inland bill of lading is a bill of lading issued by the railway carrier or trucking firm certifying carriage of goods from the place where the exporter is located to the point of exit for shipment overseas. This document is issued by exporters to consign goods to a freight forwarder who will transport the goods by rail to an airport, seaport, or truck for shipment.

Through Bill of Lading

A through bill of lading is used for intermodal transportation, that is, when different modes of transportation are used. The first carrier will issue a through bill of lading and is generally responsible for the delivery of the cargo to the final destination.

Consular Invoice

Certain nations require a consular invoice for customs, statistical, and other purposes. It must be obtained from the consulate of the country to which the goods are being shipped and usually must be prepared in the language of that country (U.S. Department of Commerce, 1990).

Certificate of Origin

A certificate of origin is required by certain countries to enable them to determine whether the product is eligible for preferential duty treatment. It is a statement as to the origin of the export product and usually is obtained from local chambers of commerce.

Inspection Certificate

Some purchasers and countries may require a certificate attesting to the specifications of the goods shipped, usually performed by a third party. Such requirements are usually stated in the contract and quotation. Inspection certificates are generally requested for certain commodities with grade designations, machinery, equipment, and so forth.

Insurance Certificate

When the exporter provides insurance, it is necessary to furnish an insurance certificate that states the type, terms, and amount of insurance coverage. The certificates are negotiable and must be endorsed before presentation to the bank.

Commercial Invoice

A commercial invoice is a bill for the merchandise from the seller to the buyer. It should include basic information about the transaction: description of the goods, delivery and payment terms, order date, and number. The overseas buyer needs the commercial invoice to clear goods from customs, prove ownership, and arrange payment. Governments in importing countries also use commercial invoices to determine the value of the merchandise for assessment of customs duties.

Dock Receipt

This receipt is used to transfer accountability when the export item is moved by the domestic carrier to the port of embarkation and left with the international carrier for export. The international carrier or agent issues it after delivery of the goods at the carrier's dock or warehouse. A similar document, when issued upon receipt of cargo by a chartered vessel, is called a mate's receipt.

Destination Control Statement (DCS)

This statement appears on the commercial invoice, bill of lading, air waybill, and shipper's export declaration. It is intended to notify the carrier and other parties that the item may only be exported to certain destinations.

Shipper's Export Declaration (SED)

A shipper's export declaration (SED) is issued to control certain exports and to compile trade data. It is required for shipments valued at more than $2,500. Carriers and exporters are also required to declare dangerous cargo.

Pro Forma Invoice

A pro forma invoice is a provisional invoice sent to the prospective buyer, usually in response to the latter's request for a price quotation. A quotation usually describes the product, states the price at a specific delivery point, time of shipment, and the terms of payment. A pro forma invoice is also needed by the buyer to obtain a foreign exchange or import permit. Quotations on such invoices are subject to change without notice partly because there is a lag between the time when the quotation is prepared and when the shipment is made to the overseas customer.

Export Packing List

An export packing list itemizes the material in each individual package and indicates the type of package (e.g., box, carton). It shows weights and measurements for each package. It is used by customs in the exporting and importing countries to check the cargo and by the exporter to ascertain the total cargo weight, the volume, and shipment of the correct merchandise. The packing list should be either included in the package or attached to the outside of a package in a waterproof envelope marked "packing list enclosed."

RISKS IN FOREIGN TRADE

Businesses conducting export-import trade face a number of risks that may adversely impact their operations, such as the following:

- Actions of legitimate government authorities to confiscate cargo, war, revolution, terrorism, and strikes that impede the conduct of international business (political risk)
- Nonpayment or delays in payment for imports (foreign credit risk)
- Loss (partial/total) or damage to shipment during transit (transportation risk)
- Depreciation of overseas customer's currency against the exporter's currency before payment or the nonavailability of foreign currency for payment in the buyer's country (foreign exchange/transfer risk)

Political Risks

Many export-import businesses are potentially exposed to various types of political risks. Wars, revolution, or civil unrest can lead to destruction or confiscation of cargo. A government may impose severe restrictions on export-import trade, such as limitation or control of exports or imports, restrictions of licenses, currency controls, and so on. Even though such risks are less likely in Western countries, they occur quite frequently in certain developing nations. Such risks can be managed by taking the following steps.

Monitoring Political Developments

Private firms offer monitoring assistance to assess the likelihood of political instability in the short and medium term. Such information can be obtained from specialized sources for specific countries such as political risk services (subsidiary of International Business Communications, Incorporated), the Economic Intelligence Unit, Euromoney, and Business International Corporation. Public agencies such as the Export-Import Bank of the United States (Eximbank) and the Department of Commerce also provide country risk reports.

Insuring Against Political Risks

Most industrialized nations provide insurance programs for their export firms to cover losses due to political risks. In the United States, Eximbank offers a wide range of policies to accommodate many different insurance needs of exporters. Private insurers cover ordinary commercial risk, but Eximbank assumes all liability for political risks. (See Chapter 14 on government export financing.)

Foreign Credit Risks

A significant percentage of export trade is conducted on credit. It is estimated that about 35 to 50 percent of exports of the United States and the United Kingdom are sold on open account and/or consignment (Seyoum and Morris, 1996). This means that the risk of delays in payment or nonpayment could have a crucial effect on cash flow and profits. Payment periods vary across countries and even within countries that have close economic relations, such as the European Common Market, payment periods range from forty-eight days in the Netherlands to ninety days in Italy. Payments are, on average, eighteen days overdue in Germany, twenty-three in the United Kingdom, nineteen in France, and twenty in Italy (Luesby, 1994). Payment practices appear to be a function of the global/local economic conditions as well as the local business culture. In many developing countries, delays may be due to foreign exchange shortages, which in turn result in delays by central banks in converting local currencies into foreign exchange. The likelihood of bad debt from an overseas customer (0.5 percent of sales) is generally less than for an American company. However, this does not provide comfort to an exporter whose cash flow and profit could be adversely affected by late payments and default. Beans Industries, once part of the British Leyland group, which makes automotive components, was taken into receivership in 1994 despite increased demand for its products, due to bad debts and late payments that had a dramatic effect on cash flow (Cheeseright, 1994). A default by an overseas customer is still costly even when the exporter has insurance to cover commercial credit risks. The exporter must follow strict procedures to obtain payment before insurance claims will be honored. The following measures will help export companies in dealing with problems of defaults and/or delays in payment.

Appropriate Credit Management

Appropriate credit management involves the review of credit decisions based on current and reliable credit reports on overseas customers. Credit reports on foreign companies can be obtained from international banks that have affiliates in various countries and private credit information sources such as Dunn and Bradstreet, Graydon America, Owens Online, TRW Credit Services, and the NACM (National Association of Credit Management Corporation). A number of foreign credit information firms also provide accurate and reliable information on overseas customers. Government agencies such as the U.S. Department of Commerce, the Eximbank, and FCIA (Foreign Credit Insurance Association) also offer credit reporting services on foreign firms. Export firms also need to have a formal credit policy that will help them recover overdue or bad debts and substantially reduce the occurrence of such risks in future.

Requiring Letters of Credit and Other Conditions

A confirmed, irrevocable letter-of-credit transaction avoids risks arising from late payments or bad debts because it ensures that payments are made before the goods are shipped to the importer. However, such requirements (including advanced payments before shipment) do not attract many customers, and exporters seeking to develop overseas markets often have to sell on open account or consignment to enable the foreign wholesaler or retailer to pay only after the goods have been sold. The exporter can also require the payment of interest when payment is not made within the time period agreed or, failing that, within a given number of days. The introduction of a similar measure in Sweden in the mid-1970s is believed to have substantially reduced the delinquency of late payments to fewer than seven days. The European Commission submitted a draft recommendation to discourage late payments in cross-border trade (European Commission, 1994). Another safeguard would be to secure collateral to cover a transaction.

Insuring Against Credit Risks

Many export firms do not insure trade receivables, and yet, such cover is as necessary as fire or car insurance. It is estimated that in most developed countries, less than 20 percent of trade debts are insured. Credit insurers tend to have extensive databases that allow them to assess the credit worthiness of an insured's customer. This helps export companies to distinguish those buyers with the money to pay for their orders from those which are likely to delay payments or default. A credit insurance policy also provides confidence to the lender and may help exporters obtain a wide range of banking services and an improved rate of borrowing.

Few private insurance firms cover foreign credit risk: American Credit Indemnity, Continental Credit Insurance, Fidelity and Deposit Company, and American Insurance Underwriters are among those that provide such coverage. Such firms could be contacted directly or through brokers stationed in various parts of the country. Policies often cover commercial and political risks, although, in some cases, they are limited to insolvency and protracted default in eligible countries. Minimum premiums range from $1,250 per policy year to $10,000.

Eximbank provides various types of credit insurance policies: credit insurance for small businesses (umbrella policy, small business policy), single and multibuyer policies, Overseas Private Investment Corporation, the bank letter-of-credit policy and so on. Its major features are U.S. content requirements and restrictions on sales destined for military use or to communist nations (see Table 9.1). (See also Chapter 14, "Government Export Financing Programs".)

Foreign Exchange Risks

Export-import firms are vulnerable to foreign exchange risks whenever they enter into an obligation to accept or deliver a specified amount of foreign currency at a future point in time. These firms could face a possibility that changes in foreign currency values could either reduce their future receipts or increase their payments in foreign currency. Different methods are used to protect against such risks, for example, shifting the risk to third parties or to the other party in an export contract (for details, see Chapter 10 on exchange rates and trade).

TABLE 9.1. Major Differences Between Eximbank and Private Insurance Programs

Eximbank Program	Private Credit Insurance Program
Products must be 51 percent U.S. content. Military goods and services are not eligible. The product must be shipped from the United States.	There is no U.S. content restriction.
Coverage of countries dependent on U.S. foreign policy. Certain countries are not eligible.	Any country is eligible for consideration.
The minimum premium payment is about $500.00 per policy year.	The minimum premium ranges from $1,250.00 per policy year to $10,000.
Insurance coverage includes commercial and political risks.	Coverage varies depending on the insurance company. Some cover commercial and political risks; others only cover commercial risks.

Transportation Risks

Inland Carriage

Transportation of merchandise almost always involves the use of an inland carrier (a trucking or rail company) to move merchandise from the exporter's warehouse to the seaport or airport. Inland transportation is governed by domestic legislation unless goods are shipped to a different country or such movement of cargo from warehouse to port is the first part of intermodal transportation to a foreign country. In the United States, different laws, including the Carmack Amendment, govern domestic transportation. Under the Carmack Amendment, rail and motor common carriers are liable for the full value of the goods lost, damaged, or delayed in transit. However, there are certain exceptions to this strict liability: act of God, act of shipper, inherent vice (defects in the goods), act of a public enemy, and intervention of law. Even though there are no universal agreements, a few regional treaties regulate transportation of goods by road and rail (Schmitthoff, 1986). Prominent among these is the Convention on the Contract for the International Carriage of Goods by Road (Convention relative au Contract de Transport International de Merchandises par Route, or CMR, 1956) and the Convention Concerning International Carriage by Rail (Convention relative au Transport Internationaux Ferroviares, or COTIF, 1980). Members include most European countries, and a few Middle Eastern nations in the case of COTIF. The respective conventions cover areas such as scope of application, liability of the carrier, the use of multiple carriers, and time limits:

- The conventions generally apply to contracts for the carriage of goods by road or rail between two countries, of which at least one is a contracting party. The convention also applies to carriage by states or public institutions.
- A carrier is required to issue a consignment note (nonnegotiable) as evidence of contract of carriage and condition of the goods. The consignee has a right to demand delivery of the goods in exchange for a receipt and to sue the carrier in its own name for any loss, damage, or delay for which the carrier is responsible. The shipper can change the place of delivery or order delivery to another consignee at any time before the delivery of the consignment note or cargo to the first consignee.
- In cases involving multiple carriers, each carrier is responsible for the entire transaction.

- Carriers are liable for loss, damage, or delays up to a liability limit insofar as the contract is governed by the CMR or COTIF. There are, however, certain exceptions to liability in cases such as inherent vice in the goods, circumstances that the carrier could not avoid, and the consequences of which he was unable to prevent, or negligence on the part of the shipper.
- There is a limitation period for bringing action (one year) and for notice of reservations (i.e., notice of damage or loss).

Carriage of Goods by Sea

International transportation of cargo by sea is governed by various conventions. The Hague Rules of 1924 have won a certain measure of global support. The U.S. law on the carriage of goods by sea is based on the Hague Rules. Subsequent modifications have been made to the Hague Rules (the Hague-Visby Rules, 1968), which are now in force in most of Western Europe, Japan, Singapore, Australia, and Canada. In 1978, the United Nations Commission on International Trade Law (UNCITRAL) was given the task of drafting a new convention to balance the interests of carriers and shippers. Although the Hague-Visby Rules were intended to rectify the procarrier inclination of the Hague Rules, many developing countries felt that the Hague-Visby rules did not go far enough in addressing the legitimate concerns of cargo owners or shippers. The commission's deliberations led to an agreement in 1978 (the Hamburg Rules). It came into effect in 1991, and its impact remains to be seen. Unlike the Hague and Hague-Visby Rules, which have been ratified by many developed and developing nations, the Hamburg Rules are mostly followed by developing nations, except Austria (Flint and O'Keefe, 1997). In view of the widespread acceptance of the Hague Rules, it is important to briefly examine some of their central features (see International Perspective 9.1).

Scope of Application. The application of the rules depends on the place of issuance of the bill of lading; that is, the rules apply to all bills of lading issued in any of the contracting states. If the parties agree to incorporate any one of the previous rules in their contract, such rules will govern the contract of carriage even when the countries where the parties reside subscribe to different rules. However, this will not be allowed if the parties are required to apply certain rules adopted by their countries. These rules apply only to bill of lading (B/L).

The Carrier's Duties Under B/L. A carrier transporting goods under a B/L is required to exercise "due diligence" in (1) making the ship seaworthy; (2) properly manning, equipping, and supplying the ship; (3) making the ship (holds, refrigerating chambers, etc.) fit and safe for reception,

---

International Perspective

9.1

THE HAGUE, HAGUE-VISBY, AND HAMBURG RULES: OVERVIEW

All three rules define the rights and duties of parties in a contract of carriage of goods by sea, insurance for goods, and transfer of title. The Hague and Hague-Visby Rules are generally identical, except for provisions dealing with limitations of liability, third parties, and a few minor areas. The Visby amendments to the Hague Rules increase the limits of the carrier's liability, change the method of expressing the limitation amount (by weight), and protect third parties acting in good faith.

The Hamburg Rules have been criticized by carriers and their insurers as favoring shippers (cargo interests). The prominent differences between the Hamburg Rules and the Hague/Hague-Visby Rules are as follows: (1) The Hamburg Rules have higher limits of liability and set higher damages against carriers; (2) under the Hamburg Rules, the carrier is liable for delays in delivery, in addition to loss or damage to goods; (3) any loss or damage to goods in transit imposes a burden of proof on the carrier to show that the latter was not at fault, whereas such burden is only triggered when the loss/damage resulted from the unseaworthy condition of the ship under the Hague and Hague-Visby Rules; and (4) the limits of the carrier's liability under the Hamburg Rules may not extend to acts of independent contractors, unlike with the other two rules.

---

carriage, and preservation of the goods; and (4) properly and carefully loading, handling, stowing, carrying, and discharging the goods. Whenever loss or damage has resulted from unseaworthiness, the burden of proving the exercise of due diligence falls on the carrier. When different modes of transportation are used, the issuer of the bill of lading undertakes to deliver the cargo to the final destination. In the event of loss or damage to merchandise, liability is determined according to the law relative to the mode of transportation at fault for the loss. If the means of loss is not determinable, it will be assumed to have occurred during the sea voyage.

Basis of Carrier's Liability and Exemptions. The carrier's liability applies to loss of or damage to the goods. It does not extend to delays in the delivery of the merchandise. The rules exempt carriers from liability that arises from actions of the servants of the carrier (master, pilot, etc.) in the management of the shipment, fire and accidents, acts of God, acts of war, civil war, insufficient packing, inherent defects in the goods, and other causes that are not the actual fault of the carrier. That loss or damage to the goods falls within one of these exemptions does not automatically absolve the carrier from liability if the damage/loss could have been prevented by the carrier's exercise of due diligence in carrying out its duties (Yancey, 1983).

Period of responsibility. The period of responsibility begins from the time the goods are loaded and extends to the time they are discharged from the ship.

Limitations of action. All claims against the carrier must be brought within one year after the actual or supposed date of delivery of the goods. This means that lapse of time discharges the carrier and the ship from all liability in respect to loss or damage. The Hague Rules also stipulate that notice of claim be made in writing before or at the time of removal of the goods.

Limits of liability. The maximum limitation of liability is $500 per package. In most cases, a container is considered as one package, and the carrier's liability is limited to $500. To ensure the application of liability limits to their agents and employees, carriers add the "Himalaya Clause" to their bills of lading. The clause entitles such agents and employees the protection of the Hague Rules. Exporters can, however, obtain full protection against loss or damage by paying an excess value charge or by taking out an insurance policy from an independent source (Force, 1996).

Carriage of Goods by Air

The international transportation of goods by air is governed by the Warsaw Convention of 1929 (original convention) and the amended convention of 1955. In certain cases, neither convention applies. Many countries, including the United States, are members of the original Warsaw Convention and did not accede to the amended convention. The major differences between the two conventions relate to the carrier's liability and limits of that liability (see International Perspective 9.2). The important aspects of the original Warsaw Convention are detailed in the following material.

Scope of the convention. The convention governs the liability of the carrier while the goods are in its charge, whether at or outside an airport. It applies when the departure and destination points set out in the contract of carriage are in two countries that subscribe to the original Warsaw Convention (i.e., both are not members of the amended convention).

Air consignment note (air waybill). A consignment note (air waybill) is a document issued by the air carrier to a shipper that serves as a receipt for goods and evidence of the contract of carriage. However, it is not a docu-

---

International Perspective

9.2

THE TWO WARSAW CONVENTIONS AND AIR CARRIAGE: MAJOR DIFFERENCES

- **Carrier's liability:** Under the Amended Convention, defense of negligent pilotage or negligence in the handling and navigation of aircraft is no longer available to carriers. The amendment also extends the benefit of liability limitations to the agents and servants of the carrier.
- **Limitation of action:** The time to give a written notice of loss or damage by consignee has been extended from seven days to fourteen days.
- **Required particulars:** Required particulars on the air waybill are fewer under the amended convention.

---

ment of title to the goods, as in the case of a bill of lading. The carrier requires the consignor to make out and hand over the air waybill with the goods. The consignor is responsible for the accuracy of the statements relating to the goods stated in the air waybill. The carrier's receipt of the consignor's goods without an air waybill or all particulars relating to the goods will not entitle the carrier to exclude or limit liability under the convention. The carrier notifies the consignee as soon as the goods arrive and hands over the air waybill upon compliance by the consignee with the conditions of carriage.

Liability of carrier. The carrier is liable for loss or damage to cargo and for damage arising from delay unless it proves that: (a) the damage was occasioned by negligent pilotage or negligence in the handling of the aircraft, and (b) the carrier and its agents have taken all necessary measures to avoid such damage. An airline can escape liability if it proves that the shipper was negligent regardless of its own negligence. In the case of intermodal transport where more than one carrier is involved, each carrier is responsible for the part of the carriage performed under its supervision. All the carriers are, however, jointly and severely liable to the consignor or consignee in the event of loss, damage or delay to cargo.

Limitation of liability. The liability of the carrier with respect to loss or damage to the goods, or delay in delivery is limited to a sum of $9 per pound ($20 per kilogram) unless the consignor has declared a higher value and paid a supplementary charge. Any agreement to lower or exclude liability is void.

Limitation of action. The right to damages will be extinguished if an action is not brought within two years after the actual or supposed delivery of cargo. Notice of complaint must be made within seven days from the date of receipt of goods (in the case of damage) or within fourteen days from the date on which the goods have been placed at the consignee's disposal (in the case of delay).

MARINE AND AVIATION INSURANCE

Export-import firms depend heavily upon the availability of insurance to cover against risks of transportation of goods. Risks in transportation are an integral part of foreign trade, partly due to our inability to adequately control the forces of nature or to prevent human failure as it affects the safe movement of goods. Insurance played an important part in stimulating early commerce. In Roman times, for example, money was borrowed to finance overseas commerce, whereby the lender would be paid a substantial interest on the loan only if the voyage was successful. The loan was canceled if the ship or cargo was lost as a result of ocean perils. The interest charged in the event of a successful voyage was essentially an insurance premium (Greene and Trieschmann, 1984; Mehr, Cammack, and Rose, 1985).

The primary purpose of insurance in the context of foreign trade is to reduce the financial burden of losses arising from the movement of goods over long distances. In export trade, it is customary to arrange extended marine insurance to cover not only the ocean voyage but also other means of transport that are used to deliver the goods to the overseas buyer. According to W. R. Vance, there are five essential elements to an insurance contract:

1. The insured must have an insurable interest, that is, a financial interest based on some legal right in the preservation of the property. The insured must prove the extent of the insurable interest to collect, and recovery is limited by the insured's interest at the time of loss.
2. The insured is subjected to risk of loss of that interest by the occurrence of certain specified perils.
3. The insurer assumes the risk of loss.
4. This assumption is part of a general scheme to distribute the actual loss among a large group of persons bearing similar risks.
5. As a consideration, the insured pays a premium to a general insurance fund. (Vance, 1951)

Since insurance is a contract of indemnity, a person may not collect more than the actual loss in the event of damage caused by an insured peril. An export firm, for example, is not permitted to receive payment from the carrier for damages for the loss of cargo and also recover for the same loss from the insurer. On paying the exporter's claim, the insurer stands in the position of the exporter (insured party) to claim from the carrier or other parties who are responsible for occasioning the loss or damage. This means that the insurer is subrogated to all the rights of the insured after having indemnified the latter for its loss. This is generally described as the principle of subrogation. Another point to consider is whether an exporter, as an insured party, can assign the policy to the overseas customer. It appears that assignment is generally allowed insofar as there is an agreement to transfer the policy with the merchandise to the buyer and the seller has an insurable interest during the time when the assignment is made.

Marine Insurance

Marine policy is the most important type of insurance in the field of international trade. This is because (1) ocean shipping remains the predominant form of transport for large cargo, and (2) marine insurance is the most traditional and highly developed branch of insurance. All other policies, such as aviation and inland carriage, are largely based on principles of marine insurance. Practices and policies are also more standardized across countries in the area of marine insurance than in insurance of goods carried by land or air (Day and Griffin, 1993).

Term of Policy

Cargo policies may be written for a single trip or shipment (voyage policy), for a specified period (time policy), usually one year, or for an indefinite period (open policy), that is effective until canceled by the insured or insurer. The majority of cargo policies are written on open contracts. Under the latter policy, shipments are reported to the underwriter as they are made and premium is paid monthly based on the shipment actually made. The time policy differs from the open contract not just in the term of the policy, but also with respect to the premium payment method. Under the time policy, a premium deposit is made based on an estimated future shipment and adjustments are later made by comparing the estimates with the actual shipment. Another version of open policy is one that is generally available to exporters/importers with larger shipments. It covers most of the shipper's needs and has certain deductibles (blanket policy). Under a blanket policy, the insured is not required to advise the insurer of the individual shipments and one premium covers all shipments.

Types of Policies

There are three basic types of policies: (1) all risks (AR), (2) free of particular average (FPA), and (3) within average (WA). All three policies generally cover the following: *total loss of cargo by loss of the vessel, or while loading or discharging; constructive total loss (total loss from a commercial point of view, although goods may be in existence); stranding, sinking, or burning of vessel; damage from fire, explosion, or collision; general average contribution, jettison, sue, and labor.*

However, in addition to these, the all risks policy protects against *hooks, rainwater, theft, pilferage, nondelivery, sweat damage, leakage, taint from other cargo, breakage, and heat damage.* All policies exclude *delay in delivery, inherent vice, strikes, riots, war, and civil commotion,* unless added by endorsement.

FPA will cover only in the event of total loss or partial loss arising from certain specified risks, such as stranding or fire.

WA covers total loss and partial losses (broader than FPA) greater than a given percentage, usually 3 percent, and the insurer is liable for the total amount lost. In view of the scope of insurance coverage, AR policies are subject to high premiums, followed by WA policies. Exporters that sell on credit and use terms of sale denoting the buyer as responsible for insurance (FAS, FOB, etc.) should consider taking out contingency insurance for the benefit of the overseas buyer, in case the latter's insurance becomes inadequate to cover the loss. By paying a small premium for such insurance, the exporter creates a favorable condition for the buyer to pay for the shipment. Contingency insurance is supplementary to the policy taken out by the overseas buyer, and recovery is not made under the policy unless the buyer's policy is inadequate to cover the loss. (See Table 9.2 for different types of losses.)

Insurance Policy versus Certificates

An insurance company may issue an insurance policy or a certificate. If the insurer issues only policies, an application must be completed by the insured for each shipment and delivered to the insurer or agent before a policy is prepared and sent to the former. This can be time-consuming.

TABLE 9.2. Types of Losses

Total Loss	
1. Actual total loss	Goods are completely damaged or destroyed or so changed in their nature as to be unmarketable.
2. Constructive total loss	Actual loss is inevitable (such as frustration of voyage for an indefinite time), or damaged cargo can only be saved at considerable cost (i.e., cost greater than its value).
Partial Loss	
1. General average loss	These are goods sacrificed as part of a general average act or as a cargo owner's contribution for the general average loss of others.
2. Particular charges	These are expenses incurred to prevent loss or damage to insured cargo from risk that is insured against. Example: expenses for extra fodder for a cargo of horses while the ship is under repair for hurricane damage that was covered under the policy.
3. Particular average loss	This includes partial losses that are not covered by general average and particular charges.

However, in the case of certificates, the insurer provides a pad of insurance certificates to the exporter or importer, and a copy of the completed certificate (with details of goods, destination, type and amount of insurance required, etc.) is mailed to the insurance company whenever a shipment is made. Certificates save time and facilitate more efficient international business transactions.

Air Cargo Insurance

A modified form of marine insurance coverage is issued for air cargo insurance. Some airlines sell their own coverage.

CLAIMS AND PROCEDURES

Claims

Shippers can claim from carriers or insurers with respect to loss or damage to their cargo. Shippers often attempt to recover from carriers when they have a reasonable basis to believe that the loss or damage was caused by the negligent act or omission of the carriers that was easily preventable through exercise of due diligence in the transportation and handling of the cargo. Another motivating factor for the insured to obtain a satisfactory settlement with carriers could be to maintain a healthy loss to premium and keep premiums low. It could also be that the loss or damage is not covered by the insurance policy. However, in most cases, shippers claim from their insurers partly because carriers reject claims received from the insured or because the shippers find that the adjustment for loss or damage is inadequate due to liability limitations. It may also be that some shippers find it more convenient and efficient to handle claims with insurance companies.

Settling losses under insurance contracts is the function of claims management. Claims management is often accomplished through employed (in-house) or independent adjusters who negotiate settlement with the insured. The claims department is responsible for ascertaining the validity of the loss, investigating, estimating the extent and amount of the loss, and finally approving payment of the claim. It is important to note the following in relation to insurance claims:

- To recover, the loss or damage incurred by the insured must be covered by the insurance policy. The insurer will avoid liability if the particular risk is specifically excluded or is not reasonably attributable to the risk insured against.
- The burden of proof falls on the insured to show that the loss or damage to the cargo is covered by the policy.
- The insured must take prudent measures to protect the merchandise from further loss or damage. Under the sue and labor clause that is incorporated in most cargo insurance contracts (see International Perspective 9.3 for other typical clauses), the insured is required to take all necessary steps to safeguard the cargo and save it from further damage, without in any way prejudicing its rights under the policy. The underwriter agrees to pay any resulting expense.
- Once the insurance company settles the insured's claim, it could exercise its subrogation right to claim from parties responsible for the loss or damage. Under the principle of subrogation, the right to re-

cover from carriers and other parties who are responsible for the loss or damage passes from the insured to the insurer on payment of the insurance money. Since the insurer stands in the shoes of the insured in claiming from third parties, the insurer does not have a better right than what the insured possessed. Any payments obtained by the insured shipper from the carrier or other parties must be transferred to the insurer (after settlement with insurer) because under the principle of subrogation, the insured is not allowed to recover more than once for the same loss.

Claims are generally valid for two years from the date of arrival for air shipments and one year in the case of ocean shipments. Claims are invalid if not initiated within this period unless legal action is pursued.

Typical Steps in Claim Procedures

Step 1

Preliminary notice of claim. The export-import firm (insured) must file a preliminary claim by notifying the carrier of a potential claim as soon as the loss is known or expected. A formal claim may follow when the nature and value of the loss or damage is ascertained.

Step 2

Formal notice of claim. The consignee must file a formal claim with the carrier and the insurance company once the damage or loss is ascertained. The claim should include costs such as the value of the cargo, inland freight, ocean/airfreight, documentation, and other items. If the insurance policy is 110 percent of the CIF value, the insured could add 10 percent of the value of the goods to the claim. Assuming that the insured intends to claim from the insurer (not the carrier), the insured should arrange for a survey with the claims agent of the insurance company. The formal claim form should be submitted with certain documents: a copy of the commercial invoice; a signed copy of bill of lading/air waybill; the original certificate of insurance; a copy of the claim against the carrier, or reply thereto; the survey report, if done by the surveyor; the packing list; and a copy of the receipt given to the carrier on delivery of the merchandise. It could also include photographs, repair invoice, and an affidavit from the carrier, if possible.

International Perspective

9.3

TYPICAL CLAUSES
IN CARGO INSURANCE CONTRACTS

1. **Inchamaree clause:** This clause covers any loss or damage to cargo due to the bursting of boilers, breakage of shafts, or any latent defect in the machinery, as well as from negligence of the captain or crew when that is the proximate cause of a loss.
2. **Free of particular average clause:** This relieves the insurer of liability for partial cargo losses, except for those caused by the stranding, sinking, burning, or collision of the vessel with another.
3. **The labels clause:** In the case of damage to labels, capsules, or wrappers, the insurer is not liable for more than the cost of the new items and the cost of reconditioning the goods.
4. **The delay clause:** This relieves the insurer of liability for loss of market due to delay in the delivery of the cargo.
5. **The general average clause:** A general average loss occurs when a sacrifice is voluntarily made or an expense is incurred in times of imminent peril to preserve the common interest from disaster. Payments of apportioned losses are secured by a general average deposit before goods are released by the carrier. When the actual shipper's share is established, appropriate adjustments are made and any excess is returned. A general average clause covers the amount of the insured shipper's contribution.
6. **Craft and lighter clause:** In this clause, the insurer agrees to provide lighters or other craft to deliver cargo within the harbor limits.
7. **Marine extension clause:** Under this clause, no time limit is to be imposed on the insurance coverage at the port of discharge while goods are delayed in transit to final destination insofar as the delay is occasioned by circumstances beyond the control of the insured.
8. **Shore clause:** This covers certain risks to cargo, such as collision, hurricane, floods, and so on, while the goods are on docks, wharves, or elsewhere on shore.
9. **Warehouse to warehouse clause:** This covers cargo while on transit between the initial point of shipment and the point of destination, subject to terms of sale and insurable interest requirement. The policy is effective from the time the goods leave the warehouse/store named in the policy for the commencement of transit to the final warehouse at the point of destination stated in the policy.

Step 3

Settlement of claim. If the claim is covered by the policy and claims procedures are appropriately followed, the insurance company will pay the insured. If the insurance company declines to approve payment, the insured could pursue arbitration or other dispute settlement procedures as provided in the insurance contract.

The claim is filed by the party that assumes the risk of loss on transit. For example, in CIF contracts, the exporter takes out an insurance policy for the benefit of the buyer and the risk of loss is transferred to the buyer once goods are put on board the vessel at the port of shipment. The exporter will send the necessary documents and detailed instructions to the overseas customer (consignee) to follow in the event of loss or damage. The consignee should be instructed to examine the goods upon delivery to determine any apparent or concealed loss or damage to cargo. Any loss or damage discovered upon such inspection should be noted on the carrier's delivery receipt or air waybill. Once the carrier obtains a clean receipt from the consignee, it becomes difficult for the latter to successfully make a claim.

The best way to deal with claims is to prevent the occurrence of loss or damage to cargo as much as is practically feasible. It is estimated that proper packing, handling, and stowage can prevent about 70 percent of cargo loss or damage. The frequent occurrence of damage or loss to cargo not only becomes a source of friction or suspicion on the part of insurance companies but also discourages the growth and expansion of trade. It could also have the effect of reducing sales abroad if overseas customers are discouraged by the frequency of such occurrences, since it could consume the parties' time and effort. If payment has already been made to the exporter, the buyer's capital is tied up with merchandise that cannot be sold.

CHAPTER SUMMARY

Documents Frequently Used in Export-Import Transactions

1. Air waybill
2. Bill of exchange
3. Bill of lading
4. Through bill of lading
5. Consular invoice

6. Certificate of origin
7. Inspection certificate
8. Insurance certificate
9. Commercial invoice
10. Dock's receipt
11. Destination control statement
12. Shipper's export declaration
13. Pro forma invoice
14. Export packing list

Risks in Foreign Trade

1. Political risks: Actions of government authorities, war, revolution, terrorism, strikes.
   a. Managing political risk: monitoring political developments, insuring against political risks.
2. Foreign credit risk: Risks of buyer's default or delays in payment.
   a. Managing foreign credit risk: appropriate credit management, letters of credit and other conditions, insurance.
3. Foreign exchange risk: Changes in currency values that could reduce future exporter's receipts or increase importer's payments in foreign currency.
   a. Managing foreign exchange risk: shifting the risk to the other party or to third parties.
4. Transportation risk: Loss or damage to merchandise during transit.

Inland Carriage

Inland carriage is the use of an inland carrier to move merchandise from the exporter's warehouse to the sea or airport. Major international rules governing inland carriage:

1. Convention on the Contract for the International Carriage of Goods by Road.
2. Convention Concerning International Carriage by Rail.

Both conventions cover areas such as liability for loss or damage to shipment, delays in delivery, and time limits for bringing action.

Carriage of Goods by Sea

Major international rules:
1. The Hague Rules (1924)
2. The Hague-Visby Rules (1968)
3. The Hamburg Rules (1978)

All three conventions cover rights and duties of parties to a contract of carriage by sea: Duty of carrier, carrier's liability, period of responsibility, limitation of action, and limits of carrier's liability.

Carriage of Goods by Air

Major international rules:

1. The Warsaw Convention (1929)
2. The Warsaw Convention—Amended (1955)

Insurance

Two essential principles:

1. The Principle of Insurable Interest: Financial interest is based on some legal right in the preservation of the insured property.
2. The Principle of Subrogation: On paying the insured's claim, the insurer stands in the position of the former (the insured) to claim from other parties who are responsible for the loss or damage.

Marine Insurance

Term of Policy

1. Voyage policy covers a single trip.
2. Time policy is coverage for a specified time.
3. Open policy covers for an indefinite period of time.

Types of Policies

1. All risks policy covers all marine risks that are insurable.
2. Free of particular average policy covers total loss and partial loss from certain specified risks insured against.
3. Within average policy covers total loss and partial losses greater than a given percentage, with the insurer liable for the total amount lost.

Claims and Procedures

Claims for loss or damage to shipment on transit can be claimed from carriers or insurers. Most cargo claims are settled with insurance companies.

Typical claims procedures: preliminary notice of claim, formal notice of claim, and settlement.

SECTION IV:
PAYMENT TERMS
AND PROCEDURES

Chapter 10

Exchange Rates
and International Trade

FOREIGN EXCHANGE TRANSACTIONS

An exchange rate is the number of units of a given currency that can be purchased for one unit of another currency. It is a common practice in world currency markets to use the indirect quotation, that is, quoting all exchange rates (except for the British pound) per U.S. dollar. *The Wall Street Journal* foreign exchange data for December 16, 1997, for example, showed the quotation for the Canadian dollar as being 1.4256 per 1 U.S. dollar (see Table 10.1). Direct quotation is the expression of the number of U.S. dollars required to buy one unit of foreign currency. The direct U.S. dollar quotation on December 16, 1997, for the Canadian dollar was U.S. $0.7017. Although it is common for foreign currency markets around the world to quote rates in U.S. dollars, some traders state the price of other currencies in terms of the dealer's home currency (cross rates), for example, Dutch guilders against Japanese yen, French francs against Spanish pesetas, and so on.

TABLE 10.1. Currency Trading, Tuesday, December 16, 1997

Selected Countries	Indirect Quotation Currency per US $	Cross Rates (per Yen/per Lira)
Canada	1.4256	0.0191/0.00082
France	5.9637	0.04559/0.0034
Germany	1.7808	0.0136/0.0010
United Kingdom	0.61143	0.0046/0.0003
Japan	130.8	—/0.0749
United States	—	0.0076/0.0005

Source: The Wall Street Journal, December 17, 1997, p. C-15.

Strictly speaking, it is reasonable to state that the rate of the foreign currency against the dollar is a cross rate to dealers in third countries.

The foreign exchange market is a place where foreign currency is purchased and sold. In the same way that the relationship between goods and money in ordinary business transactions is expressed by price, so the relationship of one currency to another is expressed by exchange rate. A large proportion of the foreign exchange transactions undertaken each day is between banks in different countries. These transactions are often a result of the wishes of the banks' customers to consummate commercial transactions, that is, payments for imports or receipts for exports. Other reasons for individual companies or governments to enter into the foreign exchange market as buyers or sellers of foreign currencies include the following:

- Foreign travel and purchase of foreign stocks and bonds; foreign investment; receipt of income, such as interest, dividends, royalties, and so on, from abroad; or payment of such income in foreign currency.
- Central banks enter the foreign exchange market to buy or sell foreign currency (in exchange for domestic currency) to stabilize the national currency, that is, to reduce violent fluctuations in exchange rates without destroying the viability and freedom of the foreign exchange market.
- Speculation, that is, purchase of foreign currency at a low rate with the hope to sell it at a profit.

Foreign exchange trading is not limited to one specific location. It takes place wherever such deals are made, for example, in a private office or even at home, far away from the dealing rooms or facilities of companies. Most of these transactions are carried out between commercial banks and their customers as well as among commercial banks themselves, which buy and sell foreign currencies in response to the needs of their clients. For example, a Canadian bank sells Canadian dollars to a French bank in exchange for French francs. This transaction, in effect, allows the Canadian bank the right to draw a check on the French bank for the amount of the deposit denominated in francs. Similarly, it will enable the French bank to draw a check in Canadian dollars for the amount of the deposit (DeRosa, 1991).

Foreign exchange rates are based on the supply and demand for various currencies, which, in turn, are derivatives of the fundamental economic factors and technical conditions in the market. In the United States, for example, the continuous deterioration in the trade deficit in the 1970s, mainly due to increased consumption expenditures on foreign goods, led to an oversupply of dollars in foreign central banks. This in turn resulted in a lower dollar in foreign exchange markets. Besides a country's balance of payments position, factors such as interest rates, growth in the money supply, inflation, and confidence in the government are important determinants of supply and demand for foreign currencies and, hence, the exchange rate. The following are some examples (see also Table 10.2):

- The German mark appreciated substantially over the recent period due to interest rate tightening by the Bundesbank (Germany's central bank). Currency traders buy currencies of countries with high interest rates to maximize their investment returns and sell those currencies with low interest rates.
- The British pound has strengthened against the dollar and other currencies in the recent period, mainly due to relatively high interest rates and low inflation, reinforced by the shift to an independent central bank. Low inflation has contributed to making its products more competitive and has increased the demand for its currency abroad.
- The Mexican peso has been depreciating in relation to other major currencies over the recent period due to a significant widening of its current account deficit, high inflation, including a mild decline in interest rates, and political uncertainty.
- The Indonesian rupiah fell by 26 percent in January of 1998 amid fears of political instability and social unrest.

TABLE 10.2. Relative Position of Major Trading Countries/Currencies, 1996

	European Union	Japan	United States
Share in world output	31%	21%	27%
Share in global reserve holdings	20%	7%	56%
Share in two-way foreign exchange transactions	70%	24%	84%
Share in world export invoicing	33%	5%	48%

Source: International Monetary Fund (IMF), 1996, pp. 10-16.

Exchange rate fluctuations can have a profound effect on international trade. Export-import firms are vulnerable to foreign exchange risks whenever they enter into an obligation to accept or deliver a specified amount of foreign currency at a future point in time. These firms are then faced with a prospect that future changes in foreign currency values could either reduce the amount of their receipts or increase their payments in foreign currency. A U.S. importer of Japanese components, for example, took a $1 million loss when the dollar took an unexpected fall against the yen in 1993 wiping out a significant portion of the company's profits. In some cases, it may also be that such changes will bring about financial benefits. In the previous example, the U.S. importer could have reduced its payments in dollars if the yen had depreciated against the dollar.

The most important types of transactions that contribute to foreign exchange risks in international trade include the following:

- Purchase of goods and services whose prices are stated in foreign currency, that is, payables in foreign currency
- Sales of goods and services whose prices are stated in foreign currency, that is, receivables in foreign currency
- Debt payments to be made or accepted in foreign currency

Most export-import companies do not have the expertise to handle such unanticipated changes in exchange rates. Banks with international trade capabilities and consultants can help assess currency risks and advise companies to take appropriate measures.

The impact of exchange rate fluctuations on export trade can be illustrated by Japanese auto sales to the United States. In 1991, when the yen appreciated against the dollar, the market share for Japanese autos in the United States declined by 25.5 percent. In 1985, when the yen was at 238 to the dollar, the Honda Civic carried a U.S. sticker price of $12,000 (2,856,000 yen). However, when the yen appreciated to 128 to the dollar a few years later, the U.S. sticker price almost doubled to $22,313. A sharp rise was also evident in the price of other Japanese exports to the United States. The Japanese responded to this by shifting factories to North America, which cushions them from currency fluctuations. For example, about 70 percent of the 700,000 Nissans sold to Americans are made in the United States. Toyota also builds more than half the 1.2 million vehicles it sells in the United States within North America. Honda's most popular model, the Accord, is built in Marysville, Ohio (Taylor, 1995).

The impact of exchange rate risks is felt more by export-import companies than domestic firms. To the extent that an exporter's inputs are domestic, a strong domestic currency could lead to loss of domestic and

Only a few countries impose no restrictions on the use of the foreign exchange market. This means that their currency is fully convertible into foreign currency for all uses—both trade in goods and services as well as international financial activities. Many Western economies, such as Canada, the United States, Japan, the United Kingdom, and Germany, have convertible currencies.

Currencies of most developing and former communist nations, however, are either not convertible or legally convertible only at artificial, government-established rates. Such exchange restrictions may be imposed for competitive reasons (keeping a lower value), to promote foreign investment, or to discharge debt payments (maintaining a high value). The most extreme form of exchange restrictions (control) is limitation of the availability of foreign currency to purchase imports. Limits could also be placed on the use of foreign currency for certain transactions, such as imports of luxury goods, to conserve foreign currency. In terms of exports, exchange control rules could require that exports are properly paid for and payment is forthcoming within a reasonable time, that is, proceeds from exports are to be repatriated to the country's bank within a given period of time after shipment.

foreign markets. Importers also face a loss of domestic markets due to the rise in the price of imports if the domestic currency weakens. In addition, such firms are vulnerable to exchange risks arising from receivables or payables in foreign currency.

PROTECTION AGAINST EXCHANGE RATE RISKS

There are several ways in which export-import companies can protect themselves against unanticipated changes in exchange rates. The risk associated with such transactions is that the exchange rate might change between the date when the export contract was made and the date of payment (the settlement date), which is often sixty to ninety days after the contract or shipment of the merchandise.

Shifting the Risk to Third Parties

Hedging in Financial Markets

Through various hedging instruments, firms could reduce the adverse impact of foreign currency fluctuations. This allows firms to lock in the exchange rate today for receipts or payments in foreign currency that will happen sometime in the future. Current foreign exchange rates are called spot prices; those occurring sometime in the future are referred to as forward prices. If the currency in question is more expensive for forward delivery (for delivery at some future date) than for ordinary spot delivery (i.e., two business days following the agreed-upon exchange date), it is said to be at a premium. If it is less expensive for forward delivery than spot delivery, it is said to be at a discount.

In Table 10.3, the forward mark is at a premium since the forward mark is more expensive than the spot. The forward Canadian dollar is at a discount because its forward price is cheaper than the spot. When viewed from the point of view of the U.S. dollar, it can also be stated that the forward dollar is at a discount in relation to the mark or that the forward U.S. dollar is at a premium in relation to the Canadian dollar.

TABLE 10.3. Hypothetical Exchange Rates, Currency per U.S. Dollar

	Deutsche Mark	Canadian Dollar
Spot rate	1.8037	1.4257
Thirty-day forward	1.7948	1.4296
Ninety-day forward	1.7887	1.4273

It is pertinent to underscore some salient points about hedging in foreign exchange markets:

- *Hedging is not always the most appropriate technique to limit foreign exchange risks:* There are fees associated with hedging, and such costs reduce the expected value from a given transaction. Export-import firms should seriously consider hedging when a high proportion of their cash flow is vulnerable to exchange rate fluctuations. This means that firms should determine the acceptable level of risk that they are willing to take. In contrast, firms with a small portion of their total cash exposed to foreign exchange rate movements may be better off playing the law of averages—shortfalls could be eventually offset by windfall gains.

- *Hedging does not protect long-term cash flows:* Hedging does not insulate firms from long-term adjustments in currency values (O'Connor and Bueso, 1990). Thus, it should not be used to cover anticipated changes in currency values. A U.S. importer of German goods would have found it difficult to adequately hedge against the predictable fall of the dollar during the 1973-1980 period. The impact of such action is felt in terms of higher dollar prices paid for imports.
- *Forward market hedges are available in a very limited number of currencies:* Most currencies are not traded in the forward market. However, many countries peg their currency to that of a major industrial country whose currency is traded in the forward market. Many Latin American countries, for example, peg their currencies to the U.S. dollar. This insulates U.S. firms from foreign exchange risk in these countries unless the country changes from the designated (pegged) official rate. Foreign firms, that is, non-U.S. firms, in these countries can reduce potential risks by buying or selling dollars (in the event of purchases or sales to these countries) forward, as the case may be.

> *Example #1.* Suppose the Colombian peso is pegged to the U.S. dollar at $1 = 1,000$ pesos. A British firm that is to make payment in pesos for its imports from Colombia, could hedge its position by buying U.S. dollars forward. On the settlement date, pounds would be converted into dollars, which, in turn, could be converted into pesos. This assumes that Colombia does not change the pegged rate during that period.

- *Hedging should not be used for individual transactions:* Since most export-import firms engage in transactions that result in inflows and outflows of foreign currencies, the most appropriate strategy to reduce transaction costs is to hedge the exported net receivable or payable in foreign currency.

> *Example #2.* Suppose a Canadian firm has receivables from two Japanese buyers amounting to 5 million yen and payables to four Japanese suppliers worth 9 million yen. Instead of hedging all six transactions, the Canadian firm should cover only the net short position (i.e., 4 million yen) in yen. This reduces the transaction cost of exchanging currencies for the firm.

Spot and Forward Market Hedge

As previously noted, a spot transaction is one in which foreign currencies are purchased and sold for immediate delivery, that is, within two business days following the agreed-upon exchange date. The two-day period is intended to allow the respective commercial banks to make the necessary transfer. A forward transaction is a contract that provides for two parties to exchange currencies on a future date at an agreed-upon exchange rate. The forward rate is usually quoted for one month, three months, four months, six months, or one year. Unlike hedging in the spot market, forward market hedging does not require borrowing or tying up a certain amount of money for a period of time. This is because the firm agrees to buy or sell the agreed amount of currency at a determinable future date, and actual delivery does not take place before the stipulated date.

Example 1: Spot market hedge. On September 1, a U.S. importer contracts to buy German machines for a total cost of 600,000 deutsche marks (DM). The payment date is December 1. When the contract is signed on September 1, the spot exchange rate is $0.5000 per DM and the December forward rate is $0.5085 per DM. The U.S. importer believes that the mark is going to appreciate in value in relation to the dollar.

The import firm could buy 600,000 DM on the spot market on September 1 for $300,000 and deposit the deutsche marks in an interest-bearing account until the payment date. If the firm does not hedge, and the spot exchange rate rises to $0.5128 per DM on December 1, the importer will suffer a loss of $7,680, or $(0.5128 - 0.5000) \times 600,000$.

The import firm could also borrow $300,000 and convert at the spot rate for 600,000 DM. The deutsch marks could be lent out, put in certificates of deposit, and so forth, until December 1, when payment is to be made to the exporter. The U.S. dollar loan will be paid from the proceeds of resale, and so on, without any foreign exchange exposure. This is often referred to as a credit hedge.

Example 2: Forward market hedge. On September 1, a U.S. exporter contracts to sell U.S. goods for SF (Swiss francs) 250,000. The goods are to be delivered and payment received on December 1. When the contract is signed, the spot exchange rate is $0.6098/SF and the December forward rate is $0.6212/SF. The Swiss franc is expected to depreciate, and the December 1 spot exchange rate is likely to fall to $0.5696/SF.

The U.S. exporter has two options: First, it can sell its franc receivable forward now and receive $0.6212 per franc on the settlement date (December). Second, it can wait until December and then sell francs on spot. Clearly, the forward market hedge is preferable, and the U.S. exporter would gain: $(0.6212 - 0.6098) \times 250,000 = \$2,850$. The decision to use the forward market is to be made upon an assessment of what the future spot rate is likely to be. It is also important to bear in mind the impact of transaction costs before a firm makes a decision on what action to take. A credit hedge could have been feasible if the spot rate in the United States had been higher than the forward rate.

Swap

A swap transaction is the simultaneous purchase and sale of a certain amount of foreign currency for two different value dates. The central feature of this transaction is that the bank arranges the swap as a single transaction, usually between two partners. Swaps are used to move out of one currency and into another for a limited period of time without the exchange risk of an open position.

Example. A U.S. firm sells semiconductor chips to Nippon, a Japanese firm, for 60 million yen, and payment was made upon receipt of shipment on October 1. The U.S. firm has payables to Nippon and other Japanese firms of about 60 million yen for the purchase of merchandise, with payments due on January 1. The spot exchange rate on October 1 is 120 yen per dollar and the January sixty-day forward rate is 125 yen per dollar.

The U.S. firm sells its 60 million yen receipts on the spot market for \$500,000 at the price of \$1 = 120 yen. Simultaneously, the firm contracts with the same or different bank to purchase 60 million yen in sixty days at the forward price of 125 yen per dollar. In addition to its normal profits on its exports, the U.S. firm has made a profit of 2.5 million yen from its swap transaction. In cases in which the delivery date to the Japanese firms is not certain, the U.S. firm could use a time option that leaves the delivery date open, while locking the exchange rate at a specified rate.

Other Hedging Techniques

Export-import companies can use different techniques to avoid foreign exchange risk:

- *Hedging receipts against payables:* An export firm that has receiv-ables in foreign currency (30 million British pounds) could hedge its receipts against a payable of 30 million pounds to the same or another firm at about the same time. This is achieved with no additional cost and without going through the foreign exchange market. The same method could be used between export-import firms and their branches or other affiliate companies abroad.

• *Acceleration or delay of payments:* If an importer reasonably believes that its domestic currency is likely to depreciate in terms of the currency of its foreign supplier, it would be motivated to accelerate its payments. This could be achieved by buying the requisite foreign currency before it appreciates in value. However, payments could be delayed if the buyer believes that the foreign currency in which payment is to be made is likely to depreciate in value in terms of the domestic currency.

Guarantees and Insurance Coverage

In certain cases, exporters require a guarantee by the importer, a bank, or another agency against the risk of devaluation or exchange controls. Certain types of insurance coverage are also available against exchange controls. In view of its high cost, hedging is a better alternative than insurance.

Shifting the Risk to the Other Party

Invoicing in One's Own Currency

Risks accompany all transactions involving a future remittance or payment in foreign currency. If the payment or receipt for a transaction is in one's own currency, the risk arising from currency fluctuations is shifted to the other party. Suppose a Korean firm negotiated to make payments (ninety days after the contract date) in its domestic currency (won) for its imports of equipment from a Canadian manufacturer. This shifts the foreign currency risk to the exporter, which will have to convert its won receipts into Canadian dollars. Payment in one's own currency shifts not only the risk of devaluation to the other party but also the risk of imposition of exchange controls by the importing country against convertibility and repatriation of foreign currency.

Invoicing in Foreign Currency

In the event that the agreement stipulates that payment is to be made in foreign currency, it is important for the exporter to require inclusion of a provision that protects the value of its receipts from currency devaluation. In the previous example, the contract could provide for an increase in payment to compensate the Canadian manufacturer/exporter for losses arising from currency fluctuations.

International Perspective

10.2

THE EURO: A BRIEF OVERVIEW

What is the Euro? The Euro is a currency designed to replace all the separate currencies of the individual countries of the European Union (EU). On January 1, 1999, the Euro became the legal currency of eleven members of the European Union.

Participating members: Austria, Belgium, Finland, France, Germany, Ireland, Italy, Luxembourg, the Netherlands, Portugal, and Spain. Denmark, Sweden, and the United Kingdom declined to participate at this stage; Greece does not yet meet the convergence criteria required for membership and is expected to join in 2001.

Convergence criteria: To participate in the single European currency, countries are required to meet certain conditions: inflation rates below 2 to 3 percent, public debt at no more than 60 percent GDP, and a budget deficit less than or equal to 3 percent GDP.

Benefits and costs: (1) For businesses that are involved in cross-border trade, the Euro will eliminate the cost of foreign exchange (hedging expenses, etc.) with regard to all intra-European transactions. There will also be no foreign currency risks in relation to cross-border investments within the EU. (2) European businesses will benefit from low inflation and interest rates, which is an important policy of the future European Central Bank. (3) Besides eliminating exchange rate uncertainty, the Euro allows consumers and businesses to compare costs and prices. This, in turn, puts a downward pressure on prices and eliminates the practice of charging different prices in different markets within Europe. The major costs associated with the Euro include: (a) conversion of cash registers and machines that accept commercial notes and (b) modification/adjustment of prices; conversion of invoicing, salary, and accounting systems, etc.

Timetable (1998-2002): (1) 1998: The creation of European Central Bank and commencement of production of Euro banknotes and coins. (2) 1999-2001: Determination of conversion rates for the Euro, establishment and execution of the single monetary policy in Euro, and commencement of foreign exchange operations and issuance of public debt in Euro. Businesses and customers may choose to use either the Euro or national currency. Increased use of the Euro for bookkeeping. (3) 2002: Changeover of the economy to Euro and circulation of Euro banknotes and coins. Withdrawal of national currencies by July 2002.

Another method would be to make certain assumptions about possible adverse changes in the exchange rate and add it to the price. If currency changes are likely to result in a 10 percent loss, the price change could be increased by that percentage.

An export contract could also provide for the establishment of an escrow account in a third country's currency (stable currency) from which payments will be made. This protects the exporter from losses due to depreciation of the importer's currency.

CHAPTER SUMMARY

Exchange Rates

An exchange rate is the number of units of a given currency that can be purchased for one unit of another currency.

Reasons for the Existence of the Foreign Exchange Market

1. Foreign travel
2. Purchase of foreign stocks and bonds
3. Foreign investment and other receipts and payments in foreign currency
4. Reduction of currency fluctuations
5. Speculation

Major Factors That Determine Foreign Exchange Rates

1. Balance of payments
2. Interest rates
3. Growth in the money supply
4. Inflation
5. Confidence in the government

Protection Against Exchange Rate Risks

1. Hedging in financial markets: spot and forward market hedge, swap, acceleration and delay of payments, etc.
2. Guarantees and insurance coverage
3. Invoicing in one's own currency
4. Invoicing in foreign currency

Chapter 11

Methods of Payment

The rapid growth and expansion in global trade cannot be sustained without efficient and timely payment arrangements. Nonpayment or delays in payment for imports could tie up limited credit facilities and create liquidity problems for many exporting companies. Advance payments by overseas customers would similarly tie up buyers' limited resources and do not necessarily guarantee delivery of agreed merchandise. The ideal payment method is one that protects the contending interests of both sellers and buyers.

Exporters often seek to develop foreign markets by using payment arrangements that are less costly to the buyer, such as consignment sales, open accounts, and documentary drafts, whereby the seller is paid by the foreign wholesaler or retailer only after the goods have been received or sold. It is estimated that about 35 to 50 percent of exports from the United States and the United Kingdom are sold on open account and/or consignment (Cheeseright, 1994). This means that the risk of delay in payment or nonpayment could have a crucial effect on cash flow and profits (see Figure 11.1).

FIGURE 11.1. Export Payment Terms Risk/Cost Tradeoff

Risk to Exporter

Least Risk < - > Highest Risk

| Cash in Advance | Confirmed Irrevocable Letter of Credit | Irrevocable Letter of Credit | Bank Collection (Sight Draft) | Bank Collection (Time Draft) | Consignment Sales, Open Account |

Highest Cost < -> Least Cost

Cost to Buyer

Export companies need access to credit reports on a global basis. There is a need to increase the existing database on companies in different parts of the world to ensure that formal reviews on credit decisions are based on current and reliable information. It is also important to consider credit insurance and other safeguards.

CONSIGNMENT SALES

This is a method in which the exporter sends the product to an importer on a deferred payment basis; that is, the importer does not pay for the merchandise until it is sold to a third party. Title to the merchandise passes to the importer only when payment is made to the exporter. Consignment is rarely used between unrelated parties, for example, independent exporters and importers (Goldsmith, 1989). It is best used in cases involving an increasing demand for a product for which a proportioned stock is required to meet such need (Tuller, 1994). It is also used when a seller wants to test-market new products or test the market in a new country.

For the exporter, consignment is the least desirable form of selling and receiving payment. The problems associated with this method include the following:

- *Delays in payment:* Buyer bears little or no risk, and payment to seller is delayed until the goods are sold to a third party. This ties up limited credit facilities and often creates liquidity problems for many exporting firms.
- *Risk of nonpayment:* Even though title to the goods does not pass until payment is made, the seller has to acquire possession of merchandise (to sell in importer's country or ship back to home country) in the event of nonpayment. This involves litigation in the importer's country, which often is time-consuming and expensive.
- *Cost of returning merchandise:* If there is limited success in selling the product, there is a need to ship it back to the exporter. It is costly to arrange for the return of merchandise that is unsold.
- *Limited sales effort by importers:* Importers may not be highly motivated to sell merchandise on consignment because their money is not tied up in inventory. They are likely to give priority to products in which they have some financial involvement.

In view of these risks, consignment sales should be used with overseas customers that have extremely good credit ratings and are well known to the exporter. They would also be satisfactory when the sale involves an affiliated firm or the seller's own sales representative or dealer (Onkvisit and Shaw, 1997). This method is frequently used by multinational companies to sell goods to their subsidiaries.

A number of issues should be considered before goods are sold on consignment between independent exporters and importers. First, it is important to verify the creditworthiness of foreign importers, including data on how long particular companies take to settle bills. Credit agencies have invested heavily in technology to improve the quantity and quality of information they provide to their clients (Kelley, 1995). Exporters can have instant access to information on overseas customers from such credit agencies. No exporting company should consider itself too small to take advice on credit matters. Bad and overdue debts erode profit margins and can jeopardize the viability of an otherwise successful company.

Information on creditworthiness should also include analysis of commercial or country risk factors such as economic and political stability as well as availability of foreign currency to purchase imports. U.S. banks and their overseas correspondents and some government agencies have credit information on foreign customers.

It is also advisable to consider some form of credit insurance to protect against default by overseas customers. Outstanding debt often makes up about 30 percent of an export company's assets, and it is important to take credit insurance to protect these assets. Credit insurance also helps exporters obtain access to a wide range of banking services and an improved rate of borrowing (Kelley, 1995). Financial institutions tend to look more favorably on businesses that are covered and are often prepared to lend more money at better terms. The parties should also agree on who will be responsible for risk insurance on merchandise until it is sold and payment is received by the seller, and who pays for freight charges for returned merchandise.

OPEN ACCOUNT

An open account is a contractual relationship between an exporter and importer in which a trade credit is extended by the former to the latter whereby payment is to be made to the exporter within an agreed period of time. The seller ships the merchandise to the buyer and separately mails the relevant shipping documents. Terms of payment range from 30 to 120 days after date of shipping invoice or receipt of merchandise, depending on the country.

As in the case of consignment sales, open account is rarely used in international trade between independent exporters and importers. Exporters are often apprehensive of potential defaults by overseas customers. They lack accurate information or may doubt the reliability of available data on foreign buyers to evaluate and determine their creditworthiness to purchase on open account. Unlike consignment sales, importers are expected to remit payment within a certain agreed-upon period regardless of whether they resold the product to third parties.

Open account is often used to increase sales by assisting foreign distributors to start new, or expand existing, product lines. It could also be used when a seller wants to test-market a new product or try a new market in a different country.

This arrangement gives the buyer/distributor enough time to resell the product to domestic customers and then pay the exporter, while generating business goodwill for future dealings. Many developing nations prohibit purchases on open account and consignment sales because of currency restrictions and lack of control over their balance of payments.

A major weakness of this method is that the importer could delay payment until merchandise is received, even when the importer is expected to pay within a specified period after shipment. There is also a greater risk of default or nonpayment by the buyer. This makes it difficult to sell the account receivable.

Open-account financing is often used for trade between parent and subsidiary companies. It is also used for sales to well-established customers with good credit ratings. When open-account sales to third parties are contemplated, it is important to verify the integrity of the buyers through a credit investigation. This should also take into account the importing country's political and economic conditions. Sources range from commercial credit agencies, such as Equifax, Dunn & Bradstreet, to chambers of commerce, trade associations, commercial banks, and public agencies, such as the Department of Commerce. It is advisable to insure trade debts to protect the seller against default by the importing company. Another safeguard would be to secure collateral to cover a transaction.

DOCUMENTARY COLLECTION (DOCUMENTARY DRAFT)

The documentary collection or documentary draft is one of the most customary methods of making payments in international trade. To facilitate the transaction, two banks are usually involved, one in the exporter's country and one in the buyer's country. The banks may be independent banks or branches of the same bank.

A draft can be drawn (documents payable) in the currency of the country of payment or in a foreign currency. This method of payment falls between the open account, which favors the buyer, and letter of credit, which protects the exporter. Bank fees are less expensive, usually a specific sum for each service, as opposed to a percentage of the transaction amount, which is used for letters of credit.

A typical documentary collection procedure includes the following steps (see also Figure 11.2):

- After the exporter (drawer) and overseas customer (drawee) agree on the terms of sale, the exporter arranges for shipment and prepares the necessary documents, such as invoice, bill of lading, certificate of origin, and draft.
- The exporter forwards the documents to its bank (remitting bank) with instructions.
- The remitting bank then forwards the documents to its overseas correspondent bank (collecting bank) in the importer's country, with the exporter's instruction letter that authorizes release of documents against payment (D/P) or acceptance (D/A) or other terms.
- The collecting bank contacts the importer to effect or accept payment. If the instruction is documents against payment (D/P), the importer pays the collecting bank in exchange for the documents. The collecting bank will then send proceeds to the remitting bank for payment to the seller. If the instructions are documents against acceptance (D/A), the collecting bank will release documents to the overseas customer only upon formal acceptance of the draft. Once accepted, the collecting bank will release the documents to the buyer. On or before maturity, the collecting bank will present the accepted draft for payment. When the buyer pays, the collecting bank will remit the funds in accordance with instructions.

The basic instructions for collection of shipping documents (in addition to those pertaining to release of documents and remittance of funds) include the following:

- Procedures as to how nonpayment or nonacceptance is to be communicated to the remitting bank
- Instructions as to who pays the bank's collection charges
- Listing of documents enclosed
- Name of a party to be contacted in case a problem arises

The banking practice relating to documentary draft is standardized by the Uniform Rules for Collections (International Chamber of Commerce [ICC], 1995). The uniform rules apply only when the parties to the con-

FIGURE 11.2. Documentary Collection

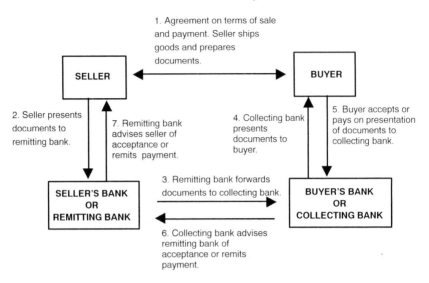

tract agree to be governed by those standards. The rules set out the rights and duties of banks and users of documentary collections.

Documents Against Payment

In a typical documents against payment (D/P) transaction, the exporter draws a draft on the foreign buyer (drawee) through a foreign bank (collecting bank) that received the collection documents from the exporter's remitting bank (Wells and Dulat, 1991). In this instance, a sight draft is presented with other documents specified by the buyer or the buyer's country and the collecting bank will provide these documents to the buyer upon payment. This means that the buyer does not receive the documents and thus will not obtain possession of the goods until payment is made to the collecting bank. This method is widely used in foreign trade and often designated as "sight draft, documents against payment" (S/D, D/P).

The original order bill of lading giving title to the goods is made out to the order of the shipper and is endorsed by the latter either in blank or the order of the collecting bank (Maggiori, 1992). This ensures that the seller retains title and control of the shipment until it reaches its destination and payment is made to the collecting bank. When the collecting bank is paid, it endorses the bill of lading and other documents to the buyer. The original bill of lading must be properly endorsed by the buyer and surrendered to the carrier before the buyer procures possession of the shipment.

Order bills of lading are not available with air shipments. If the importer's name is on the air waybill (not a negotiable document) as consignee, often nothing more is needed to hand over the merchandise to the buyer (importer) than the latter's identification, and the importer could then obtain the goods without payment. This problem can be resolved by designating a third party, such as a custom broker or, with prior permission, a collecting bank, as consignee on the air waybill. The importer's name should be mentioned as the party to be notified for identification of shipment.

In using S/D, D/P, there remains the potential risk of nonpayment by the importer. The buyer's ability or willingness to pay may change between the time the goods are shipped and the time the draft is presented for payment (McMahon et al., 1994). It could also be that the policy of the importing country may change (e.g., exchange controls), making it difficult for the importer to make payments. In the event of nonpayment by the buyer, the exporter has the choice of having the merchandise shipped back or selling it to another buyer in the importing country.

Documents Against Acceptance

In this method, the exporter allows the overseas customer a certain period of time to effect payment for the shipment. The buyer receives the documents, and thus the title, to the goods in exchange for acceptance of the draft to pay at some determinable future date. A time draft is used to establish the time of payment; that is that the payment is due within a certain time after the buyer accepts the draft. A date draft, which specifies the date of payment, is sometimes used. When a time draft is used, the customer can potentially delay payment by delaying acceptance of the draft. An exporter can prevent such delays by either using a date draft or tying the payment date to the date on the bill of lading (e.g., thirty days from the date of the bill of lading) or draft. The collecting bank holds the draft to present for payment on the maturity date.

This method offers less security than an S/D, D/P because documents that certify ownership of merchandise are transferred to an overseas customer prior to payment. Even when the customer is willing and able to pay, payment can be prolonged by delaying acceptance of the time draft. This method is quite similar to open-account sales in which the exporter extends a trade credit to an overseas customer in exchange for payment at some determinable future date. One major difference between the two methods is that in the case of documents against acceptance (for which a time or date draft is used), the draft is a negotiable instrument (unlike an account receivable in an open account) that can be sold and easily converted into cash by the exporter before maturity.

A draft drawn on and accepted by a bank is called a banker's acceptance. Once accepted, the draft becomes a primary obligation of the accepting bank to pay at maturity. If the draft is accepted by nonbank entities such as importers, it is known as a trade acceptance. The greater the creditworthiness of the party accepting the draft, the greater the marketability of the banker's or trade acceptance. They are important tools which can be negotiated or discounted to companies engaged in trade finance and which can serve the financing needs of exporters.

Direct Collection

Exporters can bypass the remitting bank and send documents directly to the foreign collecting bank for payment or acceptance. This reduces bank charges and speeds up the collection process. In this case, the collecting bank acts as the exporter's agent for follow-up and collection without the involvement of the remitting bank.

Liability and Responsibility of the Banks

The Uniform Rules for Collections (ICC, 1995) distinguish two types of collection arrangements: clean collections and documentary collections. In the case of clean collections, a draft is presented to the overseas buyer for the purpose of obtaining payment or acceptance without being accompanied by shipping documents. Documentary collections, which is the subject of this chapter, however, involve the presentation of shipping (commercial) and financial documents (draft or promissory note) by the collecting bank to the buyer. In certain cases in which a collection is payable against shipping documents without a draft (invoice is used in lieu of a draft), it is termed cash against documents.

In documentary collections, banks act as agents for collection and assume no responsibility for the consequences arising out of delay or for loss in transit of any messages, letters, or documents (ICC, 1995). They do not question documents submitted for collection and are not responsible for their form and/or content or for the authenticity of any signatures for acceptance. However, they have to act in good faith and exercise reasonable care in execution of the collection order. The bank's major responsibilities include the following:

- *Verification of documents received:* The bank checks whether the documents appear to be as listed in the collection order and advises the party in the event of missing documents.

- *Compliance with instructions in the collection order:* The exporter instructs the remitting bank on payment whether the documents shall be handed to a representative in case of need and what to do in the event of nonpayment or nonacceptance of the draft. These instructions are then sent along with other documents by the remitting bank to the collecting bank. The latter is only permitted to act upon these instructions.

In case the buyer refuses to pay, accept the draft, or pay the accepted draft at maturity, exporters often instruct the collecting bank to (1) protest, that is, to present the dishonored draft again, (2) warehouse the merchandise, or (3) send the merchandise back to the exporter. The collecting bank may be requested to contact the exporter's agent for clearance of the merchandise. All charges for carrying out these instructions are borne by the exporter. If the collecting bank releases the documents to the overseas customer contrary to instructions, the bank is liable to the seller: it has to pay the seller and collect from the buyer.

The use of documentary collections offers certain advantages. It reduces transaction costs for both parties, helps maintain suitable levels of control for exporters, and speeds up the flow of transactions. The major risk with this method, however, is the buyer being unable or unwilling to pay or accept the draft on presentation. It is thus important to check credit references, consider taking out credit insurance, or secure collateral to cover the transaction.

DOCUMENTARY LETTER OF CREDIT

A letter of credit (L/C) is a document in which a bank or other financial institution assumes liability for payment of the purchase price to the seller on behalf of the buyer. The bank could deal directly or through the intervention of a bank in the seller's country. In all types of letters of credit, the buyer arranges with a bank to provide finance for the exporter in exchange for certain documents. The bank makes credit available to its client, the buyer, in consideration of a security that often includes a pledge of the documents of title to the goods, placement of funds in advance, or a pledge to reimburse with a commission. The essential feature of this method, and its value to an exporter of goods, is that it superimposes upon the credit of the buyer the credit of a bank, often one carrying on business in the seller's country. The letter of credit is a legally enforceable commitment by a bank to pay money upon the performance of certain conditions, stipulated therein, to the seller (exporter or beneficiary) for the account of the buyer (importer or applicant).

A letter of credit (L/C) is considered an export or import L/C depending on the party. The same letter of credit is considered an export L/C by the seller and an import L/C by the buyer. The steps involved in Figure 11.3 are the following:

1. The Canadian buyer in Montreal contracts with the U.S. seller in New York. The agreement provides for the payment to be financed by means of a confirmed, irrevocable documentary credit for goods delivered CIF, port of Montreal.
2. The Canadian buyer applies to its bank (issuing bank), which issues the letter of credit with the U.S. seller as beneficiary.
3. Issuing bank sends the letter of credit to an advising bank in the United States, which also confirms the letter of credit.
4. The advising bank notifies the U.S. seller that a letter of credit has been issued on its behalf (confirmed by the advising bank) and is available on presentation of documents.
5. The U.S. seller scrutinizes the credit. When satisfied that the stipulations in the credit can be met, the U.S. seller will arrange for shipment and prepare the necessary documents, that is, commercial invoice, bill of lading, draft, insurance policy, and certificate of origin. Amendments may be necessary in cases in which the credit improperly describes the merchandise.
6. After shipment of merchandise, the U.S. seller submits relevant documents to the advising/confirming bank for payment. If the documents comply, the advising/confirming bank will pay the seller. (If the L/C provides for acceptance, the bank accepts the draft, signifying its commitment to pay the face value at maturity to the seller or bona fide holder of the draft—acceptance L/C. It is straight L/C if payment is made by the issuing bank or the bank designated in the credit at a determinable future date). If the credit provides for negotiation at any bank, it is negotiable L/C.
7. The advising/confirming bank sends documents plus settlement instructions to the issuing bank.
8. On inspecting documents for compliance with instructions, the issuing bank reimburses/remits proceeds to the advising/confirming bank.
9. The issuing bank gives documents to the buyer and presents the term draft for acceptance. With a sight draft, the issuing bank will be paid by the buyer on presentation of documents.
10. The buyer arranges for clearance of the merchandise, that is, gives up the bill of lading and takes receipt of goods.
11. The buyer pays the issuing bank on or before the draft maturity date.

FIGURE 11.3. Documentary Letter of Credit

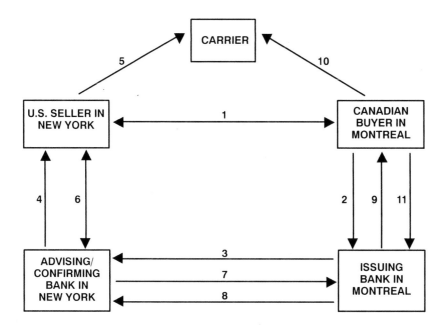

Issuing banks often verify receipt of full details of the L/C by the advising bank. This is done by using a private test code arrangement between banks. Credits are opened and forwarded to the advising/confirming bank by mail, telex, or cable. Issuing banks can also open credits by using the SWIFT system (Society for Worldwide Interbank Financial Telecommunications), which allows for faster transmission time. It also allows member banks to use automatic authentication (verification) of messages (Ruggiero, 1991).

The letter of credit consists of four separate and distinct bilateral contracts: (1) a sales contract between the buyer and seller; (2) a credit and reimbursement contract between the buyer and issuing bank, providing for the issuing bank to establish a letter of credit in favor of the seller and for reimbursement by the buyer; (3) a letter of credit contract between the issuing bank and the beneficiary (exporter), in which the bank will pay the seller on presentation of specified documents; and (4) the confirmed advice also signifies a contract between the advising/confirming bank and the seller, in which the bank will pay the seller on presentation of specified documents.

When the letter of credit is revocable, the issuing bank could amend or cancel the credit at any time after issue without consent from, or notice to, the seller. Revocable L/Cs are seldom used in international trade except in cases of trade between parent and subsidiary companies because they do not provide sufficient protection to the seller. Under the Uniform Customs and Practice for Documentary Credits (UCP), letters of credit are deemed irrevocable unless specifically marked revocable (ICC, 1993). Irrevocable credits cannot be amended or cancelled before their expiry date without express consent of all parties to the credit. The terms revocable and irrevocable refer only to the issuing bank.

In cases in which sellers do not know of, or have little confidence in, the financial strength of the buyer's country or the issuing bank, they often require a bank in their country to guarantee payment (i.e., confirm the L/C).

There are several advantages to using letters of credit. They accommodate the competing desires of the seller and overseas customer. The seller receives payment on presentation of documents to the bank after shipment of goods, unlike open-account sales or documentary collection. In cases in which the advising bank accepts the L/C for payment at a determinable future date, the seller can discount the L/C before maturity. Buyers also avoid the need to make prepayment or to establish an escrow account. Letters of credit also ensure that payment is not made until the goods are placed in possession of a carrier and that specified documents are presented to that effect.

One major disadvantage with an L/C for the buyer is that issuing banks often require cash or other collateral before they open an L/C, unless the buyer has a satisfactory credit rating. This could tie up the available credit line. In certain countries, buyers are also required to make a prior deposit before establishing an L/C. Letters of credit are complex transactions between different parties, and the smallest discrepancy between documents could require an amendment of the terms or lead to the invalidation of the credit. This may expose the seller to a risk of delay in payment or nonpayment in certain cases.

A letter of credit is a documentary payment obligation, and banks are required to pay or agree to pay on presentation of appropriate documents specified in the credit. This payment obligation applies even if a seller ships defective or nonexistent goods (empty crates/boxes). The buyer then has to sue for breach of contract. The interests of the buyer can be protected by structuring the L/C to require, as a condition of payment, the following:

- The presentation of a certificate of inspection executed by a third party certifying that the goods shipped conform to the terms of the contract of sale. If the goods are defective or nonconforming to the terms of the contract, the third party will refuse to sign the certificate and the seller will not receive payment. In such cases, it is preferable to use a revocable L/C.
- The presentation of a certificate of inspection executed or countersigned by the buyer. It is preferable to use a revocable L/C to allow the bank to cancel the credit.
- A reciprocal standby L/C issued in favor of the buyer in which the latter could draw on this credit and obtain a return of the purchase price if the seller shipped nonconforming goods (McLaughlin, 1989).

Governing Law

The rights and duties of parties to a letter of credit issued or confirmed in the United States are determined by reference to three different sources:

- *The Uniform Commercial Code (UCC):* The basic law on letter of credit is codified in article 5-101 to 5-117 of the Uniform Commercial Code. This article has been adopted in all states of the Union. However, some states (New York, Missouri, Alabama) have introduced an amendment providing that article 5 will not apply if the letter of credit is subject, in whole or in part, to the Uniform Customs and Practice for Documentary Credits.
- *The Uniform Customs and Practice for Documentary Credits (UCP):* Parties to the letter of credit frequently agree to be governed by the rules of the UCP, which is a result of collaboration between the International Chamber of Commerce, the United Nations, and many international trade banks. The UCP is periodically revised to take into account new developments in international trade and credit (the latest revision was in 1993). The Uniform Commercial Code provisions on letters of credit and the UCP complement each other in many areas. Under both the UCC and UCP, the terms of the credit can be altered by agreement of the parties.
- General principles of law: In cases in which the UCC or UCP provisions are not sufficient to resolve a dispute, courts apply general principles of law insofar as they do not conflict with the governing law (UCC or UCP) or agreement of the parties.

Role of Banks Under Letters of Credit

The buyer's bank issues the letter of credit at the request of the buyer. The details of the credit are normally specified by the buyer. Since the seller wants a local bank available to which the seller can present the letter of credit for payment, an additional bank often becomes involved in the transaction. The second bank usually either "advises" or "confirms" the letter of credit. A bank that advises on the L/C gives notification of the terms and conditions of the credit issued by another bank to the seller. It assumes no liability for paying the letter of credit. Its only obligation is to ensure that the beneficiary (seller) is advised, credit delivered, and to ensure the apparent authenticity of the credit.

An issuing bank may also request a bank to confirm the letter of credit. A confirming bank promises to honor a letter of credit already issued by another bank and becomes directly obligated to the beneficiary (seller), as though it had issued the letter of credit itself. It will pay, accept, or negotiate a letter of credit upon presentation of specific documents that comply with the terms and conditions of the credit. A confirming bank is entitled to reimbursement by the issuing bank, assuming that the latter's instructions have been properly executed. It, however, faces the risk of nonpayment if the issuing bank or the buyer is unable or unwilling to pay the confirming bank, in which case it will be left with title to the goods and obliged to liquidate them to offset its losses.

Both the confirming and issuing banks have an obligation toward the exporter (beneficiary) and the buyer to act in good faith and with reasonable care in examining the documents. The basic rule pertaining to a bank's liability to a beneficiary is that the bank should honor the L/C if the documents presented comply with the terms of the credit. The following circumstances cannot be used by banks as a basis to dishonor (refusal to pay or accept a draft) letters of credit:

- *Dishonor to serve the buyer's interests:* In this case, claims are made by a bank's customer (buyer) that the beneficiary has breached the sales contract or that the underlying agreement has been modified or amended in some way in the face of complying documents. This includes cases of dishonor based on the bank's knowledge or reasonable belief that the goods do not conform to the underlying contract of sale.
- *Dishonor to serve the bank's own interests:* This occurs when the sole reason for dishonor is the bank's belief that it would not obtain reimbursement from its insolvent customer. This involves situations

in which the buyer becomes insolvent after the L/C is issued and before the beneficiary's draft is honored.

- *Dishonor after express waiver of a particular discrepancy:* A bank dishonors an L/C after it has expressly agreed to disregard a particular discrepancy.
- *Dishonor without giving the beneficiary an opportunity to correct the discrepancy:* If the issuing bank decides to refuse the documents, it must give notice to that effect, stating the discrepancy without delay, and must also state whether it is holding the documents at the disposal of and returning them to the remitting bank or beneficiary, as the case may be (Arzt, 1991; Rosenblith, 1991).

Banks may properly dishonor a letter of credit in cases of fraud or forgery, even if the documents presented to the beneficiary appear to comply with the terms of the credit. This assumes that there are no innocent parties involved in the presentation of the letter of credit to the bank. Banks are subject to two principles in the conduct of their letter-of-credit transactions: the independent principle and the rule of strict compliance.

The Independent Principle

The letter of credit is separate from, and independent of, other contracts relating to the transaction. Each of the four contracts in a letter-of-credit transaction are entirely independent. It is irrelevant to the bank whether the seller/buyer has fully carried out its part of the contract with the buyer/seller. The bank's duty is to establish whether the stipulated documents have been presented in order to pay (accept to pay) the exporter. It is not the bank's duty to ascertain whether the goods mentioned in the documents have been shipped or whether they conform to the terms of the contract. Article 3 of the UCP states:

> Credits by their nature are separate transactions from the sales or other contract(s) on which they may be based and banks are in no way concerned with or bound by such contract(s), even if any reference whatsoever to such contact(s) is included in the credit. (ICC, 1993, p. 11)

The independent principle is subject to a fraud exception. A bank can refuse payment if it has been informed that there has been fraud or forgery in connection with the letter-of-credit transaction and the person presenting the documents is not a holder in due course (as third party who took the draft for value, in good faith, and without knowledge of the fraud). In one case, for example, a buyer notified the issuing bank not to pay the seller under the letter of credit, alleging that the seller had intentionally shipped fifty crates of rubbish in place of fifty crates of bristles. The bank's refusal of payment was accepted by the court as a justifiable reason in view of fraud in the underlying transaction (Ryan, 1990). U.S. courts have held in several cases that banks are justified in dishonoring L/Cs when the documents are forged or fraudulent. The UCP is silent on the question of fraud. Article 15 of the UCP states that banks assume no liability or responsibility for the form, sufficiency, accuracy, genuineness, or legal effect of any documents. Article 9 also states that the obligation to honor an irrevocable L/C exists provided the stipulated documents are presented (ICC, 1993, p. 12). In credit operations, all parties concerned deal in documents and not in the goods to which the documents relate. Thus, when the L/C is governed by the UCP, it appears that the bank must pay, regardless of any underlying fraud. A bank would, however, be liable for the money paid out if it participated in the fraud.

The Rule of Strict Compliance

The general rule is that an exporter cannot compel payment unless it strictly complies with the conditions specified in the credit (Rosenblith, 1991). When conforming documents are presented, the advising bank must pay, the issuing bank must reimburse, and the buyer is obliged to pay the issuing bank. In certain cases, courts have refused to recognize the substantial-compliance argument by banks to recover their payments from buyers (unless it involves minor spelling error or insignificant additions or abbreviations in drafts) (Rubenstein, 1994). The reason behind the doctrine of strict compliance is that the advising bank is an agent of the issuing bank and the latter is a special agent of the buyer. This means that banks have limited authority and have to bear the commercial risk of the transaction if they act outside the scope of their mandate (Barnes, 1994; Macintosh, 1992). In addition, in times of falling demand, the buyer may be tempted to reject documents that the bank accepted, alleging that they are not in strict compliance with the terms of the credit.

Two assumptions underlie the doctrine of strict compliance:

1. *Linkage of documents:* The documents (bill of lading, draft, invoice, insurance certificate) are linked by an unambiguous reference to the same merchandise.
2. *Description of goods:* The goods must be fully described in the invoice, but the same details are not necessary in all the other documents. What is important is that the documents, when taken together,

contain the particulars required under the L/C. This means that the invoice could include more details than the bill of lading as long as the enlarged descriptions are essentially consistent with those contained in the bill of lading (Schmitthoff, 1986).

Discrepancies

Discrepancies occur when documents submitted contain language or terms different from the letter of credit or some other apparent irregularity. Most discrepancies occur because the exporter does not present all the documents required under the letter of credit or because the documents do not strictly conform to the L/C requirements.

Example

Dushkin Bank issued an irrevocable L/C on behalf of its customer (buyer), John Textiles, Incorporated. It promised to honor a draft of KG Company (exporter) for $250,000, covering shipments of "100% Acrylic Yarn." KG Company presented its draft with a commercial invoice describing the merchandise as "Imported Acrylic Yarns." The packing list describes it as follows: "Cartons Marked: 100% Acrylic." Discrepancy: The description of the goods in the invoice does not match that stated in the letter of credit. Dushkin Bank could refuse to honor the draft and return the documents to the exporter.

To receive payment under the credit, the exporter must present documents that are in strict accord with the terms of the letter of credit. It is estimated that over 50 percent of documents presented under L/Cs contain some discrepancy.

There are three types of discrepancies:

- *Accidental discrepancies:* These are discrepancies that can easily be corrected by the exporter (beneficiary) or the issuing bank. Such discrepancies include typographical errors, omission to state the L/C number, errors in arithmetic, and improper endorsement or signature on the draft. Once these discrepancies are corrected (within a reasonable period of time: twenty-one days after shipment of merchandise and before the expiry date of the L/C), the bank will accept the documents and pay the exporter.
- *Minor discrepancies:* These are minor errors in documents that contain the essential particulars required in the L/C and can be corrected by obtaining a written waiver from the buyer. Such errors include

failure to legalize documents, nonpresentation of all documents required under the L/C, and discrepancy between the wording on the invoice and the L/C. Once these discrepancies are waived by buyer, the transaction will proceed as anticipated.

- *Major discrepancies:* These are discrepancies that fundamentally affect the essential nature of the L/C. Certain discrepancies cannot be corrected under any circumstances: presentation of documents after the expiry date of the L/C, shipment of merchandise later than the specified date under the L/C, or expiration of the L/C. However, other major discrepancies can be corrected by an amendment of the L/C. Amendments require the approval of the issuing bank, the confirming bank (in the case of a confirmed L/C), and the exporter. Examples of discrepancies that can be amended include presentation of an incorrect bill of lading, a draft in excess of the amount specified in the credit, and making partial shipments not allowed under the credit.

Discrepancies that can be corrected (accidental, minor, and certain major discrepancies) must be rectified within a reasonable period of time after shipment and before the expiry of the letter of credit. Most letters of credit require that the document be submitted within a reasonable period of time after the date of the bill of lading. If no time is specified, the UCP requires submission of shipping documents to banks within twenty-one days.

In cases in which the buyer is looking for an excuse to reject the documents (when the price of the product is falling, the product is destroyed on shipment, etc.), the buyer may not accede to a waiver or amendment of the discrepancy or may do so in consideration for a huge discount off the contract price. The buyer could also delay correction, in which case the exporter loses the use of the proceeds for a certain period of time. Besides incurring further bank charges to correct the discrepancy, the seller also faces the risk that the credit will expire before the discrepancies are corrected.

When the discrepancy stands (the discrepancy cannot be corrected or the buyer refuses to waive or amend the terms of the credit), the seller can still attempt to obtain payment by requesting the bank to obtain authority to pay or send the documents for collection (documentary collection) outside the terms of the L/C. If the buyer refuses to accept the documents, the bank will not pay the seller (exporter) and the exporter has to either find a buyer abroad or have the merchandise returned. If the confirming/issuing bank accepts documents that contain a discrepancy, then it cannot seek reimbursement from its respective customers (issuing bank/buyer, respectively).

When the issuing bank decides to refuse the document, it must notify the party from which it obtained the document (the remitting bank or the exporter) without delay, stating the reasons for the rejection and whether it holds the documents at the disposal of, or is returning them to, the presenter.

CASH IN ADVANCE

This method of payment requires the buyer to pay before shipment is effected. The seller assumes no risk of bad debt and/or delays in payment because advance payment is a precondition to shipment.

Sellers often require advance payment in cases in which the creditworthiness of the overseas customer is poor or unknown and/or the political/economic conditions of the buyer's country are unstable. Cash in advance is sometimes used between related companies. It is also common to require money in advance for samples.

OTHER LETTERS OF CREDIT

Transferable Letter of Credit

Exporters often use transferable L/Cs to pay a supplier, while keeping the identity of the supplier and the foreign customer from each other, lest they conduct the next transaction without the exporter. This method is often used when the exporter acts as an agent or intermediary. Under a transferable L/C, the exporter (beneficiary) transfers the rights and certain duties, such as shipment, under the credit to another person, usually its supplier (transferee), who receives payment, provided that the conditions of the original credit are met. The bank requested by the beneficiary to effect the transfer is under no obligation to do so, unless it has expressly consented to it.

It is important to note the following with respect to such letters of credit:

- A credit is transferred only if it is expressly designated as "transferable" by the issuing bank.
- It can be transferred only once. The credit is automatically divisible and can be transferred in fractions, provided that partial shipments are not excluded.
- The name and address of the first beneficiary may be substituted for that of the buyer. This would mask the identity of the true suppliers of the merchandise from the buyer.

- The transferee receives rights under this type of L/C. Such a transfer requires the consent of the buyer and of the issuing bank.
- The supplier might demand that the exporter actually transfer the letter of credit in its entirety, without substitution of invoices. The beneficiary (exporter) will receive a commission independent of the L/C transaction.

Example 1: A Canadian bank opens a transferable credit in the amount of $90,000 in favor of a U.S. exporter in Florida for a shipment of tomatoes. The exporter had located a supplier in Texas and had decided to use $85,000 of the credit to pay the supplier.

The exporter asks the advising bank in Florida to effect a transfer in favor of the supplier. The supplier is advised of the transfer by the advising bank. The new credit does not mention the amount of the original credit or the name of the foreign buyer but substitutes the name of the exporter (original beneficiary) as the buyer. When the supplier presents conforming documents to the advising bank in Florida, the bank substitutes the exporter's invoice for that of the supplier, pays $85,000 to the supplier, and pays the difference to the exporter. The advising bank forwards the documents to the Canadian bank, which has no knowledge of the transfer for reimbursement.

Transferable L/C is different from assignment of proceeds under the credit. In assignment, the exporter asks the bank holding the L/C to pay either the entire amount or a percentage of the proceeds to a specified third party, usually a supplier. This allows the exporter to make domestic purchases with limited capital by using the overseas buyer's credit. This is done by assigning the proceeds from the buyer's L/C. The beneficiary (exporter) of a letter of credit may assign its rights to the proceeds of the L/C, even if the L/C expressly states that it is nontransferable. Only the beneficiary (not assignee) has rights under the credit, and the overseas buyer as well as the issuing bank often have no knowledge of the assignment.

Example 2: A U.S. exporter has a letter of credit for $40,000 from a buyer in Brazil. The exporter had located a supplier within the United States that will sell the product for $25,000. However, the supplier would not release the product for shipment without some downpayment or collateral. The exporter (assignor) could assign part of the proceeds ($25,000) from the L/C to the supplier (assignee). The assignee will then provide the merchandise to the exporter, who will arrange shipment. The exporter (assignor) must submit documents that comply with the credit in order for the advising bank to pay the assignee (supplier). The remainder ($15,000) will be paid to the exporter.

Back-to-Back Letter of Credit

This is a letter of credit that is issued on the strength of another letter of credit. Such credits are issued when suppliers or subcontractors demand payment from the exporter before collections are received from the customer. The back-to-back L/C is separate from the original L/C, and the bank that issued the former is obligated to make payment to suppliers regardless of the outcome of the latter. If there is default on the original L/C, the bank is left with worthless collateral.

> *Example:* A Japanese manufacturer (exporter) of cars has a letter of credit issued for 1,000 cars by a buyer in New York. Payment is to be made ninety days after shipment. However, subcontractors require payment to be made for spare parts purchased in ten days (earlier than the date of payment provided under the L/C). The Japanese exporter presents the buyer's L/C to the advising bank in Tokyo and asks the bank to issue a new L/C to the subcontractor, payable in ten days. The first L/C is used as collateral to issue the second L/C in favor of the subcontractor.

Revolving Letter of Credit

Banks make available letters of credit with a set limit for their customers that allow for a free flow of merchandise until the expiry date of the credit. This avoids the need to open credits for each shipment. The value of the credit allowed can be reinstated automatically or by amendment. If credits designated for use during one period can be carried over to the next period, they are termed as cumulative. They are noncumulative if any unused amount is no longer available.

> *Example 1:* Queen's Bank in Fort Lauderdale opens a revolving line of credit for up to $150,000 in favor of Kegan Enterprises, Incorporated, for the importation of handicrafts. Kegan Enterprises agrees to purchase toys (for $50,000) from Korea and requests Queen's Bank to open an L/C for $50,000 in favor of the seller in South Korea. If the credit provides for automatic reinstatement, $100,000 will be readily available for other purchases. In other cases, Kegan Enterprises will have to wait for approval from the bank, reinstating the credit ($100,000) to use for another shipment.

Example 2: Suppose Queen's Bank opens a letter of credit of up to $15,000 a month for six months in favor of Kegan Enterprises. If the credit states that it is cumulative, $30,000 credit not used during the first two months could still be used during the next four months. If it is noncumulative, the credit not used during the two-month period cannot be carried over for use in the next four months.

Red-Clause Credit

Such credits provide for advance payment to an exporter before presentation of shipping documents. It is intended to provide pre-export financing to an agent or distributor for purchase of the merchandise from a supplier. When financing is conditional on presentation of negotiable warehouse receipts issued in favor of the advising bank, it is termed green-clause credit.

Deferred-Payment Credit

This is a letter of credit whereby the bank undertakes an obligation to pay at a future date stipulated on the credit, provided that the terms and conditions of the credit are met.

Example: Suppose a U.S. buyer agrees to buy lumber valued at $40 million from a Canadian seller. The parties agree to use a deferred-payment credit. In this case, the U.S. buyer asks its bank to open (issue) a letter of credit obligating itself to pay the seller sixty days after the date of the bill of lading. If the documents are as stipulated in the credit, the bank undertakes an obligation to pay the Canadian seller sixty days after the date of the bill of lading. No draft, however, need accompany the documents.

What are the major differences between an acceptance letter of credit and a deferred-payment credit?

In the case of acceptance credits, the bank undertakes an obligation to accept drafts drawn on itself provided that stipulated documents are presented. Assume that a Canadian seller and a U.S. buyer agreed to use an acceptance credit payable sixty days after presentation of shipping documents. Once the Canadian seller presents the requisite shipping documents and draft to the advising bank, the bank will stamp the draft "accepted," if it is in strict compliance with the credit. This represents the bank's obligation to pay on the maturity date of the draft. Once accepted by the bank, the draft becomes a negotiable instrument that can be discounted by the accepting bank, enabling the seller to receive payment for the goods in advance of the maturity date of the acceptance. In the case of deferred-payment credits, no draft accompanies the documents. The agreement providing for the Canadian bank to pay the seller sixty days after the date of the bill of lading represents the bank's undertaking of a deferred-payment obligation. In this case, no negotiable draft is generated and there is no way to discount the bank's deferred-payment obligation. Any advance payment by the bank to the seller often requires a collateral or security interest in the proceeds of the deferred credit.

Such credits developed primarily as a way of avoiding charges and fees associated with acceptance credits.

Standby Letter of Credit

The standby letter of credit is generally used to guarantee that a party will fulfill its obligation under a contract. Such credits are opened to cover the account party's business obligations to the beneficiary. A standby letter of credit is thus a bank's guarantee to the beneficiary that a specific sum of money will be received by the beneficiary in the event of default or nonperformance by the account party under a sales or service contract. Similar to the documentary letter of credit, a standby credit is payable against presentation of documents that comply with the terms of the standby credit. The documents required to be presented by the beneficiary often include a sight draft and the beneficiary's written statement of default by the account party.

A major problem with such credits is that payments are often required to be made upon the issuing bank's receipt of a signed statement by the beneficiary that the account party did not perform under the contract and that the credit is currently due and payable. There is a possibility of unfair and capricious calling in of the credit, despite the absence of default or nonperformance by the account party. To protect account parties under a standby credit from such unjustified demand by beneficiaries, the following steps are often recommended:

- Include a clause under the credit requiring that the beneficiary present certification by a third party or court that default has occurred.
- Take out an insurance policy that covers commercial and political risk. This would cover exporters against, inter alias contract repudiation as well as unfair callings by private entities or governments.
- Take out a surety bond issued by an insurance company (instead of a performance bond issued by a bank) to guarantee performance under

the contract. Whereas banks honor a drawing under a standby letter of credit based on the face value of the beneficiary's statement of default, insurance companies verify the validity of the claim before payment. If the claim is unfounded, the insurance company will deny payment. However, if the insured's default is proven, payment is made under the credit and thereafter the company will recover from the insured (Kozolchyk, 1996).

The standby letter of credit is commonly used in the case of contractor bids and performance bonds, advance payments, open account sales, and loan guarantees.

Contractor Bids and Performance Bonds

Bid bonds are issued to a customer to show the seller's real interest and ability to undertake the resulting contract. This is intended to protect buyers from losses incurred in accepting invalid bids. The bid would be legitimately called in if a successful bidder failed to accept the contract.

> *Example:* The Ministry of Defense of the state of Urbania want to buy 400,000 pairs of winter boots for the military. They invite domestic and foreign manufacturers to submit bids. All bidders are also required to submit a bid bond issued by a reputable surety company or a bank. Nunez Shoes, Limited, a U.S. footwear company, is awarded the contract. A few days later, Nunez Shoes writes a letter to the Ministry of Urbania, stating that it cannot carry out the contract because the company does not have enough supplies and an adequate labor force. Based on the contract, the ministry will be entitled to draw under the credit.

Standby credits are also issued to guarantee performance under a sales and service contract. Using the previous example, suppose Nunez Shoes signs the contract to deliver 400,000 winter boots to Urbania. The ministry could require Nunez Shoes to post a performance bond issued by a reputable bank as guarantee that it will live up to the terms of the sales contract. Performance bond credits are issued for a percentage of the total contract value. Suppose Nunez Shoes manages to deliver only 50 percent of the shoes before the expiry of the sales contract. The ministry will then be entitled to draw under the credit on presentation of the necessary documents.

Performance Guarantees Against Advance Payments

These are bonds issued to guarantee the return of cash advanced by the customer if the seller does not comply with the terms of the contract.

> *Example:* Using the previous example, suppose Nunez Shoes signs the contract with the Ministry of Urbania to supply the winter boots but requires an advance payment of $40,000. The ministry, in turn, could require Nunez Shoes to post an advance payment bond (a standby L/C with a bank to guarantee the return of money advanced by the ministry in the event of default by the seller). In the event that Nunez Shoes does not deliver the product as agreed under the contract, the ministry would be entitled to call in the credit, that is to recover its advance payment on presentation of complying documents.

Guarantee Against Payments on Open Account

This type of credit protects the seller in the event that the buyer fails to pay or delays payment. The seller asks the buyer to have a standby letter of credit issued in its favor. Suppose payment is to be made within ninety days to the seller under an open account transaction and the buyer fails to pay. The seller could then request payment under the credit against presentation of stipulated documents, such as a sight draft, commercial invoice, and the seller's signed written statement.

Loan Guarantees

Standby credits are often issued by banks when an applicant guarantees repayment of a loan taken by another party. Suppose a subsidiary of Nunez Shoes, in England, borrows 200,000 British pounds from a bank in London. If the applicant's financial position is not well-known to the bank, the bank could agree to extend the loan, provided the parent company (Nunez Shoes in the United States) guarantees payment. Under this arrangement, Nunez Shoes, United States, would have a standby L/C issued in favor of the bank in London. Upon receiving the credit, the London bank will grant the loan to the subsidiary. If Nunez Shoes, England, defaults in repaying the loan, the bank will draw on the credit. In addition to this situation, standby credits are employed to cover rental payments, custom duties, royalties, and tax shelter transactions.

CHAPTER SUMMARY

Consignment Sales

Exporter sends product to importer on a deferred-payment basis. Importer pays seller upon sale of product to a third party. Exporter retains title to goods until payment.

Open-Account Sales

Exporter ships merchandise to overseas customer on credit. Payment is to be made within an agreed time after receipt of merchandise.

Documentary Draft

This is a service offered by banks to sellers to facilitate payment of a sale of merchandise on an international basis. Under this method, the exporter draws a draft on a buyer after shipment of the merchandise, requesting payment on presentation of documents (documents against payment) or acceptance of the draft to pay at some future determinable date (documents against acceptance).

Banker's (Trade) Acceptance

If a draft is drawn on and accepted by a bank, it is called banker's acceptance. If a draft is accepted by nonbank entities, such as importers, it is trade acceptance.

Role of Banks

1. Verification of documents: This is to determine whether the documents appear as listed in the collection order and to advise the party in the event of missing documents.
2. Compliance with instructions in the collection order.
3. Act as agents for collection and assume no responsibility for damages arising out of delay or for the substance and form of documents. However, they have to act in good faith.

Clean Collections

This is a documentary draft presented to buyer for payment or acceptance without being accompanied by shipping documents.

Documentary Collections

This is a documentary draft accompanied by shipping documents.

International Rules Governing Documentary Collections

Uniform Rules for Collections, 1995, International Chamber of Commerce Publication No. 522.

Documentary Letter of Credit (L/C)

A document in which a bank or other financial institution assumes liability for payment of the purchase price to exporter on behalf of overseas customer.

Parties to the L/C Contract

1. Sales contract: Exporter (beneficiary) and importer (account party).
2. Credit reimbursement contract: Importer and issuing bank.
3. L/C contract: Opening bank and beneficiary.
4. Confirmation agreement: Confirming bank and beneficiary.

International Rules on L/C

The Uniform Customs Practices for Documentary Credits (UCP), 1993 revision, International Chamber of Commerce Publication No. 500.

Role of Banks

1. Banks should act equitably and in good faith.
2. Independent principle: Credits are separate transactions from sales or other contracts, and banks are in no way concerned with, or bound by, such contracts. The independent principle is subject to a fraud exception.
3. Rule of strict compliance: Exporter cannot compel payment by banks unless the documents presented strictly comply with the terms specified in the credit.

Discrepancies

Accidental Discrepancies

Discrepancies that can easily be corrected by the beneficiary or the issuing bank.

Minor Discrepancies

Discrepancies that can be corrected by a written waiver from the buyer.

Major Discrepancies

Discrepancies that either cannot be corrected or can only be corrected by an amendment to the L/C.

Cash in Advance

A method of payment requiring the buyer to pay before shipment is effected.

LETTERS OF CREDIT

1. *Irrevocable.* L/Cs that cannot be amended or canceled without the agreement of all parties to the credit, i.e., the beneficiary, the buyer, and the issuing bank.
2. *Revocable.* L/Cs that may be amended or canceled by issuing bank without prior notice to the exporter (beneficiary). However, issuing banks must honor drafts duly negotiated by other banks prior to revocation.
3. *Confirmed.* A credit in which another bank, usually the advising bank, confirms its obligation to honor drafts and documents presented by the beneficiary, in accordance with the terms of the credit. This applies only to an irrevocable L/C, as the revocable L/C would become irrevocable if another bank added its confirmation.
4. *Transferable.* L/Cs that permit a beneficiary to transfer the credit to a second beneficiary. Similar to back-to-back L/Cs, but only one credit is issued.
5. *Back-to-Back.* A letter of credit that is issued on the strength of another L/C.
6. *Revolving.* An agreement in which the buyer is allowed to replenish the credit after it is drawn down by a seller.
7. *Red-clause credit.* Advances or pre-export financing provided to an agent or distributor for the purchase of merchandise from a supplier. Such advances are made without presentation of documents.
8. *Green-clause credit.* When advances are made on presentation of warehouse receipts.

9. *Deferred-Payment credit.* The seller agrees not to present a sight draft until after a specified period following presentation of documents. No draft need accompany the documents. When it is accompanied by a draft, it becomes an acceptance L/C.

10. *Standby.* A credit used to guarantee that a party will fulfill its obligation under a sales or service contract. Types of standby L/Cs: contractor bids and performance bonds, performance guarantees against advance payments, guarantee against payments on open account, and loan guarantees.

11. *Straight.* An L/C that is payable at the issuing bank or at a designated bank nominated in the letter of credit.

12. *Negotiable.* An L/C that can be negotiated at any bank. This means that the issuing bank will reimburse any bank that pays against the documents stipulated in the credit.

Chapter 12

Countertrade

ORIGINS OF COUNTERTRADE

Countertrade is any commercial arrangement in which sellers or exporters are required to accept, in partial or total settlement of their deliveries, a supply of products from the importing country. In essence, it is a nation's (or firm's) use of its purchasing power as leverage to force a private firm to purchase or market its marginally undesirable goods or to exact other concessions to finance its imports, obtain needed hard currency, or acquire technology. Although the manner in which the transaction is structured may vary, the distinctive feature of such arrangements is the mandatory performance element that is either required by the importer or the importer's government or made necessary due to competitive considerations (Verzariu, 1992; 1985).

The origins of countertrade can be traced to ancient times when international trade was based on the free exchange of goods. Barter flourished in northern Mesopotamia as early as 3000 B.C. when inhabitants traded in textiles and metals. The Greeks also profited by the exchange of olive oil and wine for grain and metals sometime before 2000 B.C. (Brinton et al., 1984; Anyane-Ntow and Harvey, 1995). Even with the flourishing of a money economy, barter still continued as a medium of exchange. Present-day countertrade involves more than the use of simple barter. It is a complex transaction that includes the exchange of some currency as well as goods between two or more nations. A countertrade transaction may, for example, specify that the seller be paid in foreign currency on the condition that the seller agrees to find markets for specified products from the buyer's country.

The resurgence of countertrade has often been associated with East-West trade. At the start of the 1950s, the former communist countries of Eastern Europe faced a chronic shortage of hard (convertible) currency to purchase needed imports. In their dealings with Western countries, they insisted that their products be taken in exchange for imports from the latter countries. This practice also proved quite attractive to many developing nations, which also suffer from a shortage of convertible currency. The use of countertrade has steadily increased and is presently estimated to account for about 15 to 20 percent of world trade (Hennart and Anderson, 1993). By the end of 1995, the number of countries using countertrade exceeded 100. Although there may be disagreements concerning the current volume of countertrade, the broad consensus is that countertrade constitutes a significant and rapidly growing portion of world commerce (McVey, 1984; Bost and Yeakel, 1992).

For example, an agreement was reached between the former Soviet Union and Occidental Petroleum in 1973 for the exchange of ammonia for superphosphoric acid. Occidental shipped the acid to the Soviet Union in payment for the ammonia. As another example, PepsiCo traded drink concentrate for basmati rice in India and for silk and mushrooms in China. The mushrooms are used in PepsiCo's Pizza Hut chain and the silk is dyed, printed, and sold for profit (Welt, 1990).

In the 1980s, countertrade was mainly used as a vehicle for trade finance. It is now used to meet a broad range of business objectives: capital project financing, production sharing, repatriation of profits from countries with hard currency shortages, and competitive bidding on major government procurements (Egan and Shipley, 1996; Caves and Marin, 1992).

Recent Examples of Countertrade

- In 1997, Menatep-Impex, a trading division of a Russian banking and investment group, took receipt of 450,000 tons of Cuban raw sugar and, in exchange, shipped 1.15 million tons of crude oil.
- Indonesia negotiated for a power station project with Asea Brown Boveri and for an air traffic control system with Hughes Aircraft. Counterpurchase obligations were to be 100 percent of the FOB values. The firms have, through a trading company, so far exported $12 million worth of Indonesian products: cocoa to the United States, coal to Japan, and fertilizer to Vietnam and Burma.
- Lockheed Martin agreed to sell F-16 military aircraft to Hungary in exchange for large investment and counterpurchase commitments. The firm plans to buy $250 million worth of Hungarian goods by the year 2000. It has already established an office in Budapest in order to participate in tendering and to procure the country's industrial goods for export.

- Taiwan purchased sixty Mirage 2000-5 from a French aviation company, Dassault, in 1997. In return, Dassault undertook a joint venture with Taiwan's aerospace company, Chenfeng, for the production of key aircraft parts and components for local aircraft and export. (Anonymous, 1997a, b, c)

BENEFITS OF COUNTERTRADE

Benefits for Buyers

Transfer of Technology

In exchange for a guaranteed supply of raw materials or other scarce resources, a developed nation will provide the capital, equipment, and technology that is needed to develop such resources. Western firms, for example, assisted Saudi Arabia in the development of its refinery and petrochemical industry in exchange for the right to purchase a certain amount of oil over a given period of time.

Alleviating Balance-of-Payments Difficulties

The debt crisis of the 1980s, coupled with adverse movements in the price of key export commodities such as coffee or sugar, left many developing countries with severe balance-of-payments difficulties. Countertrade has been used as a way of financing needed imports without depleting limited foreign-currency reserves. Some countries have even used it as a way of earning hard currency by promoting the export of their domestic output. Countertrade has thus helped these nations avoid the burden of additional borrowing to finance imports as well as the need to restrict domestic economic activity. After the debt crisis, private lending by commercial banks has virtually dried up and now represents about 5 percent of long-term capital flows to developing nations, compared with 40 percent a decade ago. Countertrade is also used as a method of entering a new market, particularly in product areas that invite strong competition.

Maintenance of Stable Prices for Exports

Countertrade allows commodity exporters to maintain nominal prices for their products even in the face of limited or declining demand. The price of the product that is purchased in exchange could be increased to take into account the inflated price of exports. In this way, an exporter can dispose of its commodities without conceding the real price of the product in a competitive market. In the case of cartels, such as OPEC (Organization of Petroleum Exporting Countries), a member could attract customers for countertrade opportunities without violating price guidelines.

Benefits for Exporters

Increased Sales Opportunities

Countertrade generates additional sales that would not otherwise be possible. It also enables entry into difficult markets.

Access to Sources of Supply

Countertrade provides exporters access to a continuous supply of production components, precious raw materials, or other natural resources in return for sales of manufactured goods or technology.

Flexibility in Prices

Countertrade enables the exporter to adjust the price of a product in exchange for overpriced commodities.

THEORIES ON COUNTERTRADE

A limited number of empirical studies on countertrade have been conducted. The following findings characterize some of the theoretical studies on countertrade practices:

- Countertrade is positively correlated with a country's level of exports. This means that a higher level of international commercial activity is associated with a high level of countertrade (Hennart and Anderson, 1993).
- Countertrade is often used as a substitute for foreign direct investment (FDI). Even though foreign direct investment reduces market

transaction costs (i.e., by internalizing sources of raw materials and components through vertical integration), multinational companies resort to countertrade as a second-best solution when host countries impose restrictions on inward FDI. Countries engaged in heavy countertrade tend to be those that severely restrict inward FDI. FDI may also be less attracted to politically risky countries, in spite of their positive attitudes toward foreign investment. Such countries are likely to have a high level of countertrade activity (Hennart, 1990).

• The stricter the level of exchange controls, the higher the level of countertrade activity. This appears to be a response to the restrictions imposed on the acquisition of foreign currency. Some studies also show that a significant percentage of countertrade has little to do with foreign exchange shortages, but rather is intended to reduce high transaction costs that affect the purchase of technology or intermediate products.

FORMS OF COUNTERTRADE

Countertrade takes a variety of forms (see Figure 12.1). Such transactions can be divided into two broad categories:

• Transactions in which products and/or services are traded in exchange for other products and/or services: these include barter, switch trading, and clearing arrangements.
• Transactions that feature two parallel money-for-goods transactions: these include buyback, counterpurchase, and offset arrangements. (Barter Publishing Staff, 1992)

Exchange of Goods (Services) for Goods (Services)

Barter

A classic barter arrangement involves the direct exchange of goods/services between two trading parties (see International Perspective 12.1). An exporter from country A to country B is paid by a reciprocal export from country B to country A and no money changes hands. The transaction is governed by a single contract. In view of its limited flexibility, barter accounts for less than 15 percent of countertrade contracts. The major problems with barter relate to the determination of the relative value of the goods traded and the reluctance of banks to finance or guarantee such transactions.

Example: In 1996, Ukraine agreed to barter its agricultural products for 2 million tons of oil from Iran. A Macedonian company agreed to pay 30 percent of the price for the purchase of Russian gas in goods/services such as medicines, pipes, and construction work.

Switch Trading

This is an arrangement in which a switch trader will buy or market countertraded products for hard currency (see Figure 12.2). The switch trader will often demand a sizable fee in the form of a discount on the goods delivered.

International Perspective

12.1

THE MECHANICS OF A BARTER TRANSACTION

Suppose a private firm is selling drilling equipment to country A in exchange for ten tons of basmati rice. One method is to use reciprocal performance guarantees, such as performance bonds or standby letters of credit. Each party posts a guarantee, and this provides payment to the aggrieved party in the event of failure by the other party to perform its part of the contract (i.e., failure to deliver the goods or delivery of nonconforming goods). However, the fees charged by banks for such guarantees are quite high. Another method is to use an escrow account to secure performance of an obligation by each party. The steps used are as follows:

- The firm opens a documentary letter of credit in favor of country A. In cases in which the product is passed to a trading company, the letter of credit is opened by the trading company in favor of the nation.
- Country A delivers the rice to the firm or trading company and the title is transferred.
- When the title passes to the firm, funds equal to the value of the rice shipped are transferred by the firm under the letter of credit into an escrow account.
- The firm makes delivery of the drilling equipment simultaneously, or at a later date, to country A and title is transferred to the nation.
- Funds in the escrow account are released to the firm.
- In the event that the firm delivers nonconforming goods or fails to deliver the goods, the funds in the escrow account are paid to the nation.

FIGURE 12.1. Classification of Countertrade Forms

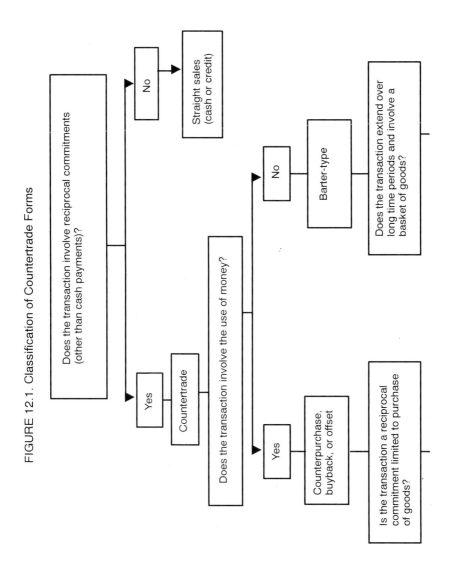

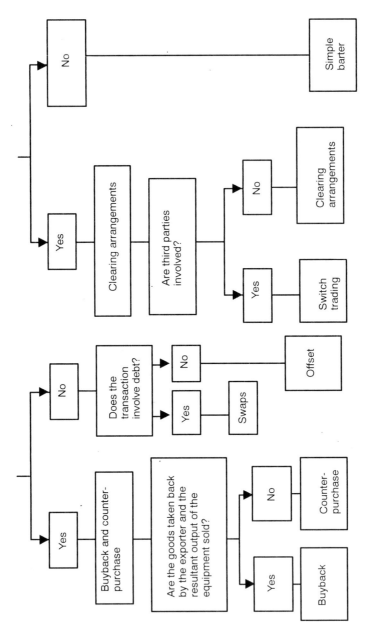

Source: Figure 12.1 originally appeared in Hennart, J. (1990), "Some Empirical Dimensions of Countertrade," *Journal of International Business Studies*, 21(2), p. 245; The Academy of International Business. Reprinted by permission.

FIGURE 12.2. Switch Trading

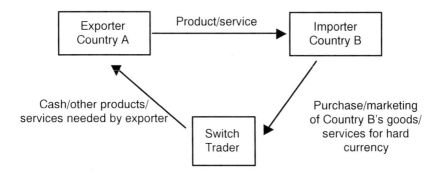

Example: A U.S. company exported fertilizer to Pakistan. However, the goods to be counterdelivered by Pakistan were of little interest to the U.S. seller. A Romanian company (switch trader) converted the Pakistani goods into cash, paid the U.S. exporter, and retained a commission.

Clearing Arrangements

Under these arrangements, two governments agree to purchase a certain volume of each other's goods and/or services over a certain period of time, usually a year. Each country sets up an account in one currency, for example, clearing dollar, franc, or local currency. When a trade imbalance exists, settlement of accounts can be in the form of hard-currency payments for the shortfall, transfer of goods, issuance of a credit against the following year's clearing arrangement, or by switch trading. In switch trading, the creditor country can sell its credit to a switch trader for a discount and receive cash payment. The switch trader will subsequently sell the corresponding goods to third parties (see Figure 12.3).

Example: In 1990, a Swedish company, Sukab, accumulated a large surplus in its clearing account with Pakistan. Sukab sold its credit to Marubeni, a Japanese company, at a discount, and Marubeni in turn liquidated this imbalance by purchasing Pakistani cotton and exporting it to a third county for hard currency.

FIGURE 12.3. Clearing Arrangement

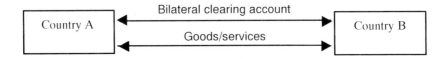

Parallel Transactions

Buyback (Compensation Agreement)

In a buyback or compensation transaction, a private firm will sell or license technology or build a plant (with payment in hard currency) and agree to purchase, over a given number of years, a certain proportion of the output produced from the use of the technology or plant. The output is to be purchased in hard currency. However, since the products are closely related, a codependency exists between the trading parties (see Figure 12.4). The duration of a compensation arrangement could range from a few years to thirty years or longer in cases in which the technology supplier (seller) is dependent upon the buyer's output for itself and its subsidiaries. The arrangement involves two contracts, each paid in hard currency, that is, one for the delivery of technology and equipment and another for the buyback of the resulting output. The two contracts are linked by a protocol that, inter alia, stipulates that the output to be purchased by the technology supplier is to be produced with the technology delivered. Since the agreement entails transfer of proprietary technology, it is quite important to pay special attention to the protection of patents, trademarks, and know-how, as well as to the rights of the technology recipient (importer/buyer) with respect to these industrial property rights.

> *Example:* A Japanese company exported computer chip processing and design technology to Korea, Singapore, and Taiwan, with a promise to purchase a certain percentage of the output over a given period of time. Levi Strauss transferred its know-how and trademark to a Hungarian firm for the production and sale of its products, with an agreement to purchase and market the output in Western Europe.

Counterpurchase

As in compensation arrangement, counterpurchase consists of two parallel hard currency-for-goods transactions (see Figure 12.5). However, in

FIGURE 12.4. Buyback

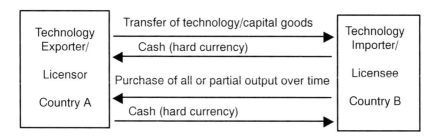

FIGURE 12.5. Counterpurchase

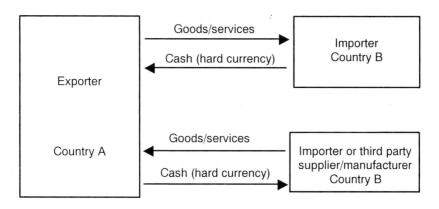

counterpurchase, a firm sells goods and/or services to an importer, promising to purchase from the latter or other entities in the importing nation goods that are unrelated to the items sold. The duration of such transactions is often short (three to five years), and the commitment usually requires a reciprocal purchase of less than the full value of the original sale. In cases in which the reciprocal purchase involves goods that are of low quality or in excess supply, the firm usually resells them to trading companies at a discount. Since the arrangement is often governed by two separate contracts, financing can be organized in a way that is similar to any other export transaction. In addition to flexibility in financing, the contractual separation also provides for separate provisions with regard to guarantee coverage, maturity of payments, and deliveries. As in compensation agreements, the two contracts are linked by a third contract that ties the purchase and sales contracts together and includes terms such as the ratio between purchases and sales, starting time of both contracts, import-export verification system, and so forth (Welt, 1990).

> *Examples:* In 1989, Pepsi and the former Soviet Union signed a $3 billion deal in which Pepsi agreed to purchase and market Russian Vodka and ten Soviet-built ocean vessels in return for doubling its Soviet bottling network and nationwide distribution of soft drinks in aluminum and plastic bottles. Rockwell and the Government of Zimbabwe signed a contract in which Rockwell offered to purchase Zimbabwe's ferro chrome and nickel in exchange for its sale of a printing press to Zimbabwe.

Offsets

An offset is a transaction in which an exporter allows the purchaser, generally a foreign government, to "offset" the cost of purchasing its (the exporter's) product (Cole, 1987) (see Figure 12.6). Such arrangements are mainly used for defense-related sales, sales of commercial aircraft, or sales of other high-technology products. Offsets are used by many countries as a way to compensate for the huge hard-currency payments resulting from the purchase as well as to create investment opportunities and employ-

FIGURE 12.6. Offsets

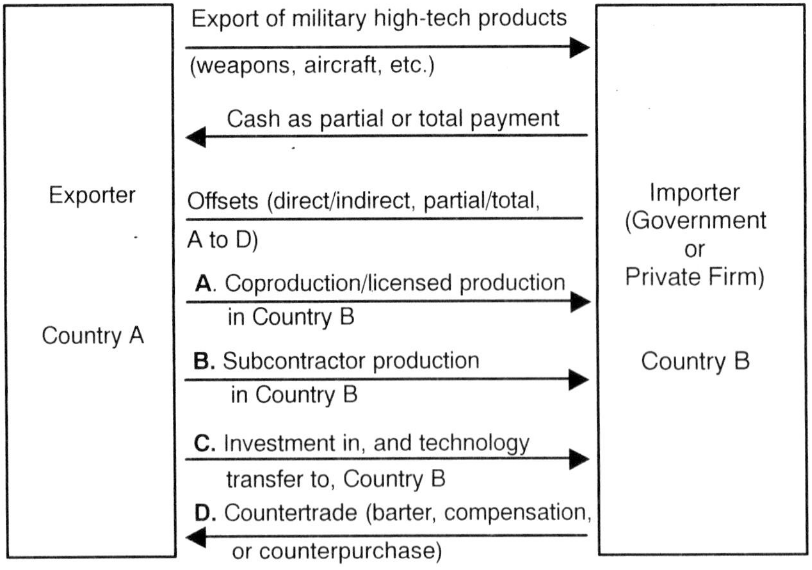

ment. Such arrangements became widespread after 1973 when OPEC sharply increased the price of oil and countries were left with limited hard currency to pay for major expenditures (Schaffer, 1989).

> *Example:* In 1975, the U.S. sale of F-16s to Norway, Denmark, Belgium, and the Netherlands was accomplished by an offset transaction. The purchase of F-16s priced at \$2.8 billion was to be offset by coproduction in the Netherlands of 10 percent of the value of the initial purchase of 650 aircraft, 15 percent of the value of all third-country F-16 purchases from the United States, and 40 percent of the value of their own purchases from the United States. (Schaffer, 1989)

Offset practices generally fall into two major categories: direct and indirect. Direct offsets include coproduction, subcontractor production, investments, and technology transfer.

Coproduction. This is an overseas production arrangement, usually based on a government-to-government agreement, that permits a foreign government or producer to acquire the technical information to manufacture all or part of an equipment or component originating in the exporting country. It may include a government-to-government production under license. The essential difference between coproduction and licensed production is that the former is normally a joint venture, while the latter does not entail ownership and/or management of the overseas production by the technology supplier. In coproduction, there is usually a government-to-government negotiation, whereas licensed production is based on direct commercial arrangements between the foreign manufacturer and host government or producer. In most cases, coproduction and licensed production are direct offsets because the resulting output directly fulfills part of the sales obligation.

> *Example:* In 1986, France purchased the AWACS (airborne warning and control system) aircraft from Boeing, based on a coproduction arrangement between the U.S. and French governments. According to the agreement, 80 percent of the contract value was to be offset by the purchase of engines produced through a joint venture between General Electric and a French firm.

Subcontractor production. This is usually a direct commercial arrangement between a manufacturer and an overseas producer (in the host country) for the production of a part or component of the manufacturer's export article to the host country. Such an arrangement does not often involve licensing of technological information.

> *Example:* In 1996, Italy announced plans to purchase four U212 submarines from Germany. The industrial cooperation agreement

will give Italian companies substantial subcontracting work in building the submarines and their systems. Indirect offsets (i.e., arrangements involving goods and services unrelated to the exports) will
also be utilized as compensation for the predominance of German-
supplied subsystems and components.

Overseas Investments. These are investments arising from the offset
agreement that usually take the form of capital investment to establish or
expand a company in the purchasing country.

> *Example:* In 1984, the Greek government purchased forty F-16s, and
> as part of the offset, the U.S. supplier firms were required to undertake
> investment, trade, and technology transfer programs. The U.S. firms
> agreed to contribute $50 million in capital over a ten-year period.

Technology transfer. Even though technology transfer provisions could
be included in coproduction or licensed production arrangements, they are
often distinct from both categories. A technology transfer arrangement usually involves the provision of technical assistance and R&D capabilities to
the joint venture partner or other firms as part of the offset agreement.

> *Example:* In the 1980s, Spain purchased F-18 aircraft under an offset
> arrangement that required the transfer of aerospace and other high
> technology to Spain, as well as the promotion of Spanish exports and
> tourism. (U.S. International Trade Commission, 1985)

Indirect offsets are contractual arrangements in which goods and services unrelated to the exports are acquired from, or produced in, the host
(purchasing) country. These include, but are not limited to, certain forms
of foreign investment, technology transfer, and countertrade.

> *Example:* As part of the cooperative defense agreement, the Nether-
> lands purchased patriot fire units from Raytheon Corporation of the
> United States for $305 million in 1986. Raytheon agreed to provide
> $115 million in direct offsets and $120 million in indirect offsets.
> The latter obligation was to be discharged through the purchase of
> goods and services in the Netherlands before 1999. (Office of Man-
> agement and Budget, 1986)

Arms sales account for a substantial part of offset transactions, which,
in turn, make up the largest percentage of countertrade deals.

COUNTERTRADE AND THE GATT/WTO

The prevalence of countertrade practices has directed the attention of policymakers to its potentially disruptive effects on international trade. Trade experts claim that countertrade represents a significant departure from the principles of free trade and could possibly undermine the delicate multilateral trading system that was carefully crafted since WWII. This movement toward bilateral trading arrangements deprives countries of the benefits of multilateral trade that GATT/WTO negotiated to confer upon members. Private countertrade transactions, however, fall outside the purview of the GATT, which regulates only governmental actions.

In addition, countertrade tends to undermine trade based on comparative advantages and prolongs inefficiency and misallocation of resources. A country, for example, may have to purchase from a high-cost/low-quality overseas supplier to fulfill its obligation under the export arrangement. Countertrade also slows down the exchange process and results in higher transaction costs, in the form of converting goods into money, warehousing, and discounting to a trader when the importer cannot use the goods received.

International Perspective

12.2

ORGANIZING FOR COUNTERTRADE

Once a firm has made a decision to countertrade, it has two organizational options: to use third parties such as consultants and trading houses or establish a countertrade department within the company. Each approach has its own benefits and disadvantages.

The following is a brief overview of the benefits and costs of establishing a countertrade unit within the firm.

Advantages	Disadvantages
Direct contact with the customer	Costly and mostly suitable for Multinational companies with broad-based product lines
Opportunity for learning and flexibility	
Confidentiality and control over the operation	Complex and involves corporate planning and coordination of staff
	Limited expertise; problems with disposing of countertraded goods

---

Countertrade is also inconsistent with the national treatment standard that is embodied in most international and regional trade agreements. The national treatment standard of the GATT/WTO, for example, requires that imported goods be taxed and regulated in the same manner as domestically produced goods. Any commercial transaction that requires the overseas supplier (exporter) to purchase a specified portion of the value of the exports from the purchaser would violate the national treatment standard (Roessler, 1985).

Countertrade constitutes a restriction on imports. The GATT/WTO prohibits restrictions other than duties, taxes, or other charges applied to imports. This means that if import licenses are granted on the condition that the imports are linked to exports, such countertrade practices would constitute a trade restriction prohibited under the general agreement. Without this government restriction, the producer would be able to import any amount of a product that efficiency and consumer demand dictated. Such restrictions would be in conformity with the agreement if they are imposed to safeguard a country's balance of payments (external financial position), as well as to protect against a sudden surge in imports of particular products (emergency actions).

COUNTERTRADE AND THE INTERNATIONAL MONETARY FUND

The International Monetary Fund (IMF) imposes a dual regime: on the one hand, it attempts to deter members from restricting international payments and transfers for current international transactions, while, on the other hand, it permits its members to regulate international capital movements as they see fit. Payments for current transactions involve an immediate quid pro quo (i.e., payments in connection with foreign trade, interest, profit, dividend payments, etc.), while capital payments are unilateral (loans, investments, etc.). A governmental measure requiring or stimulating countertrade would constitute an exchange restriction on current transactions if it involved a direct limitation on the availability or use of foreign currency.

GOVERNMENTS' ATTITUDES TOWARD COUNTERTRADE

Consistent with their commitment to a nondiscriminatory trading system, many countries are opposed to government-mandated countertrade because it distorts the free flow of trade and investment. Yet, they do not publicly discourage firms from engaging in countertrade.

The U.S. policy on countertrade was developed in 1983 by an interagency working group. The policy does the following:

- It prohibits federal agencies from promoting countertrade in their business or official contracts.
- It adopts a hands-off approach toward those arrangements which do not involve the U.S. government or are pursued by private parties. This means that the U.S. government will not oppose participation of U.S. companies in countertrade deals unless such activity has negative implications on national security.
- It provides no special accommodations for cases involving such transactions. The Export-Import Bank (Eximbank) will not provide financing support for the countertrade component of a transaction or accept countertrade as security, but the U.S. export component is eligible for all types of Eximbank support. Any repayment to Eximbank must be in hard currency and not conditional on the fulfillment of a side contract associated with countertrade.

In view of congressional concern with respect to such practices, the 1998 Trade Act mandated the establishment of an office of barter within the Department of Commerce's International Trade Administration and of an interagency group on countertrade. The Barter and Countertrade Unit established within the Department of Commerce now provides advisory services to firms interested in such transactions, while the interagency group on countertrade reviews and evaluates U.S. policy on countertrade and makes recommendations to the president and Congress.

Some countries have officially instituted mandatory countertrade requirements for any transaction over a certain value. Australia, for example, mandates local content and other investment requirements for all defense purchases valued at $5 million and above (Liesch, 1991). Certain countries have passed laws providing for counterpurchase operations and the extension of bank guarantees in the form of performance bonds. Indonesia, for example, established a countertrade division within the Ministry of Trade and has mandated countertrade requirements for any transaction exceeding $500,000 (Liesch, 1991; Verdun, 1985). Other countries may not have an official policy on countertrade or may even be opposed to it due to their position on free trade. However, this opposition often yields to the realities of international trade and competition, and a number of these countries are seen providing tacit approval to such transactions.

| International Perspective |

12.3

NEGOTIATING COUNTERTRADE CONTRACTS: POINTERS

Costs: All costs are included in one price. The price also includes the commission payable to dispose of the countertraded goods.

Contract(s): One or separate contracts can be used. Separate contracts are signified by three legal documents: the original sales contract, which is similar to any standard export contract; the subsequent agreement to purchase from the original buyer a certain amount of goods over a given time period and some type of protocol that ties the two contracts together.

Barter contract: Barter usually requires one contract. Key provisions include (1) description of goods to be sold and countertraded; (2) guarantee of quality; (3) penalty or other arrangements in the event of late delivery, failure to deliver, or delivery of nonconforming goods, including a bank guarantee or other guarantee in the form of standby letter of credit in the event of default, and providing for full payment; and (4) provisions for settlement of disputes.

Buybacks, counterpurchases, or offsets: Such contracts require the use of one or separate contracts. Key provisions include the following: (1) The Compensation ratio: this establishes the counterpurchase commitment by the original exporter; (2) range of products to be countertraded: parties must agree on the list of products to be purchased; (3) assignment clause: this enables the original seller to transfer its counterpurchase or buyback obligation to a trading house or a barter business club; (4) the penalty clause: this provides for penalties in the event that the original seller fails to fulfill its obligations (i.e., quality specifications and delivery schedules; (5) marketing restrictions: it may be important to secure the right to dispose of the countertraded goods in any market; and (6) provisions on force majeure (delay or default in performance caused by conditions beyond the party's control), applicable law (i.e., the law governing the contract), and dispute settlement.

CHAPTER SUMMARY

What Is Countertrade?

Countertrade is any commercial arrangement in which the exporter is required to accept in partial or total settlemennt of its deliveries, a supply of products from the importing country. Barter could be traced to ancient times. Presently, countertrade is estimated to account for 15 to 20 percent of world trade.

Benefits of Countertrade

Benefits for Buyers

1. Transfer of technology
2. Alleviation of balance-of-payments difficulties
3. Market access and maintenance of stable prices

Benefits for Exporters

1. Increased sales opportunities
2. Access to sources of supply
3. Flexibility in prices

Theories on Countertrade

1. Countertrade is positively correlated with a country's level of exports.
2. Countertrade is partly motivated by its use as a substitute for foreign direct investment.
3. The stricter the level of exchange controls, the higher the level of countertrade activity.

Forms of Countertrade

Exchange of Goods/Services for Goods/Services

1. Barter: Direct exchange of goods and services between two trading parties.
2. Switch trading: An arrangement in which the switch trader will buy or market countertraded goods for hard currency.
3. Clearing arrangement: A method in which two governments agree to purchase a certain volume of each other's goods/services over a given period of time. In the event of trade imbalance, settlement could be in hard-currency payments, transfer of goods, issuance of credit, or use of switch trading.

Two Parallel Transactions

1. Buyback: An arrangement in which a private firm will sell or license technology to an overseas customer, with an agreement to purchase part

of the output produced from the use of such technology. The agreement involves two contracts, both of which are discharged by payment of hard currency.

2. Counterpurchase: Two parallel transactions in which a firm exports a product to an overseas buyer with a promise to purchase from the latter or other parties in the country goods not related to the items exported.

3. Offset: A transaction in which an exporter allows the purchaser, usually a foreign government, to reduce the cost of purchasing the exporter's product through coproduction, subcontracting, investments, and transfers of technology.

Offsets

Direct Offsets

1. Coproduction: Joint venture or licensing arrangements with overseas customers.

2. Subcontractor production: Arrangement for production in the importing country of parts or components of the export product destined to the latter.

3. Investments and transfer of technology: Certain offset agreements provide for investments and technology transfer to the importing country.

Indirect Offsets

Offset arrangements in which goods and services unrelated to the exports are acquired from, or produced in, the importing country.

Countertrade and the GATT/WTO

Concerns of the GATT/WTO with countertrade:

1. Countertrade represents a significant departure from the principles of free trade based on comparative advantage.

2. Countertrade results in higher transaction costs.

3. Countertrade is inconsistent with the national treatment standard that is embodied in most trade agreements.

Governments' Attitudes Toward Countertrade

U.S. government policy toward countertrade:

1. U.S. government prohibits federal agencies from promoting countertrade in their business.
2. U.S. policy adopts a hands-off approach in relation to private transactions.

Some countries have a countertrade requirement for certain purchases exceeding a given amount. Such transactions are quite common in defense-related purchases.

SECTION V:
FINANCING TECHNIQUES
AND VEHICLES

Chapter 13

Capital Requirements
and Private Sources of Financing

Many small and medium-sized businesses suffer from undercapitalization and/or poor management of financial resources, often during the first few years of operation. The entrepreneur typically either overestimates demand for the product or severely underestimates the need for capital resources and organizational skills. Undercapitalization may also be a result of the entrepreneur's aversion to equity financing (fear of loss of control over the business) or the lender's resistance to provide capital due to the entrepreneur's lack of credit history and a comprehensive business plan (Hutchinson, 1995; Gardner, 1994).

Large corporations have an advantage in raising capital compared with small businesses. They have greater bargaining strength with lenders, they can issue securities, and they have greater access to capital markets around the world. However, major changes are taking place in small/medium-sized business financing due to three important factors: technology, globalization, and deregulation. Information technology enables the financial world to operate efficiently, to decentralize while improving control. It also provides businesses seeking capital to choose from a vast range of financial instruments (Grimaud, 1995). Globalization allows businesses to turn increasingly to international markets to raise capital. With a touch of a button, businesses will have access to individual or corporate sources of finance around the world. With deregulation, in many countries, competition in financial products is allowed across all depository institutions. The distinction between investment and commercial banking is quite blurred, and both sectors now compete in the small business financing market.

It is important to properly evaluate how much capital is needed, in what increments, and over what time period. First are the initial capital needs to start the export-import business. Start-up costs are not large if the exporter-importer begins as an agent (without buying for resale) and uses his or her own home as an office. Initial capital needs are for office supplies and

equipment—telephone, fax, computer—and a part-time assistant. The
business could also be started on a part-time basis until it provides sufficient revenues to cover expenses, including the owner's salary. However,
when the business is commenced with the intention of establishing an
independent company with products purchased for resale (merchant, distributor, etc.), a lot more capital is needed to prepare a business plan,
travel, purchase and distribute the product, and exhibit in major trade
shows. Second, capital is needed to finance growth and expansion of the
business. It is thus critical to anticipate capital needs during the time of
growth and expansion as well as during abnormal increases in accounts
receivable, inventory levels, and changes in the business cycle.

The capital needs and financing alternatives of an export-import business are determined by its stage of evolution, ownership structure, distribution channel choice, and other pertinent factors. A very small sum of
money is often needed to start the business as an agent because no payments are made for merchandise, transportation, or distribution of the
product. However, initial capital needs are substantial if a person starts the
business as a merchant, distributor, or trading company with products
available for resale. This entails payments for transportation, distribution,
advertising and promotion, travel, and other expenses.

Capital needs at the start-up stage may be smaller compared to those
needed during the growth and expansion period. However, this depends on
the degree of expansion and the capital needed to support additional marketing efforts, inventories, and accounts receivable. The ownership structure of an export-import firm tends to have an important influence on
financing alternatives and little or no influence on capital needs. Studies
on small business financing indicate the following salient features:

- Incorporated companies are more likely to receive equity (and other
  nondebt) financing than debt financing because lenders perceive the
  incorporated entity as having a greater incentive to take on risky ventures due to its limited liability (Brewer et al., 1996).
- Younger firms are more likely to obtain equity (nondebt) than debt
  financing. The probability of receiving debt financing increases with
  age. This is consistent with standard theories of capital structure,
  which state that such businesses have little or no track record on
  which to base financing decisions and are often perceived as risky by
  lenders.
- Firms with high growth opportunities, a volatile cash flow, and low
  liquidation value are more likely to finance their business with equity than debt. In firms with high growth opportunities, conflicts are
  likely between management and shareholders over the direction and

pace of growth options, and this reduces the chances of debt financing. However, businesses with a good track record and high liquidation value (with assets that can be easily liquidated) have a greater chance of financing their business with debt rather than equity (Williamson, 1988; Schleifer and Vishny, 1992; Stulz, 1990).

CAPITAL SOURCES FOR EXPORT-IMPORT BUSINESSES

Capital needs to start the business or to finance current operations or expansion can be obtained from different sources. Internal financing should be explored before resorting to external funding sources. This includes using one's own resources for initial capital needs and then retaining more profits in the business or reducing accounts receivables and inventories to meet current obligations and finance growth and expansion. Such reductions in receivables or inventories should be applied carefully so as not to lead to a loss of customers or goodwill, both of which are critical to the viability of the business.

External financing takes different forms, and businesses use one or a combination of the following:

1. *Debt or equity financing:* Debt financing occurs when an export-import firm borrows money from a lender with a promise to repay (principal and interest) at some predetermined future date. Equity financing involves raising money from private investors in exchange for a percentage of ownership (and sometimes participation in management) of the business. The major disadvantage with equity financing is the owner's potential loss of control over the business.
2. *Short-term, intermediate, or long-term financing:* Short-term financing involves a credit period of less than one year, while intermediate financing is credit extended for a period of one to five years. In long-term financing, the credit period ranges between five and twenty years.
3. *Investment, inventory, or working capital financing:* Investment financing is money used to start the business (computer, fax machine, telephone, etc). Inventory capital is money raised to purchase products for resale. Working capital supports current operations such as rent, advertising, supplies, wages, and so on. All three could be financed by debt or equity.

Several sources of funding are available to existing export-import businesses that have established track records. However, financing is quite limited for initial capital needs, and the entrepreneur has to use his/her own resources or borrow from family or friends. It is also important to evaluate funding sources not just in terms of availability (willingness to provide funding) but also in regard to the capital's cost and its effect on business profits, as well as any restrictions imposed by lenders on the operations of the business. Certain loan agreements, for example, prevent the sale of accounts receivable or equipment or require the representation of lenders in the firm's management. The following is an overview of possible sources of capital for export/import businesses.

Internal Sources

This is the best source of financing for initial capital needs or expansion because there is no interest to be paid back or equity in the business to be surrendered. Start-up businesses have limited chances of obtaining loans so self-funding becomes the only alternative. Internal sources include the following:

- Money in saving accounts, certificates of deposit, and other personal accounts
- Money in stocks, bonds, and money market funds

External Sources

Family and Friends

This is the second-best option for raising capital for an export-import business. The money should be borrowed with a promissory note indicating the date of payment and the amount of principal and interest to be paid. As long as the business pays a market interest rate, it is entitled to a tax deduction and the lender gets the interest income. In the event of failure by the business to repay the loan, the lender may be able to deduct the amount as a short-term capital loss. Such an arrangement protects the lender and also prevents the latter from acquiring equity in the business.

Banks and Other Commercial Lenders

The largest challenge to successful lending is the turnover rate of small businesses. In general, fewer than half of all small businesses survive beyond the third-year mark. However, the survival rate for export-import businesses is generally higher than that of other businesses. Due to the level of risk, banks and other commercial lenders tend to avoid start-up financing without collateral. A 1994 IBM consulting group survey of small businesses revealed that bank credit was the most popular primary source of capital in the United States, followed by internally generated funds. Credit cards were not a significant source of financing. Of the businesses, 58 percent maintained a working capital line of credit, followed by term loans (42 percent). Only 3 percent of the businesses used Small Business Administration (SBA) loans (Anonymous, 1995).

Banks remain the cheapest source of borrowed capital for export-import firms as well as other small businesses. To persuade a bank to provide a loan, it is essential to prepare a business plan that sets clear financial goals, including how the loan will be repaid. Banks always review the ability of the borrower to service the debt, whether sufficient cash is invested in the business, as well as the nature of the collateral that is to be provided as a guarantee for the loan. Bankers always investigate the five Cs in making lending decisions: character (trustworthiness, reliability), capacity (ability and track record in meeting financial obligations), capital (significant equity in the business), collateral (security for the loan), and condition (the effect of overall economic conditions) (Lorenz-Fife, 1997). Even though it is often difficult to obtain a commercial loan for start-up capital, a good business plan and a strong, experienced management team may entice lenders to make a decision in favor of providing the loan. The following are different types of financing.

Asset-based financing. Banks and other commercial lenders provide loans secured by fixed assets, such as land, buildings, and machinery. For example, they will lend up to 80 percent of the value of one's home minus the first mortgage. These are often long-term loans payable over a ten- year period. Business assets, such as accounts receivable, inventories, and personal assets (savings accounts, cars, jewelry, etc.), can be used as collateral for business loans. With accounts receivable and inventories, commercial lenders usually lend up to 50 percent and 80 percent of their respective values. Use of saving accounts as collateral could reduce interest payment on a loan. Suppose the interest on the savings account is 4 percent and the business loan is financed at 12 percent. The actual interest rate that is to be paid is reduced to 8 percent $(12 - 4)$.

Lines of credit. These are short-term loans (for a period of one year) intended for purchases of inventory and payment of operating costs. They may sometimes be secured by collateral such as accounts receivable based on the creditworthiness and reputation of the borrower. A certain amount of money (line of credit) is made available, and interest is often charged on the amount used. Certain lenders do not allow use of such lines of credit until the business's checking account is depleted.

Personal and commercial loans. Owners with good credit standing could obtain personal loans that are backed by the mere signature and guarantee of the borrower. They are short-term loans and subject to relatively high interest rates. Commercial loans are also short-term loans that are often backed by stocks, bonds, and life insurance policies as collateral. The cash value of a life insurance policy can also be borrowed and repaid over a certain period of time.

Credit cards. Credit cards are generally not recommended for capital needs for new or existing export-import businesses because they are one of the costliest forms of business financing. They charge extremely high interest rates and there is no limit on how much credit card issuers can charge for late fees and other penalties (Fraser, 1996). If financing options are limited, credit cards could be used if the probability of the business succeeding is very high (if you have made definite arrangements with foreign buyers, etc). One should shop for the lowest available rates and plan for bank or credit union financing at a later date, if the debt cannot be retired within a short time period, possibly with an account receivable or inventory as collateral. A survey of small and medium-sized businesses, by Arthur Anderson and Company, in 1994, showed that 29 percent of businesses use credit cards for capital needs (Field, Korn, and Middleton, 1995).

Small Business Administration (SBA)

The SBA has several facilities for lending that can be used by export-import businesses for capital needs at different stages of their growth cycle (see Table 13.1).

Small business investment companies (SBICs). SBICs are private companies funded by the SBA that were established to provide loan (sometimes equity) capital to small businesses. Even though they prefer to finance existing small businesses with a track record, they also consider loans for start-up capital. Members of a minority group could also consider a similar lending agency funded by the SBA that is intended to finance minority start-up or existing businesses.

The SBA guaranteed loan (7(a) Loan Guarantee Program). The guarantee by the SBA permits a lending institution to provide long-term loans to start-up or existing small businesses. Export-import businesses can use the money for their working capital needs, for example, to purchase inventory and help carry a receivable until it is paid, to purchase real estate to house the business, and for acquisition of furniture and fixtures. The SBA guarantee is available only after the business has failed to obtain financing on reasonable terms from other private sources. It is considered to be a lender of last resort.

TABLE 13.1. SBA Funding for Export-Import and Other Small Businesses

Program	Brief Overview
1. The 7(A) Loan Guarantee: Start-up/expansion/ working capital	Loans made by private lenders are guaranteed up to $750,000, which could cover up to 90 percent of the loan. Funds could be used to buy land and buildings, to expand facilities, to purchase equipment, or for working capital.
2. Certified Development Company (CDC) Loan	CDCs are nonprofit economic development agencies, certified by the SBA. The owner is to contribute a minimum of 10 percent equity in the business. The loans are available up to $750,000. Loans can be used to purchase land, for improvement or renovation of facilities, and to purchase machinery or equipment. Project assets are often used as collateral. It cannot be used for working capital. (Up to 40 percent cost of fixed assets.)
3. Small Business Investment Companies (SBICs)	They are licensed by SBA and lend their own capital as well as funds borrowed through the federal government to small businesses, both new and already established. SBICs make either equity investments or long-term loans to companies with growth potential. Investment is not to exceed 20 percent of its private capital in securities or guarantees in any one concern. (Loans for start-up or expansion.)
4. Low Documentation	Designed to increase the availability of funds under $100,000 and to expedite the loan review process. (Loan guarantees for start-up or expansion/working capital.)
5. International Trade Loan	Used for businesses preparing to engage in, or are already engaged in, international trade or for those adversely affected by competition from imports. Used to develop and expand export market or for working capital. Loans are guaranteed up to $1,250,000. (Loan guarantees to expand market/working capital.)
6. Fast trak	This was designed to increase capital available to businesses seeking loans up to $100,000. It is currently offered as a pilot with a limited number of lenders. (Loan guarantee for start-up/expansion/working capital.)
7. Export Working Capital	This was designed to provide short-term working capital to exporters. Maximum loan guarantee is $750,000. Loan requests above $833,333 are processed by Exim-bank. (Loan guarantee.)
8. Microloans	These range from $100 to $25,000. Funds available to nonprofit intermediaries, who in turn make loans to small business borrowers. Collateral and personal guarantee are required. Loan maturity may be as long as six years. (Loan for start-up/expansion/working capital.)

The Certified Development Company. The Certified Development Company (CDC 503/504) Program assists in the development and expansion of small firms and in the creation of jobs. This program is designed to provide fixed-asset financing and cannot be used for working capital or inventory or for consolidating or repaying debt. (For an overview of SBA loans, see International Perspective 13.1.)

Finance Companies

The following are different ways of raising capital from finance companies to start or expand an export-import business.

Loans from insurance companies and pension funds. Life insurance policies can be used as collateral to borrow money for capital needs. Pension funds also provide loans to businesses with attractive growth prospects. Pension funds and insurance company loans are intermediate and long-term credits (five to fifteen years). Banks often introduce such lending agencies to their clients when the funds are needed for longer than the banks' maximum maturity period.

International Perspective

13.1

SBA LOANS AND THEIR FEATURES

1. Guarantee Loans: The loans are made and disbursed by private lenders and guaranteed by SBA up to a certain amount. This means that if the borrower defaults on the loan, SBA will purchase an agreed-upon percentage of the unpaid balance. Direct and participation loans (loans made jointly by SBA and other lenders) are quite few and have even decreased over the years.

2. Interest Rates: Unless otherwise stated, maximum rates for guaranteed loans are 2.25 percent above prime for a loan greater than $50,000 with maturity of less than seven years and 2.75 percent above prime for loans from seven to twenty-five years. Rates on loans under $50,000 may be higher.

3. Guarantee Fee: Payment of a guarantee fee is required for all guaranteed loans. Loans are to be secured by a collateral and personal guarantee.

4. Guarantees of Last Resort: SBA loans are provided as a matter of last resort (i.e., when borrowers cannot obtain credit without SBA guarantee). The borrower is expected to have some personal equity to operate the business on a sound financial basis.

Commercial finance companies. These companies grant short-term loans using accounts receivable, inventories, or equipment as collateral. They can also factor (buy) accounts receivable at a discount and provide the export-import firm the necessary capital for growth and expansion. Factoring is a way of turning a firm's accounts receivable into immediate cash without creating new debt. The factoring company will collect the accounts receivable (A/R), assume credit risks associated with the A/R, conduct investigations on the firm's existing and prospective accounts, as well as do the bookkeeping with respect to the credit. In most cases, a factoring company will advance 50 to 90 percent of the face value of the receivables and later pay the balance less the factor's discount (4 to 7 percent of face value of receivables) once the receivables are collected. An export-import firm could easily factor its receivables so long as it sells to government clients or to major companies that have good credit. The disadvantage with this method is that it is expensive and could absorb a good part of the firm's profits.

Equity Sources

For many export-import businesses, the ability to raise equity finance is quite limited. Although such funding provides the owner with initial capital needs, money for expansion, or working capital, it means some dilution of ownership and control. Finding compatible business partners and shareholders is always difficult. There are three sources for equity funding:

- *Family and friends*
- *Business angels (invisible venture capitalists):* Business angels provide start-up or expansion capital and are the biggest providers of equity capital for small businesses. They can be found through networking advertisements or newspapers or the World Wide Web. This segment is estimated to represent about 2,000 individuals or businesses investing between $10 billion to $20 billion each year in over 30,000 businesses (Lorenz-Fife, 1997).
- *Venture capitalists:* Venture capitalists provide equity capital to businesses that are already established and need working or expansion capital. The Small Business Administration (SBA) estimates that 500 venture capital firms are currently investing about $4 billion a year in some 3,000 ventures. They may not be suitable for small export-import firms because

1. their minimum investment is about $50,000 to 100,000;
2. they seldom provide funding for start-up capital because they are

interested in companies with a proven track record and market position; and

3. they expect high returns (10 to 15 percent) on their investments over a relatively short period of time.

PRIVATE SOURCES OF EXPORT FINANCING

In many export transactions, the buyer is unable or unwilling to pay for the goods at the time of delivery. This means that the seller has to agree to payment at some future date or that the buyer should seek financing from third parties. The seller may seek financing from the buyer or third parties for purchasing goods from suppliers, to pay for labor, or to arrange for transportation and insurance (preshipment financing). The exporter may also need postshipment financing of the resulting account or accounts receivable or both (Silvester, 1995).

Competitive finance is a crucial element in export strategies, especially for small and medium-sized companies. Exporters should carefully consider the type of financing required, the length of time for repayment, the loan's effect on price and profit, as well as the various risks that may be associated with such financing.

In extending credit to overseas customers, it is important to recognize the following:

1. Normal commercial terms range from 30 to 180 days for sales of consumer goods, industrial materials, and agricultural commodities. Custom-made or high-value capital equipment may warrant longer repayment periods.
2. An allowance may have to be made for longer shipment periods than are found in domestic trade because foreign buyers are often unwilling to have the credit period start before receiving the goods.
3. Customers are usually charged interest on credit periods of a year or longer and seldom on short-term credit of up to 180 days. Even though the provision of favorable financing terms makes a product more competitive, the exporter should carefully assess such financing against considerations of cost and risk of default.

Financing by the Exporter

Open Account

Under this arrangement, an exporter will transfer possession or ownership of the merchandise on a deferred-payment basis (payment deferred for an agreed period of time). This can be done in the case of creditworthy customers who have proven track records. In the case of customers who are not well-known to the exporter, such arrangements should not be undertaken without taking out export credit insurance.

Consignment Sales

Importers do not pay for the merchandise until it is sold to a third party. Exporters could take out an insurance policy to cover them against risk of nonpayment.

Financing by the Overseas Customer

Advance Payment

The buyer is required to pay before shipment is effected. The advance payment may comprise of the entire price or an agreed-upon percentage of the purchase price. An importer may secure the advance payment through a performance guarantee provided by a third party. Export trading or export management companies, for example, often purchase goods on an advance-payment or cash-on-delivery basis, thus eliminating the need for financing. They can also use their vast international networks to help the exporter obtain credit and credit insurance.

Progress Payment

Payments are tied to partial performance of the contract, such as production, partial shipment, and so on. This means that a mix of advance and progress payments meets the financing needs of the exporter.

Financing by Third Parties

Short-Term Methods

Loan secured by a foreign account receivable. An exporter can borrow money from a bank or finance company to meet its short-term working capital needs by using its foreign account receivable as collateral. In most cases, the overseas customer is not notified about the loan. As the customer makes payment to the exporter, the exporter, in turn, repays the loan to the lender. It is also possible to notify the overseas customer about the collateral and instruct the latter to pay bills directly to the lender. This may, however, put to question the financial standing of the exporter in the eyes of the overseas buyer.

An exporter can usually borrow 80 to 85 percent of the face-value of its accounts receivable if the receivables are insured and the exporter and overseas customer have good credit ratings.

Most banks are reluctant to lend against receivables that are not insured. The bank's security is effected through assignment of the exporter's foreign accounts receivable. Documentary collections are easier and less expensive to finance than sales on open accounts because the draft in documentary collections is a negotiable instrument (unlike open account sales, which are accompanied by an invoice and transport documents) that can easily be sold or discounted before maturity. Although most lenders are interested in providing a loan against foreign receivables, it is not uncommon to find some that would purchase them with full or limited recourse. In both cases, most banks require insurance. (Once the receivables are sold, the exporter will be able to remove the receivables and the loan from its balance sheet.)

Trade/banker's acceptance. This arises when a draft drawn by the seller is accepted by the overseas customer to pay a certain sum of money on an agreed-upon date. The exporter could obtain a loan using the acceptance as collateral or discount the acceptance to a financial institution for payment. In cases in which the debt is not acknowledged in the form of a draft, the exporter could sell or discount the invoice (invoice acceptance) before maturity. In both cases, the acceptances are usually sold without recourse to the exporter and the latter is relieved from the responsibility of collection.

A draft drawn on, and accepted by, a bank is called a banker's acceptance. Once accepted, the draft becomes a primary obligation of the accepting bank to pay at maturity. This occurs in the case of documents against acceptance (documentary collection or acceptance credit), whereby payment is to be made at a specified date in the future. The bank returns the draft to the seller with an endorsement of its acceptance, guaranteeing payment to the seller (exporter) on the due date. The exporter may then sell the accepted draft at a discount to the bank or any other financial institution. The exporter could also secure a loan using the draft as collateral. The marketability of a banker's or trade acceptance is dependent on the creditworthiness of the party accepting the draft.

Letter of credit. In addition to the acceptance credit discussed previously, the letter of credit could be an important instrument of financing exports:

1. *Transferable letter of credit:* Using this method, the exporter transfers its rights under the credit to another party, usually a supplier, who receives payment. When the supplier presents the necessary documents to the advising bank, the supplier's invoice is replaced with the exporter's invoice for the full value of the original credit. The advising bank pays the supplier the value of the invoice and will pay the difference to the exporter.
2. *Assignment of proceeds under the letter of credit:* The beneficiary (exporter) may assign either the entire amount or a percentage of the proceeds of the L/C to a specified third party, usually a supplier. This allows the exporter to make purchases with limited capital by using the overseas buyer's credit. It does not require the assent of the buyer or the buyer's bank.
3. *Back-to-back letters of credit:* A letter of credit is issued on the strength of another letter of credit. Such credits are issued when a supplier or subcontractor demands payment from the exporter before collections are received from the customer. The exporter remains obligated to perform under the original credit, and if default occurs, the bank is left holding a worthless collateral.

Factoring. Factoring is a continuous arrangement between a factoring concern and the exporter, whereby the factor purchases export receivables for a somewhat discounted price (usually 2 to 4 percent less than the full value). The amount of the discount depends on a number of factors, including the kind of products involved, the customer, the factoring entity, and the importing country. Factoring enables exporters to offer terms of sale on open account without assuming the credit risk. Importers also prefer factoring because by buying on open account, they forgo costly payment arrangements such as letters of credit. It also frees up their working capital. In the case of importers that have not yet established a track record, banks often will not issue letters of credit and open account sales may be the only available option.

In export factoring, the exporter receives immediate payment and the burden of collection is eliminated. Factors have ties to banks and financial institutions in other countries through networks such as Factors Chain International, which enables them to check the creditworthiness of an overseas customer, to authorize credit, and to assume financial risk.

Increases in global trade and competition have resulted in the search for alternative forms of financing to accommodate the diverse needs of customers. In highly competitive markets, concluding a successful export deal often depends on the seller's ability to obtain trade finance at the most favorable terms for the overseas customer.

International factoring has grown by about 500 percent during the last ten years, amounting to $20 billion in 1994. In the United States, the factoring industry handles about $2 billion in foreign trade (Ioannou, 1995). The export factoring business grew by 14 percent in 1991, compared with a 9 percent increase in domestic factoring (Ring, 1993). It is now available in about forty countries, mostly concentrated in North America, Western Europe, and Asia. Even though export factoring has been traditionally associated with the sale of textiles and apparel, footwear, or carpets, it is now used for a host of diversified products.

A typical export factoring procedure includes the following steps: Upon receipt of an order from an overseas customer, the exporter verifies with the factor, through its overseas affiliate, the customer's credit standing and determines whether the factor is willing to authorize credit and to assume financial risk. If the factor's decision is in favor of authorizing credit to the overseas customer, then the parties follow the procedure described in Figure 13.1.

Arrangements with factors are made either with recourse (exporter liable in the event of default by buyer or other problems) or without recourse, in which case a larger discount may be required because the exporter is free of liability. (For advantages and disadvantages of this financing method, see Table 13.2.)

Intermediate- and Long-Term Methods

Buyer credit. Some export sales, such as those involving capital equipment, often require financing terms that extend over several years. The importer may obtain credit from a bank or other financial institution to pay the exporter. The seller often cooperates in structuring the financing arrangements to make them suitable to the needs of the buyer.

Forfaiting. Forfaiting is the practice of purchasing deferred debts arising from international sales contracts without recourse to the exporter. The exporter surrenders possession of export receivables (deferred-debt obligation from the importer), which are usually guaranteed by a bank in the importing country, by selling to a forfaiter at a discount in exchange for cash. The deferred debt may be in the form of a promissory note, bill of exchange, trade acceptance, or documentary credit, which are unconditional and easily transferable debt instruments that can be sold on the secondary market.

The origins of forfaiting date back to the 1940s, when Swiss financiers developed new ways of financing sales of West German capital equipment to Eastern Europe. Since Eastern European countries did not have enough

FIGURE 13.1. Export Factoring

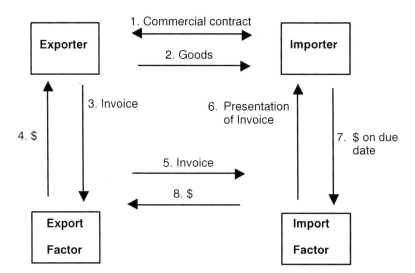

1. The exporter and importer enter into a commercial contract and agree on the terms of sale (i.e., open account).
2. The exporter ships the goods to the importer.
3. The exporter submits the invoice to the export factor.
4. The export factor provides (cash in advance) funds to the exporter against receivables until money is collected from the importer. The exporter often receives up to 30 percent of the value of the receivables ahead of time and pays the factor interest on the money received, or the factor pays the exporter, less a commission charge, when receivables are due (or shortly thereafter). The commission often ranges between 1 and 3 percent.
5. The export factor passes the invoice to the import factor for assumption of credit risk, administration, and collection of the receivables.
6. The import factor presents the invoice to the importer for payment on the agreed-upon date.
7. The importer pays the import factor.
8. The import factor pays the export factor. In cases in which the export factor advanced funds up to a certain percentage (e.g., 30 percent) of the export-er's receivables, the remaining portion (70 percent of receivables less interest or other charges) is paid by the export factor to the exporter.

Source: Ring, 1993, p. 11.

TABLE 13.2. Advantages and Disadvantages of Export Factoring

Advantages	Disadvantages
• Factoring allows immediate payment against receivables and increases working capital.	• Factoring is not available for shipments with a value of less than $100,000. It is appropriate for continuous or repetitive transactions (not one-shot deals). Factors often require access to a certain volume of the exporter's yearly sales.
• Factors conduct credit investigations, collect accounts receivable from the importer, and provide other bookkeeping services.	
• Factors assume credit risk in the event of the buyer's default or refusal to pay (nonrecourse).	• Factors do not work for receivables with a maturity of over 180 days.
• Factoring is a good substitute for bank credit when the latter is too restrictive or uneconomical.	• Factors generally do not work with most developing countries because of their inadequate legal and financial frameworks.
	• Exporters could be liable for disputes concerning merchandise (quality, condition of goods, etc.) and contract of sale.

hard currency to finance imports, they sought intermediate-term financing from their suppliers. The leading forfait houses are still located in Europe.

In a typical forfaiting transaction, the overseas customer does not have hard currency to finance the sale and requests to purchase on credit, usually payable within one to ten years. The exporter (or exporter's bank) contacts a forfaiter and provides the latter with the details of the proposed transaction with the overseas customer. The forfaiter evaluates the transaction and agrees to finance the deal based on a certain discount rate and other conditions. The exporter then incorporates the discount into the selling price. Discount rates are fixed and based on the London Interbank Offered Rate (LIBOR), on which floating interest rates are based. The forfaiter usually requires a guarantee or aval (letter of assurance) from a bank in the importer's country and often provides the exporter with a list of local banks that are acceptable as guarantors. The guarantee becomes quite important, especially in cases of receivables from developing countries. Once an acceptable guarantor is found, the exporter ships the goods to the buyer and endorses the negotiable instruments in favor of the forfaiter, without recourse. The forfaiter then pays the exporter the discounted proceeds.

Although export factoring and forfaiting appear quite similar, there are certain differences in terms of payment terms, products involved, continuity of transaction, and overall use:

1. Factors are often used to finance consumer goods, whereas forfaiters usually work with capital goods, commodities, and projects.
2. Factors are used for continuous transactions, but forfaiters finance one-time deals.
3. Forfaiters work with receivables from developing countries whenever they obtain an acceptable bank guarantor; factors do not finance trade with most developing countries because of unavailability of credit information, poor credit ratings or inadequate legal and financial frameworks.
4. Factors generally work with short-term receivables, whereas forfaiters finance receivables with a maturity of over 180 days. (See Table 13.3 for advantages and disadvantages of this financing method.)

TABLE 13.3. Forfaiting

Advantages
1. Forfaiters purchase receivables as a one-shot deal without requiring an ongoing volume of business, as in the case of factoring.
2. Financing can cover 100 percent of the sale. This improves cash flow and reduces transaction costs for the exporter because responsibility for collection is assumed by the forfaiter. Forfaiter also assumes all of the payment risk (i.e., credit risk of the guarantor bank, the interest rate risk, as well as the buyer's country risk).
Disadvantages
1. This is not available for short-term financing (less than 180 days). Terms range from one to ten years.
2. Transaction size is usually limited to $250,000 or more.
3. Interest and commitment fees (if advance payment is required by exporter) may be high.
4. Exporter is responsible for quality, condition of goods, delivery, overshipment, and other contract disputes.
5. Exporter is responsible for obtaining a bank guarantee for the buyer.

The following are some examples of forfaiting transactions:

- The Bankers Association for Foreign Trade (BAFT) arranged with a cotton machinery company to sell over $500,000 worth of cotton lint removal machinery payable eleven months from the date on the bill of lading. A Greek commercial bank issued the letter of credit, which called for acceptance drafts. Bankers Trust of New York confirmed the letter of credit, and Midland Bank undertook the forfaiting transaction.

- Morgan Grenfell Trade Finance Limited purchased receivables from U.S. exporters to Peru. The finance company required the guarantee of one of the large Peruvian banks and accepted a repayment period of up to five years.
- Morgel Grenfell also financed the down payment in cash (forfaiting) of the sale of electric turbines to Mexico, which was financed by Eximbank. The Eximbank required a 15 percent down payment.
- The Export Development Corporation (EDC) of Canada purchases accounts receivable from Canadian exporters provided the promissory notes issued by the overseas customer are guaranteed by a bank acceptable to the EDC, the transaction complies with the Canadian content requirement, and the promissory note does not exceed 85 percent of the contract price.

Export leasing. This is a financing scheme in which a third party, be it an international leasing entity or a finance firm, purchases and exports capital equipment with a view to leasing it to the importer in another country on an intermediate- to long-term basis. This arrangement is suitable for the export of capital goods. The lessor could be located in the exporting or importing country. Whether it is an operating or finance lease, the legal ownership of the asset remains with the lessor and only possession passes to the lessee. Under the operating lease, the lease rentals are not intended to amortize the capital outlay incurred by the lessor when the equipment was purchased. Instead, the capital outlay and profit are intended to be recovered through the re-leasing of the equipment and/or through its residual value on its eventual sale. It is not a method of financing the acquisition of the equipment, but a lease for a specified period. The lease is reflected in the balance sheet of the lessor and not the lessee. Under the finance lease, the lease rentals are intended to amortize the capital costs of acquisition as well as to provide profit. Usually, the lessee chooses the equipment to be leased and bears the cost of maintenance and insurance. The lease is reflected in the balance sheet of the lessee and not the lessor.

For businesses that need new equipment but lack the necessary resources or hard currency to purchase, leasing becomes an attractive option. It requires little or no down payment, and the equipment can be bought at the end of the lease agreement for a nominal price. Lease payments are tax deductible in many countries. Since such payments do not appear as liabilities in the financial statements, they preserve the lessee's financial position and do not reduce its ability to borrow for other reasons. Other advantages of leasing are that (1) one can lease up-to-date equipment that may be too expensive to purchase, and (2) the lessee can always trade in the old equipment in the event of obsolescence and obtain new even before the end of the lease. There are, however, certain disadvantages: (1) it may attract adverse tax consequences in certain countries, and (2) the cost of leasing is often higher than other financing methods.

CHAPTER SUMMARY

Major Changes in Small Business Financing

Technology, globalization, and deregulation

Determinants of Capital Needs and Financing Alternatives

Stage of evolution, ownership structure, and distribution channels

Internal Financing

Using one's own resources, retaining more profits in the business, and reducing accounts receivable and inventories

External Financing

Forms of External Financing

Debt or equity financing; short-term/intermediate/long-term financing; investment, inventory, or working capital financing

Sources of External Financing

Family and friends, banks (asset-based financing, lines of credit, personal and commercial loans, credit cards), Small Business Administration, finance companies, and equity sources

Financing by the Exporter

1. Open account: Payment is deferred for a specified period of time.
2. Consignment contract: Importer pays after merchandise is sold to a third party.

Financing by the Importer

1. Advance payment: Payment is before shipment is effected.
2. Progress payment: Payment is related to performance.

Financing by Third Parties

Short-Term Methods

1. Loan Secured by a foreign accounts receivable: Account receivable used as collateral to meet short-term financing needs.
2. Trade/banker's acceptance: A draft accepted by the importer is used as collateral to obtain financing.
3. Letter of credit: Transferable letter of credit (L/C), assignment of proceeds under an L/C, and a back-to-back L/C used to secure financing.
4. Factoring: An arrangement between a factoring concern and exporter whereby the factor purchases export receivables for a discount.

Intermediate- and Long-Term Methods

1. Buyer credit: Importer obtains a credit from a bank or financial institution to pay the exporter.
2. Forfaiting: Purchase of deferred debts arising from international sales contracts without rcourse to the exporter.
3. Export leasing: A firm purchases and exports capital equipment with a view to leasing.

Chapter 14

Government Export Financing Programs

Exporters prefer to be paid on or before shipment of the goods, whereas buyers want to delay payment until they have sold the merchandise. To expand export sales, many governments offer a wide choice of financing programs. Such assistance increases the exporter's credit line needed for corporate and domestic transactions, neutralizes financing as a factor, and creates a level playing field with competitors in other countries who also benefit from similar financing programs.

Programs are usually categorized as short-term (usually under two years), intermediate-term (usually two to five years), and long-term (usually over five years) financing. Government financing could be in the form of supplier credit or buyer credit. Supplier credits are extended to the buyer by the exporter; that is, the exporter arranges for government financing. Such credits also include a direct extension of credit by the exporter, as well as the latter's arrangement of financing from other private sources. Buyer's credits are extended to the buyer by parties other than the exporter. Banks, government agencies, or other private parties (domestic or foreign) could provide buyer credits. This chapter is primarily devoted to supplier or buyer credits that are extended by government agencies.

Government financing generally includes the provision of insurance or guarantees to exporters or lending institutions, as well as the extension of official credit, interest, or subsidies to the exporter or overseas customer. Either of these financing schemes may be combined in a single transaction. Some governments provide a whole range of services (e.g., guarantees, insurance, credit, etc.) while others provide some or all of these services, insofar as they are not readily available in the market.

The OECD (Organization for Economic Cooperation and Development) has developed guidelines on export credits for its members. These are intended to provide the institutional framework for an orderly export credit market, thus preventing an export credit race in which exporting countries compete on the basis of who provides the most favorable financing terms rather than on the basis of who provides the best-quality product at the lowest price. The guidelines provide for the following:

- A minimum of 15 percent of the contract price to be paid in cash
- Maximum repayment term of eight and a half years, with exceptions for poor countries
- Minimum interest rates for set periods of up to five, eight and a half, and ten years
- Gradual abolition of subsidized interest rates and adjustment of discount rates for aid loans to better reflect market realities
- The establishment of related conditions for certain sectors, including agriculture, that are not covered by the guidelines

EXPORT-IMPORT BANK OF THE UNITED STATES (EXIMBANK)

The Eximbank was created in 1934 and established under its present law in 1945, with the aim of assisting in the financing of U.S. export trade. It was originally established to finance exports to Europe after World War II. Eximbank's role in promoting U.S. exports is likely to be more significant now than in the past few decades because (1) the U.S. economy is more internationalized and exports constitute a growing share of the GNP, and (2) there has been a substantial increase in the volume of international trade and competition for export markets is quite intense.

Eximbank is intended to supplement, but not compete with, private capital. It has historically been active in areas in which the private sector has been reluctant to provide export financing. Eximbank has three main functions: (1) provide guarantees and export credit insurance so that exporters and their bankers give credit to foreign buyers, (2) provide competitive financing to foreign buyers, and (3) negotiate with other countries to reduce the level of subsidy in export credits (Eximbank, 1997a).

Over the last few years, Eximbank has focused on a broad range of critical areas, such as provision of greater support to small businesses, export promotion to developing nations, and promoting exports of environmentally beneficial goods and services. It has also been engaged in expanding project finance capabilities as well as in reducing trade subsidies of other governments through bilateral or multilateral negotiations.

Eximbank provides assistance to U.S. exporters of goods and/or services insofar as the exports include a minimum of 50 percent U.S. (local) content and are not military related. Its financing decision is determined, inter alia, upon an assessment of the borrower's capability to repay the loan (for Eximbank's other criteria for financing, see International Perspective 14.1). Eximbank offers four major export financing programs:

- Working capital loan guarantees for U.S. exporters
- Credit insurance
- Guarantees of commercial loans to foreign buyers
- Direct loans to foreign purchasers

International Perspective

14.1

**GENERAL EXIMBANK CRITERIA
FOR LOANS AND LOAN GUARANTEES**

Foreign Content Policy: To be eligible for support, items must be shipped from the United States and the foreign content (cost of foreign components incorporated in the item in the United States) must be less than 50 percent of the total cost to produce the item. In the case of U.S. items supplied to a foreign project under long-term program support, Eximbank support is available even though the U.S. items aggregate less than 50 percent of the total project cost (intermediate-term to long-term loans and guarantees).

Repayment Terms: Repayment usually begins about six months after shipment or project completion, and payments of principal and interest must be made semiannually. Applicable payment term for a transaction can be determined by (a) identifying the country group (I or II) in the list where the product is exported, (b) finding the standard term that applies to the country group and the contract price of your transaction, and (c) reviewing the terms in chart II and shorter/longer than standard terms.

Scope of Coverage: Eximbank's loans, guarantees, and intermediate-term insurance cover 85 percent of the contract price. The foreign buyer is required to make a 15 percent cash payment. Fees charged are based on the risk assessment of the foreign buyer or guarantor, the buyer's country, and the terms of the credit.

Interest Rates and Shipping: Interest rates and maximum maturity terms are subject to OECD guidelines. The lender sets the rate in guarantee programs, while loans are often negotiated at fixed rates. Eximbank supported sales of more than $10 million in loans or loan guarantees must be shipped in a vessel of U.S registry unless a waiver has been obtained by the foreign buyer from the U.S. Maritime Administration. This applies in the case of long-term financing programs.

Source: Eximbank, 1997a, pp. 1-3.

Working Capital Guarantee Program

The availability of adequate working capital is critical for the maintenance and expansion of a viable export-import business. Banks are often reluctant to make financing available because the businesses either have reached the borrowing limits set by their banks or do not have the necessary collateral. The working capital guarantee program is intended to encourage commercial lenders to make loans for various exports–related activities (see Figure 14.1). Such loans may be used for the purchase of raw materials and finished products for export, to pay for overhead, as well as to cover standby letters of credit, such as bid bonds, performance bonds, or payment guarantees (Eximbank, 1997b, c).

Exporters may apply to the Eximbank for a preliminary commitment for a guarantee. The lender also may apply directly for a final authorization. In the case of preliminary commitment, the Eximbank will outline the general terms and conditions under which it will provide the guarantee to the exporter, and this can be used to approach various lenders to secure the most attractive loan package. This commitment is valid for six months. The lender must apply for the final commitment. Applications for a loan amount below $833,333 are processed by the Small Business Administration. Guarantees may be approved for a single loan or a revolving line of credit. The major features of the working capital guarantee program are as follows.

Guarantee Coverage and Term of the Loan

In the event of default by the exporter, Eximbank will cover 90 percent of the principal of the loan and interest, up to the date of claim for payment, insofar as the lender has met all the terms and conditions of the guarantee agreement. Guaranteed loans generally have maturities of twelve months and are renewable.

FIGURE 14.1. Working Capital Guarantee Program

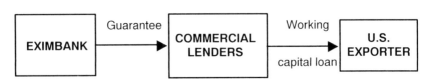

Collateral

Guaranteed loans are to be secured by collateral. Acceptable collateral may include export-related inventory, export-related accounts receivable, or other assets. Inventory and accounts receivable include goods purchased or sales generated by use of the guaranteed loan. For service companies, costs such as engineering, design, or allocable overhead may be treated as collateral.

Qualified Exporters and Lenders

Exporters must be domiciled in the United States (regardless of domestic/foreign ownership requirements), show a successful track record of past performance, including an operating history of at least one year, and have a positive net worth. Financial statements must show sufficient strength to accommodate the requested debt.

Any public or private lender may apply under the program. Eligibility is determined on many factors, including the lender's financial condition, knowledge of trade finance, and ability to manage asset-based loans. Lenders may be approved as priority lenders or delegated authority lenders. Approved lenders under the priority lender program submit final commitment applications to Eximbank and receive a decision within ten business days. The lender, prior to submission to Eximbank, must approve the loan application. However, approved delegated authority lenders are allowed to approve loans and receive a guarantee from Eximbank without having to submit individual applications for approval.

Export Credit Insurance Program (ECIP)

The purpose of the ECIP is to promote U.S. sales abroad by protecting exporters against loss in the event of default by a foreign buyer or debt arising from commercial or political risks. The policy also enables exporters to obtain financing more easily because, with prior Eximbank approval, the proceeds of the policy can be readily assigned to a financial institution as collateral. Eximbank offers a wide range of policies to accommodate many different insurance needs of exporters and financial institutions. For example, insurance policies may apply to shipments to one buyer or to many buyers, cover short-term (180 days or less) or intermediate-term (generally one to five years) credit, and provide comprehensive coverage for commercial as well as specific or all political risks. There are also policies specifically geared to small businesses that are beginning to export their goods or services (Small Business Policy, Small Business Environmental Policy, and the Umbrella Policy). Some export credit insurance program (ECIP) highlights include the following:

- *U.S. contents requirements:* To be eligible for support, the products sold must be produced in the United States. For short-term and intermediate-term sales, at least 50 percent of the value of the product must be of U.S. origin (excluding price markup). In the case of service exports, services must be performed by U.S.-based personnel or U.S. personnel temporally assigned in the host country.
- *Restrictions on sales:* ECIP may not be provided for exports destined for military applications (with some exceptions) or to communist nations unless it is determined by the president to be in the U.S. national interest.
- *Insurance programs under ECIP:* (1) Single-buyer/multibuyer policies and (2) policies for small businesses.
- *Other policies:* Other policies include Financial Institution Buyer Credit Policy, Bank Letter of Credit Policy, and Policies for Financing and Operating Leases.

Single-Buyer Versus Multibuyer Policy

Single-buyer policies insure short-term, intermediate-term, or combined (i.e., short and medium) -term sales to one buyer. The multibuyer policy, however, is intended to provide coverage for short-term export sales to many different buyers. Besides repayment terms, which typically range up to 180 days, the short-term single-buyer and short-term multiple-buyer policies have many similarities (see also Figure 14.2):

1. In both cases, eligible exports usually include consumables, agricultural commodities, raw materials, consumer durables, spare parts, and services.
2. Eligible exporters are U.S. firms or foreign companies doing business in the United States and foreign sales corporations controlled by U.S companies. Buyers must be creditworthy and located in an acceptable country. Only exporters may apply for both types of policies.
3. The risks covered include commercial and specified political risks. Commercial risks generally include buyers' insolvency or failure to pay when an obligation is due. Political risks include losses caused by war, revolution, cancellation of an export-import license, or inability to transfer money.

FIGURE 14.2. Single-Buyer and Multibuyer Policies

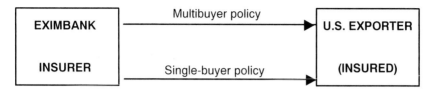

The intermediate-term single-buyer policy is intended to cover one-time or repetitive transactions. It covers sales of capital goods and services. Eligible policyholders/exporters may include financial institutions besides those mentioned in the case of short-term buyers. In other areas, such as risks covered, eligible buyers, and country restrictions, the intermediate-term single-buyer policy is identical to the short-term single, or multibuyer policy (see Figure 14.2).

Policies for Small Business Exporters

Eximbank offers a short-term insurance policy (Small Business Insurance Policy) that is intended to meet the credit requirements of small, less experienced exporters. The coverage is available for companies with average annual export credit sales of less than $3 million for the two years prior to application that meet the eligibility requirements for small business.

The Umbrella Policy allows administrators to act as intermediaries between Eximbank and their client in assisting the latter to obtain export credit insurance. The following entities may apply to be administrators under this policy: banks, export trading companies, insurance brokers, and export finance companies. An administrator must hold a current fidelity bond as well as error and omissions insurance policy. The program is suitable for small business exporters with no or limited experience in international trade and that are less familiar with the necessary paperwork and supervision of policy. The Small Business Environmental Policy insures sales of environmentally related goods and services. There are no restrictions on the level of export credit sales activity to qualify for the policy.

All three policies are identical in many areas, such as repayment terms, risk coverage, assignment of policy proceeds, and credit limits (see also Figure 14.3). Repayment terms range from 180 days for most products to 360 days for capital goods and certain consumer durables. They are one-year policies (renewable) insuring all short-term export credit sales. Risk coverage usually includes 100 percent political risk protection and 95 percent commercial risk protection. There is no annual commercial-risks first-

FIGURE 14.3. Policy for Small Business Exporters

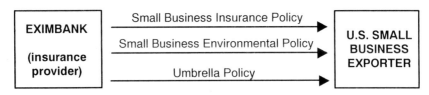

loss deductible (i.e., insured must absorb the first loss before making a valid claim for payment). Political-risk-only coverage is also available. Policy proceeds are assignable with prior approval. A special "hold harmless" assignment of proceeds makes financing of insured receivables quite attractive to banks. The assignment greatly improves assurance of payment to the assignee irrespective of most policy violations by the exporter. This is done within the limits of coverage and given that the assignee complies with its responsibilities under the assignment agreement. Experienced exporters may receive discretionary credit limits (DCLs). The DCL represents the highest insurance credit that could be extended by a U.S. exporter to a foreign buyer, at any given time, without obtaining approval from Eximbank in the form of a special buyer credit limit (SBCL). No DCLs are available under the Umbrella Policy; that is, the exporter must apply for a special buyer credit limit (SBCL) on each buyer through the administrator. The premium varies with each sale, according to repayment term and type of buyer.

Other Policies

Eximbank also provides other policies that serve the special needs of some U.S. exporters and financial institutions (see Figure 14.4). These include the Trade Association Policy, Financial Institution Buyer Credit Policy, Bank Letter of Credit Policy, and Policies for Financing or Operating Leases. The Trade Association Policy encourages associations to assist their members in the expansion of their exports. The individual association member is the insured party. However, the association helps members in obtaining and administering the insurance policy, thus relieving members of the burden of paperwork and other administrative duties. The association is responsible for obtaining approval for individual members as exporters under the policy, seeking buyer credit approvals, collecting premiums, reporting shipments, completing claim forms, and so on. The association generally holds a fidelity bond and an errors and omissions policy.

FIGURE 14.4. Other Policies for Exporters and Financial Institutions

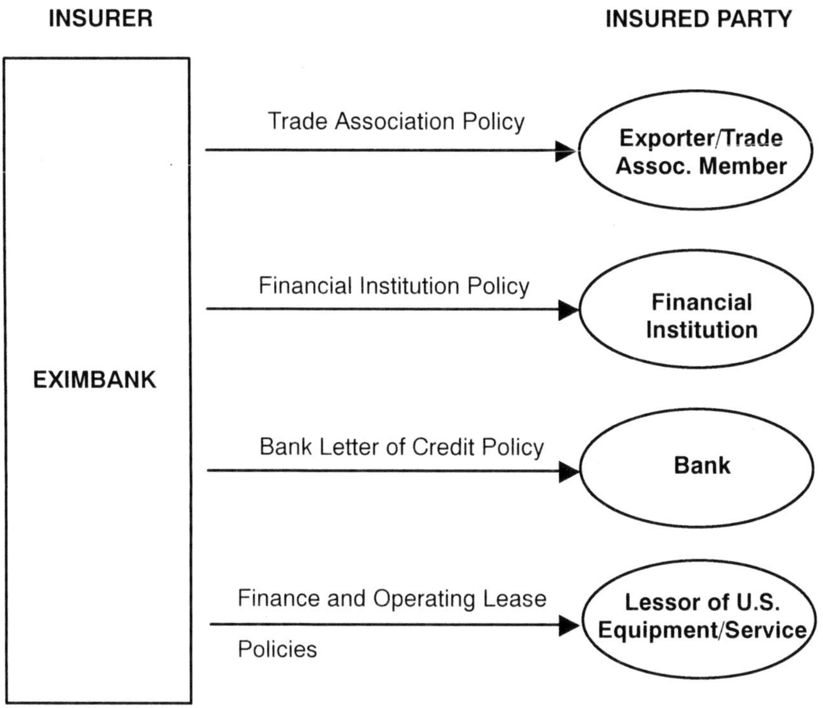

INSURER   **INSURED PARTY**

EXIMBANK	Trade Association Policy →	Exporter/Trade Assoc. Member
	Financial Institution Policy →	Financial Institution
	Bank Letter of Credit Policy →	Bank
	Finance and Operating Lease Policies →	Lessor of U.S. Equipment/Service

The Financial Institution Buyer Credit Policy protects financial institutions against losses on short-term direct-credit loans or reimbursement loans to foreign entities for importing U.S. goods and services. The direct-buyer credit loan is a loan extended to a foreign entity by a financial institution for the importation of U.S. goods and services; the reimbursement loan is the financial institution's reimbursement of a buyer's payments to U.S. suppliers. The policy covers against commercial and political risks.

The Bank Letter of Credit Policy is intended to encourage banks to support U.S. exports by protecting them against loss on irrevocable letters of credit issued by foreign banks for the purchase of U.S. goods. This provides coverage against the failure of a foreign financial institution (the issuing bank) to honor its letter of credit to the insured bank. The policy can only be used with irrevocable letters of credit and for eligible exports. The policy covers against commercial and political risks.

Financing and Operating Leases are two separate lease policies that are intended to insure both the stream of lease payments and the fair market value of the leased products. The major difference between financing and operating leases is that in the case of the former, little residual value remains in the leased product and ownership is transferred to the lessee at the end of the lease, and in the case of an operating lease, a residual value remains at the end of the lease and the lessor repossesses, sells, or otherwise disposes of the product as it sees fit. The title to the leased product, which can be either new or used equipment, must be maintained by the lessor who takes out the insurance policy. The policies cover against political and commercial risks or against political risks only.

Guarantees

Eximbank guarantees provide repayment protection for private-sector loans to creditworthy buyers of U.S. exports (see Figure 14.5). The program covers 100 percent of the commercial and political risks (85 percent of U.S. contract amount). The foreign buyer is required to make at least a 15 percent cash payment. Exports supported under this program are capital equipment, services, and projects, and the loan guarantees are offered for intermediate- and long-term sales. Guarantees of $10 million or less do not require shipment on U.S.-registered vessels. The credit may be for any amount. The guarantee is unconditional and transferable (see Figure 14.5).

There is also a special coverage or guarantee (Credit Guarantee Facility) extended by Eximbank to U.S or foreign lenders on lines of credit to foreign banks or large foreign buyers (see Figure 14.6). The products supported, as well as the coverage and terms, are identical with the guarantee program just discussed. The facility can finance small transactions with minimal paperwork. When a financing institution is extending a loan of $10 million or less to a borrower with Eximbank's guarantee, Eximbank requires only that a note be issued in favor of the financing institution; that is, a credit agreement is not often required.

FIGURE 14.5. Guarantees

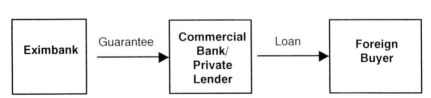

FIGURE 14.6. Credit Guarantee Facility

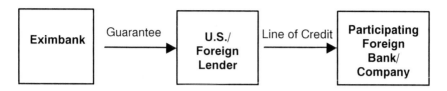

Direct Loans Program

Under this program, Eximbank provides a fixed-rate loan directly to creditworthy foreign buyers for the purchase of U.S. capital equipment, projects, and related services (see Figure 14.7). The loan covers up to 85 percent of the U.S. export value. The buyer is; however, required to make a cash payment for the difference, that is, 15 percent of the value. The loan is often used by buyers when the financed portion exceeds $10 million. A loan agreement as well as shipment on U.S.-registered vessels is required. The program supports intermediate- and long-term sales. Transactions normally range from five to ten years, depending on the export value, the product, the importing country, and the terms offered by the competition.

FIGURE 14.7. Direct Loan Program

Project Finance Program

This program supports exports of U.S. capital equipment and related services for projects whose repayment depends on project cash flows, as defined in the contract. It is suitable for major U.S. suppliers and sponsors that do not have adequate access to bank or government guarantees. There is no limit on the size of the transaction. Any combination of either direct loans or guarantees for commercial bank loans, with political-risk-only or comprehensive coverage, are available. The basic coverage and terms are as follows:

1. The foreign buyer makes a 15 percent cash payment. Direct loan and/or guarantee covers up to 85 percent of the U.S. contract amount.
2. Political-risk-only coverage is available during construction and for postcompletion financing.
3. Repayment terms are subject to OECD guidelines.
4. No coverage is provided for precompletion commercial risks.
5. Approvals are subject to Eximbank's environmental procedures and guidelines. (For program selection guide, see Table 14.1.)

TABLE 14.1. Program Selection Guide

PRE-EXPORT	POST-EXPORT		
	Spare Parts/ Consumables/ Raw Materials	Capital Goods	
		Sales of $10 million or less	Sales of Over $10 million
Need: Cash flow support	Finance and protect receivables/extend credit to foreign buyers/cash flow support	Extend credit to foreign buyers/ competition for markets	Extend credit to foreign buyers/competition for markets
Policy or Program • Working capital guarantee • Small business programs (assignment of proceeds)	• Short-term multibuyer (experienced exporters) • Small business program (qualified exporters) • Short-term single-buyer (all exporters) • Bank L/C (banks) • Financial institution buyer credit (banks)	• Intermediate-term insurance • Leasing • Guarantee • Credit guarantee facility	• Leasing • Guarantee • Direct loan • Project finance

Source: Eximbank, 1997a, pp. 2-10.

SMALL BUSINESS ADMINISTRATION

The Small Business Administration (SBA) also provides a few programs for U.S. exporters. To qualify for the programs, applicants must meet the definition of a small business under SBA's size standards and other eligibility requirements. The SBA Act defines an eligible small business as one that is independently owned and operated and not dominant in its field of operation. It has established size standards that define the maximum size of an eligible small business. The following represent general guidelines to determine a small business:

Industry	Maximum Size
Retail and service	$3.5 to $13.5 million
Construction	$7.0 to $17.0 million
Agriculture	$0.5 to $3.5 million
Wholesale	No more than 100 employees
Manufacturing	500 to 1,500 employees

Some of the SBA programs that are intended to promote exports are detailed in the following material.

Export Working Capital Program Loans (EWCP)

The EWCP is a combined effort of the SBA and Eximbank to provide short-term working capital to U.S. exporters. To be processed by the SBA, loan guarantee requests must be equal to or less than $833,333. Loan requests greater than that amount are processed by Eximbank. The applicant must be in business for one year (not necessarily exporting) at the time of application. The agency can guarantee up to 80 percent of loans of $100,000 or less, and up to 75 percent of loans above $100,000 (generally up to a maximum guarantee amount of $750,000). The loan may be used for purchase of inventory or raw material or for the manufacture of a product. A borrower must give SBA a first security interest equal to 100 percent of the EWCP guaranty amount. Collateral must be located in the United States (Eximbank, 1997b, c; Tuller, 1994; Wells and Dulat, 1996).

International Trade Loan Program

This program assists small businesses that are already engaged or preparing to engage in international trade and those which are adversely affected by import competition. The SBA can guarantee as much as $1,250,000 in combined working capital (provided under the EWCP) and facilities and equipment loans. No more than $250,000 can be used for working capital. The guarantee percentage and amount is similar to the EWCP. Collateral is required and must be located in the United States.

In both programs, the SBA provides loan guarantees only if the exporter is unable to obtain financing from private sources without its support.

OVERSEAS PRIVATE INVESTMENT CORPORATION

The Overseas Private Investment Corporation (OPIC) is a wholly owned U.S. government corporation that supports American private investment in developing nations and emerging-market economies. OPIC programs are presently available for new and expanding businesses in some 140 countries worldwide. The program has generated positive net income for every year of operation since its inception in 1971 and has accumulated reserves of over $2.6 billion. Since 1971, OPIC has supported investments worth nearly $100 billion and generated about $43 billion in U.S. exports. Although OPIC is primarily intended to promote U.S. investment abroad, it has played a significant role in expanding American exports. OPIC-backed projects in 1996, for example, were estimated to generate $9.6 billion in U.S. exports and to create or support about 30,000 jobs. A recent OPIC-supported power project in Indonesia, for example, is expected to purchase more than $1 billion in U.S. equipment and supplies and to support more than 3,000 American jobs. OPIC-backed investments in these countries are also likely to depend on a constant supply of U.S. components, supplies, or raw materials. In short, OPIC helps developing nations expand their economies and become viable markets for U.S. goods and services (U.S. Department of Commerce, 1990).

OPIC assists American investors through four principal activities designed to promote overseas investment and to reduce associated risks. They are detailed as follows.

Financing of Business Through Loans and Loan Guarantees

OPIC provides intermediate- and long-term project financing through loans and loan guarantees in countries where conventional financial institutions often are reluctant or unable to provide financing. All projects considered for financing must be commercially and financially sound and managed by people with a proven track record of success in the same or related business. OPIC, for example, carefully reviews whether the project will generate adequate cash flow to pay all operational costs, to service all debt, and provide owners with an adequate return on their investments. The proceeds of OPIC financing may be spent for capital goods and services in the United States, the host country, or other less-developed countries. The following are the major features of the program.

Ownership

Projects wholly owned by governments are not eligible. OPIC finances overseas ventures wholly owned by U.S. companies or joint ventures in which the U.S. investor has at least 25 percent equity. As a rule, at least 51 percent of the voting shares of the overseas venture must be held by the private sector. Financing is provided in cases in which the government holds majority ownership, insofar as management remains in private hands.

OPIC Participation

OPIC assists in designing and coordinating the financial plan with other lenders and investors. OPIC usually participates by providing up to 50 percent of the total cost of a new venture. The percentage is often higher in the case of an expansion of an existing business.

Financing and Loan Terms

For projects sponsored by U.S. small businesses or cooperatives, financing is provided through direct loans ranging from $2 million to $10 million. Loan guarantees are often used for large-scale projects and range from $10 million to $200 million. The guarantees are issued to U.S financial institutions that are more than 50 percent owned by U.S. citizens, corporations, or partnerships. Foreign corporations that are at least 95 percent U.S. owned are also eligible. Funding sources include commercial banks, pension funds, and insurance companies. OPIC loans typically provide for a final maturity of five to fifteen years, following a certain grace period during which only interest is payable. For loan guarantees, OPIC charges the borrower a guarantee fee that may include an income-sharing provision.

Providing Support to Private Investments

OPIC provides finance to a number of privately owned and managed investment funds so that these funds extend equity capital to facilitate business formation and expansion. Some funds invest primarily in small companies, whereas others invest in larger projects. Participation in equity ownership ranges from 5 to 40 percent of the company's portfolio. To be eligible for funding, the overseas company must have a significant business connection with the U.S. economy and a positive impact on U.S. employment, the environment, and workers' rights. OPIC-supported investment funds presently operate in Africa, East Asia, South America, and Eastern Europe.

Insuring Investments Against a Broad Range of Political Risks

OPIC offers many programs to insure investments in developing nations against political risk. The following risks are covered:

1. *Currency inconvertibility:* This is the inability to convert profits, debt services, and other remittances from local currency into U.S. dollars.
2. *Expropriation:* This involves loss of investment due to expropriation, nationalization, or confiscation by the host government.
3. *Political violence:* This relates to loss of assets or income due to war, revolution, civil war, terrorism, and so forth. An investor may purchase a separate policy for loss of business, loss of assets, or both. Coverage is available for new or existing investments. Special insurance programs are available for the following sectors: financial institutions, leases, oil and gas projects, natural resource projects, contractors, and exporters.

OPIC insurance is available to citizens of the United States, businesses created under U.S. law with majority ownership by U.S. citizens, and foreign companies with a minimum ownership of 95 percent equity by U.S citizens.

Engaging in Outreach Activities

This is mainly designed to inform the U.S. business community of investment opportunities abroad.

Investments by OPIC clients may take many forms, including equity investments, loans, service contracts, leases, joint ventures, franchises, and other arrangements. In the event that the project is foreign owned, OPIC insures the portion of the project (investment) made by the U.S. investor. OPIC does not participate in projects subject to performance requirements that would substantially undercut U.S trade benefits from the investment (e.g., local content, maximum import and minimum export requirements imposed by host states).

PRIVATE EXPORT FUNDING CORPORATION

The Private Export Funding Corporation (PEFCO) is a major source of capital for intermediate- and long-term fixed-rate loans for U.S. exports. It acts as a supplemental lender to traditional sources by making loans available for foreign purchasers of U.S. goods and services.

PEFCO is a private corporation owned by banks and industrial and financial companies. It works closely with Eximbank. Eximbank, for example, unconditionally guarantees all PEFCO loans. PEFCO often lends in conjunction with one or more commercial banks and will cover up to

85 percent of the export value. PEFCO generally does not make loans of less than $1 million, and this makes it suitable for high-cost purchases, such as aircraft, industrial plants, and so on, that require large amounts of money for extended terms. PEFCO has a program for small business exporters to provide short-term working capital through private lenders or directly to small business exporters as a lender of last resort.

U.S. DEPARTMENT OF AGRICULTURE

The U.S. Department of Agriculture (USDA) provides financial support for U.S. agricultural exports through various programs, such as the following:

- GSM-102 program provides credit guarantees for up to three years and will cover 98 percent of the export value and up to 2.8 percentage points of interest on the guaranteed value.
- GSM-103 program offers credit guarantees with terms of greater than three but not more than ten years. Both guarantees cover commercial and noncommercial risks.
- Public Law 480 authorizes U.S. government financing of sales of U.S. agricultural products to friendly countries on concessional terms.

In addition to government programs, more than a dozen state governments have introduced export financing programs. Some of the programs implemented in California and Illinois have the following essential features: (1) state-funded loan guarantee programs, (2) preshipment and postshipment assistance in the form of loans to lenders and loan guarantees to exporters and their banks, and (3) state agency acting as a delivery agent for Eximbank programs.

CHAPTER SUMMARY

Eximbank

Eximbank is an idependent agency of the U.S. government, the purpose of which is to aid in financing and to facilitate trade between the United States and other countries. The bank, which is expected to be self-sustaining (except for the initial capital of $1 billion to start operations), makes loans and guarantees with reasonable assurance of repayment. It complements private sources of finance.

Working Capital Guarantee Program

This enables exporters to meet critical pre-export financing needs, such as inventory build up or marketing. Eximbank will guarantee 90 percent of the loan provided by a qualified lender. The guarantee has a maturity of twelve months and is renewable.

Export Credit Insurance Program

A wide range of policies to accommodate different insurance needs. Its major features are: U.S. content requirements, restrictions on sales destined for military use and to communist nations.

1. Short-term single-buyer policies: These cover a single sale or repetitive sales over a one-year period to a single buyer. They provide coverage against political and commercial risks. They support products such as consumables, raw materials, spare parts, low-cost capital goods, etc.
2. Short-term multibuyer policies: These cover short-term export sales to many different buyers against political and commercial risks. Product coverage is the same as above.
3. Small business policy (graduate to short-term multibuyer when annual export credit sales exceed $3 million): This short-term policy covers small businesses with average annual export credit sales of less than $3 million. It provides coverage against political and commercial risks.
4. Small business environmental policy: This short-term policy provides coverage to small businesses that export environmental goods and services against political and commercial risks.
5. Umbrella policy: This short-term policy covers small businesses against political and economic risks. Insurance brokers, state development agencies, etc., will administer the policy on behalf of the small business. Product coverage is similar to that of short-term single buyer policies.
6. Trade association policy: A trade association administers the policy on behalf of members.
7. Financial institution buyer credit policy: This protects financial institutions against losses on short-term direct credit loans or reimbursement loans to foreign buyers of U.S. goods and services.
8. The bank letter of credit policy: This provides coverage against the failure of a foreign financial institution (the issuing bank) to honor its letter of credit to the insured bank.

9. Financing and operating lease policy: These two separate leases provide coverage against political and/or commercial risks—policies protect lessor against loss of a stream of lease payments and fair market value of the leased product.

Guarantees

The program provides repayment protection for private-sector loans to creditworthy buyers of U.S. goods and services. There is also special coverage for U.S. or foreign lenders on lines of credit extended to foreign banks or foreign buyers.

Direct Loan Program

This is an intermediate/long-term loan provided to creditworthy foreign buyers for the purchase of U.S. capital goods and services.

Small Business Administration (SBA)

The SBA provides certain programs for small business exporters.

Export Working Capital

This guarantees short-term working capital loans to U.S. small business exporters.

International Trade Loan Program

Guarantees loans to small businesses that are already engaged or plan to engage in international trade as well as those which are adversely affected by import competition.

Overseas Private Investment Corporation (OPIC)

This self-supporting agency of the U.S. government insures U.S. investors against political and commercial risks and provides financing through loans and loan guarantees.

Private Export Funding Corporation (PEFCO)

This private corporation works in conjunction with Eximbank in the financing of foreign purchases of U.S. goods and services. PEFCO loans are guaranteed by Eximbank.

Department of Agriculture

The USDA provides financial support for export of U.S. agricultural products through GSM-102, GSM-103, and Public Law 480.

State and Local Export Financing Programs

States provide different programs to expand exports: loans, loan guarantees. They also act as delivery agents for Eximbank programs.

SECTION VI:
EXPORT REGULATIONS
AND TAX INCENTIVES

Chapter 15

Regulations and Policies Affecting Exports

EXPORT LICENSING AND ADMINISTRATION

Export Controls

Governments use export controls for a variety of reasons. Such controls are often intended to achieve certain desired political and economic objectives. The first U.S. export control was introduced in 1775 when Continental Congress outlawed the export of goods to Great Britain. Since then, the United States has restricted exports to certain countries through legislation such as the Embargo Act, Trading with the Enemy Act, the Neutrality Act, and the Export Control Act.

The Export Control Act of 1949 represents the first comprehensive export control program enacted in peacetime. Export controls prior to this time were almost exclusively devoted to the prohibition or curtailment of arms exports (arms embargoes). The 1949 legislation was primarily intended to curtail the export of certain commodities to communist nations during the cold war era. Export controls were thus allowed for reasons of national security, foreign policy, and short supply. Given America's dominant economic position in the postwar era, the country provided leadership in international economic relations and pursued an active foreign policy (Stenger, 1984; Moskowitz, 1996).

In 1969, the often stringent and far-reaching restrictions were curtailed, and the new law (Export Administration Act, 1969) attempted to balance the need for export controls with a recognition of the adverse effects of an overly comprehensive export control system on the country's economy. This came at a time when the United States was losing ground to other nations in economic performance, such as balance of trade, exports, and so on. The overvalued dollar and inflation, for example, had adversely affected its competitiveness in foreign markets and shrank its trade surplus from $6.8 billion in 1964 to a mere $400 million in 1969. The promotion of exports was considered essential to improving the country's declining trade surplus and overall competitiveness, as well as to reducing growing unemployment. The general trend in 1969, and thereafter, has been to ease and/or strengthen the position of exporters and increase the role of Congress in implementing export control policy. Some examples are as follows:

1. The Equal Export Opportunity Act of 1972 curtailed the use of export controls if the product (that is subject to such restrictions) was available from sources outside the United States in comparable quality and quantity. This was because export controls would be ineffective if certain commodities were available from foreign sources. The 1977 amendment prohibited the president from imposing export controls without providing adequate evidence with regard to its importance to U.S. national security interests. In the event that the president decided to prohibit or control exports, the law required him to negotiate with other countries to eliminate foreign availability.

    The scope of presidential authority to regulate U.S. foreign transactions, including the imposition of export controls, was restricted to wartime only. A statute (the International Emergency Economic Powers Act, 50 U.S. Code 1701 4 seq.) was also passed to regulate presidential powers in the area of export controls during national emergencies. As of 1998, restrictions based on national emergencies have been imposed against Angola, Iraq, Libya, North Korea, Iran, Haiti, and Yugoslavia. In short, the president can impose export controls outside emergency and wartime periods only upon extensive review and consultation with Congress.

2. In 1977, Congress introduced limitations on the power of the executive branch to prohibit or curtail agricultural exports. Any prohibition of such exports was considered ineffective without the approval of Congress by concurrent resolution.

3. The 1979 Export Administration Act (EAA) also emphasized the important contribution of exports to the U.S. economy and acknowledged the necessity of balancing the need for trade and exports and national security interests. The law also gave legal effect to the agreement of the Coordinating Committee for Multilateral Export Controls (COCOM). COCOM was established in 1949 to coordinate export controls of technology to communist countries. It was dissolved in 1994.

4. The 1985 amendments to the Export Administration Act further restricted the power of the president to impose foreign policy controls that interfere with contracts entered into before the decision to restrict exports, except under very specific circumstances. Congress also established validated licenses for multiple exports, allowing exporters to make successive shipments of the same goods under a single license, waived licensing requirements for certain low-tech goods exports to COCOM nations, and shortened by one-third the time period for issuing licenses for exports to non-COCOM members. In view of certain international incidents, such as the downing of the Korean aircraft by the former Soviet Union, the law, however, tightened export controls on the acquisition of critical military goods and technology by the former Soviet Union and its allies.

Current Developments in Export Controls

Export controls were originally intended to be used against former communist countries. However, with the end of the cold war, no longer was there a clearly defined, single adversary, and it became necessary to adjust the system of export controls to take into account the new reality in international relations. Export controls are now primarily aimed at, inter alia, restricting a narrow range of transactions that could assist in the development of weapons of mass destruction by certain irresponsible countries. Thus, the control system essentially focuses on a small group of critical goods and technology, on specific end uses and end users, in addition to certain "reckless" nations that must be stopped from acquiring weapons of mass destruction. In view of these developments, significant changes have been made in the implementation of the export control system.

Liberalization of Outdated Controls

There has been substantial liberalization of controls on high-performance computers, semiconductors, chemicals, beta-test software, telecommunication equipment, and so on. The government has developed a Special Comprehensive License (SCL) that allows experienced, high-volume exporters to export a broad range of items. The SCL, which was introduced in lieu of special licenses, allows exportation of all commodities (except those controlled for missile technology) to all destinations. There are, however, exceptions for embargoed countries and those which support terrorism. As the list of controlled products, technologies, and countries is significantly reduced, the number of license applications has dropped from about 50,000 in 1991 to less than 10,000 in 1996. In the area of computers and telecommunications, for example, such liberalization freed over $42 billion in exports from the requirement of advance government approval.

Simplifications and Efficiency in the Control Process

The classification of general and validated licenses was dropped. Under the present system, there are two categories: exports for which licenses are required or exports for which licenses are not required. No license is required unless it is expressly stated under the regulations.

Average license processing time has been reduced from forty days (for referred cases) in 1994 to less than thirty days in 1998. Cases that are not referred to other departments are now processed in about ten days.

Strengthening of the Multilateral Regime

An effective system of export controls cannot be sustained without the cooperation of other exporting countries. So far, multilateral agreements have established controls on exports of conventional arms and sensitive dual-use equipment (Wassenaar Agreement, 1996), chemical and biological weapons (Australia Group Agreement, 1985), and missile technology regime (1987).

Export Administration Regulations

Administration and Purpose of Export Controls

The Export Administration Regulations (EAR) are designed to implement the Export Administration Act (EAA) of 1979 and subsequent amendments. The EAR is administered by the U.S. Department of Commerce, Bureau of Export Administration (BXA), under laws relating to the control of certain exports, re-exports and activities. The EAR is not permanent legislation. When it lapsed, presidential executive orders under the Emergency Powers Act directed and authorized the continuation of the EAR. The regulations also implement antiboycott law provisions.

The core of the export control provisions of the EAR concerns exports from the United States. However, the term 'exports' has been given broad meaning to include activities other than exports or to apply to transactions outside the United States. The scope of EAR covers the following:

- Exports from the United States.
- Re-exports by any party of commodities, software, or technology exported from the United States.
- Foreign products that are the direct products of technology exported from the United States.
- U.S. person activities: The EAR restricts the involvement of "U.S. persons," that is, U.S. firms or individuals, from exporting foreign-origin items or from providing services that may contribute to the proliferation of weapons of mass destruction. The regulations also restrict technical assistance by U.S. persons with respect to encryption commodities or software.

Export controls are primarily imposed for the following reasons: (1) to protect national security; (2) to further foreign policy goals such as human rights, antiterrorism, and regional stability or to implement unilateral or international sanctions, such as those imposed by the United Nations or the Organization of American States; (3) to prevent the proliferation of weapons of mass destruction, such as nuclear weapons technology, which is often maintained as part of multilateral control arrangements; and (4) to prevent exports that would excessively drain scarce natural resources (e.g., export of some crude oil and other petroleum products or unprocessed western red cedar).

Determining License Requirements

The Bureau of Export Administration is the primary licensing agency for dual-use exports. The term dual use distinguishes items (i.e., commercial items with military applications) covered by EAR from those covered by the regulations of certain other export licensing agencies, such as the Departments of State and Defense. Although dual use is often employed to refer to the entire scope of the EAR, the EAR also applies to some items that have solely civilian uses. It is also important to note that the export of certain goods is subject to the jurisdiction of other agencies, such as the Food and Drug Administration (drugs and medical devices), the Department of State (defense articles), and the Nuclear Regulatory Commission (nuclear materials).

.   The following steps are helpful in determining whether a potential U.S. exporter needs a license for a product or service.

Step 1: Is the transaction subject to EAR? The potential exporter should determine whether the item or activity is subject to the exclusive jurisdiction of another federal agency. If this is the case, there is no need to comply with the EAR; the exporter should comply with the regulations of the particular agency. Publicly available technology and software, phonograph records, magazines, and so on, are also excluded from the scope of the EAR.

Transactions subject to EAR include all items in the United States (regardless of their country of origin), U.S.-origin items anywhere in the world, foreign products with U.S. content exceeding certain minimum levels, and certain foreign commodities produced using U.S. technology or software. Exports/re-exports to certain denied parties are also subject to EAR.

Step 2: Is an export license required? A small percentage of exports and re-exports subject to the EAR require a license from the Department of Commerce, Bureau of Export Administration (BXA). License requirements are dependent upon an item's product classification, which is based on its technical characteristics, destination, end use, end user, and other activities of the end user.

- *Product classification:* All commodities, technology, or software subject to the licensing authority of the BXA are included in the Commerce Control List (CCL).

  Individual items are identified on the CCL by an Export Control Classification Number (ECCN). To classify a product or service, it is important to review the general characteristics of the item. This will usually lead to the appropriate category on the CCL and then to the specific ECCN based on its particular characteristics and function. It will also help determine whether a product or service is subject to the export licensing authority of the Department of Commerce and/or other agencies.

  If the potential exporter is not completely certain of the export licensing jurisdiction for an item, a request can be made for a commodity jurisdiction determination. Such determination could also be requested if an item has been incorrectly classified and should be transferred to another agency.

- *Destination of the product/service:* If the product or service is listed on the CCL and the country chart, then a license is required for exports to that country. The country chart allows one to determine if a license is needed to export or re-export an item to a particular destination. There are only two instances in which the country chart cannot be used for this purpose: (1) when items are controlled for short-supply reasons, since such matters are governed by self-contained regulations, and (2) when items under all or certain entries are subject to license requirements for all or specific destinations. A license is required for embargoed destinations, such as Cuba or Libya, with respect to all exports of items listed on the CCL.

- *Prohibited end uses and end users:* The EAR requires an exporter to submit an individual validated license application if the latter knows that the export (which otherwise is exempt from licensing requirements) is for end uses involving nuclear, chemical, and biological weapons (NCBW) in named destinations listed in the regulations. There is a provision against exports without a license to certain end users involved in the export of such items. A license is required for exports or re-exports to certain entities that have been determined to present an unacceptable risk of diversion of export products to developing weapons of mass destruction or the missiles that deliver those weapons. The 1997 list of such entities, for example, includes the All Russian Scientific Research Institute of Technical Physics, Bhaba Atomic Research Center in India, Chinese Academy of Engineering Physics, Pakistan Institute for Nuclear Science and Technology, and Ben Gurion University in Israel (for computers between 2,000 and 7,000 million theoretical operations per second [Mtops]).*
- *Conduct of U.S. persons:* Is the transaction or activity by a US person in any way supportive of known prohibited proliferation activities (NCBW)? If the answer is in the affirmative, the transaction or activity is prohibited without a license.
- *In-transit shipments:* A transaction for exports or re-exports that involves an in-transit shipment through certain destinations (former and current communist countries) is prohibited without a license.
- *Violation of EAR:* Does the export transaction involve a violation of the EAR? If yes, the transaction is prohibited.

Step 3: Are there exceptions to the license requirements? A "license exception" is an authorization that allows a party to export or re-export an item that would otherwise require a validated license. If the ECCN for the item and the country chart does not show an "X," no export license is required. The availability of license exception is considered when both columns (item and country chart) indicate that a license is required for the shipment. License exceptions are permitted for certain export transactions that involve shipment of the following items: items of limited value (LVS); civil end users (CIV); temporary imports, exports, and re-exports (TMP); technology and software (TSU); gift parcels and humanitarian donations (GFT).

---

*The U.S. government, however, intends to update the regulations by raising the threshold for computers subject to export controls. This is because powerful computers exceeding the capabilities of existing export control thresholds are widely available from non-U.S. sources.

Step 4: Applying for an export license. The Bureau of Export Adminis-tration provides formal classification for a product or service, advisory opinion, or licensing decision upon review of a completed application submitted in writing or electronically (for basic application guidelines, see International Perspective 15.3). Even though it is the applicant's responsi-bility to classify the export, the BXA could be requested to provide infor-mation on whether the item is subject to the EAR and, if so, its correct ECCN. In addition to classification requests, potential applicants could also seek advisory opinions on whether a license is required or likely to be granted for a particular transaction. Such opinions, however, do not bind the BXA from issuing a license in the future.

Step 5: Destination control statement, shipper's export declaration, and record keeping. A Destination Control Statement (DCS) is intended to prevent items licensed for export from being diverted while in transit or thereafter. A typical DCS reads as follows:

> These commodities, technology, or software were exported from the United States in accordance with the Export Administration Regula-tions for ultimate destination (name of country). Diversion contrary to U.S. law is prohibited.

International Perspective

15.1

EXPORTING MEDICAL ITEMS TO CUBA

All exports of medical items to Cuba require a specific license from the BXA unless the transaction qualifies for a license exception.

Exports that are eligible for a license exception:

- Gift parcels (GFT) of low value to an individual or a religious, charitable, or educational organization in Cuba for the use of the recipient or the re-cipient's immediate family. Each parcel may not exceed $200.00 in retail value.
- Personal effect (BAG): personal items can be taken for one's own use.

Exports requiring an export license:

- Donations of medicines to nongovernmental organizations
- All other donations and commercial sales
- Temporary exports of demonstration items

A DCS must be entered on all documents covering (1) exports under license (including the special comprehensive license), (2) exports under certain license exceptions, and (3) exports requiring no license because the reason for control of the item is national security or nonproliferation. The DCS must be shown on all copies of the bill of lading, the air waybill, and the commercial invoice. However, a DCS is not required for exports/re-exports from abroad to approved destinations.

Even though there are a few exemptions, submission of a Shipper's Export Declaration (SED) to the U.S. government is generally required under the EAR. Information on the SED, such as value of shipment, quantity, and so on, is also used by the Census Bureau for statistical purposes. The exporter or the authorized forwarding agent submits the SED, which includes information such as criteria under which the item is exported (e.g., license exception, no license required, license number and expiration date), ECCN, and other relevant information.

The exporter is required to keep records for every export transaction for a period of five years from the date of export. The records to be retained include contracts, invitation to bid, books of account, financial records, restrictive trade practices, and boycott documents or reports.

Sanctions and Violations

The enforcement of the EAR is the responsibility of the U.S. Customs Service (Department of the Treasury) and the Office of Export Enforcement (Department of Commerce). There are criminal and administrative penalties for persons who violate the EAR. Individuals or companies who violate the EAR could be subject to fines of up to $100,000 for each violation, seizure of goods intended for export/re-export, or denial of export/re-export privileges by placing them on the denied persons list.

The EAR also provides certain indicators to help exporters recognize and report a possible violation. It reminds exporters to look for the following in export transactions:

- If one of the parties to the transaction has a name or address that is similar to an entity on the U.S. Department of Commerce's list of denied persons.
- If the transaction has "red flags," that is, the customer or purchasing agent is reluctant to offer information about the end user of the item or the product's capabilities do not fit the buyer's line of business, delivery dates are vague, or routine installation is declined by customer.

International Perspective

15.2

BASIC GUIDELINES
WITH RESPECT TO LICENSE APPLICATIONS

Applicant to be Subject to U.S. Jurisdiction: A license application to export items from the United States may be made only by a person subject to the jurisdiction of the United States. The importer's agent or other person subject to U.S. jurisdiction could be accepted as applicant and exporter.

Disclosure of Facts: The applicant is required to make a complete disclosure of all parties to the transaction and other relevant facts pertaining to the export.

Items on License Applications: It is recommended to limit items on each license application to those which are similar and/or related. There are additional requirements for the export of certain items such as chemicals, digital computers, nuclear proliferation items, or in-transit shipments.

Multiple Shipments: A license application need not be limited to a single shipment but may represent a reasonable estimate of items to be shipped throughout the validity of the license. A new application needs to be submitted prior to the expiration of the current license to ensure uninterrupted shipping.

Emergency Processing: A request for emergency processing could be made to the BXA explaining the reasons for such action. This procedure does not apply to SCLs for which multiple licenses will be required over a short period of time. Such licenses are granted only after extensive evaluation by the BXA.

Supporting Documents for License Applications: License applications not exempt from accompanying documentary requirements must often be supported by sufficient written information concerning the disposition of the items intended for export and re-export.

ANTIBOYCOTT REGULATIONS

The U.S. antiboycott provisions of the Export Administration Act prohibit U.S. firms from participating in foreign boycotts or embargoes not authorized by the U.S. government. Even though this law was primarily aimed at the Arab boycott against Israel, it prevents U.S. firms from being used to implement foreign policies of other nations that are inconsistent or contrary to U.S. policy. The law requires companies to report boycott-related requests by other nations and imposes a range of sanctions in the

---

| **International Perspective** |

15.3

AUTOMATED SERVICES

ELAIN (Export License Application and Information Network): ELAIN allows exporters to submit license applications electronically to the BXA.

When the application is approved without conditions, STELA allows exporters to ship their goods without the need to wait for a formal letter from the BXA.

STELA (System for Tracking Export License Applications): STELA is an automated voice response system that provides applicants with the status of their license and product classification applications.

ERIC (Electronic Request for Item Classification): This allows exporters to submit commodity classification requests electronically to the BXA.

---

event of violations. In February 1998, for example, a New Orleans shipping agent agreed to pay penalties totaling $12,000 for alleged violations of the antiboycott law. The transactions involved a sale to Lebanon in 1993 in which the agent agreed to decline to do business with ships blacklisted by the countries that participate in the Arab League's boycott of Israel. The company also furnished information about another company's business relationships with such blacklisted ships in violation of the regulations. International Paper Company, a Memphis-based manufacturer and exporter of paper and paper products also agreed to pay a penalty for similar violations of the antiboycott regulations in January 1998. In both cases, the companies paid the penalty without admitting or denying the allegations.

Scope of Coverage

Who Is Covered by the Laws?

The sources of U.S. antiboycott regulations can be found in the Export Administration Act (EAA) and its implementing regulation, the Export Administration Regulations (EAR), and the Internal Revenue Code. The EAR applies to all "U.S. persons" (individuals and companies located in the United States). It also covers foreign subsidiaries that are controlled by a U.S. company in terms of ownership or management. In such cases, the foreign affiliate will be subject to the antiboycott laws and the U.S. parent will be held responsible for any noncompliance. The regulations cover the activities of individuals or companies relating to the sale, purchase, or transfer of goods or services between the U.S. and a foreign country. This includes U.S. exports, imports, financing, forwarding and shipping, and certain other transactions that may take place outside the United States. To trigger the application of the antiboycott laws, the activity must involve U.S. commerce with foreign countries.

What Do the Laws Prohibit?

Refusals to do business. The statute prohibits any U.S. person from refusing to do business (expressly or implicitly) with any person pursuant to a request, agreement, or requirement from a boycotting country. The use of a designated list of persons also constitutes a refusal to do business prohibited under the act.

Discriminatory actions. The statute prohibits any U.S. person from discriminating against an individual (who is a U.S. person) on the basis of race, religion, gender, or national origin. It also prohibits similar action against a U.S. corporation based on the race, religion, and so forth, of the owner, officer, director, or employee. Such prohibitions apply when the action is taken in order to comply with or support an unsanctioned foreign boycott.

Furnishing information to a boycotting country. The statute prohibits furnishing information about any business relationship with or in a boycotted country or with blacklisted firms or persons. It also prohibits actual furnishing of, or agreements to furnish, information about the race, religion, sex, or national origin of another U.S. person or any U.S. person's association with any charitable organization that supports the boycotted country.

Implementing letters of credit with prohibited conditions or requirements. The statute also prohibits any U.S. person from implementing a letter of credit that contains a condition or requirement from a boycotting country. This includes issuing, honoring, paying, or confirming a letter of credit. The prohibition applies when the beneficiary is a U.S. person and the transaction involves the export of U.S. goods (i.e., shipment of U.S.-origin goods or goods from the United States).

Some exceptions to the prohibitions include the following:

- Compliance with import requirements of a boycotting country
- Compliance with unilateral and specific selections by buyers in a boycotting country

- Compliance with a boycotting country's requirements regarding shipment and transshipment of exports
- Compliance with immigration, passport, visa, employment, and local requirements of a boycotting country

Reporting Requirements

The regulations require U.S. persons to report quarterly to the U.S. Department of Commerce any requests they have received to take any action to comply with, further, or support an unsanctioned foreign boycott (for nonreportable requests, see International Perspective 15.4). The U.S. Treasury also requires taxpayers to report activities in or with a boycotting country and any requests to participate in a foreign boycott.

Penalties for Noncompliance

The law provides both criminal and civil penalties for violations of the antiboycott statute. On the criminal side, a person who knowingly violates the regulations is subject to a fine of up to $50,000 or five times the value of the exports involved, whichever is greater. It may also include impris-

---

International Perspective

15.4

REQUESTS THAT ARE NOT REPORTABLE

- To refrain from shipping on a carrier owned or leased by a particular country or its nationals or a request to certify to that effect.
- To ship goods via a prescribed route or refrain from shipping via a prescribed route or to certify to that effect.
- To supply information regarding the country of origin of goods, the name of the supplier, provider of services, or the destination of exports.
- To comply with the laws of another country other than one that requires compliance with the country's boycott laws.
- To supply information about the exporter or the exporter's family for immigration, passport, or employment purposes.
- To supply a certificate by owner/master that the vessel, aircraft, etc., is eligible to enter a particular port pursuant to its laws.
- To supply a certificate from an insurance company stating that the company has an agent or representative in the boycotting country including the name and address of such agent.

onment of up to five years. In cases in which the violator has knowledge that the items will be used for the benefit of countries or persons to which exports are restricted for national security or foreign policy purposes, the criminal penalty varies. For individuals, a fine may be imposed of up to $250,000 and/or imprisonment of up to ten years. For firms, the penalty for each violation can be $1 million or up to five times the value of the exports involved, whichever is greater. Administrative or civil penalties may include any or all of the following: revocation of export licenses, denial of export privileges, exclusion from practice, and imposition of fines of up to $10,000 per violation or $100,000, if the violation involves items controlled for national security reasons. The treasury may also deny all or part of the foreign tax benefits.

FOREIGN CORRUPT PRACTICES

The Foreign Corrupt Practices Act (FCPA) of 1977 was enacted as a public response to the Watergate Scandal and the disclosure of corrupt payments by U.S. multinationals to foreign government officials in order to obtain business. The Security Exchange Commission (SEC) investigations revealed that 117 Fortune 500 companies had paid millions of dollars to foreign governments. Substantial payments were made by companies such as Exxon ($56.7 million), Northrop ($30.7 million), and Lockheed Martin ($25 million) to foreign officials (Impert, 1990). The overriding public concern was that this practice could tarnish the reputation of the United States in the world and was not in the best interest of U.S. corporations.

The legislation represents an attempt to enforce morality and ethics in the conduct of international business transactions. The FCPA was enacted as an amendment to the Securities and Exchange Act of 1934. It was later amended, in 1988, as part of the Omnibus Trade and Competitiveness Act.

The principal objectives of the legislation are to

- prohibit the bribery of foreign officials by U.S. individuals and corporations to obtain or retain a business and
- establish standards for maintaining corporate records and internal accounting control objectives. The antibribery provision applies to all publicly held corporations registered with SEC and all domestic concerns. The accounting standards and objectives apply only to SEC registrants.

Scope of Coverage

Who Is Subject to the FCPA?

The act applies to all publicly held corporations registered with the Security Exchange Commission and other domestic concerns. Domestic concerns are broadly defined to include all U.S. citizens and residents as well as any entity whose principal place of business is in the United States or incorporated under the laws of the United States.

A U.S. parent company may be liable for corrupt payments by its foreign subsidiary if the U.S. parent company knew or participated in the subsidiary's corrupt action or took no measures to discourage such payments.

What Is Covered by the FCPA?

The antibribery provision prohibits American businesses from using interstate commerce to pay off foreign officials to obtain or retain a business.

Payments to any foreign official to obtain the performance of routine governmental action is explicitly exempted. The 1988 amendments to the FCPA changed the knowledge requirement and the definition of grease payments, added certain defenses to charges of bribery under the statute, increased penalties, and authorized the president to negotiate an international agreement prohibiting bribery.

The knowledge requirement. The 1977 act prohibited any payments while knowing or having reason to know that they would be used to bribe foreign officials. It was believed that a broad application of the "reason to know" standard would put many multinational companies under the risk of liability for the actions of their sales agents who engage in bribery without their approval. Such a standard would also invite unwarranted scrutiny of distributors or sales agents in countries that are considered to be corrupt. Given such legitimate business concerns, the "reason to know" standard was removed from the act and objective criteria established with respect to such conduct. This standard is narrower and holds businesses liable only if they are substantially certain that the illicit payments are to occur or that such a circumstance exists (Hall, 1994).

Exemption of payments for ministerial or clerical duties. The amendment based permissible bribes on the purpose for which payment is made, as opposed to the official position of the recipient. It excludes payments for routine governmental actions from the application of the act.

Additional defenses against charges of bribery. Payments are not considered corrupt if they are lawful under the laws of the foreign country and if they are used to reimburse foreign officials for reasonable expenditures, such as visits to manufacturing facilities, promotion, and so on.

Increased penalties. The maximum fine for a corporation was increased from $1 million to $2 million. For individuals, the maximum fine was also increased from $10,000 to $100,000. Individuals and corporate employees were made criminally liable even when the corporation is not in contravention of the FCPA.

Authorization to negotiate an international agreement. The act authorizes the president to negotiate an international agreement with countries that are members of the OECD to prohibit bribery.

The accounting provisions of the FCPA are intended to prevent companies from escaping detection by maintaining dubious accounts or slush funds. It requires any corporation that has certain classes of shares with the SEC to (1) make and keep accurate books and accounts that fairly reflect the transactions and (2) maintain a system of internal accounting controls in order to prevent the unauthorized use of corporate assets and transactions and to ensure the accuracy of corporate records.

Enforcement and Penalties

Enforcement of the FCPA is the joint responsibility of the SEC and the Department of Justice. The Department of Justice has authority for civil enforcement of violations by domestic concerns with respect to the antibribery provisions. It also has exclusive jurisdiction over criminal prosecution in relation to the accounting as well as antibribery provisions of the statute. The SEC has similar authority for civil enforcement of violations of the antibribery and accounting provisions.

Criminal penalties may reach up to $2 million for public corporations and domestic concerns and $100,000 and/or a maximum of five years for officers, directors, or employees who commit willful violations of the antibribery provisions. With regard to civil penalties, a maximum of $10,000 may be levied against any company, employee, officer, or director. Injunctive relief is also available to forestall a violation. Violations of the accounting provisions can result in a fine of $2.5 million for companies or up to ten years of imprisonment for individuals.

Since the introduction of the FCPA, several U.S. companies have been investigated for bribing foreign officials to obtain contracts. Over the last few years, some companies were indicted and fined for bribing foreign officials in order to use their influence to secure government contracts. Here are some examples:

- In 1995, Lockheed Martin was indicted for paying an Egyptian legislator $1 million through a consulting firm for helping Lockheed secure the sale of three transport planes. The company agreed to a settlement by paying a $24.8 million penalty (Anonymous, 1995).
- In 1990, Young and Rubicam, a New York-based advertising firm, entered a guilty plea and paid a $500,000 fine for bribing a former official of the Jamaican Ministry of Tourism to secure a contract with the Jamaican Tourist Board (Lipman, 1990).

U.S. companies could seek an advisory opinion from the Department of Justice (DOJ) on whether a particular transaction would violate the FCPA. Any opinion by the DOJ that sanctions a proposed transaction would create a presumption of legality.

Measures for Compliance with the FCPA

Implementing Due Diligence Procedures

It is advisable to prepare internal procedures to evaluate and select foreign partners and agents. Once an appointment has been made consistent with the internal procedures, a written agreement is needed to govern the relationship between the parties. Such an agreement should generally state that the agent/partner has no authority to bind the exporter and that the agreement is valid insofar as the foreign agent/partner complies with the FCPA and the foreign country's laws. It should also stipulate that the agent/partner is not an employee, officer, or representative of any government agency. The exporter should be promptly notified of any changes in representation.

Seeking an Advisory Opinion from the Government

The Department of Justice provides an advisory opinion on the legitimacy of a proposed transaction. Other federal agencies also provide an advisory opinion.

Adopting Internal Measures and Controls

Internal procedures should be established to guide employees. Such programs include procedures for reporting and investigations; seeking the opinion of counsel; policies for employees, agents, or joint venture partners; and training programs for officers and employees.

International Efforts to Control Corruption

- The OECD Antibribery Recommendation, 1994
- The OECD Convention on Combating Bribery, 1997
- The ICC Rules of Conduct to Combat Extortion and Bribery, 1977 (revised in 1996)
- Transparency International (TI), which has as its mission to enhance public transparency and accountability in international business transactions and in the administration of public procurement

---

International Perspective

15.5

MEASURES OF CORRUPTION WITHIN THE POLITICAL SYSTEM OF SELECTED COUNTRIES (JANUARY 1998)

Country	Level of Corruption	Country	Level of Corruption
Argentina	2	Japan	3
Australia	5	Kenya	2
Brazil	3	Mexico	3
Canada	6	Nigeria	2
China	2	Pakistan	3
Colombia	1	Russia	2
Costa Rica	5	Thailand	2
Egypt	2	United States	4
France	4	Uruguay	3
India	3	Venezuela	3
Indonesia	1	Zimbabwe	2

Source: The Political Risk Services Group, 1998, pp. 4-6.

Note: The measure is taken out of 6 points. Countries with 2.5 points or less are considered to have a high level of corruption.

ANTITRUST LAWS AND TRADE REGULATION

Antitrust laws are intended to enhance efficiency and consumer welfare by proscribing practices that lessen competition or create a monopoly. Such laws also meet the sociopolitical objective of dispersing economic power. Historically, monopolies were often sanctioned in the area of trade and commerce.

During the colonial period, for example, private companies such as the East India Company (1600), The Dutch West India Company (1621), and The Hudson Bay Company (1670) received charters from governments that granted them a monopoly of trade. In North America, British merchants were given monopolies over the export and import of goods.

The idea of monopoly rights was soon found unacceptable, as it restricted the rights of individuals from competing freely. In many European countries, it was viewed as incompatible with the competitive integrity of markets and free trade. By 1860, Britain had unilaterally abrogated the rights of commercial monopolies given to particular companies (Johns, 1988). In the United States, there was a call for legislation to control "dangerous conspiracies against the public good" (Shenefield and Stelzer, 1993). The Sherman Act was passed in 1890.

Antitrust laws are often referred to as the Magna Carta of free enterprise because they preserve free competition in domestic and foreign trade as well as minimize government intervention in business affairs.

U.S. Antitrust Regulations

U.S. antitrust laws can be grouped into three categories:

1. *General prohibitions:* The Sherman Act, the Federal Trade Commission (FTC)
2. *Specific prohibitions:* The Clayton Act and amendments
3. *Exemptions*

General Prohibitions

The Sherman Act outlaws certain concerted activity in restraint of trade between two or more parties. The U.S. Supreme Court has developed certain criteria to determine the lawfulness of a given restraint: the per se rule and the rule of reason. The per se rule applies to those restraints of trade which are prohibited regardless of their effect on competition or economic welfare.

Per se violations include price-fixing, division of markets (market sharing) between competitors, and certain boycotts by sellers or buyers (i.e., an agreement between competitors not to deal with a customer or supplier). Restraints that are not categorized as per se violations are subject to the rule of reason; that is, practices are restricted only if they have an adverse effect on competition. This often requires analysis of the competitive structure of the firm, the firm's market share and/or power, and other relevant factors. The Sherman Act also prohibits monopoly abuse and attempts or conspiracies to monopolize trade or commerce with foreign nations. If a firm has a high market share as a result of improved productivity, it is not considered objectionable unless it is obtained through systematic conduct designed to harm competitors.

The Federal Trade Commission proscribes unfair competitive practices even though they do not violate specific provisions of either the Sherman Act or the Clayton Act. It also prohibits unfair or deceptive practices in or affecting foreign commerce. The commission has authority to issue interpretative rules and general statements of policy, rules, and guidelines that define unfair or deceptive business practices.

Specific Prohibitions

The Clayton Act proscribes any acquisition of the stocks or assets of another entity affecting commerce in any part of the United States that results in the creation of a monopoly or a substantial lessening of competition. The Clayton Act is not limited to the acquisition of a competitor. It also prohibits price discrimination between two purchasers without just cause or exclusive dealing in foreign commerce that tends to create a monopoly or lessen competition in the United States. Exclusive dealing (tying) occurs when the seller sells a product only on the condition that the purchaser will not deal in the goods of the seller's competitor.

Exemptions

Certain export activities of U.S. companies are exempt from the reach of U.S. antitrust laws. These exemptions came in the wake of increasing U.S. trade deficits and were intended to encourage U.S. companies to form alliances in order to increase exports overseas. The development of export trading companies (ETCs) was sought to benefit export firms through the creation of economies of scale and diffusion of risk. The following are some of the exemptions in the area of export trade.

The Webb-Pomerene Act. The Webb-Pomerene Act allows U.S. firms to establish export cartels for the sole purpose of marketing their products overseas. This exemption from the antitrust laws allows competing firms to set prices, allocate orders, consolidate freight, or arrange shipments and, until 1982, applied only to merchandise exports. The Export Trading Company Act (ETC) of 1982 extended the application of the Webb-Pomerene Act to services.

Export trade certificate of review. The ETC Act provides a procedure for issuing a certificate of review exempting U.S. applicants from antitrust liability. Under this procedure, applicants disclose their plans for overseas trade with the government and obtain preclearance, that is, obtain the government's approval for their future export activity. The Commerce and Justice Departments issue the certificate to potential exporters after establishing that their conduct or activity does not substantially lessen competition or unreasonably affect prices in the United States. Applicants are exempt from antitrust laws so long as the minimum standards are met under the act. The ETC Act also provides protection to certificate holders against frivolous lawsuits by competitors that are intended to forestall their export activities.

Application of antitrust laws to international business transactions. Title IV of the ETC Act exempts exporting and other international business transactions from the application of the Sherman and Federal Trade Commission Acts unless the export conduct has a direct, substantial, and reasonably foreseeable effect on domestic trade or commerce. Anticompetitive acts directed at exports without effect on domestic commerce of a U.S. person are treated as foreign transactions and out of reach of U.S. antitrust laws. In the absence of this legislation, the antitrust laws would otherwise have extended to any anticompetitive conduct (agreements, conspiracy, etc.), regardless of its effect on U.S. import, export, or domestic commerce. Although this exemption could be used as an alternative to export certification or preclearance, it does not provide the immunity from prosecution that is available under the latter arrangement.

The following are generally considered to be a checklist of practices that businesses should avoid:

1. Discussing prices with competitors
2. Pricing below cost to drive out a competitor or discourage a new entrant
3. Dividing markets with other competitors
4. Compelling dealers to charge a given price
5. Tying the sale of one product to another
6. Charging customers different prices without reasonable justification
7. Terminating a customer without reasonable justification
8. Abusing market power to the disadvantage of consumers and competitors
9. Joining with a competitor to the disadvantage of other competitors
10. Suggesting that a supplier purchase from another division of the subsidiary

It is also important for companies to establish an antitrust compliance program.

International Perspective

15.6

MATSUSHITA COMPANY LIMITED
VERSUS ZENITH RADIO CORPORATION

Background and Facts: In 1974, Zenith filed a suit against a group of Japanese firms, including Matsushita, claiming that they had engaged in predatory pricing (pricing below cost) as part of a collusive plan to drive U.S. firms out of the color television market (CTV). It was alleged that the Japanese producers had agreed to limit the number of U.S. distributors to five and to set minimum prices in the U.S. market. It was also alleged that, notwithstanding the minimum prices, the companies agreed to provide substantial rebates to their U.S. distributors. In Japan, the producers controlled the retail outlets and used their control to fix retail prices and retail market shares and to restrict retailers from selling competitive products. It was also found that the Japanese firms never gained more than 45 percent of the U.S. market share and did not raise prices in twenty years. The district court held for Matsushita and other defendants and Zenith appealed. The appellate court reversed the trial court's decision. Matsushita and others appealed to the U.S. Supreme Court.

Decision: The Supreme Court reversed the decision of the appellate court. The court stated that Zenith's accusations that Japanese firms were conspiring to drive U.S. industry out of business in order to monopolize the U.S. CTV market not only were untrue but could not have been possibly true. Elaborating on this issue, the court stated:

"If predatory pricing conspiracies are generally unlikely to occur, they are especially so, where, as here, the prospect of attaining monopoly power seems slight. . . . Two decades after their conspiracy is alleged to have commenced, petitioners appear to be far from achieving this goal: the two largest shares of the retail market are held by RCA and the respondent Zenith. The alleged conspiracy's failure to achieve its ends in the two decades of its asserted operation is strong evidence that the conspiracy does not in fact exist. . . . Petitioners had every incentive not to engage in the conduct with which they are charged, for its likely effect would be to generate losses for the petitioners with no corresponding gains."

Source: 106 S. Court 1349 (1986).

Extraterritorial Application of U.S. Antitrust Laws

The U.S. antitrust laws are not limited to transactions that take place within U.S. borders. Overseas transactions with a substantial and foreseeable effect on U.S. commerce are subject to U.S. antitrust laws. Efforts by the United States to exercise its jurisdiction outside its borders have often been frustrated by foreign governments that did not want any infringements of their sovereignty. Some countries have enacted legislation to block the enforcement of U.S. laws within their countries, including any cooperation with respect to submission of evidence, documents, and so on. In view of such opposition, the U.S. government has resorted to bilateral antitrust agreements with various countries concerning the extraterritorial application of national antitrust laws. The agreements generally provide for the exchange of information, prior notification of enforcement actions, consultation on policy matters, and so forth.

Enforcement and Penalties

The Department of Justice and the Federal Trade Commission enforce U.S. antitrust laws. Whereas the Department of Justice can initiate civil or criminal suits against alleged violators, the Federal Trade Commission or states, through the attorney general, are empowered to bring only civil cases. Private parties that have been adversely affected by a violation of antitrust laws can also sue in federal court for an injunction or damages.

Penalties in criminal cases may involve fines up to $100,000 and imprisonment for up to three years for individuals. Corporations may be fined up to $1 million. Civil penalties could also result in hefty fines.

INCENTIVES TO PROMOTE EXPORTS

From the 1870s until 1971, U.S. exports typically exceeded U.S. imports, except during World War II. Even during this period, U.S. exports fell below imports because a substantial percentage of the exports was not sold, but provided to allies under the Marshall Plan. All this began to change in the 1970s. The U.S. registered a trade deficit in 1971. The merchandise trade balance showed a $2.27 billion deficit (1971) in contrast to the previous decades when exports exceeded imports. Some of the contributing factors to this state of affairs included the overvalued dollar and increased government expenditures at home and abroad that often resulted in purchases of foreign products and services. This situation was further exacerbated in 1973 when oil prices sharply increased and worsened the U.S. trade deficit due to large increases in expenditures for imports for petroleum products (Stein and Foss, 1992).

DISC and the GATT

In an effort to remedy the worsening trade imbalance, the government enacted the Revenue Act of 1972. The act created the Domestic International Sales Corporation (DISC) to promote U.S. exports by providing tax incentives that would lower the cost of exporting goods in foreign markets. The legislation was also intended to remove the disadvantage of U.S. companies engaged in export activities through domestic corporations.

The DISC statute was also intended to offset the competitive disadvantage faced by U.S. firms in view of the various incentives provided by major trading nations to their export firms. Under the DISC scheme, a U.S. corporation could export its products through a subsidiary (DISC) organized in the United States (a shell corporation) with minimum capital of $2,500. The DISC was required to engage almost exclusively in export sales. The tax implications of a corporation that elected to be treated as a DISC were as follows:

- Approximately half of DISC's earnings were taxed at the shareholder level regardless of whether they were distributed to shareholders (constructive dividends).
- The remainder of DISC's earnings was not taxable to the shareholder until actually distributed. This allowed for an indefinite deferral of tax. In effect, this amounted to a de facto tax exemption on about half of DISC's earnings because deferred taxes may never become due.
- Deferred taxes became due when distributed to shareholders, when a shareholder disposed of its DISC stock, or the corporation ceased to qualify as a DISC.

The DISC came under increasing attack by U.S. trading partners as an unfair and illegal subsidy to U.S. exporters. In a complaint by the EEC and Canada against the United States, the GATT panel issued a report stating that the DISC scheme conferred a tax benefit to exports and resulted in the price of exports being lower than similar goods for domestic consumption. The panel concluded that the scheme was in violation of the GATT treaty (GATT, 1977). Even though the United States never conceded to the inconsistency of the DISC with the GATT agreement, it nevertheless proceeded to replace the DISC with an alternative scheme that was acceptable to the GATT.

The Tax Reform Act of 1984 created the Foreign Sales Corporation (FSC) to promote U.S. exports. Once the FSC is incorporated outside the United States and satisfies other requirements in the statute, its earnings are exempt from U.S. taxation. Although the FSC provides a benefit to U.S. exporters comparable to the DISC, it is permitted under the GATT because the GATT treaty does not require member countries to tax "economic processes" that take place outside their territory.

Foreign Sales Corporations in General

The FSC is intended to provide economic incentives mainly for the export of manufactured goods. To qualify as an FSC, a firm must meet certain requirements, such as foreign incorporation, foreign presence, and other technical tests. In addition, special provisions for small business exporters provide similar incentives without requiring the stringent standards applied to regular FSCs (i.e., small FSCs and interest-charge DISCs) (Mandell, 1995).

In short, an FSC is an offshore company with a main office in a U.S. possession or qualified foreign country. It can be organized by a manufacturer or service business for the purpose of buying or selling U.S.-made products abroad for its own account or as a commission agent. The FSC is eligible for a tax rate of 15 to 32 percent. The greatest number of FSCs have been set up in the U.S. Virgin Islands (about 80 percent of over 5,000 FSCs incorporated abroad), followed by Barbados, Jamaica, and Guam. These countries have attracted most of the FSCs because of their special incentives that provide FSCs exemptions from income tax and dividend withholdings. A small number of FSCs have also been established in Belgium, Canada, Ireland, and the Netherlands (Bernet, 1991). The list of qualifying countries includes another twenty-five states, and competition to attract FSCs is likely to intensify among these nations. FSCs provide substantial benefits to U.S. export firms. For example, Aerotech World Trade Company, based in New York, sells about two-thirds of its airplane parts, worth about $67 million, outside the United States. In 1984, it set up an FSC in the U.S. Virgin Islands, and this reduced Aerotech's taxes by almost $300,000. Similarly, Dranetz Technologies, a New Jersey manufacturer of instruments that measure power quality, was able to save $100,000 by using its Guam-based FSC in 1985. The company exports about 25 percent of its sales (Mandell, 1995).

Formal Requirements for FSC Status

Organizational Requirements

A corporation must meet the following criteria to be considered an FSC under the statute.

Foreign incorporation. A company must be incorporated under the laws of a qualified foreign country or under the laws of any U.S. possession, except Puerto Rico. A qualified foreign country is one that has a bilateral agreement, such as the Caribbean Basin Initiative, or income tax treaty with the United States that the Internal Revenue Service certifies as providing an exchange of information adequate to prevent tax avoidance.

The countries that have been certified to host FSCs include Australia, Austria, Belgium, Canada, Costa Rica, Denmark, the Dominican Republic, Egypt, Finland, France, Germany, Grenada, Iceland, Ireland, Jamaica, South Korea, Malta, Morocco, the Netherlands, New Zealand, Norway, Pakistan, the Philippines, Saint Lucia, South Africa, Sweden, and Trinidad and Tobago.

Foreign presence. An FSC must maintain an office in a qualifying foreign country or in any U.S. possession. It is also required to keep a set of permanent books of account, including invoices of transactions at said office.

Limited shareholders. An FSC may have no more than twenty-five shareholders at any time during the taxable year.

Stock limitation. An FSC must not have any outstanding preferred stock at any time during the year. The regulations allow for different classes of common stock.

Domestic presence. An FSC is required to maintain its business records at a location within the United States or any of its possessions.

Foreign director. An FSC is required to include at least one individual who is not a U.S. resident on the board of directors. The individual could be a U.S. citizen and does not have to be a resident of the country of incorporation.

No controlled group with DISC. An FSC cannot be a member of any controlled group of corporations of which a DISC is a member.

FSC election. A corporation must also elect to be treated as an FSC within ninety days of the beginning of its taxable year.

Foreign Management Requirements

Meetings. All board and shareholder meetings must be held outside the United States. Even though the meetings have to comply with the laws of the country of incorporation, they need not be held in the place of incorporation.

Bank account. The main corporate bank account must be maintained outside the United States in a qualifying jurisdiction or a U.S. possession. The main or principal account is considered to be one from which dividends, legal and accounting fees, and officers' and directors' salaries are disbursed. The regulations do not require maintenance of a minimum balance in the form of cash or in the form of a percentage of working capital.

Disbursements. Disbursements of all dividends, legal and accounting fees, salaries of officers and directors must be out of the principal bank account maintained outside the United States.

Foreign Economic Process Requirements

An FSC must conduct economic activities outside the United States with respect to qualifying transactions (except for small FSCs). This requirement has two parts.

Foreign sales activity. The FSC must participate outside the United States in the solicitation (other than advertising), negotiations, or making of the contract related to the transaction (Marcus and Hoff-Patrinas, 1984).

Foreign direct cost. For purposes of the direct-cost test, 50 percent or more of the direct costs incurred by the FSC in a transaction must be attributable to activities such as advertising, promotion, and so on (see the following list) occurring outside the United States. A corporation will also be treated as satisfying the foreign 50 percent of the direct-costs requirement if at least 85 percent of the direct cost is incurred in at least two of the following five categories:

1. Advertising and sales promotion
2. The processing of customer orders and the arranging for delivery of the export property
3. Transportation from the time of acquisition by the FSC to delivery to the customer
4. Assumption of risk
5. The determination and transmittal of a final invoice or statement of account and the receipt of payment

Most companies tend to use the 85 percent of selected direct-costs test instead of the 50 percent of all direct-costs test.

Qualifying transactions. The FSC tax benefit is only available to qualifying transactions, which include the following:

- The sale, exchange, or other disposition of export property
- The lease or rental of export property for use by a lessee outside the United States
- The rendering of services relating to such sales or leases
- The rendering of engineering or architectural services for construction projects located outside the United States
- The rendering of managerial services for an unrelated FSC so long as at least 50 percent of the gross receipts of the FSC that renders such

services is derived from its own sales or leases of export property and the rendering of related services

Export property generally includes products grown, manufactured, or extracted in the United States by a party other than an FSC for sale, lease, or rental outside the United States. No more than 50 percent of the fair-market value of the property or item can be attributed to articles imported into the United States. The definition of export property excludes intellectual property rights (other than those embodied in products such as tapes, films, or records); lease or rental to a member of a controlled group of companies of which the FSC is a member; oil, gas, or any primary product; and products curtailed for reasons of short supply.

Tax Benefits

A properly structured FSC will qualify for a tax exemption of 34 to 74 percent of its income, depending on the nature of the transaction. The remainder of the export income is subject to U.S. taxes. After paying its reduced tax, an FSC can pay its earnings from qualified sales as a dividend without any further U.S. taxes. The level of tax exemption depends on the pricing method used and the type of ownership. If one of the two administrative pricing methods (to determine taxable income) is used, the exclusion is $^{15}/_{23}$ to $^{16}/_{23}$ of qualified gross income (foreign trade income). The higher exemptions apply if the FSC is owned by individual shareholders. Investment income such as dividends, royalties, or gains on sales of securities is taxed as U.S. source income.

FSCs with a corporate shareholder can exempt $^{15}/_{23}$ of their foreign trade income (using administrative pricing rules, i.e., gross-receipts pricing or the combined-taxable-income method). The remainder and any investment income is taxed as U.S. source income at the current tax rate. The following example is used to show how foreign trade income is determined.

Determination of Foreign Trade Income

Foreign trade income can be calculated in one of the following three ways:

1. *Arms-length pricing method:* For products purchased by an FSC from an unrelated party, transactions are based on the price that was actually paid by the FSC for the export property to, or the commission received from, the unrelated party. For transactions with related parties, prices or commissions declared could be taken if they satisfy the arms-length transaction requirements.

2. *Administrative pricing (gross-receipts method):* The taxable income that can be earned by an FSC is an amount not exceeding 1.83 percent of the foreign trade gross receipts derived by the FSC from the sale.

3. *Administrative pricing (combined-taxable-income method):* Under this method, taxable income is an amount not exceeding 23 percent of the combined taxable income of the FSC and the related supplier attributed to the foreign trade gross receipts.

Determination of exempt foreign trade income. Once taxable income is determined under one of the pricing methods, exempt foreign trade income is $^{16}/_{23}$ of total foreign trade income, except for corporate shareholders, which is computed at a lower rate ($^{15}/_{23}$). If the arms-length pricing method is used, the exemption is 30 percent of foreign trade income for corporate shareholders. (For example computations of exempt trade income, see Table 15.1.)

Which of the pricing methods should be used? The choice of the pricing method to measure taxable income depends on its impact on the size of the allowable tax exemption. The arm's-length method tends to produce the largest taxable income and hence a lower allowable exemption than the pricing rules used under the administrative method. When we compare the gross-receipts method with the combined-income approach, the latter is the most advantageous, unless the exporter's profit margin falls below 8 percent, in which case 1.83 percent of an FSC's gross sales will exceed 23 percent of export profits (see Illustrative Example, p. 318).

FSC Dividends and Taxation

When the FSC pays dividends to its U.S. shareholders, the dividend is subject to a 100 percent dividends-received deduction. This applies to the exempt foreign trade income regardless of the pricing method used to compute taxable income. However, although the 100 percent dividends-received deduction applies for the entire dividend (exempt or nonexempt foreign trade income), when administrative pricing is used, no such exemption is available for the nonexempt part of foreign trade income in the case of arm's-length pricing (Kramer, Pope, and Phillips, 1997).

Small FSC

The small FSC is designed for the small business exporter. To obtain small FSC status, a corporation has to make an election to be treated as a small FSC, and it cannot be a member of a controlled group of corporations which includes an FSC unless the latter is a small FSC. In cases involving a group of FSCs connected to a large parent firm, they would all be treated as a single small FSC. The major advantage of filing as a small FSC is that a small FSC does not have to comply with the stringent foreign management and process requirements. However, FSC benefits are allowed on a

---

Illustrative Example

Nova FSC was incorporated as an FSC in Guam in 1997. It is owned by Nova, Incorporated, a U.S. corporation that manufactures pharmaceutical products. In 1997, Nova FSC earned taxable income of $20,000 from commissions on sales of pharmaceutical products in Asia. Nova FSC received income of $800,000 from the sale of pharmaceutical products. Assume that it cost $450,000 to manufacture the goods, $150,000 for insurance and transportation to Nova FSC. The FSC also spent $120,000 in sales expenses.

Establishing Taxable Income
Arm's-length pricing method: For transactions with related parties, prices or commissions declared could be taken if it satisfies the arms-length transaction requirements.

In the previous example, the taxable income derived by the FSC under the arm's-length pricing method is $20,000.

Administrative pricing method: Under the gross-receipts method, taxable income is 1.83 percent of FSC's foreign trading gross receipts (i.e., 1.83 percent of $800,000 = $14,640). However, taxable income under the combined-income method is 23 percent of combined taxable income of Nova FSC and Nova, Incorporated (i.e., 23 percent of $800,000 less $450,000 manufacturing costs, $150,000 insurance and transportation, and $120,000 sales expenses = $18,400).

Establishing the Transfer Price
The transfer price is established by deducting FSC's taxable income and sales expenses from its foreign trading gross receipts. For example, under the arm's-length pricing method, the transfer price is $800,000 – ($20,000 + $120,000) = $660,000. Foreign trade income then is $800,000 – $660,000 = $140,000.

Determination of Exempt Foreign Trade Income
Once taxable income is determined under one of the pricing methods, exempt foreign trade income is $16/23$ of total foreign trade income, except for corporate shareholders, which is computed at a lower rate ($15/23$). If the arm's-length pricing method is used, the exemption is 30 percent of foreign trade income for corporate shareholders.

TABLE 15.1. Computing Exempt Trade Income and Tax Savings Under Various Pricing Methods

	Arms-length pricing method	Gross receipts pricing method (1.83% FSC's gross sales)	Combined tax-able income method (23% combined tax-able income)
Foreign trade gross receipts (FTGR)	$800,000	$800,000	$800,000
Less taxable income	(20,000)	(14,640)	(18,400)
Less FSC sales expenses	(120,000)	(120,000)	(120,000)
Transfer price (TP)	660,000	665,360	661,600
FTGR less TP = foreign trade income (FTI)	140,000	134,640	138,400
Exempt FTI $^{15}/_{23}$ (FTI)	42,000 (30% FTI)	87,809	90,261
Less expenses allocable to exempt FTI $^{15}/_{23}$ (FSC expenses)	36,000 (30% sales expenses)	78,261 $^{15}/_{23}$ sales expenses	78,261 $^{15}/_{23}$ of sales expenses
Tax exempt income tax savings—34% corporation tax	6,000 34% (6,000)= 2,040	9,548 3,246	12,000 4,080

maximum of $5 million sales abroad. A corporation that initially organized as a small FSC can later convert to a regular FSC if its export receipts increase above $5 million. If the small FSC prefers to use the administrative pricing rules, it must meet the process requirements, that is, sales activity and direct-cost tests. However, none of the activities are required to be done offshore. In all other respects, the small FSC is subject to the same operational rules as a regular FSC. Small FSCs are often considered attractive for firms with foreign sales of about $1 million and a gross margin of around 20 percent. The savings would amount to approximately 15 percent of the $200,000 taxable income, or $30,000.

Shared FSC

The foreign activity as well as the reporting requirements of an FSC are often cumbersome and costly for many small and midsized exporters. Shared FSCs were introduced under the tax code to reduce this burden by enabling several exporters to join together to form and operate as a shared

FSC. The shared FSC will be eligible for the tax benefits of a regular FSC, while greatly reducing organizational, start-up, and operational costs by spreading these costs among several exporters/shareholders (Wilson, 1989). The important features of this incentive program are as follows.

Shareholders

A shared FSC must have twenty-five or fewer unrelated exporters as shareholders.

Sponsors

A shared FSC can be sponsored by the state or regional authority, trade associations, banks, export management companies, or shippers. Sponsors promote a shared FSC for their members in return for a fee. Delaware, for example, developed a model program to attract businesses from outside the state. This is done by encouraging exporters to establish FSC holding companies and service firms in Delaware. Delaware-based shared FSCs and shareholders are exempt from state taxes.

Exporters Share the Expenses of the FSC and Not Its Benefits

The shared FSC is not managed by the U.S. exporters (shareholders). The shared FSC, such as an export management company, incorporates, organizes, and operates the FSC in return for a fee (the fee is usually about $500 for a one-time start-up cost and an annual maintenance fee of a minimum of $ 3,000 or $1/10$ of 1 percent of export receipts, whichever is greater). The shared FSC will be responsible for all aspects of compliance with federal and local laws. Each exporter, however, will be required to provide the necessary documents, such as invoice and expenses, to the shared FSC to enable the latter to file its tax return and comply with other regulations.

Shared FSCs or Their Sponsors Do Not Get Involved in the Participating Exporters' Business

The shared FSCs or their sponsors do not participate in the exporters' business, profits, or tax benefits. Since each exporter receives its own class of stock in the shared FSC, it is treated as a separate corporation with its own proprietary information, risk, or benefit.

Formal Requirements for Shared FSC Status

The organizational, foreign management, and foreign economic process requirements are identical to that of a regular FSC.

Tax Benefits

The tax benefit amounts to a 15 percent exemption in corporate taxes on exports. Unlike the small FSC, there are no limits on the amount of profits that can qualify for the exemption, since the shared FSC is technically considered regular FSC. Typically, a portion of export income, such as commission to the shared FSC, is allocated to the latter and part of the income is exempted in the hands of the FSC and the exporter/shareholder. This exemption amounts to about 15 percent of combined taxable income of the exporter and the FSC.

> *Example:* Suppose Otoro Incorporated, a New Jersey export firm, is a member of MTI, a shared FSC. In 1998, Otoro made a profit of $165,000. At the end of 1998, Otoro allocated 23 percent of its profit ($37,950) as commission to the FSC. The amount exempt from tax equaled 15 percent of Otoro's overall profit, i.e., $15/23$ of $37,950 = $24,750. The $24,750 and other receipts after tax are not taxable when paid as a dividend to the exporter.
>
> Without using the shared FSC, Otoro would be subject to the full corporate tax, i.e., 0.34 ($165,000) = $56,100. However, when it uses the shared FSC, only $140,250 (i.e., $127,050 + $13,200 [i.e., $37,950 - $24,750]) will be subject to the full rate: 0.34 ($140,250) = $47,685. The tax savings amounts to $8,415 (i.e., $56,100 - $47,685).

Major Participants in a Shared FSC

The major participants include the exporter/shareholder, the sponsor that develops and implements the shared FSC (individual, public, or private agency), and the manager that is responsible for daily operations and coordination of activities among shareholders. To meet the FSC regulations, it is also important to establish an overseas service organization that assists with incorporation of the shared FSC and to fulfill other managerial and process requirements. Besides an overseas service organization, banks (overseas and domestic banks) and accounting firms (to prepare tax returns, etc.) are significant participants that ensure the successful operation of shared FSCs.

Interest-Charge Domestic International Sales Corporations (IC-DISCs)

IC-DISCs are set up to defer the imposition of taxes for up to $10 million in export sales. The taxpayer must make an election to be treated as an IC-DISC. The shareholders, however, must pay interest at U.S. treasury bill rates on their proportionate share of the accumulated taxes deferred. Interest payments by shareholders are tax deductible. In other respects, its operational rules are identical to that of pre-1985 DISCs.

International Perspective

15.7

AGRICULTURAL EXPORT INCENTIVES

- **Market Development:** The largest promotional programs are those pertaining to foreign market development and access to foreign markets. The programs allow for reimbursement of expenses incurred in approved activities.

- **Commercial Export Financing:** Provision of short- and intermediate-term commercial financing through the Commodity Credit Corporation. A buyer/supplier-guarantee program is available for the purchase of U.S. agricultural exports.

- **Concessional Sales:** Under Public Law 480, the U.S. government provides food aid under different arrangements (Title I, II & III).

- **Programs to Offset the Effects of Unfair Trade Practices:** Such programs are intended to expand U.S. agricultural exports and to challenge unfair trade practices through the provision of subsidies, and so on.

CHAPTER SUMMARY

Objectives of Export Controls

These include national security, foreign policy, nonproliferation of weapons of mass destruction, and prevention of excessive draining of scarce natural resources.

Export Controls and Major Developments

With the end of the cold war, controls have been substantially liberalized and simplified. Present controls focus on a small group of critical goods, technology, and countries.

Scope of Export Administration Regulations (EAR)

The EAR covers exports, re-exports, foreign products that are made using U.S. technology, and U.S. person activities.

Determining License Requirements

Step 1: Is the transaction subject to Export Administration Regulations (EAR)?

Step 2: If so, is an export license required based on product characteristics, destination, and use/user and the general prohibitions?

Step 3: If yes, is there a license exception?

Step 4: If no, apply for a license. If yes, no license required.

Step 5: Whether export is made under a license or not, exporters have to comply with SED/DCS and record-keeping requirements.

Indicators That Help Identify and Report Possible Violations

One of the parties to the transaction is on the list of denied persons or the transaction has red flags.

The U.S. Antiboycott Law

The law prohibits U.S. firms from participating in foreign boycotts not authorized by the U.S. government.

Who Is Covered by the Laws?

Individuals and companies located in the United States, foreign subsidiaries controlled by a U.S. company, and all activities involving U.S. commerce with foreign nations are covered.

What Do the Laws Prohibit?

Prohibitions include refusals to do business, discriminatory actions against a U.S. individual or company in order to support an unsanctioned foreign boycott, furnishing information to a boycotting country, implementing letters of credit with prohibited conditions.

Exceptions to the Prohibitions

These include compliance with import/shipping and documentary requirements of boycotting country, compliance with shipment/transshipment/specific carrier or route selection requirements of boycotting country, compliance with immigration/passport/employment and other local law requirements of boycotting country.

Enforcement and Penalties

Penalties for noncompliance:

1. Criminal penalties: Fines and/or imprisonment
2. Civil penalties: Revocation of export license, denial of export privileges, imposition of a fine, denial of tax benefits

The Foreign Corrupt Practices Act (FCPA)

Principal objectives behind FCPA: To prohibit bribery of foreign officials by U.S. individuals and corporations to obtain or retain a business; to establish standards for maintaining corporate records and internal accounting control objectives

Who Is Subject to the FCPA?

1. All U.S. citizens and residents
2. All entities with their principal place of business in the United States or incorporated in the United States.

Enforcement and Penalties

FCPA is enforced by the Securities Exchange Commission and the U.S. Department of Justice.

Criminal penalties: $2 million for corporations and/or a maximum of five years for officers, directors, or employees who commit willful violations of the FCPA.

Civil penalties: Fine of $10,000 against any company, employee, or officer, $2.5 million fine imposed for violating the accounting provisions. Injunctive relief is also available.

Measures for Compliance with the FCPA

These include implementing due diligence procedures, seeking an advisory opinion from the government, and adopting internal measures and controls.

Antitrust Regulation and U.S. Trade

There are three categories of antitrust laws:

1. General prohibitions: The Sherman Act, The Federal Trade Commission.
2. Specific prohibitions: The Clayton Act. The latter covers restraints to commerce through mergers, acquisitions, exclusive dealing, and similar arrangements that lessen competition.
3. Exemptions: Exemptions from antitrust laws in the area of export trade include the Webb-Pomerene Act, Export Trade Certificate of Review, Title IV of the ETC Act.

Extraterritorial Application of U.S. Antitrust Laws

Overseas transactions with a substantial and foreseeable effect on U.S. commerce are subject to U.S. antitrust laws.

Enforcement and Penalties

Institutions that enforce U.S. antitrust laws:

1. The Department of Justice initiates civil or criminal suits against alleged violators.
2. The Federal Trade Commission initiates only civil cases.

Penalties:

1. Criminal penalties: Fines up to $100,000 and imprisonment for up to three years (individuals); fines of up to $1 million for corporations.
2. Civil penalties: Hefty fines.

Incentives to Promote Exports

1. DISCs: DISCs were introduced to promote exports by providing tax incentives. They were abandoned due to accusations by other trading partners that they constituted an unfair and illegal export subsidy.
2. FSCs: Economic incentives mainly for the export of manufactured goods. To qualify, a firm must meet certain organizational, foreign management, and foreign economic process requirements. An FSC will quality for a tax exemption of 34 to 74 percent of its income, depending on the nature of the transaction.

3. Small FSCs: Small FSCs are designed for the small business exporter. A small FSC does not have to comply with the stringent foreign management and process requirements. Tax benefits are allowed on a maximum of $5 million of sales abroad.

4. Shared FSCs: These are intended to allow several exporters to join together to form and operate as a shared FSC, which reduces organizational and operational costs. The formal requirements are the same as for regular FSCs.

5. Interest-charge DISCs: Under this arrangement, taxes on export sales can be deferred. However, shareholders must pay interest on their proportionate share of the accumulated taxes deferred. Operational rules are similar to pre-1985 DISCs.

SECTION VII:
IMPORT PROCEDURES
AND TECHNIQUES

Chapter 16

Import Regulations, Trade Intermediaries, and Services

IMPORT RESTRICTIONS IN THE UNITED STATES

Tariffs

All goods imported into the United States are subject to duty or duty-free entry, depending on their classification under the applicable tariff schedule and their country of origin. For dutiable products, three different methods are used to levy tariffs:

1. *Ad valorem duty:* The duty levied is a percentage of the value of the imported product. It is the type of duty most often applied. An example would be a 2 percent ad valorem on imports of leather shoes. The duty obligation is proportional to the value of the dutiable cargo and bears no relation to the quantity imported.
2. *Specific duty:* This duty rate is based on the physical unit or weight or other quantity. Such duty applies equally to low- and high-priced goods. To the extent that the same duty rate is applied to similar goods with different import prices, specific duties tend to be more restrictive of low-priced goods. When the price of imports rises, the rate remains unchanged, and, subsequently, the effect of the specific duty declines. Examples would be a $9.00 per ton (wheat) or $2.50 per dozen (fountain pens) charges.
3. *Compound duty:* Compound duty combines both ad valorem and specific duty. An example would be $2.00 per pound and 4 percent ad valorem (chicken imports).

Most merchandise imported into the United States is dutiable under the most-favored-nation (MFN) rate. The MFN principle is expressed in Article I of the GATT and in a number of bilateral and other treaties. Under this principle, any advantage or favor granted by the United States (a member of the GATT) to any import originating from any other country shall be accorded, unconditionally, to the like product originating from all other GATT/WTO members. If the MFN treatment is provided as a result of a bilateral treaty (MFN treatment for goods from China, not a member of the GATT/WTO), an obligation arises to treat imports from that country as favorably as imports from any other member of the GATT/WTO. Certain communist countries, such as Cuba and North Korea, are not accorded MFN status and thus denied the benefit of the low rates of duty resulting from trade agreements entered into by the United States.

Nontariff Barriers

Even though most goods freely enter the United States, there are some restrictions on the importation of certain articles (see International Perspective 16.1 and Tables 16.1 and 16.2). The rules prohibit or limit the entry of some imports; limit entry to certain ports; restrict routing, storage, or use; or require treatment, labeling, or processing as a condition of release from customs. U.S. nontariff barriers fall into the following categories (U.S. Department of Commerce, 1995):

Prohibited Imports

These imports include certain narcotics and drug paraphernalia (materials used to make or produce drugs); counterfeit articles; products sold in violation of intellectual property rights; obscene, immoral, and seditious matter; and merchandise produced by convicts or through forced labor.

Imports Prohibited Without a License

These include arms and ammunition, and products from certain countries, such as Cuba, Iran, and North Korea.

Imports Requiring a Permit

Such imports include alcoholic beverages, animal and animal products, plant products, and trademarked articles. For example, all commercial shipments of meat and meat food products offered for entry into the United States are subject to the regulations of the Department of Agricul-

---

International Perspective

16.1

CONSUMER PRODUCTS AND IMPORT RESTRICTIONS IN THE UNITED STATES

Products or product categories with no import restrictions:

Artwork, crafts, gems and gemstones, glass and glass products, household appliances, jewelry and pearls, leather goods that are not from endangered species, metals, musical instruments, optics and optical instruments, paper and paper products, plastics and plastic products, rubber and rubber products, sporting goods, tools and other utensils.

Products or product categories subject to certain restrictions or requirements:

Aerospace products, live animals and animal products, beverages, chemicals, combustibles, cosmetics, drugs and explosives, foods, radioactive and radio frequency devices, used merchandise, vehicles.

Products or product categories that are generally prohibited:

Food products grown or produced in disease-ridden regions, products derived from endangered species, products that infringe on intellectual property rights, obscene or pornographic materials, as well as national treasures.

Source: U.S. Department of Commerce, 1995, p. 60.

ture and must be inspected by the USDA Inspection Service before release by customs.

Imports with Labeling, Marking, and Other Requirements

Certain imports require special labeling. For example, wool and fur products must be tagged, labeled, or otherwise clearly marked to show the importer's name and other required information. All goods imported must be marked individually with the name of the country of origin in English.

Imports Limited by Absolute Quotas

These imports include dairy products, animal feed, chocolate, some beers and wines, textiles and apparel, cotton, peanuts, sugars, syrups, molasses, cheese, and wheat.

Table 16.1. Import Permits/Other Requirements and Respective Government Agencies

Agricultural commodities	
• Cheese, milk and dairy products, fruits and vegetables, meat and meat products (from sources other than cattle, sheep, swine, goats, and horses), plant and plant products	U.S. Department of Agriculture (USDA) and the Food and Drug Administration (FDA)
• Insects, livestock and animals, meat and meat products (from cattle, sheep, etc.), plant and plant products, poultry and poultry products, seeds	USDA
Arms, ammunition, and radioactive materials	
• Arms, ammunition, explosives, and implements of war	Department of State and Department of the Treasury
Consumer and electronic products	
• Household appliances such as washers, dryers, air conditioners, refrigerators, heaters, etc.	U.S. Department of Energy
• Flammable fabrics	U.S. Consumer Safety Commission
• Electronic products such as microwave ovens, X-ray equipment, TV receivers	FDA
Foods, drugs, cosmetics, and medical devices	
• Foods and cosmetics	FDA
• Biological drugs	FDA
• Biological drugs for animals	USDA
• Narcotic drugs and derivatives	U.S. Department of Justice (USDJ)
• Pesticides and toxic substances	U.S. Customs
Textile, wool, and fur products	Federal Trade Commission
Wildlife and pets	U.S. Department of the Interior
Motor vehicles and boats	U.S. Department of Transportation
Alcoholic beverages **All bottle jackets made of plant materials**	FDA USDA
Administering agency for quotas and tariff quotas on imports	U.S. Customs

Source: U.S. Department of Commerce, 1995, pp. 47-56.

TABLE 16.2. Import Barriers in Selected Countries

Country	Tariffs	Nontariff Barriers
Brazil	Average tariff is about 15 to 25 percent ad valorem. High tariffs imposed in certain protected sectors, such as autos and computers.	Import licensing required for all products. Sanitary, photo-sanitary requirements for agricultural imports. Subsidies provided for export products. Inadequate protection and enforcement of certain intellectual property rights.
Canada	Average tariff is 4 to 6 percent ad valorem. Tariff increases as goods become more processed. No or low tariffs for U.S. and Mexican products.	Cost of service markups and other barriers to imports of wines and spirits. Import license required for certain commodities. Tariff quotas on dairy products, poultry, eggs, and barley products. Restrictions on certain publications.
Germany	Tariffs range from 0 to 14 percent ad valorem and less than 10 percent for most manufactured goods.	Special licenses for imports of pharmaceutical and military equipment. European Union Quotas on textiles. Local buying preferences, restrictive packaging, food and drug trademark laws.
Japan	Average tariff is 1.5 percent ad valorem. Tariffs are high on certain imports, such as agricultural products, semiprocessed products, etc.	Slow and cumbersome import clearance procedures; product standards, testing, and certification requirements. Highly regulated, inefficient distribution system. Inadequate protection and enforcement of certain intellectual property rights.

Imports Limited by Tariff Quotas

The tariffs rates on these imports are raised after a certain quantity has been imported. This applies to cattle, whole milk, motorcycles, certain kinds of fish, and potatoes.

The Buy American Act of 1933

This act provides for the purchase of goods by the U.S. government (for use within the country) from domestic sources unless they are not of satisfactory quality, are too expensive, or are not available in sufficient quantity. The procurement regulations allow for the purchase of domestic goods even though they are more expensive than competing foreign merchandise, insofar as the price differential does not exceed 6 percent (12 percent in high-unemployment areas) in favor of domestic goods.

PREFERENTIAL TRADE ARRANGEMENTS

One of the prominent exceptions to the MFN principle of nondiscrimination in the treatment of imports is that of free-trade areas and other preferential arrangements. This means that imports from countries with which the U.S. has free-trade or similar arrangements are accorded low- or duty-free status.

The North American Free Trade Agreement (NAFTA, 1993)

NAFTA eliminates tariffs on most goods originating in Canada, Mexico, and the United States over a maximum transition period of fifteen years (i.e., 2008). For most of Mexico-U.S. trade, NAFTA will either eliminate existing duties immediately or phase them out over a period of five to ten years. On a few sensitive items, the agreement will phase out tariffs over fifteen years. NAFTA duty treatment is applicable only to goods wholly produced or obtained in the NAFTA region, that is, goods produced in the NAFTA region wholly from originating materials. Goods processed or assembled from imported merchandise must contain 60 percent regional value content (transaction value method) or 50 percent value content using the net cost method.

The U.S./Israel Free Trade Agreement (FTA, 1985)

This agreement provides for free or low rates of duty for merchandise imports from Israel insofar as the imports meet the rules of origin requirements. For the preferential tariff rate, the product must be grown, produced, or manufactured in Israel and imported directly into the United States, and the cost or value of the materials produced in Israel plus the direct costs of processing operations in Israel must be no less than 35 percent of the import value.

Other Preferential Arrangements

Generalized System of Preferences (GSP)

The GSP is a special arrangement by developed nations, agreed under the United Nations, to provide special treatment for imports from developing nations to encourage their economic growth. Under the GSP, tariff exemptions and reductions are provided by industrialized countries on a specified range of commodities exported from developing nations. The GSP scheme was first implemented in the United States in 1976 when the government specified some 2,700 articles that were to receive duty-free treatment if imported from 140 designated developing nations. The scheme has been extended since, with certain modifications and limitations.

Imports from eligible countries are subject to tariff exemptions or reductions if

1. the merchandise is destined to the United States without contingency for diversion at the time of exportation,
2. the cost or value of materials produced in the beneficiary country and/or the direct cost of processing performed is no less than 35 percent of the appraised value of the goods, and
3. the United Nations (United Nations Conference on Trade and Development) certificate of origin is prepared and signed by the exporter and filed with the entry of the goods.

There are two important limitations to the application of the GSP. First, the president is required to suspend GSP eligibility on imports of specific article from a particular country when the latter supplied more than $25 million in value of the article during the previous calendar year or over 50 percent of the value of U.S. imports. Since the $25 million limitation was based on the GDP of 1974, appropriate adjustments are made in light of the GDP for the current year. Such limitations do not apply to an eligible least-developed country. Second, the provision of GSP is restricted for the more advanced developing nations. For example, many products from countries such as Israel, Korea, Singapore, and Taiwan were graduated from GSP duty-free treatment.

The Caribbean Basin Initiative (CBI)

The CBI is a program intended to provide duty-free entry of goods from designated Caribbean nations to the United States. The program was implemented in 1984 and has no expiration date. For CBI duty-free treatment, the merchandise must be wholly produced or substantially transformed in the beneficiary country, be destined to the United States without contingency for diversion at the time of exportation, and meet the 35 percent value-added requirement, similar to the GSP scheme. Value attributable to Puerto Rico, the U.S. Virgin Islands, and the U.S. customs territory may be counted toward the 35 percent value-added requirement. In the latter case, the attributable value is counted only up to a maximum of 15 percent of the appraised value of the imported article.

The Andean Trade Preference (ATP)

This program was enacted in 1991 and is scheduled to expire on December 4, 2001. It provides duty-free treatment for imports of merchandise from designated beneficiary countries, e.g., Bolivia and Colombia, to the United States. The eligibility requirements are similar to the CBI. A similar arrangement was also made with Marshall Islands and the Federated States of Micronesia in 1989 and has no expiration date.

TRADE INTERMEDIARIES AND SERVICES

Customs Brokers

Customs brokers are persons who act as agents for importers for activities involving transactions with the customs service concerning (1) the entry and admissibility of merchandise, (2) its classification and valuation, and (3) the payment of duties and other charges assessed by customs or the refund or drawback thereof. A customs broker could be an individual, partnership, or corporation licensed by the U.S. Department of the Treasury. Finding an honest and knowledgeable broker is crucial to the success of an import firm (see International perspective 16.2). Dishonest brokers have, for example, been known to make incorrect entries at higher rates of duty and to bill the importer and later seek and pocket the refund. Brokers' failure to make timely filing can be costly to the importer (Serko, 1985).

International Perspective

16.2

CRITERIA FOR SELECTING THE RIGHT CUSTOMS BROKER OR FREIGHT FORWARDER

- Competitive rate
- Knowledge of the product
- Reputation
- Service and flexibility

Duties and Responsibilities of Customs Brokers

Record of transactions. Customs brokers are required to keep a correct and itemized record of all financial transactions and supporting papers for at least five years after the date of entry. Such books and papers must be available for inspection by officials of the Treasury Department. Brokers are required to make a status report of their continuing activity with customs.

Responsible supervision. Licensed brokers must exercise responsible supervision and control over the transaction of the customs business.

Diligence in correspondence and paying monies. Each licensed broker is required to exercise due diligence in making financial statements, in answering correspondence, and in preparing and filing records of all customs transactions. Payments of duties and other charges to the government are to be made on or before the date that payments are due. Any payment received by a broker from a client after the due date is to be transmitted to the government within five working days from receipt by the broker. A written statement should be made by the broker (to the client) accounting for funds received for the client from the government, as well as those received from the client when no payment has been made or received from a client in excess of charges properly payable within sixty days after receipt.

Improper conduct. The regulations prohibit the filing of false information, the procurement of information from government records to which access is not granted, the acceptance of excessive fees from attorneys, or the misuse of a license or permit.

License Requirements

To obtain a customs broker license, an individual must be (1) a citizen of the United States (but not an officer or employee of the United States), (2) at least twenty-one years of age, (3) of good moral character, and (4) able to pass an examination to determine that he or she has sufficient knowledge of customs and related laws.

To obtain a broker's license, a partnership or corporation must have one member who is a licensed broker and must establish that the customs transactions are performed by a licensed member or a qualified employee under the supervision and control of the licensed member. Disciplinary action for infractions, such as making false or misleading statements in an application for a license, conviction after filing of a license application, violation of any law enforced by the customs service, and so on, could result in a monetary penalty as well as the revocation or suspension of a license or permit.

A license is not required to transact customs business by the exporter or importer on his or her own account. This also extends to authorized employees or officers of the exporter/importer or customs broker. A license is also not required by a person transacting business in connection with the entry or clearance of vessels or by any carriers bringing merchandise to port.

Free-Trade Zones

Free-trade or foreign trade zones (FTZ) are areas usually located in or near customs ports of entry and legally outside the customs territory of the United States. Foreign goods brought into these zones may be stored, broken up, sorted, or otherwise manipulated or manufactured. While conducting these operations, duty payments are delayed until products officially enter into the customs territory.

Merchandise may be admitted into an FTZ upon issuance of a permit by the district director, unless the merchandise is brought in solely for manipulation after entry, is transiting the FTZ (for which a permit is granted), or is domestic merchandise.

FTZs are operated as public utilities under the supervision of the Foreign Trade Zones Board, which is authorized to grant the privilege of establishing a zone. Regulations are issued by the board covering the establishment and operation of FTZs. The Board, which is composed of the Secretary of Commerce (chairperson), the Secretary of the Treasury, and the Secretary of the Army, evaluates applications by public and private corporations for a zone based on the following criteria: the need for zone services in the area, suitability of the site and facilities, justification in support of a zone, extent of state and local government support, views of persons or firms to be affected, as well as regulatory policy and other applicable economic criteria. The board also accepts applications for subzones, that is, special-purpose zones established as adjuncts to a zone for a limited purpose. Such zones are single-user facilities, usually accommodating the manufacturing operations of an individual firm at its plant. Every port of entry is entitled to at least one FTZ (Rossides, 1986; U.S. Department of Commerce, 1990).

Economic Advantages

- Merchandise admitted into the zone is not subject to customs duty until it is admitted into the customs territory. There is no time limit as to the storage or handling of the merchandise within the zone.

- Businesses can import a product subject to a high rate of duty and manipulate and manufacture it into a final product that is classified under a lower rate of duty when imported into the customs territory. Importers can also bring in products for display to wholesalers or items restricted under a quota until the next quota period. A quota item may also be transformed in an FTZ into an item that can be freely imported without quota restrictions.
- The importer can establish the duty of foreign merchandise when entered into a zone by applying for a "privileged status." Under this scheme, only the duty previously fixed is payable upon entry of the merchandise into the customs territory at a later date even though its conditions may have changed or resulted in an article subject to a higher rate of duty.
- Duties are paid only on the actual quantity of such foreign goods incorporated in merchandise transferred from a zone of entry into the customs territory. This means that allowances are made for any unrecoverable waste resulting from manufacture or manipulation, thereby limiting the duty to articles actually entered. Savings in duties and taxes may thus result from moisture taken out or dirt removed, and so on. Savings in shipping and taxes may also be possible from shipping unassembled parts into a zone for assembly.
- Merchandise may be remarked or reconditioned to conform to certain requirements for entry into the customs territory.

The popularity of FTZs has grown not only in the United States but also in different parts of the world. By 1998, the number of such zones in the Unites States exceeded 200. Similar growth in the number of FTZs is observed in Africa, Asia, and Eastern Europe. A substantial part of the merchandise (over 80 percent) entered under FTZs in the United States is imported into the United States for domestic consumption, while the rest is exported to foreign markets.

Bonded Warehouses

Bonded warehouses are secured, U.S. customs-approved warehouse facilities in which imported goods are stored or manipulated without paying duty until the goods are removed and entered for consumption. Duty is not payable when goods under bond are exported, destroyed under customs supervision, or withdrawn as supplies for vessel or aircraft. Merchandise may be kept in the warehouse for up to five years from the date of importation. The advantages of a bonded warehouse are quite similar to those of FTZs.

Any person desiring to establish a bonded warehouse must submit an application to the district director where such facility is located. On approval of the application, a bond is executed to protect the duty liability. Customs regulations provide for different types of bonded warehouses.

The major differences between a bonded warehouse and an FTZ are as follows: (1) costs for the use of bonded warehouses are generally less than for FTZs, (2) bonded warehouses may be established on a user's facilities and with a limited degree of difficulty as compared with FTZs, and (3) the permitted types of manipulation are more limited in the case of a bonded warehouse than for an FTZ. For example, goods may be stored or otherwise manipulated in a bonded warehouse as long as the process does not involve manufacturing. The assembly of watch heads by combined domestic and foreign components is a manufacture (not a manipulation) prohibited under customs regulations. However, the repackaging of spare watch parts is a manipulation that is allowable.

CHAPTER SUMMARY

Tariffs and Nontariff Barriers As Import Restrictions

Methods of Levying Tariffs

1. Ad valorem: Duty based on value of the imported product
2. Specific: Duty based on quantity or volume
3. Compound: Duty that combines both ad valorem and specific

Nontariff Barriers

Nontariff barriers include quotas, tariff quotas, labeling requirements, licensing requirements, prohibiting the entry of certain imports, and requirements to purchase domestically produced goods.

Preferential Trading Arrangements

NAFTA, U.S./Israel FTA, the Caribbean Basin Initiative, the Andean Trade Preference, the Generalized System of Preferences

Trade Intermediaries and Services

Customs brokers, free-trade zones, and bonded warehouses

Customs Brokers

Customs brokers act as agents for importers with regard to (1) the entry and admissibility of merchandise, (2) its classification and valuation, and (3) the payment of duties and other charges assessed by customs or the refund or drawback thereof.

Free-Trade Zones (FTZ)

Free-trade zones are certain designated areas, usually located in or near a customs port of entry, where merchandise admitted is not subject to a tariff until it is entered into the customs territory. Foreign goods brought into an FTZ may be stored, sorted, or otherwise manipulated or manufactured. FTZs are legally considered to be outside the customs territory of a country.

Bonded Warehouses

Bonded warehouses are secured, government-approved warehouse facilities in which imported goods are stored or manipulated without payment of duty until they are removed and entered for consumption.

Chapter 17

Selecting Import Products and Suppliers

TYPES OF PRODUCTS FOR IMPORTATION

One of the most important import decisions is the selection of the proper product that serves the market need. In the absence of the latter, one is left with a warehouse full of merchandise with no one interested in buying it. Nevertheless, importing can become a successful and profitable venture so long as sufficient effort and time is invested in selecting the right product for the target market.

How does one find the right product to import? The following are different types of products to consider.

Unique Products

Products that are unique and different can be appealing to customers because they are a welcome change from the standardized and identical products sold in the domestic market. The fact that a product is imported and different, is in itself, sufficient for many people to purchase the item.

Less Expensive Products

It is quite common to find imports that perform identically to the competitor's product but can be sold at a much lower price. As customers quickly switch allegiance to buy the imported item, it is quite possible to capture a substantial share of the domestic market.

Products with Proven Demand

Keeping abreast of market trends often helps identify products that are in great demand. For example, increases in the immigrant populations from

Asia and Latin America have encouraged growth in the import of more and greater variety of spices. The United States imported an annual average of 530 million pounds of spices in 1990 to 1994, compared with 362 million pounds in 1980 to 1984 (Buzzanell and Lipton, 1995). In cases involving a continuous increase in demand for a product, imports become a major source of domestic supply because the product is either not produced in the country or not produced in sufficient quantities to satisfy the growing demand.

Products of Better Quality

Many products are manufactured abroad that are of better quality than those produced domestically. German machine tools, Japanese cars, and French perfumes have proven market demand because of high quality. In some cases, certain designs could best be manufactured overseas. Identifying a quality product has the potential to increase profits.

Any one of these types of products can be carefully selected based on one's background and expertise. Someone who likes gardening can import gardening utensils, decorations, and so on, while the computer technician could find imports of, for example, peripherals, software, enjoyable, and easy to handle.

FINDING THE PRODUCT

Any one or a combination of the following can be used to find, assess, and select the right product for importation.

Domestic Market Research

Primary market research can be conducted by a consulting firm to identify the best line of products for the domestic market. A variety of statistical sources provide data on projected total demand for certain products. Trade flows can also be examined to gather information on domestic demand and growth trends for various products. Some secondary sources also provide important market information, such as domestic market overviews, market share data, and opinions of industry experts. Such secondary market research studies and surveys can be purchased for a fraction of the cost of primary research. Online data can also provide industry and product information.

Trade Publications

Trade publications such as *Trade Channel, Asian Sources,* and *General Merchandise* provide business and trade opportunities in various countries. They include various advertisements of products and services available for import from all parts of the world (Weiss, 1987). Certain banks with international departments often publish newsletters with offers to buy and sell. The prospective importer can also use electronic bulletin boards of the World Trade Centers to find out what products are available for import.

Foreign Travel

Whenever one visits a foreign country, it is important to look for products that may have a market at home. If a good product is obtained, it could create a profitable business opportunity. One could find new and exciting products that are not currently imported in the public markets, bazaars, or gift stores. Once a good product is identified, a few samples can be purchased. The manufacturer's address could be obtained from the country's trade department or from local vendors, usually for a small referral fee. If one does not travel overseas, it is always possible to ask friends or agents abroad for product information.

Trade Fairs and Shows

One way of finding a product is to attend trade fairs and trade shows. Many exporters find such shows to be an effective means of promoting their products. It is estimated that almost 2,000 trade shows took place in over seventy-five countries in 1991 (Vanderleest, 1994). Many exporters introduce their products to the foreign market with the hope of writing orders at the show or of finding suitable distributors or manufacturers' agents who will handle their products in overseas markets. Major shows in the United States are published in the *Exhibits Guide.* The Department of Commerce publishes information on upcoming trade fairs and trade shows in the United States and abroad. There are also online sources on various shows and exhibitions in certain product areas to be held in various parts of the world. A recent online announcement, for example, invites buyers and sellers of artworks to the leading arts and antique fair in Maastricht, the Netherlands, where 125 major dealers from around the globe are expected to offer their antiques and works of art from all periods.

Foreign Countries' Trade Offices

Most countries have export promotion offices abroad. A trade promotion office provides important information on a country's major export products or services, suppliers, and other helpful contacts. In the absence of a trade promotion office for a nearby country, the embassy could be a good source of information on potential products to import.

International Perspective

17.1

QUALITY CONTROL FOR IMPORTS

Ensuring quality is the best means of winning consumer confidence and sales. Many manufacturing firms find that they must meet new and different standards criteria (national, corporate, regional, or international) to compete in the global marketplace. Even though the majority of industrial standards are voluntary, there are mandatory government-imposed standards in the fields of health and safety, food and drugs, and the environment. In many European countries, consumers often base their purchasing decisions on proof of certification for the product or service. European community directives also mandate that companies meet certain product certification standards in order to sell in the European Union.

In the area of imports, quality standards provide a basis for assessing quality of products and services. Suppliers are provided with a guide as to the quality of the product to be manufactured, while buyers are provided with the confidence that the goods are safe and meet high quality standards. It is important to establish quality testing and inspection procedures, and in the case of large orders, the importer could appoint a quality inspector at the supplier's location to assess and advise the supplier on quality. Acceptance and payment on a letter of credit can be made conditional on receipt of a satisfactory inspection certificate. An example of a quality control program for imports is the one jointly created by Chrysler, GM, and Ford (the QS-9000). The QS-9000 employs the ISO 9000 international quality assurance standard coupled with industry-specific criteria. The program mandates the use of the QS-9000 quality standard by suppliers around the world.

Regardless of the method used to find the potential product to import, it is advisable to buy a sample or a small order to determine whether there are any prohibitions or restrictions to entry and whether the product can be sold at a competitive price. The sample can be inspected by a customs broker to establish whether the product can be freely entered and, if allowed entry, the applicable duty rate. The sample could also be shown to a freight forwarder to obtain an estimate of the shipping and insurance cost in order to calculate the price at which the merchandise will be sold. It is important to realistically evaluate the price in terms of competing products in the market. When calculating the total cost plus a decent profit margin, if the price is much higher than a competing product in the market, it may be necessary to go back to the drawing board and try another product.

Suppose the product is not subject to prohibitions or restrictions and can be sold at a competitive price. The next step is to presell the product to likely buyers. This will determine whether people will buy the product and how much they are willing to pay for it. This can be done by the potential importer or salespeople. The process of supplier selection and negotiation to purchase the first shipment should be done only after making an assessment of how much one can realistically sell.

WHAT DETERMINES IMPORT VOLUME

Much of the literature on imports underlines the importance of high per capita incomes and population size in determining import levels. All other things being equal, countries with higher per capita incomes will be able to import more per person than countries with lower levels (Lutz, 1994). Larger countries (in terms of population) import fewer manufactured goods on a per capita basis because they tend to have a diversified industrial base, as investment will be attracted to these countries to take advantage of their big markets. This view can be exemplified by the case of the United States and Japan, both of which have low import propensities compared to countries such as Belgium or the Netherlands. Economic theory also suggests that import levels are affected by other factors, such as the price of imports denominated in foreign currency, the exchange rate, as well as the price of domestic goods relative to imports (Deyak, Sawyer, and Sprinkle, 1993; Warner and Kreinin, 1983). While relative prices have a predictable and systematic impact on imports, price elasticities tend to be low, in most instances well below unity. This suggests that large relative price swings are required to have an appreciable impact on trade patterns (Reinhart, 1995). For developing countries, however, determinants of import demand include government restrictions on imports and availability of foreign exchange (Sarmad, 1989). The study by Sarmad (1989) examining the factors influencing import demand in Pakistan from 1959 to 1986 found that the policy of devaluation or raising tariffs was not significant in reducing imports except in the case of imports of machinery and transport equipment. In countries with successful import-substitution strategies, the impact of relative prices and tariffs tends to decline in terms of their influence on import demand. Import substitution is a policy that taxes and restricts imports to protect and subsidize domestic industries. This policy, which paradoxically led to more import dependence (e.g., for purchases of raw materials, components, etc.), remains a popular economic strategy among developing nations (Lindert and Pugel, 1996).

SELECTING THE SUPPLIER

The product selected for importation may be manufactured by several firms in different countries or within the same country. The next important

step is to assess and select the right supplier based on a number of critical
factors, such as quality, delivery time and supplier reliability, transportation cost, import duty implications, protection of intellectual property
rights, and ability to meet standard requirements.

A study conducted in 1983 on the decision process of U.S. purchasing
agents suggests timely delivery, product brand name, and style as important factors that determine purchasing decisions (Ghymn, 1983). A major
concern in the minds of many U.S. importers is the quality of the imported
product. In today's marketplace, where many firms are competing for the
buyer's attention, it is the customer who defines quality in terms of his or
her needs. To be successful, an importer should select a supplier who can
deliver a product that satisfies consumer needs, has minimum defects, and is
priced competitively. Also adding to the importance of quality and the local
market appeal of the product is the availability of core supplier benefits,
such as warranties, timely delivery, favorable transportation terms, as well
as after-sales service and reliability. Low-cost suppliers can also be identified based on their proximity to raw materials, labor costs, current exchange
rates, or transportation costs.

Import duties could be eliminated or substantially reduced by selecting
suppliers located in countries that participate in a preferential trade arrangement. In the United States, for example, most products imported from
Canada, Mexico (NAFTA), Caribbean countries (CBI), Israel (FTA), and
countries eligible for GSP benefits are subject to duty-free treatment. For
example, ceramic tile imported from Italy is subject to a 13.5 percent duty,
whereas an identical tile coming from Israel would cost the importer only
4.3 percent duty. To qualify for such favorable treatment, it is necessary to
mark the country of origin of the import.

Selection of the supplier should also be based on the integrity of the
product. Integrity of the product includes the assumption that the import
does not violate any intellectual property rights registered in the country,
such as patent, trademark, design, or copyright, and that it meets certain
regulatory requirements, such as product compliance with the various
import laws relating to marking, labeling, inspections, and safety. There
has been a rise in the production and sale of counterfeit and pirated goods
in many parts of the world. Industry experts, for example, estimate lost
sales from unauthorized use of U.S. intellectual property rights at $60
billion annually. It is also important to select suppliers that use certain
product safety standards. For example, food service ceramics must be
tested for lead, and toys must meet labeling and safety standards.

A potential importer should be aware of any foreign laws that might
affect purchase, such as export restrictions or quotas. The importer also

needs to ascertain whether the supplier has already appointed other distributors or sales agents in the territory and whether the distribution channels available are acceptable in terms of overall profitability and risk. For example, an agent is likely to realize limited profits if the supplier has a distributor in the market.

Once a small number of potential suppliers are identified, a personal visit can be made to perform the necessary evaluation and selection of the right supplier. Final selection will be made based on factors such as (1) international knowledge and experience of supplier, (2) supplier's willingness to devote sufficient time to develop the market, (3) supplier's willingness to provide necessary training, and (4) provision of certain market exclusivity and acceptable payment arrangement. It is also important to obtain a credit report of the supplier. Such evaluation is critical regardless of the marketing channels adopted by the importer.

International Perspective

17.2

A TYPICAL IMPORT TRANSACTION

Step 1—Once a product is selected (see Finding the Product), the importer writes to overseas suppliers to send price lists and product catalogs.

Step 2—Upon receipt of the price lists and catalogs, the importer then shows the catalogs to potential customers without disclosing the supplier's name and address.

Step 3—If there is a favorable response from potential customers, the importer contacts the overseas supplier to request product samples and pays for their shipment by air. In the meantime, their importer checks with customs for the applicable duty and other import requirements for the product.

Step 4—Suppose the product sample received is found acceptable by the importer. The importer then orders a trial shipment by air and makes an advance payment to the supplier. The importer should communicate domestic marking, labeling, and other requirements to overseas supplier. The supplier's credit references can be obtained from the supplier, banks, and the U.S. Department of Commerce. Potential customers are approached to place orders for the product.

Step 5—As the goods arrive at the airport, the importer arranges with a customs broker to clear customs. The importer sets the selling price.

Step 6—If the trial shipment sells easily, the importer orders large shipments by sea freight and prepares a formal price list and product catalog.

INTERNATIONAL SOURCING

The outsourcing of products and services to external suppliers continues to expand, as firms search for ways to lower costs while improving their products to remain competitive. By the end of 1998, it is estimated that U.S. companies have spent more than $100 billion on outsourcing. Outsourcing is commonly used by firms in the areas of communications, computers, and semiconductors Firms that outsource often realize cost savings and an increase in capacity and quality. In spite of its fast growth, outsourcing is frequently perceived to be poorly controlled, high in cost, and a drain on quality and service performance (Domberger, 1999) (for advantages and disadvantages, see International Perspective 17.3). A firm can undertake outsourcing under various arrangements.

Wholly Owned Subsidiary

A firm may move production of parts or components to an affiliate established in a low cost location abroad. The firm will then import the output as it is needed. For example, IBM outsources production of parts to its manufacturing plants located around the world.

International Perspective

17.3

ADVANTAGES AND DISADVANTAGES OF OUTSOURCING

Advantages	Disadvantages
1. Lower price 2. Higher-quality products 3. Supply of products not available domestically 4. Advanced technology available from foreign sources	1. Difficulty in evaluating and selecting qualified suppliers 2. Effort should be made to ensure quality and delivery time 3. Political and labor problems 4. Paperwork and extra documentation as well as added costs such as freight, insurance, import duties, cost of letter of credit, travel, marking, etc. 5. Currency fluctuations and payment problems 6. Harder to quickly respond to market changes

---

Overseas Joint Venture

A firm can import supplies made under a joint venture arrangement. For example, Fujitsu imports parts for its DRAMs production from its joint venture partner in Taiwan. Mitsubishi Electric and Toshiba have also contracted DRAM manufacturing to Taiwanese partners.

In-Bond Plant Contractor

A firm sends raw materials and components to be processed or assembled in a low-cost location by an independent contractor. No customs duty is imposed by the country where the goods are assembled (temporarily imported under bond) and when the products are re-exported to the home country, import duties are imposed only on the value added abroad. The most popular is the maquiladora, which allows U.S. or other foreign companies to combine their technology with low-cost labor in Mexico. The raw materials or components imported in bond and duty free are processed or assembled for eventual re-export. The maquiladora can also be established as a wholly owned operation of the foreign firm.

Contract Manufacturing

A company enters into a contract with a foreign supplier to import a given quantity of products according to specifications. The supplier manages the day-to-day operation of the production process and allows the importer to focus on other core activities. The contract will provide for assurance of quality and quality control. Nortel, a Canadian-based manufacturer of communications equipment, outsources nearly $1 billion worth of components to contract manufacturers abroad.

PRICING THE IMPORTED PRODUCT

Knowledge of the price structure for imported goods makes it possible to determine the appropriate price to be charged for the merchandise. The price structure in Table 17.1 could be used as a general guide.

IMPORT MARKETING CHANNELS

One of the fundamental decisions for foreign suppliers is whether to sell their products direct or through intermediaries. Relying on an intermediary relieves the producer of international marketing activities. However, the producer forgoes part of the export profit and does not obtain firsthand

TABLE 17.1. Landed-Cost Survey, DM Import Company, Davie, Florida

Supplier: V. Maundo, Nairobi, Kenya	
Quantity: 150 Makonde carvings	
Gross sales price	**$3,500.00**
Less cash discount (15%)	525.00
Net sales price	2,975.00
Landed cost	
Purchase price	2,975.00
Packing	------
Inland freight	------
Duty $2,975 − (insurance [$50]+	
freight [800]) = 7% ($2,125.00)	148.75
Brokerage and banking charges	160.00
Custom bond fee	50.00
Merchandise processing fee	8.00
Harbor maintenance fee	2.00
Total landed cost (CIF Miami)	**3,343.75**
Expenses	
Advertising	------
Repacking	15.00
Interest	10.00
ABI (Automatic broker interface fee)	10.00
Total landed costs and expense	**3,378.75**
Unit cost	$22.52 per item
Suggested selling price	$45.00
Net Profit $6,750 ($45 × 150) − $3,378.75 (22.52 × 150) = $3,371.25	

Note: Markup is generally 60 to 100 percent for consumer items; 20 to 30 percent for industrial goods; 250 to 300 percent for mail-order items.

information on the market, and this, in turn, may reduce the firm's product adaptation capacity.

Two of the important developments in marketing channels have been the involvement of large retail groups in direct importation and subcontracting of production abroad by major manufacturing companies. In this age of intense competition, firms that manufacture standardized products can no longer rely on firm-specific advantages arising solely from technology. They should focus on ways of minimizing costs by manufacturing certain components (or subcontracting such production) in low-cost countries.

Direct Channel of Distribution

If a direct channel is adopted, the foreign producer exports through its subsidiary, the joint venture representative serving as importer, distributor, and/or wholesaler. This channel also includes imports manufactured under a subcontracting arrangement.

Indirect Channel of Distribution

This entails exporting the product to an intermediary, usually an import distributor, who serves as channel leader on behalf of the foreign manufacturer. It also includes a commission agent or an import merchant.

In short, a product can be imported by a firm wholly or partly owned by the foreign producer or by independent distributors or agents. Depending on the channel structure, imported merchandise is sold through various outlets: it may be sold to a wholesaler, retailer, or directly to the consumer. Wholesaling may bring in less money per item than retail, but it has the advantage of faster inventory turnover, less sales effort, and lower warehousing costs. However, since the wholesaler's sales effort is often spread among dozens of other products, a product may not be given individual attention. A product can be sold directly to retailers, for example, supermarkets, convenience stores, and specialty or discount stores. The importer could also set up his or her own store and sell the merchandise directly to the consumer. Several importers also sell at the various swap shops and flea markets around the country. Over the last few years, there has been an increase in the use of mail order or direct response TV/radio. Even though this approach can be very expensive, it allows the importer to reach millions of consumers in a very short time and possibly make a substantial number of sales very quickly if the product is successful.

FINANCING IMPORTS

Imports can be financed by using methods such as documentary collection, letters of credit, transferable letter-of-credit, or back-to-back letters of credit. Read the section dealing with the various types of letters of credit.

CHAPTER SUMMARY

Type of Products to Consider for Importation

Products that are unique, are less expensive, have proven market demand, and are of better quality.

```
┌─────────────────────────────────────────────────────────────┐
│              ┌──────────────────────────┐                     │
│     ═════════│  International Perspective │═════════          │
│              └──────────────────────────┘                     │
│                                                               │
│                          17.4                                 │
│                                                               │
│                THE TEN MOST COMMON MISTAKES                    │
│                   OF POTENTIAL IMPORTERS                       │
```

1. Failure to develop sufficient knowledge of the import process before starting the business, including import regulations
2. Insufficient knowledge of the product to be imported
3. Insufficient knowledge of the costs involved in obtaining, importing, and marketing a product
4. Neglecting to seek quality products at the lowest possible price
5. Failure to maintain a good working relationship with suppliers, banks, customs brokers, and other intermediaries
6. Inability to develop an appropriate price structure
7. Insufficient knowledge of the market
8. Insufficient working capital
9. Unwillingness to modify products to meet regulations or consumer preferences
10. Failure to invest sufficient time and effort to develop the business

Means of Finding, Assessing, and Selecting the Product

1. Domestic market research: using primary or secondary market research
2. Trade publications: Advertisements in various trade publications, international bank newspapers, and electronic bulletin boards
3. Foreign travel: Identifying promising import products during visits abroad
4. Trade fairs and shows: Import products found by attending various trade shows and trade fairs domestically and abroad
5. Trade offices: Seeking information from trade promotion offices and embassies of various countries on their major export products, as well as from other helpful contacts

Other Steps Before Selecting the Product and Supplier

1. Purchase a sample of the promising item
2. Request inspection by customs to determine if there are any restrictions to entry of the product and establish the applicable duty
3. Check with a freight forwarder about shipping and insurance cost

4. Estimate the price and determine whether the product can be sold at a competitive price

Determinants of Import Volume

1. High per capita income
2. Population size
3. Price of imports denominated in foreign currency
4. Exchange rates
5. Price of domestic goods relative to imports
6. Price elasticity
7. Government restrictions, availability of foreign exchange

Selecting the Supplier: Important Considerations

1. Product quality, brand name
2. Market appeal, minimum defects
3. Other supplier benefits: Timely delivery, warranties, after-sales service, reliability
4. Protection of intellectual property rights

Import Marketing Channels

1. Direct
2. Indirect

Financing Imports

1. Open account
2. Consignment
3. Documentary collection
4. Letter of credit

Chapter 18

The Entry Process for Imports

All goods entering the United States are subject to certain customs procedures regardless of their value or dutiable status. Duties accrue upon the imported merchandise on arrival of the vessel within the customs port (or on arrival of the merchandise within U.S. Customs territory for other means of transport). The making of an entry is generally required within five working days after arrival of the importing vessel or aircraft. "Entry" is the act of filing the necessary documentation with the customs officer to secure the release of imported merchandise. If entry is not made within five days, the goods are placed in a warehouse at the risk and expense of the importer. They may be sold at public auction if entry is not made within one year from the date of importation.

Goods may be entered by the owner, purchaser, his authorized regular employee, or by a licensed customs broker. When the goods are consigned to "order," the bill of lading, properly endorsed by the consignee, may serve as evidence of a right to make entry. An air waybill may be used for merchandise arriving by air. A foreign corporation in whose name a product is entered must have a resident agent at the place where the port of entry is located.

The importer or agent pays the estimated duty at the time of making entry even though customs has not yet liquidated the entry (i.e., final assessment of duty has not been made). Imported goods are not legally entered until after the shipment has arrived within the port of entry, delivery of merchandise has been authorized by customs, and estimated duties have been paid. It is the responsibility of the importer to arrange for examination and release of the goods. The required documentation can now be transmitted electronically to customs. U.S. Customs is in the process of moving toward a new paperless system in which importers can file their entries from a single location and clear shipments in hours instead of days.

U.S. Customs collected about $22 billion in tariffs, taxes, and user fees in 1996. Its revenues from user fees approached $700 million in 1997.

Additional revenues accrue from confiscations of cash allegedly involved in money laundering, penalties for violations of import quotas, and so forth (Bovard, 1998). In addition to the U.S. Customs Service, importers should contact other agencies when questions regarding particular commodities arise. Questions with respect to imports of products regulated by the Food and Drug Administration (FDA), for example, should be forwarded to the nearest FDA district office. Similarly, the respective federal agencies should be consulted whenever an imported product is subject to their regulatory regimes.

THE ENTRY PROCESS

Filing Entry Papers

The entry process requires filing the necessary documents to enable customs to determine whether the merchandise may be released from its custody, as well as for duty assessment and statistical purposes. Both of these processes can be accomplished electronically via the Automatic Broker Interface Program. What are entry documents? Entry documents generally consist of (1) an entry manifest (Form 7533) or application and special permit for immediate delivery (Form 3461), (2) a commercial invoice (or pro forma invoice when the commercial invoice cannot be produced), (3) a bill of lading, air waybill, or other evidence of right to make entry, (4) a packing list, if appropriate, and (5) other documents necessary to determine the admissibility of the merchandise. This may include information to determine whether the imported merchandise bears an infringing trademark. If the goods are to be released from customs on entry documents, an entry summary for consumption must be filed. An entry summary includes the entry package returned that allows for release of merchandise and other forms (Form 7501).

Release of Merchandise and Deposit of Estimated Duty

Once the complete entry is made by filing with customs (i.e., the declared value, classification, and rate of duty applicable to the merchandise as well as an entry summary for consumption), the product is released by customs and the estimated duty deposited. A bond must be posted before filing the entry summary to guarantee payment of duties or taxes upon the final assessment of duties or other fees by customs (liquidation of entry).

A bond is different from a carnet because the latter serves as a customs entry document and as a customs bond. Carnets are ordinarily acceptable without posting further security. Institutions that issue carnets or guarantee the payment obligation under carnets must be approved by customs. In cases in which a carnet is not used, a bond is usually required to secure a customs transaction. A single entry bond application is made by the importer or designated person to secure the entry of a single customs transaction, whereas a continuous bond application is made for multiple transactions. Such applications are made to the port director. Bonds may be secured through a resident U.S. surety company, a resident and citizen of the United States, or in the form of cash or other government obligations. The list of corporations authorized to act as sureties on bonds and the limits of their bonds is published by the Treasury Department. If individuals sign as sureties, customs often requires two sureties on a bond to protect the revenue and ensure compliance with the regulations. There are also other requirements that individuals have to meet to act as sureties: U.S. residency and citizenship, evidence of solvency and financial responsibility, and ownership of property that could be used as security within the limits of the port where the contract of suretyship is approved. The current market value of the property, and so on, less any debts, and so on, must be equal to or greater than the amount of the bond. In the event of default by the importer, the surety and importer are liable to pay liquidated damages to customs (Serko, 1985).

Liquidation, Protests, and Petitions

Liquidation is the final ascertainment of the duties and drawback accruing on an entry by customs. Liquidation is required for all entries of imported merchandise except the following: temporary importation bond entry, transportation in bond, and imports that are subject to immediate exportation. The liquidation procedure involves determination of the value of imports, ascertainment of their classification and applicable rate of duty, as well as computation of the final amount of duty to be paid. Customs will then establish whether any additional (excess) duty has to be paid (refunded) to the importer, as the case may be, and notify such liquidation to the importer, consignee, or agent by posting a public notice. It is also important to note the following:

Limitation on Liquidation

If imported merchandise is not liquidated within one year from the date of entry, it is considered liquidated at the rate and amount of duty stated at the time of entry.

International Perspective

18.1

AVOIDING ERRORS IN INVOICING

Any inaccurate or misleading representation or omission of required information in an invoice presented to customs pertaining to an entry may result in delays in release of merchandise or claims against the importer (unless he/she can establish due diligence). The invoice should reflect the real nature of the transaction. All invoices must include the following information:

•Description of port of entry and detailed description of merchandise (i.e., grade, quality, quantity, marks, and numbers, for products and/or packages, as the case may be) under which the product is sold.

•Description of the name of actual seller, importer, place and date of sale. It should also include the purchase price in the currency of sale. In the event that the product is shipped other than in pursuance of a purchase agreement, the invoice must state the value that the owner or shipper would have received in the ordinary course of trade.

•All charges included in the invoice price including commissions, insurance, etc., as well as any rebates or drawbacks allowed upon exportation of the merchandise. It should also state the value of any materials supplied by the importer.

•Any discounts as well as charges incurred by seller or consignee to deliver the merchandise to buyer and not just the FOB price.

Voluntary Reliquidation by Customs

Customs could reliquidate any entry within ninety days from the date of notice of the original liquidation.

Liquidation for Informal, Mail, and Baggage Entries

The effective date of liquidation for such entries is the date of payment of estimated duties upon entry of merchandise or the date of release by customs under free duty or permit for immediate delivery (Rossides, 1986).

Conversion of Currency

The date of exportation of the goods is the date used to determine the applicable rate of exchange for customs purposes.

Liquidation is not final until any protest that has been filed against it has been decided. If an importer disagrees with the liquidation of an entry, a protest may be filed in writing within ninety days after the date of notice of liquidation. The protest could be with respect to any one or more of the following: the appraised value of the merchandise, classification, duties and other charges, the exclusion of a product from entry, or the refusal to reliquidate an entry. If a protest is denied by the district director, the importer can appeal to the Court of International Trade. The parties have a right to further appeal to the Court of Appeals for the Federal Circuit and from there to the highest court in the country, the Supreme Court of the United States. An importer can also request for a further review of the protest other than that provided by the district director. If the protest is denied by the latter, the matter is forwarded for review by the regional commissioner.

Any interested party could file a petition with the secretary of the treasury if the individual/group believes that the appraised value, classification, or rate of duty for an imported merchandise is not correct. The term interested party includes manufacturers, producers, wholesalers, or trade unions in the United States.

THE HARMONIZED TARIFF SCHEDULE
OF THE UNITED STATES

In 1988, the Harmonized Tariff Schedule of the United States (HTSUS) was adopted. This was a commodity description and coding system that is predominantly used by other nations. The Harmonized System was developed under the auspices of the Customs Cooperation Council, with the active participation of governments and private organizations. The major benefits of adopting the Harmonized system are as follows:

- The HTSUS will be in line with the tariff determination procedures of most countries of the world.
- It facilitates the shipment and documentation of merchandise into the United States and creates a uniform and familiar system for U.S. exporters shipping to other countries.
- Such uniformity in classification and coding across countries simplifies the conduct of international trade negotiations and increases the accuracy of international trade statistics.

The HTSUS classifies goods according to their "essential character" or, in the case of apparel, on the basis of the fiber of chief weight. It is a

International Perspective

18.2

TYPES OF ENTRY

Entry for Consumption: This is the most common type of entry. Merchandise that is not held for examination is released under bond. Even in cases in which examination is required (e.g., to determine value, dutiable status, proper markings, or whether shipment contains prohibited articles), certain packages are designated for examination and the rest of the shipment is released under bond.

Entry for Warehouse: Imported goods may be placed in a customs bonded warehouse, and payment of duties is deferred until the goods are removed for consumption. No duty is payable if they are re-exported or destroyed under customs supervision. Goods may be manipulated, sorted, or repackaged in the bonded warehouse for eventual consumption or export. In this case, the duty payable is for the manipulated or new product at the time of withdrawal. Goods may remain in a bonded warehouse up to five years from the date of importation.

Entry for Transportation in Bond: Merchandise may be entered for transportation in bond without appraisement to any other port of entry designated by the importer. Only an entry for consumption is accepted if more than a year has elapsed since the date of original importation.

Informal Entry: Under this category are commercial entries valued at under $1,250, household and personal effects, and tools of trade. It does not require the same formalities as consumption entry and is also liquidated at entry.

Mail Entry: Merchandise that is imported by mail. No entry is required on duty-free merchandise not exceeding $1,250 in value. There is also no need to clear shipments for imports of under $1,250 (e.g., parcel delivered by a letter carrier).

Temporary Importation Under Bond: Certain types of goods that are not imported for sale (or sale on approval) are admitted without payment of duty, under bond, for exportation within one year (could be extended up to three years upon application to the port director) from the date of importation. This generally includes merchandise imported for repair, articles used as models, samples, animals and poultry imported for breeding, and so on. The ATA carnet can be used for this purpose.

Drawback Entry: A refund of 99 percent of all customs duties is allowed under certain conditions: (1) if the imported material is exported in the same condition as when imported or if destroyed under customs supervision within three years of the date of importation, or (2) if the imported merchandise is used in the manufacturing process and exported within five years from the date of importation.

detailed classification system containing approximately 5,000 headings and subheadings organized into ninety-six chapters and twenty sections (see Table 18.1).

Goods imported are subject to duty or duty-free status in accordance with their classification under the HTSUS. Duty-free status, for example, is available under certain conditional exemptions provided in column 1 of

TABLE 18.1. Harmonized Tariff Schedule of the United States

Heading/ Subheading	Stat. Suffix	Article Description	Unit of Quantity	Rates of Duty General	Special	2
4902		Newspapers, journals, and periodicals, whether or not illustrated or containing advertised material: appearing at least four times a				
4902.10.00	00	week	Kg	free	free	free
4902.90		Other: Newspaper supplements printed by				
4902.90.10	00	a granure process	No	1.6%	Free (A, CA E, IL, J, MX)	25%
4902.90.20		Other:	free	free		
	20	Newspapers appearing less than four times a week	Kg			
	40	Other business and professional journals and periodicals	No			
	60	Other (including single issues tied together for shipping purposes)	No			

Note: A = GSP countries, CA = Canada (import from Canada), E = Caribbean Basin countries, IL = Israel, J = Andean Preference Pact, MX = Mexico.

Rates of Duty
General: GATT members and others obtaining such status by a bilateral agreement.
Special: Imports from countries accorded special duty treatment: Canada, Mexico, GSP countries, etc.
2: Countries not friendly to the United States: Libya, North Korea, etc.

the tariff schedule. Column 2 is intended for countries that do not qualify for the most-favored-nation (MFN) duty rate, and imports under this category are subject to the highest rate. In cases in which the correct classification is not certain or the product falls under more than one classification, it is important to resort to the body of interpretative rules provided under the HTSUS or to seek a binding tariff classification ruling from customs that can be relied on before placing or accepting orders. Although the average tariff rate in the United States is now around 5 percent, some imports are subject to high tariffs: watch parts (151.2 percent), some shoe imports (67 percent). In certain cases, it is also possible for customs to reverse its classification even after the product has been imported and used. The customs service reversed its decision on imports of muffin mix toppings in 1996 and informed the importer to pay $750,000 penalty for violating the U.S. sugar quota (the decision was, however, reversed for the second time). In another case, imports of large antique red telephone booths were blocked on the grounds that the product was actually a steel product restricted by import quotas (Bovard, 1998). Thus, one cannot overemphasize the importance of obtaining an expert opinion, seeking an advance ruling by customs, or establishing reliable procedures on the correct description and classification of a given merchandise before importation.

CUSTOMS VALUATION

In 1979, the United States adopted the customs valuation system that was the result of the Tokyo Round negotiations of the GATT. Valuation of a product is important because most imported products are subject to tariffs based on the percentage of the value of the import (ad valorem rate). It also helps countries to maintain accurate and comparable records of their international trade transactions.

Imported merchandise is appraised on the basis, and in the order, of the following:

1. Transaction value
2. Deductive value
3. Computed value

The Transaction Value

Transaction value is the invoice price of the goods as they enter the United States. In determining transaction value, the price actually paid or payable will be considered without regard to its method of derivation. The value includes various costs that enhance the good's value to the importer i.e. packing costs, sales commissions, and royalties. It also includes any direct or indirect items provided by the buyer free of charge or at a reduced cost for use in the production or sale of merchandise for export to the United States. In short, the transaction value is the price actually paid or payable for imported merchandise, excluding international freight, insurance and other CIF charges. Transaction value cannot be used in the following situations:

- In cases in which the transaction value cannot be determined (proceeds of subsequent sales, etc.) or is not acceptable (related-party transactions)
- In cases involving restrictions on the sale or use of the product

Example 1

A foreign shipper sold merchandise at $1,500 to a U.S. buyer. The seller subsequently increased the price to $1,650. The invoice price is $1,500.00 because that was the price agreed to and actually paid by the importer. The merchandise should be appraised at $1,500 because the latter was the price actually paid by the buyer—the transaction value.

Example 2

DM, Incorporated, a firm located in Miami, Florida, purchased 10,000 barrels of crude oil from a Venezuelan oil company, Soto, Incorporated, for $250,000. The price consists of $200,000 for the oil and $50,000 for ocean freight and insurance. Soto would have charged $210,000 for the oil. However, since it owes DM $10,000, Soto charged DM only $200,000 for the oil. The transaction value is $210,000, that is, the sum of ($200,000 + $10,000), excluding CIF charges of $50,000 for ocean freight and insurance.

If the transaction value cannot be determined, the transaction value of an identical merchandise or, in the absence of the latter, the transaction value of a similar merchandise (commercially interchangeable) will be used. The transaction value of identical and similar merchandise (ISM) will be used under the following circumstances:

- The products (ISM) must have been sold for export to the United States at or about the same time as the merchandise being appraised.

- Value must be based on sales of ISM at the same commercial level and substantially the same quantity as the sale of the merchandise being appraised.
- The ISM must be produced in the same country and by the same person (if not available, by a different person) as the merchandise being appraised.
- In cases involving two or more transaction values for ISM, the lowest value will be used as the appraised value of the imported merchandise.

Deductive Value

This method is used when the transaction value cannot be determined, such as sales between related parties. However, if the importer designates computed value as the preferred method of appraisement, the latter can be used as the next basis of determining value. Deductive value is essentially the resale price of an imported product, with deductions for commissions, profit and general expenses, transportation and insurance costs (from the country of export to the United States), import duties and taxes, and any cost of further processing after importation. The deductive value is generally calculated by starting with the unit price and making additions to (such as packing costs), and deductions from, that price (see International Perspective 18.3).

Example 1

Merchandise is sold to an unrelated person from a price list that provides favorable unit prices for purchases in larger quantities:

Total Quantity Sold	Unit Price
65	$90.00
50	95.00
60	100.00
25	105.00

In this example, the unit price used in determining deductive value is $90 because the greatest quantity is sold at that price.

Example 2

A foreign parent company sells parts to its U.S. subsidiary in Texas. The product is not sold to unrelated parties and there is no similar or

```
┌─────────────────────────────────────────────────────────────────┐
│  ┌─────────────────────────────────┐                             │
│  │      International Perspective   │                             │
│  └─────────────────────────────────┘                             │
│                                                                   │
│                              18.3                                 │
│                                                                   │
│               UNIT PRICE IN DEDUCTIVE VALUE                       │
│                                                                   │
│   One of three prices is used based on time and condition of sale:│
│                                                                   │
```

•If the merchandise is sold in the condition as imported at or about the date of importation of the merchandise being appraised, the unit price used is the one at which the greatest quantity of the product is sold.

•If the merchandise is sold in the condition as imported, but not sold at or about the date of importation of the merchandise being appraised, the unit price used is the one at which the greatest quantity of the merchandise is sold before the ninetieth day after the date of importation.

•If the merchandise is not sold in the condition as imported and not before the close of the ninetieth day after the date of importation of the merchandise being appraised, the unit price used is the one at which the greatest quantity (after processing) is sold before the eightieth day after the date of importation. An amount equal to the value of the further processing is deducted from the unit price in arriving at the deductive value. This method cannot be used if further processing destroys the identity of the merchandise.

identical merchandise from the country of production. The U.S. subsidiary further processes the product and sells to an unrelated buyer in Florida within 180 days after importation.

In this example, the merchandise should be appraised under deductive value, with allowances for profit and general expenses, freight and insurance, duties and taxes, and the cost of processing.

Computed Value

The computed value starts with the costs of the materials, labor, and overhead in producing the imported goods. Customs then adds profits and general expenses incurred by the producer (based on average estimates for similar goods in the same country) as well as the prorated value of any materials supplied by the buyer free of charge or at reduced price and packing costs (U.S. Department of Commerce, 1995).

Example

Suppose under the previous Example 2, the U.S. importer requested the shipment to be appraised under computed value. The merchandise is appraised using the company's profit and general expenses if not inconsistent with sales of merchandise of the same class or kind.

If none of the previous methods can be used to appraise the imported merchandise, the customs value is based on a value derived from one of these methods, reasonably adjusted or administered flexibly. If an identical or similar product, for example, is not available in the exporting country, customs could appraise an identical or similar product from a third country to determine value.

RULES OF ORIGIN
AND OTHER MARKING REQUIREMENTS

Imported articles are to be marked with the name of the country of origin to indicate to the ultimate purchaser the name of the country in which the product was manufactured. Country-of-origin determination is important because imports are subject to selective tariffs and nontariff barriers depending on the origin of the merchandise. Most imports, for example, from Canada and Mexico, enter duty free, whereas those from other nations are subject to a higher tariff, a quota, or even an import ban (e.g., Cuba, and North Korea). Customs uses the "substantial transformation test" to determine the country of origin of a product that is made up of components or materials from several different countries. The country of origin is determined to be the one where the product was substantially transformed in its current state (Buonafina and Haar, 1989).

In the case of certain articles for which marking is not required, such as artworks, lumber, sugar, and so forth, their containers must be marked to indicate the English name of the country of origin. There are also special marking requirements for certain articles, for example, watches, surgical instruments, and vacuum containers. However, marking is not required for imports not intended for sale (personal use items), products used for further processing, or items that are incapable of being marked or cannot be marked without injury or prohibitive expense. Notwithstanding the exemption, the containers must be marked to show the country of origin of such articles.

| International Perspective |

18.4

AUTOMATED SERVICES IN THE UNITED STATES TO FACILITATE INTERNATIONAL TRADE

• **Automated Broker Interface (ABI):** The Automated Broker Interface is a component of the U.S. Customs Service's Automated Commercial System that permits participants to electronically file required import data with Customs. ABI participants include brokers, importers, carriers, port authorities, or independent service centers. Presently, over 96 percent of all entries are filed through ABI. ABI speeds up the release of merchandise. Entry summaries are electronically transmitted, validated, confirmed, corrected, and paid. Participants are also informed of current information and can request quota status, visa requirements, entry, or entry summary status. ABI allows filers to pay for multiple entries with one payment transaction.

• **Automated Clearinghouse (ACH):** The Customs Automated Clearinghouse is an electronic payment option that allows participants to pay customs fees, duties, and taxes electronically. Participants' banks must belong to the National Clearinghouse Association. The accuracy and speed of ACH results in a higher volume of transactions.

• **Automated Export System (AES):** The Automated Export System is a joint undertaking between the Bureau of Export Administration, U.S. Customs and other federal agencies intended to ensure compliance with U.S. export regulations and to improve trade statistics. Its objective also includes introduction of a paperless reporting system for export information by 2002.

• **Automated Information Systems Security Policy (AIS):** This policy provides guidance for the protection of AIS resources by establishing uniform policies and procedures for the Customs AIS Security program. It provides security for information that is collected, processed, stored or transmitted.

• **Automated Manifest System (AMS):** This is a cargo inventory control and release notification system. AMS interfaces with other systems such as ABI to allow for faster identification and release of low-risk shipments. It speeds the flow of cargo and entry processing and provides participants with electronic authorization of cargo release prior to arrival. It also facilitates the intermodal movement and delivery of cargo.

• **AMS Paperless Master In-Bond Participants:** This program is designed to take advantage of the detailed information available within the AMS to control the movement and disposition of master in-bond shipments from the custody of the ocean carrier at the port of unlading to the same carrier's custody at the port of destination. AMS tracks and records such merchandise.

CHAPTER SUMMARY

Entry of Imports

Entry is the act of filing the necessary documentation with customs to secure release of imported merchandise.

Accrual of Duties on Imports

1. On arrival of the vessel: Upon arrival of vessel within the U.S. Customs territory
2. Arrival of merchandise: Upon arrival of merchandise within the U.S. Customs territory (for other means of transport)

Who May Enter the Goods

Owner, purchaser, authorized regular employee, or a licensed customs broker

Documentation Required to Enter Merchandise

Entry manifest, commercial invoice, pro forma invoice, packing list, and other necessary documents

Release of Merchandise

After complete entry is made, product is released by customs and estimated duty paid. A bond must be posted to guarantee payment of duty upon final assessment of duty. A bond may be secured through a resident surety company, resident, citizen, or posted in the form of cash or other government obligations.

Liquidation and Protests

1. Liquidation: This involves the final ascertainment of the duties and drawback accruing on an entry by customs.
2. Protests: If an importer disagrees with the liquidation of an entry, it is possible to file a protest in writing with the district director within ninety days after notice of liquidation. The decision can be appealed to the Court of International Trade, the Court of Appeals for the Federal circuit, and the Supreme Court of the United States.

Harmonized Tariff Schedule of the United States (HTSUS)

HTSUS is a commodity description and coding system that is used by many countries. It classifies goods according to their essential character.

Customs Valuation

Imported merchandise is appraised on the basis and in order of the following:
1. The transaction value: Invoice value of the goods as they enter customs
2. The deductive value: Resale price of imported merchandise with deductions for profit and general expenses
3. The computed value: Cost of materials, labor, and overhead in producing the imported product plus profits and general expenses incurred by the producer and value of any items supplied by buyer

Rules of Origin and Other Marketing Requirements

Marking requirements: Every imported article must be legibly marked with the English name of the country of origin unless otherwise indicated.

Chapter 19

Import Relief to Domestic Industry

The U.S. trade policy is based on combating unfairly traded imports. There are regulations in place to provide relief to domestic producers that are adversely affected by imports that benefit from government subsidies in home countries or are dumped at low prices in the U.S. market.

ANTIDUMPING AND COUNTERVAILING DUTIES

U.S. antidumping and countervailing duty laws have been subject to several changes over the years; the most recent amendments were made to implement the Uruguay Round Agreements of the GATT. It is important, however, to describe the terms that are often used in the analysis of unfair trade practices, that is, dumping, subsidies, and material injury.

Dumping is defined as selling a product in the United States at a price that is lower than the price for which it is sold in the home market in the ordinary course of trade (certain adjustments are made for differences in the merchandise, quantity purchased, or circumstances of sale). In the absence of sales or sufficient sales of the like product in the domestic market of the exporting country, dumping may be measured by comparison (1) with a comparable price of a like product sold in a third country or (2) with the cost of production in the country of origin plus a reasonable amount for administrative, selling, and other costs and for profits (constructed value). Selection of third a country is often based on the similarity of merchandise to the one exported in the United States, volume of sales (country with largest volume of sales), and similarity of market in terms of organization and development to that of the United States. In calculating constructed value, transactions with related parties that do not fairly reflect the usual market price, as well as sales that are made at less than the cost of production, are disregarded. In cases in which the economy of the home market is state-controlled and does not reflect the market value of the product, foreign market value can be determined based on, in order of preference, (1) the price at which such or similar merchandise produced in a non-state-controlled economy is sold either for consumption in that country, or another country including the United States, or (2) the constructed value of such and similar merchandise in a non-state-controlled economy country. Where the price comparison requires a conversion of currencies, such conversion is made using the rate of exchange on the date of sale.

There is no agreed-upon definition of subsidies anywhere in the GATT or domestic law. However, it is reasonable to infer from the list of practices that are considered as subsidies that a subsidy is a preferential benefit given by the government to domestic producers. The benefit could be in the form of income or price support of any direct or indirect financial contributions (e.g., grants, loans, tax credits, loan guarantees, etc.).

Export subsidies are benefits intended to increase exports; domestic subsidies are granted on a product regardless of whether it is exported or consumed at home. Governments provide domestic subsidies to achieve certain socioeconomic goals, such as optimum employment or location of industries in depressed regions, that could not be attained by the sole efforts of the private sector. Although domestic subsidies may increase the subsidizing country's trade flow, they do not attract international condemnation as export subsidies.

It is important to review the rules with respect to permitted or actionable subsidies. If an actionable subsidy is found in a country that is a signatory to the GATT Subsidies Code and that subsidy causes injury to a domestic industry, a countervailing duty is imposed on the subsidized imported product. Proof of injury is not required if the subsidized import comes from a country that is not party to the Subsidies Code or similar agreement. A countervailing duty is imposed to offset the subsidy, that is, equal to the net amount of the subsidy.

Actionable Subsidies

These are subsidies conferred upon a producer to encourage exports (export subsidy) or to promote the use of domestic goods (import-substitution subsidies). They are considered to be industry specific, as opposed to noncountervailable (nonactionable) subsidies that are broadly available and widely used throughout the economy. National programs of subsidies that are designed to specifically assist selected national regions are now considered actionable and subject to retaliation. In all these cases, the benefits obtained are not countervailable if they cannot be calculated in monetary terms. Actionable subsidies include domestic subsidies bestowed on input products used in the production of an imported item (upstream subsidies). However, the input subsidy must be provided in the country of manufacture of the imported product for the application of trade remedy. Countervailable subsides that are small *(de minimis)* subsidies, that is, less that 0.5 percent or 2 to 3 percent for developing nations, are disregarded. The Department of Commerce does not make an affirmative countervailing duty determination in such cases.

Nonactionable Subsidies

Nonspecific Subsidies

The determination of whether a subsidy is specific is based on a number of factors, such as the number or proportion of particular industries using the subsidy program as well as the manner in which authorities exercise discretion in providing the subsidy.

Subsidies for Industrial/Research and Competitive Development

These include assistance for research activities conducted by firms or by higher education establishments if such subsidies cover (1) not more than 75 percent of the costs of industrial research or (2) not more than 50 percent of the costs of precompetitive development activity (e.g., translation of industrial research findings into a blueprint or plan for new or improved products or processes).

Subsidies to Entities in Disadvantaged Regions

These subsidies should be part of a general framework of regional development, and they are not provided specifically to an enterprise or industry.

Environmental Subsidies

A nonrecurring subsidy for the adaptation of existing facilities (up to 20 percent of the cost) to new environmental requirements.

> *Example 1.* An Italian firm sells a pair of leather shoes manufactured in Milan for $250 in Italy. The same pair of shoes when exported is

sold for $150 in the U.S. market. There is no evidence that the firm obtained any financial help from the Italian government. This is a case of dumping.

Example 2. A Colombian firm obtained a low interest loan from a governmental-owned bank to buy chemical imports that are used for the production of textiles that are exported to the United States. The price of linen textiles (1 foot) is $20 in Colombia, whereas the same type of textile is sold at $12 a foot in New York. This involves upstream subsidies and dumping.

Proof of Injury and Remedies

In both antidumping and countervailing duty investigations, it is important to establish causation: material injury, threat of material injury, or retardation of a U.S. industry producing similar products because of the importation of subsidized and dumped products. Imports do not have to be the sole or even major cause of injury. Typically, the U.S. International Trade Commission (USITC) considers the collective impact of all imports of a product from a given country in arriving at its injury determination. However, in countervailing duty investigations, there is no injury determination for imports from countries that are not signatories of the Subsidies Code or an equivalent arrangement with the United States, unless the goods are entered duty free.

In determining whether there is injury to a U.S. industry, the ITC will consider import volumes, price effects, and impact on domestic producers of similar products as well as all other relevant economic factors that have a bearing on the domestic industry. Lost sales to the domestic industry have traditionally served as an important element of injury (USITC, Publ. 1691, Inv. No. 731-TA-254, May 1985). Injury may be shown even in cases involving an improvement in the condition of the industry or a decrease in import volume. ITC's determination of threat of material injury is made on the basis of evidence that the threat is real and the actual injury imminent and not based on "mere conjectures and suppositions" (19 U.S. Code S.1677).

Once it is established that foreign merchandise is being sold in the United States at less than fair market value and injury to domestic industry is established, an antidumping duty is imposed on the product i.e. an amount by which the foreign market value exceeds the U.S. price of the merchandise. Similarly, if a subsidy is shown to exist and material injury or threat thereof to U.S. industry is found, then a duty equal to the subsidy (countervailing duty) is imposed. In the case of agricultural products, injury could still be established even though the prevailing market price is at or above the minimum support price. This is intended to ensure that injury analysis is not distorted by the beneficial effects of government assistance programs.

ANTIDUMPING AND COUNTERVAILING DUTY PROCEEDINGS

Antidumping (AD) and countervailing duty (CVD) investigations are conducted either on the basis of a petition filed with the Department of Commerce (Commerce) through the International Trade Administration (ITA) and the International Trade Commission (ITC) on behalf of a domestic industry or by Commerce upon its own initiative. In the latter case, Commerce must notify the ITC. In a countervailing duty investigation, the ITC plays an active role only when the foreign government conferring the subsidies has entered into a trade agreement such as the Subsidies Code or a similar arrangement with the United States (U.S. International Trade Commission [USITC], 1996a). The procedural steps of a typical investigation are as follows (see Table 19.1).

TABLE 19.1. Antidumping and Countervailing Duty Investigations

Day	Event
0	Petition Filed
20	Decision on Initiation
45	Preliminary Injury Determination by ITC*
AD:160	Preliminary Determination by ITA
CVD:85	Preliminary Determination by ITA
AD:235	Final Determination by ITA*
CVD:160	Final Determination by ITA*
AD:280	Final Injury Determination by ITC*
CVD:205	Final Injury Determination by ITC*
AD:287	Publication of Order
CVD:212	Publication of Order

Note: AD= Antidumping duty; CVD = Countervailing duty.
*If the determination is negative, the investigation is terminated.

Initiation of Investigation by Commerce

Once a petition is filed or an investigation started at the initiative of Commerce (ITA), ITC begins to investigate material injury or threat of material injury, etc. to the domestic industry. In the case of a petition, Commerce determines within twenty days whether to initiate or terminate the investigation based on whether the petition adequately alleges material injury or threat thereof, with sufficient information supporting the allegations, and whether the petition has been filed by or on behalf of the industry (domestic producers or workers supporting the petition must account for at least 25 percent of total production and more than 50 percent of production of those supporting or opposing the petition). If Commerce (ITA) determines to initiate an investigation, it will begin to establish whether there is a subsidy or dumping in the U.S market, and the commission continues its investigation on injury to domestic industry.

Preliminary Phase of ITC's Investigation

Within forty-five days after a petition is filed or an investigation is begun by Commerce, the ITC makes its preliminary determination, that is, whether there is a reasonable indication of injury to domestic industry. If the determination is negative, or the imports subject to the investigation are negligible, the proceedings terminate.

Preliminary Phase of Commerce's Investigation

If the ITC's determination is affirmative, Commerce makes its preliminary determination based on the information available at the time whether there is a reasonable basis to believe or suspect that a countervailable subsidy or sales at less than fair market value exists.

If commerce finds a reasonable basis, it estimates the dumping or subsidy margin within 140 and 65 days, respectively, of initiating an investigation. However, such deadlines can be extended if the petitioner requests or the case is extraordinarily complicated.

If Commerce's preliminary determination is affirmative, commerce (1) suspends liquidation of the investigated merchandise subsequently entered into the United States or withdrawn from warehouse, (2) requires bonds or cash deposits to be posted for each entry of the merchandise in an amount equal to the estimated net subsidy or dumping margin, and (3) continues the investigation. In addition, the ITC institutes a final investigation concerning injury, threat, or retardation. If Commerce's preliminary determination is negative, Commerce's investigation simply continues (USITC, 1996b).

Final Phase of Commerce's Investigation

Within seventy-five days after its preliminary determination, Commerce makes a final determination as to whether a subsidy is being provided or sales at less than fair value are being made. If the final determination is negative, the proceedings end, and any suspension of liquidation is terminated, bonds or other security released, and deposits refunded. Any party to the proceedings can request a hearing before final determination by Commerce. If the final determination by Commerce is affirmative, the ITC will then make its determination on injury.

Final Phase of ITC's Investigation

The ITC makes its final determination with respect to material injury, threat thereof, or retardation of domestic industry because of sales at less than market value or subsidies. The investigations must be completed within 120 days after Commerce's affirmative preliminary determination (if Commerce's preliminary determination is affirmative) or within seventy-five days after Commerce's affirmative final determination (if Commerce's preliminary determination is negative).

Issuance of an Order

If the final determination of the ITC is affirmative, Commerce issues an antidumping or countervailing duty order, usually within a week of ITC's determination. The order requires the deposit of estimated antidumping (AD) or countervailing duty (CVD) at the same time as other estimated customs duties pending calculation of the final AD or CVD. If the final determination by the ITC is negative, no AD or CVD is imposed, and any suspension of liquidation is terminated, bonds released, and deposits refunded (USITC, 1996a). If the petitioner alleges in an investigation the existence of critical circumstance, that is, massive entry of subsidized imports or imports sold at less than fair value in a relatively short period, Commerce's final determination, if affirmative, will include a retroactive suspension of liquidation for all unliquidated entries of merchandise entered into the United States, including those withdrawn from warehouse.

Suspension of Investigation

An investigation can be suspended prior to a final determination by Commerce if the parties (exporting or subsidizing government) involved agree to cease exports or eliminate the dumping margin or subsidy within a few months after suspension of the investigation. At the same time as it suspends a proceeding, Commerce must issue an affirmative preliminary determination. Suspensions are reviewed by the ITC to ensure the injurious effect of imports is eliminated by the agreement. If the ITC determines that the injurious effect is not eliminated, the investigation, if not yet completed, will resume.

Appeal of Determinations

Any interested party adversely affected by a determination by Commerce or ITC may appeal to the U.S. Court of International Trade. In the case of NAFTA members, an interested party may appeal for a review by a binational panel set up under the agreement (for the type/number of investigatons, see Table 19.2).

Table 19.2. Antidumping (Countervailing) Duty Investigations (1991-1996)

	1991	1992	1993	1994	1995	1996
Initiations	66(11)	84(22)	37(5)	51(07)	14(2)	21(01)
Preliminaries	43(09)	54(26)	67(01)	46(07)	23(03)	16(00)
Finals	28(05)	28(07)	80(20)	31(02)	38(06)	2(02)
Duty Orders	19(02)	16(04)	42(16)	16(01)	24(02)	09(02)
Revocations	07(06)	01(00)	03(01)	29(05)	12(35)	06(01)

Source: USITC, 1996a, p. 5.

OTHER TRADE REMEDIES

Unfair Trade Practices in Import Trade

The ITC is authorized, upon the filing of a complaint or on its own initiative, to investigate alleged violations of section 337 and to determine whether such violations exist. Section 337 of the Tariff Act of 1930 pro-

```
┌──────────────────────────────────────────────────────────────┐
│                  ┌────────────────────────────┐               │
│                  │   International Perspective │               │
│                  └────────────────────────────┘               │
│                                                                │
│                            19.1                                │
│                                                                │
│              ECONOMIC EFFECTS OF ANTIDUMPING                   │
│                AND COUNTERVAILING DUTIES                       │
└──────────────────────────────────────────────────────────────┘
```

A study by the ITC published in 1995 on the economic effects of unfair imports and of remedies imposed under antidumping (AD) and countervailing duties (CVD) laws indicates the following: (1) the removal of outstanding AD/CVD orders in 1991 resulted in a welfare gain of $1.59 billion; (2) while domestic companies and their workers receiving AD/CVD protection earned $658 million more profits and wages, terminating this protection would have increased overall American business profits and wages by $1.85 billion in industries that were not receiving such protection; (3) U.S. prices of goods subject to AD/CVD rose when the duties were applied. For example, domestic steel pipe and tube prices rose by 10 percent, lamb meat prices went up by 10 percent; U.S. consumers paid $11 million in higher prices for orange juice concentrate in the 1984-1985 crop year (USITC, 1995). The economic effects of AD/CVD orders are ranked third behind the Multifiber Arrangement restrictions and the Jones Act maritime restrictions in their net costs to the economy.

hibits (1) the importation of articles that violate a valid and enforceable U.S. patent, trademark, copyright, and so on, for which an industry exists or is in the process of being established in the United States and (2) unfair methods of competition by the importer or consignee that could adversely affect a U.S. industry (19 U.S. Code S.1337). ITC's investigations also include gray-market imports (i.e., products manufactured abroad by the owner or under license that are imported by unauthorized sources into the United States). The strict definition of gray-market goods is: products that are authorized by the owner of production rights to be made and sold in one market are diverted and sold in another, often unauthorized market. The problem with such goods in import trade is that they are often purchased at discounted prices abroad and imported into the United States, taking away the market from authorized dealers.

A large percentage of Section 337 cases involve patent infringement; others pertain to violation of other forms of intellectual property. Such actions can also be raised with the U.S. Patent and Trademark Office. The remedies for such violations include the following:

1. A general or limited exclusion order that directs customs to deny entry of certain goods
2. A cease and desist order that enjoins a person from further violation of Section 337

These remedies may be ordered by the ITC in the case of imports infringing upon U.S. intellectual property rights without finding injury. ITC determinations may be appealed to the US. Court of Appeal for the Federal Circuit.

Market Disruption by Imports from Communist Nations

The ITC conducts investigations to establish whether imports of products made in a communist country are causing market disruption to a domestically produced article (19 U.S. Code S.2436). "Market disruption" is defined as a rapid increase in imports that causes material injury or threat thereof to a domestic industry producing a product similar to, or in direct competition with, the imported article. Such investigations may be requested by the president, the U.S. Trade Representative (USTR), Congress, or any interested party. The President may order remedial action in the form of imposition of duties, quotas, and so forth, after receiving the recommendation of the ITC.

Unjustified Foreign Trade Practices

Section 301 of the Trade Act of 1974 was introduced in order to seek open access to U.S. exports in foreign markets. It is directed at foreign government practices that restrict U.S. exports or artificially direct goods or services to the United States. It is applicable to the export of goods and services, investment practices, and intellectual property rights. Under Super 301 Clause of the 1988 Trade Act (renewed in 1994), the U.S. Trade Representative (USTR) is required to examine annually unreasonable or discriminatory restrictions on U.S. exports and then prepare a list of foreign trade practices of foreign countries. If the offending practice remains in place one year after unsuccessful negotiation, punitive tariffs can be imposed equal to the estimated value of lost sales by U.S. firms. Super 301 negotiations have been conducted with many countries, including China and Japan.

Special 301 is another version of Super 301 applicable to intellectual property rights. Priority countries (countries that do not provide adequate protection for intellectual property rights) are identified for bilateral negotiations. A Special 301 investigation is similar to an investigation initiated in response to an industry Section 301 petition. Trade sanctions for noncompliance could be imposed in the event that the country declines bilateral consultations or fails to implement an agreement to open its market or provide adequate protection for U.S. intellectual property rights.

Example 1

In June 1995, the Committee on Pipe and Tube Imports filed a petition alleging that the Korean government restricts exports of domestically produced steel sheet and controls domestic prices of steel sheet at levels well below world prices. It also complained of restricting exports to the European Union of pipe and tube products, which are thereby diverted to the U.S. market. In July 1995, the committee withdrew their petition in response to a binding agreement between the United States and South Korea establishing a consultative mechanism.

Example 2

In 1996, the following countries were identified for their trade policies and practices that have the greatest adverse effect on U.S. products:

1. *China:* Piracy of U.S. intellectual property rights, export of infringing goods (illegal production and export of CDs, videos, CD-ROMs, etc.) (priority foreign country).
2. *Argentina, Greece, India, Indonesia, Korea:* Lack of adequate and effective protection of intellectual property rights and market access (countries under a priority watch list).
3. *Australia, Brazil, Canada, Colombia, Italy:* Monitored to ensure the implementation of agreements on intellectual property and market access (countries under a watch list). (U.S. Trade Representative [USTR], 1997)

In 1999, the office of the USTR released its annual report on foreign trade barriers, covering the practices of fifty-four trading partners. The report identifies many countries as having unfair trade practices and barriers to American exports of goods, services, and farm products. Countries covered include Canada (in the areas of agricultural regime, cultural industries, inadequate protection of patents and copyright); China (problems of market access, inadequate enforcement of its laws against piracy of IPR); the European Union (protectionist agricultural policy, standard-setting procedures); and Japan, Korea, and Mexico (problems of market access in certain sectors) (USTR, 1999).

Import Interference with Agricultural Programs

The ITC conducts investigations at the direction of the president to determine whether imports interfere with or render ineffective any program of the Department of Agriculture. The ITC makes its findings and recommendations to the president, who may take appropriate remedial action, including the imposition of a fee or quota on the imports in question. However, fees or quotas may not be imposed on imports from nations that are members of the WTO (USITC, 1997).

Trade Adjustment Assistance

For companies and workers adversely affected by fairly traded imports, trade adjustment assistance is provided in the form of retraining or relocation assistance for workers or certain forms of technical and financial assistance to companies. The Department of Labor (adjustment assistance for workers) or Commerce (adjustment assistance for firms) makes an affirmative determination insofar as imports constitute an important contributing factor to declines in production and sales as well as loss of jobs in the affected industries. Such assistance could be pursued before or in tandem with escape clause proceedings.

The Escape Clause

Under Section 201 of the U.S. Trade Act, 1974, the ITC assesses whether U.S. industries are being seriously injured by fairly traded imports and can recommend to the president that relief be provided to those industries to facilitate positive adjustment to import competition. Relief could take the form of increased tariffs or quotas on imports and/or adjustment assistance for the domestic industry. Such relief is temporary and may be provided for up to five years, with one possible extension of not more than three years. Such actions can be appealed to the U.S. Court of International Trade then to the Court of Appeals for the Federal Circuit and from there to the U.S. Supreme Court.

Import Relief Based on National Security

The Tariff Act (19 U.S. Code S.1862) gives the president discretion to restrict imports that threaten national security. The Department of Com-

---

International Perspective

19.2

THE SEMICONDUCTOR INDUSTRY

The semiconductor industry has been a target of industrial policy in many countries. In the United States, the government has paid a large share of R&D expenditures since the 1950s. In Japan, the industry was protected by high tariffs, restrictive quotas, and approval of licensing arrangements. Even after the abolition of formal barriers in the 1970s, the Japanese government provided R&D support, preferential procurement policies, and so forth. In Europe, stiff tariff rates on imports were used to protect domestic firms.

The Semiconductor Accord: The first agreement (1986) between the United States and Japan focused on improving market share, increasing access to the Japanese market, and terminating unfair trade practices such as dumping by Japanese companies. The Reagan administration applied some $165 million in retaliatory duties on Japanese imports in 1987. The Japanese were compelled to raise prices for their semiconductors sold in the United States in order to avoid the imposition of special tariffs and duties resulting from U.S. anti-dumping investigations.

The agreement resulted in a rise in U.S. foreign market share (U.S. market share in Japan grew from 9 to 14 percent in 1991). The price of Japanese chips sold in the United States increased by over 30 percent. The agreement was extended in 1991, endorsing the desirability of increasing the foreign market share in Japan by more than 20 percent by the end of 1992. It also paved the way for U.S. and Japanese firms to enter into joint ventures.

As the 1991 agreement expired in 1996, the two governments announced new industry and government agreements on semiconductors. The key provisions of the new agreement include the continuation of existing cooperative activities between users and suppliers as well as new cooperative activities among suppliers from the two countries. These activities include international standards, designs, and environmental data (imports, exports, market size, market growth, openness of market, etc.). U.S. and Japanese industries will collect and submit data to their respective governments for review in bilateral consultations.

Problems with Managed Trade: The major shortcomings with such arrangements are that they are arbitrary and, once established, they become institutionalized and perpetuated. They may also distort competition in the semiconductor industry with adverse effects on users, such as the computer industry.

merce makes findings and recommendations to the president who may order the imposition of a quota, fee, tariff, or other remedies. Although such remedies are rarely invoked, they could conceivably be used by companies in some strategic sectors. Such remedies are available only if it is established that a strategically important industry is adversely affected by imports and that supplies may not be available during a crisis either from domestic or foreign sources.

CHAPTER SUMMARY

Dumping Subsidies

Dumping is the selling of a product in a foreign market at a price that is lower than the price for which it is sold in the home market.

Subsidies are any benefit given by the government to domestic producers.

Domestic subsidies are provided to achieve certain socioeconomic goals, such as optimum employment.

Export subsidies are intended to promote exports.

Proof of Injury and Remedies

In both cases, remedies are subject to proof of injury of subsidized or dumped imports. Injury is generally established by considering import volumes, lost sales, and impact on domestic producers of similar products.

Antidumping and Countervailing Duty Proceedings

1. Initiation of investigation by commerce
2. Preliminary phase of ITC investigation
3. Preliminary phase of Commerce investigation
4. Final phase of investigation by commerce
5. Final phase of investigation by ITC

Other Categories of Trade Remedies

1. Unfair trade practices, S.337
2. Market disruption by imports from communist countries
3. Unjustified foreign trade practice, S.301
4. Import interference with agricultural programs
5. Trade adjustment assistance
6. The escape clause

Chapter 20

Intellectual Property Rights

Intellectual Property Rights (IPRs) are associated with patents, trademarks, copyrights, trade secrets, and other protective devices granted by the state to facilitate industrial innovation and artistic creation (Wolfhard, 1991). The grant of exclusive property rights provides owners with personal incentives to make the most productive use of their assets and facilitates transfer by making possible a high degree of exchange. Intellectual property rights are one form of exclusive rights conferred by the state to promote science and technology. The issue of intellectual property has received wider attention compared to other property rights for the following reasons:

- The volume of trade in goods protected by intellectual property rights is becoming increasingly significant as more countries produce and consume products that result from creative activity and innovation (Gadbaw and Richards, 1988).
- The globalization of markets has created opportunities for the production and/or sale of unauthorized copies to supply the newly generated demand. The value of lost sales resulting from unauthorized copying of U.S.-patented, -copyrighted, or -trademarked materials is estimated at $40 billion to $60 billion per year (U.S. Congress, 1995).

WHAT ARE INTELLECTUAL PROPERTY RIGHTS?

Intellectual property rights are exclusive rights given to persons over the use of their creation for a given period of time. Such rights are customarily divided into various areas, as detailed in the following material.

Patents

A patent is a proprietary right granted by the government to inventors (and other persons deriving their rights from the inventor) for a fixed period of years to exclude other persons from manufacturing, using, or selling a patented product or from utilizing a patented method or process. At the expiration of the time for which the privilege is granted, the patented invention is available to the general public, or falls into public domain.

Patents may be granted for new and useful products as well as processes for the manufacture (or methods of use) of new or existing products. The basis for patent protection is promotion of innovative activity, dissemination of technical knowledge, and facilitation of transfer of technology. Even though patents are granted as a recognition of the concept of a natural right in inventions, they provide an incentive for the encouragement of inventions and the promotion of economic development. With the monopoly grant, the patent owner can divulge the invention to the public and still retain exclusive use of it for the period of the patent. At the end of the monopoly period, the patent becomes available for the unrestricted use of the public. Patent protection also encourages transfer of technology through direct investment or licensing. In the United States, patents are valid for a period of twenty years from the filing date. Patent violations are generally referred to as patent infringement or piracy.

Trademarks

A trademark is a word, name, symbol, or device or any combination of these used by a manufacturer or seller of goods to identify and distinguish the particular manufacturer's/seller's goods from goods made or sold by others (Ladas, 1975). In general, trademarks perform three functions:

1. Identify one seller's goods and distinguish them from goods sold by others
2. Signify that all goods bearing the trademark come from a single source and are of an equal level of quality
3. Serve as a primary instrument in advertising and selling the goods

An important part of the advertising effort is to develop goodwill. Trademark rights can be acquired by registration or use (reputation). Registered marks are renewable. Once a trader acquires a reputation in respect of a mark, that is, an unregistered mark, it becomes part of that trader's goodwill and is protectible as a registered mark. Violation of trademarks consists of counterfeiting and other forms of infringement, such as advertising, sales, or distribution of goods bearing a similar mark (to that of the owner) that results in deception or confusion. Counterfeiting is the unauthorized use of a mark. In the United States, trademarks are valid for ten years from the date of registration.

Trade Secrets

A trade secret involves a formula, method, or technique that derives independent economic value from not being generally known or available to other persons who can obtain economic value from its disclosure or use (Kinter and Lahr, 1983). The historical roots of trade secrets protection can be traced to ancient China, where death by torture was prescribed for revealing the secret of silkmaking to outsiders, and to ancient Rome, where enticing a competitor's servant to disclose business secrets was a punishable offense. In England, the movement of artisans to other countries was prohibited by a series of statutes aimed at preventing knowledge of British processes from reaching possible competitors in Europe and America, and employers sued would-be emigrants and those who tried to seduce them (Ashton, 1988). Violation of trade secrets includes acquisition of a trade secret by improper means or disclosure without the consent of the owner.

In most developed nations, however, protection is afforded through laws pertaining to contracts, criminal law, or torts, such as breach of confidence (Seyoum, 1993). Protection of trade secrets does not expire after a set period of time, as in the case of other intellectual property rights. The owner, in effect, has perpetual monopoly on the innovation. A large part of technology being developed now, perhaps with the exceptions of pharmaceuticals and specialty chemicals, does not get patented. Many high-technology innovations, such as aircraft and automobiles, and most low-technology innovations, such as detergents or food products, are not patented (Williams, 1983). In some countries, a formula might be patentable, while methods of production based on personal skills are not patentable. Patent protection also ends at some point, even if one is able to obtain and keep the patent. Thus, companies prefer to maintain new innovations as trade secrets and protect their technology by contract rather than by patent.

Copyrights

A copyright is a form of protection granted to authors of original works, including literary, dramatic, musical, artistic, and certain other intellectual works. The owner of the copyright has the exclusive right to reproduce, distribute, sell, or transfer the copyrighted work to other persons. In the United States, copyrights are protected for a minimum period of fifty years after the death of the author. The core copyright industries (i.e., business and entertainment software) are second only to motor vehicles and automotive parts in terms of estimated sales and exports ($53.25 billion of exports in 1995) and also have grown twice as fast as the rest of the U.S. economy.

INTELLECTUAL PROPERTY RIGHTS
AND INTERNATIONAL TRADE

An important feature of intellectual property rights (IPRs) is their exclusiveness and territorial dimension. This means that a patent holder or licensee is the person solely entitled to manufacture and market the patented product within a given territory of the state in which the patent is granted. The exclusive and territorial character of such rights is capable of creating obstacles to both the free movement of goods and competition. For example, a patent or trademark owner in country A may be entitled to block the importation of a product legally manufactured in country B by its own licensee or subsidiary. Although such restrictive use of intellectual property rights interferes with free trade, the grant of monopoly rights is considered an acceptable trade-off to encourage research and the diffusion of new knowledge and technology. In short, free trade between countries as a result of an agreement such as NAFTA, EEC, or WTO does not preclude prohibitions or restrictions on imports, exports, or goods in transit justified on the grounds of the protection of intellectual property rights.

A number of issues pertaining to intellectual property rights have important implications to the conduct and growth of international trade. They are as follows.

The Growth of Trade in Counterfeit Goods

The globalization of markets, the increased demand for new products, and the nearly prohibitive R&D costs to develop such products have created incentives for the unauthorized use of intellectual property rights. For example, counterfeiting (false labeling for sale in export markets) has spread from strong brand-name consumer goods to a variety of consumer and industrial goods. Related violations include copyright, patent infringement, and unfair competition.

Lack of Adequate Protection for IPRs in Many Countries

An important contributing factor to trade in counterfeit/pirated goods is the lack of adequate protection and effective enforcement of intellectual property rights in many countries. Furthermore, some new technologies do not fit within any of the existing types of intellectual property. For example, in many developing countries, the protection of computer software, biotechnology, and semiconductor chips remains unclear. The International Intellectual Property Alliance estimates that U.S. industries lose about $18 to $20 billion annually due to inadequate copyright protection and enforcement around the world.

Piracy of IPRs As a Trade Barrier

Given the fact that counterfeit/pirated goods displace those of legitimate producers, such action distorts international trade and has the long-term effect of reducing trade in technology-intensive goods. Piracy leads to the misallocation of resources by diverting trade from legitimate producers to pirates. Trade experts believe that elimination of piracy abroad of U.S. intellectual property could easily wipe out a majority of the U.S. trade deficit.

PROTECTION OF INTELLECTUAL PROPERTY RIGHTS

Protection Under Domestic Laws

Most countries have domestic laws to protect intellectual property rights (for examples, see International Perspective 20.1). In the United States, Section 337 of the Tariff Act of 1930 authorizes the International Trade Commission (ITC) to institute an investigation into the importation of articles that may infringe on U.S. patents, trademarks, or copyrights. If the ITC determines that a violation exists, the U.S. Customs Service is then charged to enforce an exclusive order, that is, to stop the article from entering the United States, or upon a subsequent violation, the property may be seized and forfeited to the U.S. government.

The Special 301 Provision of the 1998 Omnibus Trade and Competitiveness Act requires the U.S. Trade Representative (USTR) to identify countries that fail to provide adequate protection and enforcement for intellectual property rights or deny fair and equitable market access to persons that rely on IPR protection. The USTR classifies countries that fail to provide adequate protection or enforcement into the following three categories.

Priority Foreign Countries

A country may be designated as a priority foreign country if

- its policies or practices have the greatest adverse impact (actual or potential) on the relevant U.S. products, and
- it is not engaged in good-faith negotiations to address these problems.

USTR is required to initiate a Section 301 investigation within thirty days after identification of a priority foreign country. If negotiations are not successful within six to nine months, the USTR may retaliate against the exports of the country by withdrawing trade agreement concessions and imposing duties or other restrictions on imports.

International Perspective

20.1
PROTECTION AND ENFORCEMENT OF IPRs:
SELECTED COUNTRIES

Argentina: Argentina does not provide patent protection for pharmaceutical products. Video piracy remains a severe problem, and pirated products presently account for about 30 percent of the sound-recording market. U.S. industry losses on pharmaceutical products and copyright piracy are estimated to be over $795 million a year. Enforcement of trademark piracy is also limited by the inability to seek criminal prosecution or monetary damages against counterfeiters. The U.S. government suspended 50 percent of Argentina's GSP benefits effective in April 1997 due to its lack of patent protection for pharmaceuticals.

India: India does not provide product patent protection to drugs, food, and chemical substances. Patents could be licensed to third parties by the government or revoked in the event of failure to exploit them in India within a given period.

Japan: Japan has inadequate protection for trademarks and trade secrets. Software piracy is widespread, and the narrow interpretation of patents by domestic courts has allowed local competitors to conduct activity that violates the rights of legitimate patent owners.

China: Inadequate protection and enforcement of IPRs has led to widespread sale of counterfeit/pirated goods. Losses in 1995 by foreign owners of IPRs were estimated at $2.2 billion. However, the 1995 and 1996 U.S.-China agreement has resulted in an improvement in the protection and enforcement of IPRs. Recent efforts to crack down on piracy included closing fifteen illegal CD factories and over 500 laser disc cinemas nationwide. Customs authorities have also increased IPR enforcement at the border.

Source: U.S. Trade Representative (USTR), 1997, pp. 8-45.

Priority Watch List

In this category are countries whose protection and enforcement of IPRs warrants close monitoring and resolution. The 1996 list of countries under this category included Argentina, Greece, India, Indonesia, Japan, South Korea, and Turkey.

Watch List

This category includes countries that warrant special attention because they maintain certain practices or barriers to market access for intellectual property products that are of particular concern. The 1996 list includes Australia, Brazil, Canada, Chile, Egypt, and Venezuela.

As a result of the 1999 Special 301 review, the USTR placed seventeen countries on "the priority watch list" (including Argentina, the Dominican Republic, Egypt, the European Union, Greece, Guatemala, India, Indonesia, Israel, Italy, Kuwait, Macau, Peru, Russia, Turkey, and Ukraine). Thirty-seven countries (some of which are Australia, Bolivia, Brazil, Canada, Chile, Colombia, Costa Rica, the Chech Republic, Denmark, Hungary, Ireland, Japan, Korea, Mexico, New Zealand, Singapore, and South Africa) were put on "the watch list." Although no country was identified under the "priority foreign country" category, the USTR has initiated WTO dispute settlement proceedings against Argentina, Canada, and the European Union. The 1999 review emphasized three critical issues: proper and timely implementation of the WTO TRIP agreement; cracking down on pirated production of optical media such as CDs, VCDs, and CD-ROMs; and ensuring that government ministries only use authorized software (USTR, 1999).

It is important to note that a Special 301 investigation is similar to an investigation initiated in response to an industry Section 301 petition (unfair foreign trade practices), except that the maximum time for the latter is shorter (in cases involving violation of TRIPs) than other Section 301 investigations. Special 301 is potentially an effective tool to protect U.S. IPRs abroad because it allows the administration to use a variety of trade sanctions (e.g., removal of GSP or MFN status) against a priority foreign country. However, its implementation has been sporadic and inconsistent over the years. For example, certain countries with gross violations of IPRs are not added to the priority country list and, in some cases, when identified, sanctions are not imposed. Russia is classified under the "Watch List" category despite its rampant black markets in videocassettes, films, music, and so forth. India was classified under the "Priority Foreign Country" category in 1991; however, no sanctions were imposed, even though there was no resolution of the problem through bilateral negotiations.

INTERNATIONAL/REGIONAL PROTECTION

The Paris Convention

The Paris Convention is used in connection with two separate treaties: (1) international protection of industrial property and (2) international copyright protection (the Universal Copyright Convention). The Paris convention for the protection of industrial property was concluded in 1883 and has gone through various revisions. It applies to industrial property in

394 EXPORT-IMPORT THEORY, PRACTICES, AND PROCEDURES

the widest sense, including patents, trademarks, trade names, and so on. The treaty sets forth three fundamental rules:

1. *National treatment:* The principle of national treatment provides that nationals of any signatory nation shall enjoy in all other countries of the Union the advantages that each nation's laws grant to its own nationals.
2. *Right of priority:* The right of priority enables any resident or national of a member country to apply for protection in any other member state of the convention within a certain period of time (twelve months for patents and six months for trademarks and industrial designs) after filing the first application in one of the member states to the treaty. These later applications will then be regarded as if they had been filed on the same day as the first application. A major advantage of this is that applicants wishing protection in multiple countries need not file all applications at the same time but have six to twelve months from the first application to decide in which countries to apply for protection.
3. *Minimum standards:* The convention lays down minimum standards common to all member countries.

The Universal Copyright Convention

The convention (1952, revised in 1971) establishes the national treatment standard and minimum rules common to all member countries. It also allows countries to set formalities or conditions for the acquisition or enjoyment of copyright in respect to works first published in its country or works of its nationals wherever published.

The Paris Convention is administered by the World Intellectual Property Organization (WIPO). WIPO's mission is to promote the protection of intellectual property throughout the world. WIPO membership includes over 130 countries.

The Patent Cooperation Treaty

The Patent Cooperation Treaty (PCT) allows for a single application and a worldwide search for novelty in all member countries; that is, a search is made in one of the designated offices based on a single application without the need to file applications in all other member states. The application with the search report will be forwarded to the countries where the applicant seeks patent protection. Although such a system eliminates duplication of filing and patent examination in each patent office of a member country, each country retains full jurisdiction to grant or refuse a patent in accordance with its own domestic legislation. The PCT has been signed by ninety-six countries and regional patent systems such as the European Patent Office (EPO) and the African Regional Industrial Property Organization (ARIPO).

Trade-Related Aspects of Intellectual Property (TRIPs)

The developed countries criticize the intellectual property conventions administered by WIPO because their minimum standards are considered insufficient and they contain no provisions for dispute settlement. They contend that the deficiencies in the protection of intellectual property rights distort international trade and reduce the value of concessions negotiated in various rounds of trade negotiations. In response to this, the Uruguay Round of the GATT (1994) established multilateral obligations for the protection and enforcement of IPRs and provided a dispute settlement mechanism under the World Trade Organization (WTO).

The TRIPs agreement covers almost all forms of intellectual property including patents, trademarks and service marks, industrial designs, trade secrets, and layout designs of integrated circuits.

The three fundamental features of the agreement are as follows:

1. *Standards:* The agreement sets out minimum standards of protection to be provided by each member country. It also requires members to comply with existing agreements such as the Paris Convention and the Berne Convention for the protection of literary and artistic works. It further supplements additional obligations on matters where the preexisting conventions are silent or inadequate.
2. *Enforcement:* The TRIPs agreement lays down domestic procedures and remedies for the enforcement of IPRs.
3. *Dispute settlement:* The agreement makes disputes between WTO members subject to the WTO's dispute settlement procedures.

Regional Conventions

The major regional agreement in the area of IPRs is the European Patent Convention (1973), which under a single application may result in the grant of a European patent valid in all member countries. It is a centralized patent-granting system administered by the European Patent Office (EPO) in Munich, Germany, on behalf of member countries. A similar regional organization is the African Regional Industrial Property Organization (ARIPO), located in Harare, Zimbabwe. ARIPO was established in 1976 to grant regional patents having effect in all designated member countries.

CHAPTER SUMMARY

Intellectual Property Rights (IPRs)

Intellectual property rights are associated with patents, trademarks, copyrights, trade secrets, and other protective devices granted by the state to facilitate industrial innovation and artistic creation.

Major Issues Pertaining to IPRs and International Trade

1. The growth of trade in counterfeit goods
2. Lack of adequate protection and enforcement of IPRs in many countries
3. The long-term effect of piracy on trade in technology-intensive goods

U.S. Classification of Countries That Do Not Provide Adequate Protection to IPRs

1. Priority foreign countries: Countries that do not provide adequate protection to IPRs and whose policies have the greatest adverse impact on U.S. commerce
2. Priority watch list: countries that warrant close monitoring and resolution
3. Watch list: Countries that warrant special attention

Regional/International Protection

International Protection

The Paris Convention, the Universal Copyright Convention, the Patent Cooperation Treaty, trade-related aspects of IPRs (the TRIP) agreement

Regional Protection

The European Patent Convention, the African Regional Industrial Property Organization

Appendix A

Export Sales Contract
(Basic Clauses)

1. **PRICES**
    A. Prices include the following costs:
      (i)   Seller's usual inspection and factory tests
      (ii) Seller's usual packing (or containerizing if applicable) for export
      (iii) Freight by Seller's usual means to alongside vessel at the point of export designated by Seller (but not the cost of insurance or charges for pier handling, marshaling, lighterage, and heavy lifts). Insurance to cover the inland shipment shall be arranged by Seller at Buyer's expense if Seller is arranging for the export shipment pursuant to Article 3 . . .
    B. Unless otherwise stated, prices are quoted in Canadian funds.

2. **TAXES, DUTIES, AND EXCHANGE RATES**
    A. Prices quoted include all applicable Canadian taxes except for sales, use, excise, value-added, and similar taxes. If sales, use, excise, value-added, or similar taxes are levied against the Seller, the Buyer shall reimburse the Seller upon presentation of invoices therefor. However, where a refund of such taxes may be applied for, the Seller, if promptly furnished by the Buyer with evidence of exportation, will apply for a refund. If the Buyer has reimbursed the Seller, the Buyer shall be credited with the refund.
    B. Prices quoted do not include Canadian import duties. All rights in drawback of customs duties paid by the Seller belong to and shall remain in the Seller. At the Seller's request, the Buyer shall provide documents and assistance necessary to process the Seller's drawback claims, failing which, the Buyer shall reimburse the Seller for such import duties. Such reimbursement shall be payable upon presentation of Seller's invoice therefor.

C. Prices quoted herein are based upon the prevailing rates for taxes and freight at the date of the Proposal and, with respect to the purchase price of goods to be bought by the Seller in foreign countries, on duty and exchange rates current at the .date of the Proposal. Any increase or decrease in these rates or the imposition of any new duties or taxes between the date of the Proposal and the date of payment by the Seller will be paid by the Buyer, upon presentation of Seller's invoices therefore, or will be credited to the Buyer.

D. Any taxes, duties, fees, charges, or assessments of any nature levied by any governmental authority other than of Canada in connection with this contract, whether levied against the Buyer, against the Seller or its employees, or against any of the Seller's subcontractors or their employees shall be for the Buyer's account and shall be paid directly by the Buyer to the governmental authority concerned. If the Seller, its subcontractors, or the employees of either are required to pay any such taxes, duties, fees, charges, or assessments in the first instance or as a result of the Buyer's failure to comply with any applicable laws or regulations governing the payment of such levies by the Buyer, the amount of any such payment so made shall be reimbursed by Buyer, payable upon presentation of Seller's invoice therefor.

3. PAYMENT

A. Payment shall be made in Canadian dollars at Toronto, Canada, as follows:

  (i)   On all orders of ten thousand dollars ($10,000) or less, payment in full shall be made simultaneously with the giving of the order.

  (ii) On orders of over ten thousand dollars ($10,000), payment shall be made through a Letter of Credit to be established by the Buyer at its expense (including any bank confirmation charges). All Letters of Credit shall be in favor of and acceptable to the Seller, shall be maintained in sufficient amounts and for the period necessary to meet all payment obligations, shall be irrevocable and issued or confirmed by a Canadian chartered bank in Toronto within fifteen days after the date of this contract, shall permit partial deliveries, and shall provide for pro rata payments, payable upon presentation of Seller's invoices and Seller's certificate of delivery FOB factory or of delivery into storage with cause therefor.

B. If the Buyer fails to fulfill any payment obligation, the Seller may suspend performance (and any costs incurred by the Seller as a result thereof shall be paid by the Buyer, payable upon presentation of invoices therefor) or may complete performance if Seller deems it reasonable to do so. Seller shall be entitled to an extension of time for performance of its obligations equaling the period of Buyer's nonfulfillment, whether or not the Seller elects to suspend performance. If such nonfulfillment is not rectified by the Buyer promptly upon notice thereof, the Seller may, in addition to its other rights, terminate this contract, and the Buyer shall pay to the Seller its charges for termination, payable upon presentation of Seller's invoice therefor and determined according to the TERMINATION CHARGES clause.

4. DELIVERY, TITLE, AND RISK OF LOSS

A. Except as stated in paragraph C below, Seller shall deliver the goods FOB factory. Partial delivery shall be allowed. Any delivery dates given are approximate and are based upon prompt receipt by Seller of all information necessary to permit Seller to proceed with work without interruption.

B. Title and risk of loss and damage shall pass to the Buyer on delivery.

C. If the goods or any part thereof cannot be delivered when ready due to any cause referred to in the EXCUSABLE DELAY clause, the Seller may place such goods into storage (which may be at the place of manufacture). In such event:

    (i)   seller's delivery obligations shall be deemed fulfilled and title and risk of loss and damage shall pass to Buyer,

    (ii)   any amounts payable to the Seller on delivery shall be payable upon presentation of Seller's invoices and its certification as to such cause, and

    (iii)   all expenses incurred by the Seller, including, but not limited to, all expenses of preparation and shipment into storage, handling, storage, inspection, preservation, and insurance shall be for Buyer's account and shall be payable upon Seller's presentation of invoices therefor.

5. EXCUSABLE DELAY

A. The Seller shall not be in breach of any of its obligations under this contract where failure to perform or delay in performing any obligation is due, wholly or in part, to:

    (i)   a cause beyond its reasonable control;

    (ii) an act of God, an act or omission of the Buyer or of any governmental authority (de jure or de facto), wars (declared or undeclared), governmental priorities, port congestion, riots, revolutions, strikes or other labor disputes, fire, flood, sabotage, nuclear incidents, earthquake, storm, epidemic; or

    (iii) inability due to a cause beyond the Seller's reasonable control to obtain necessary or proper labor, materials, components, facilities, energy, fuel, transportation, governmental authorizations or instructions, material or information required from the Buyer. The foregoing shall apply even though any such cause exists at the time of the order or occurs after the Seller's performance of its obligations is delayed by another cause.

B. The Seller will notify the Buyer of any failure to perform or delay in performing due to a cause set out in paragraph A and shall specify, as soon as practicable, when the obligation will be performed. Subject to paragraph C, the time for performing the obligation shall be extended for the period lost due to such a cause.

C. Where the period lost is at least sixty days and the parties have not agreed upon a revised basis for performing the obligation, including the adjustment of the prices, then, either party may, upon thirty days' written notice, terminate this contract, whereupon the Buyer shall pay to the Seller termination charges determined in accordance with the TERMINATION CHARGES clause.

6. TERMINATION CHARGES

A. In the event that this contract is terminated by the Seller pursuant to any of its terms, the termination charges payable by the Buyer shall be calculated as follows:

    (i)   material, labor, and indirect expenses committed or incurred to date of termination;

    (ii) all costs incurred in the execution of the termination;

    (iii) reasonable profit on (i) and (ii) herein above cited;

    (iv) the greater of 10 percent of the unbilled portion of the contract price or the unrecoverable, ongoing, fixed costs and expenses due to discontinuities in operation plus loss of reasonable anticipated profit; and

    (v) interest at the rate of 1.5 percent per month on the amount of the claim as cited in (i) to (iv) inclusive, if the termination charges are not paid as invoiced.

B. The termination charges shall be payable upon presentation of Seller's invoice therefor.

7. EXPORT SHIPMENT

If the Seller agrees to make export shipment, all fees and expenses, including, but not limited to, those covering preparation of consular documents, consular fees, storage, marine insurance (including war risk, if available) and other insurance, ocean freight, and Seller's then current fees for such services shall be payable by the Buyer upon presentation of invoices therefor. Unless otherwise instructed by the Buyer, the Seller shall prepare consular documents according to its best judgment but without liability for fines or other charges due to error or incorrect declarations.

8. GOVERNMENT AUTHORIZATIONS

The Seller shall, without any assumption of liability therefor, apply for an export permit on behalf of the Buyer where a permit is required by law. In the event that an export permit is denied or revoked, the Buyer shall have the right to elect to terminate the contract subject to the payment to the Seller of termination charges determined according to the TERMINATION CHARGES clause. The Buyer shall be responsible for obtaining any import permit, exchange permit, or other governmental authorization required by the law of the country of importation.

9. NUCLEAR USE

The goods sold are not intended for nor shall they be used for or as any part of any activity or process involving any use or handling of any radioactive material, including any nuclear material (as that term is defined in the Nuclear Liability Act of Canada). If the goods or any part thereof are used by the Buyer contrary to the aforesaid, the Buyer shall provide, at its own expense, insurance and indemnity satisfactory to the Seller protecting the Seller and all of its subcontractors and suppliers from all loss, expense, damages, costs, or liability of every kind, whether in contract or in tort (including negligence), and the Seller may terminate this contract. Upon such termination, the Buyer shall pay to the Seller termination charges determined according to the TERMINATION CHARGES clause.

10. PATENTS

A. The Seller shall, if notified promptly in writing and given authority, information, and assistance, defend, at its own expense, any suit or proceeding brought against the Buyer so far as based on a claim that the goods, or any part thereof, sold under this contract infringe any patent of Canada, and the Seller shall pay all damages and costs awarded therein against the Buyer. In the event that the goods, or part thereof, are in such a suit held to constitute an infringement and use of the goods, or part thereof, is enjoined for the intended use, the Seller shall, at its expense and option:

(i)   procure for the Buyer the right to continue using the same;

(ii) replace the same with noninfringing goods or part thereof;

(iii) modify the same so as to eliminate infringement; or

(iv) remove the same and refund the purchase price (less reasonable depreciation for any period of use) and any transportation costs and installation costs paid by the Buyer.

B. The preceding paragraph shall not apply to any goods, or any part thereof, manufactured to the Buyer's design. As to such goods, or part, the Seller assumes no liability whatsoever for infringement.

C. The rights and obligations of the parties with respect to patents or any other industrial property rights are solely and exclusively as stated herein, and the foregoing states the entire liability of the Seller for patent infringement.

11. WARRANTIES

A. The Seller warrants to the Buyer that the goods manufactured by the Seller will be free from defects in material, workmanship, and title and will be of the kind and quality described in the contract.

B. If a failure to meet any of the foregoing warranties, except as to title, appears within one year from the date of shipment or within one year after completion of installation, if the latter is supervised by or performed by the Seller, and provided that completion of installation is not unreasonably delayed by the Buyer, then the Buyer shall not be entitled to terminate or rescind this contract, but the Seller shall correct any such failure by either, at its option, repairing any defective or damaged part or parts of the goods or by making available, FOB Seller's plant or other points of shipment, any necessary repaired or replacement part or parts. Where a failure cannot be corrected by the Seller's reasonable efforts, the parties shall negotiate an equitable adjustment in price. In the event of a failure to meet the warranty as to title, the Buyer shall not be entitled to elect to terminate or rescind this contract but the Seller shall correct such failure. The foregoing sets out the Seller's sole obligation for failure to comply with the foregoing warranties. The Seller shall have no obligation whatsoever and the Buyer shall have no right to make a claim against the Seller in respect of the failure to meet any of the foregoing warranties, except as to title, which appears after the one-year period set out in this clause.

C. The obligations set forth in this clause are conditional upon:

    (i)   proper storage, installation (except where installation is supervised by or performed by the Seller), use, maintenance and compliance with any applicable recommendations of the Seller; and

    (ii)   the Buyer promptly notifying the Seller of any defect and, if required, promptly making the goods available for correction.

D. There is no warranty whatsoever with respect to goods normally consumed in operation or that have a normal life shorter than the warranty period set out in this clause.

E. With respect to goods not manufactured by the Seller (except for integral parts of the goods sold, to which the warranties given in this clause shall apply), the Seller gives no warranty whatsoever, and only the warranty, if any, given by the manufacturer shall apply.

F. The foregoing is exclusive and in lieu of all other warranties and conditions, regardless of whether they be oral, written, express, or implied by statute, including the implied conditions of reasonable fitness for purpose, merchantability, and correspondence with description.

12. LIMITATION OF LIABILITY

A. In no event, whether as a result of a breach of contract or a tort (including negligence), shall the Seller be liable to the Buyer for:

    (i)   loss of profit or revenue, loss of use, cost of capital, downtime costs, cost of substitute goods, facilities, services or replacement power;

    (ii)   property damage external to the product and loss arising out of such damage;

    (iii) special or consequential damages; and

    (iv) any of the foregoing suffered by a customer of the Buyer.

B. Except as may be provided in the PATENTS clause, in no event, whether as a result of a breach of contract or a tort (including negligence) shall the liability of the Seller to the Buyer exceed the price of the goods, or part thereof or to the service, which gives rise to the claim.

C. If the Buyer transfers title to or leases the goods sold hereunder to, or otherwise permits or suffers use by, any third party, Buyer shall obtain from such third party a provision affording Seller and its suppliers the protection of paragraph A.

D. If the Seller furnishes Buyer with advice or other assistance that concerns the goods supplied hereunder or any system or equipment in which any such goods may be installed and which is not required pursuant to an express term of this contract, the furnishing of such advice or assistance is done without any assumption of responsibility or liability therefore, and the Buyer shall not institute a claim in contract or in tort (including negligence) arising out of or in any way connected therewith.

13. GENERAL

A. Unless otherwise stated in this contract, the goods shall be installed by and at the expense of the Buyer.

B. The delegation or assignment by the Buyer of any or all of its duties or rights without the Seller's prior written consent shall be void.

C. No waiver, alteration, or modification of any of the provisions of this contract shall be binding on the Seller unless it is in writing and signed by a duly authorized representative of the Seller.

D. Any goods sold shall comply with federal and provincial laws and regulations applicable to the manufacture, packing, and shipment of such goods as of the date of the Seller's Proposal and shall comply with any amendments thereto that may have come into effect prior to the time such goods are shipped, provided that the price and, if necessary, delivery shall be equitably adjusted to compensate the Seller for having to comply with such amendments.

E. The invalidity, in whole or in part, of any of the foregoing clauses will not affect the remainder of such clauses or any other clauses in this contract.

F. Any reference to "goods" in this contract shall, where the context requires, be a reference to a single chattel personal or to a part of such single chattel personal.

G. No trade usage or course of dealing will be binding on the Seller unless specifically referred to in the contract.

H. This contract and any amendments thereto shall be governed in all respects including, but not limited to, validity, interpretation, and effect, by the laws of the Province of Ontario and of Canada.

EXHIBIT A
PRICE ADJUSTMENT CLAUSE (Manufacturing Only)

All prices stated herein are subject to adjustments, upon completion of this agreement, for changes in labor and material costs. Such adjustments, involving increases or decreases in the prices stated herein, are to be determined in accordance with the following:

1. **LABOR**
    A. For the purpose of adjustment, the proportion of the price representing labor is accepted as 50 percent thereof.
    B. The above amount accepted as representing labor will be adjusted for changes in labor cost. Such adjustment will be based upon the Index Numbers of the *Average Hourly Earnings in the Electrical Industrial Equipment Manufacturing Industry,* published monthly by Statistics Canada.

2. **MATERIAL**
    A. For the purpose of adjustment, the proportion of the price representing material is accepted as 40 percent hereof.
    B. The above amount accepted as representing material will be adjusted for changes in material costs. Such adjustment will be based upon the *Combined Index of Wholesale Prices for Iron and Non-Ferrous Metals Groups* (excluding gold), or any similar mutually agreed-upon index published monthly by Statistics Canada.

The averages of the monthly indices for labor and material referred to above for the period from a date six months preceding shipment to date of shipment of order under this agreement will be computed separately, and percentage increases or decreases will be established for labor and material by comparison with corresponding indices in effect at the time this proposal was made in the month of _____.

The adjustments for changes in labor and material will be obtained by applying the respective percentages of increase or decrease to the amounts covering labor and material as specified above, and the results will be accepted as an increase or decrease in the aforementioned price.

If Field Construction is involved, refer for Price Adjustment Clause for Field Labor to_____ on page_____.

EXHIBIT B
PRICE ADJUSTMENT PROVISIONS

Upon completion of the work, the total contract price for the apparatus to be supplied under this contract shall be subject to an increase or decrease due to fluctuation in the cost of material and/or labor. Adjustments shall be determined in accordance with the following, and the results shall be accepted as an increase or decrease in the Contract price.

1. **LABOR**
   A. For the purpose of adjustment, the proportion of the contract price representing labor is accepted as 50 percent.
   B. The amount so accepted as representing labor will be adjusted for changes in labor costs. Such adjustment will be based upon Table 18 "Average Hourly Earnings, Machinery—Except Electrical, Canada" as shown in *Employment Earnings and Hours*, published monthly by Statistics Canada. An average of those published monthly/hourly earnings for the period from a date six months before complete shipment to the date complete shipment of the apparatus is made from the Company's works will be calculated, and the percentage increase or decrease will be calculated by a comparison with such published hourly earnings for the month during which the Company's tender was submitted. The adjustment for changes in labor costs will be obtained by applying such percentage of increase or decrease to the amount representing labor above mentioned.

2. **MATERIAL**
   A. For the purpose of adjustment, the proportion of the contract price representing material is accepted as _____ percent hereof.
   B. The amount so accepted as representing material will be adjusted for changes in material costs. Such adjustment will be based upon Table 2 "General Wholesale Index—Iron Products (1,935 – 39 = 100)" as shown in *Industry Price Indexes*, published monthly by Statistics Canada. An average of those published indexes for the period from the date six months before complete shipment to the date complete shipment of the apparatus is made from the Company's works will be computed, and the percentage increase or decrease will be calculated by a comparison with such published index for the month during which the Company's tender was submitted. The adjustment for changes in material costs will be obtained by applying such percentage of increase or decrease to the amount representing material above mentioned.

3. **SUBCONTRACT**
   To carry out this contract, the Company will purchase the components or material listed below, which may increase or decrease in price due to increases or decreases in the cost of labor or material.

The Purchaser shall reimburse the Company the amount of any increase and the Company shall credit the Purchaser the amount of any decrease due to such adjustment from date of submission of the Company's tender.

EXHIBIT C
PRICE ADJUSTMENT CLAUSE (Field Labor Only)

Prices stated herein applicable to construction or assembly of the equipment provided, at the Purchaser's site, are subject to adjustments upon completion of this agreement for changes in labor costs. Such adjustments, involving increases or decreases in the prices stated herein, are to be determined in accordance with the following:

1. **FIELD LABOR**
   A. For the purpose of adjustment, the proportion of the price representing labor is accepted as _____ percent thereof.
   B. The above amount accepted as representing labor will be adjusted for changes in labor cost. Such adjustment will be based upon the *Average Hourly Earnings in the Construction Industry, Other Engineering Group* published monthly by Statistics Canada, for the area of _____.

The monthly average hourly earnings for labor referred to above for the period of construction under this agreement will be computed separately, and percentage increases or decreases will be established for labor by comparison with corresponding average hourly earnings in effect at the time this proposal was made in the month of _____.

The adjustments for changes in labor will be obtained by applying the respective percentage of increase or decrease to the amounts covering labor as specified above, and the result will be accepted as an increase or decrease in the aforementioned price.

Appendix B

Sample Distributorship Agreement

This Distributorship Agreement is entered into this _____ day of _____ between ABC 2 _____ Company, hereinafter referred to as "Company," having its principal place of business at Naples, Florida, and XYZ Company of Mexico City, Mexico, hereinafter referred to as "Distributor."

1. **DEFINITIONS**
   A. Product(s): Product or products refers to products manufactured or marketed by the company, that including spare parts which are listed in Exhibit A. Exhibit A is subject to change by mutual agreement of the parties.
   B. Territory: Territory shall mean the geographical area designated under Exhibit B. Exhibit B may be revised from time to time by mutual agreement of the parties.
   C. Contract year: Contract year shall mean the period commencing January 1 and ending on December 31. The first contract year shall commence as of the date of this contract, and subsequent years shall commence on January 1 thereafter.
   D. Trade terms: Trade terms such as FOB, CIF, etc., shall be interpreted according to the latest version of International Chamber of Commerce (ICC) Rules.
   E. Purchaser: Purchaser shall mean a purchaser of goods for consumption and not for resale as a distributor.

2. **APPOINTMENT AND ACCEPTANCE**
   A. Company hereby appoints Distributor as the sole importer-distributor of products in the territory and Distributor accepts such appointment.
   B. Company shall not appoint any third person to import, sell, or otherwise deal with products in the territory during the time when the agreement is in effect.

3. **TERM OF THE AGREEMENT**

The term of this agreement shall be from _____ to _____ unless sooner terminated or further extended as hereinafter provided.

4. **MINIMUM ANNUAL PURCHASES**

Distributor shall purchase from Company during the _____ contract year such minimum dollar or unit amount of products as specified in Exhibit C attached thereto. Minimum sales for subsequent periods shall be specified in an addendum to this agreement. Should no agreement be reached between the parties, the minimum annual sales for the new contract year shall be deemed to be _____ percent of the minimum annual sales for the preceding contract year.

5. **PRICES FOR THE PRODUCTS**

A. Company reserves the right to establish or revise at its sole discretion, from time to time, upon thirty days, prices and terms of its sales of products to distributor, including the right at any time to issue new price lists and to change the prices, terms, and provisions therein contained. The price to be paid by the Distributor, excluding spare parts, shall be the price quoted on the Company's current international price list, less a discount of 12 percent.

B. Company shall provide an additional discount of 3 percent percent when Distributor takes responsibility at the company's request to service products during the guarantee period. Company shall provide replacement parts free of charge to Distributor during the guarantee period.

C. Distributor shall bear the cost of freight, insurance, and duties for such parts. Distributor shall make no charge for the replacement parts to customer.

D. After the end of the guarantee period, spare parts shall be sold to Distributor at the company's current international price, less a discount of 20 percent.

6. **PAYMENTS TO DISTRIBUTOR FOR DIRECT SALES**

A. Where the Company sells products direct to a customer, the Company shall pay Distributor such commission as is agreed between the parties. In the event that no specific commission is agreed, company shall pay Distributor 8 percent of the net selling price for the products.

B. Any sums earned by Distributor shall be paid by Company thirty days after receipt by the Company of payment for any such order, provided that no such sums shall be payable by the Company to Distributor in respect of any orders received by the Company after termination of this agreement, except where orders are accepted from potential customers within six months after termination of this agreement and at the time of termination the Distributor has provided the Company with a written list of such potential customers, including evidence to show potential customer's communication and intent to buy the products.

7. GOVERNMENT LICENSES AND PERMITS

The Company shall secure the necessary licenses and permits for the sale and export of the products. It is also incumbent on the Distributor to obtain the necessary licenses and permits required for purchase and importation of the products.

8. INTELLECTUAL PROPERTY RIGHTS

A. The Distributor shall not remove or obliterate any marks or symbols affixed on the goods without the written permission of the Company. A small label bearing the words "supplied by" together with the name and address of the Distributor, shall be applied to the goods.

B. The Distributor shall advertise the goods solely under the trademarks of the Company. However, it shall not act in any manner, whether by advertising or other means, that might adversely affect the validity of any intellectual property rights belonging to the Company.

C. The Distributor shall, at all times, do all in its power to protect the Company's intellectual property rights and shall ensure that the same remain connected only with the products as defined in this agreement and as the Company may indicate from time to time.

D. The Distributor shall notify the Company in writing as soon as it becomes aware of any infringements of the latter's intellectual property rights in the territory. The Distributor shall bring an action to prevent infringement of such rights at the Company's expense. However, the Company shall not be liable for any infringement caused by the actions of the Distributor.

9. WARRANTY AND LIABILITY

A. The Company guarantees that products sold to Distributor are free from defects in material and workmanship and agrees to reimburse all costs of repairs, including reasonably necessary related labor charges, or, at Company's option, to replace any or all defective products within the period of such warranty.

B. The period of the warranty shall extend for one year after the date of sale to the customer for products and ninety days from the date of sale to customer for parts. The Company shall not be liable for the acts or defaults of the Distributor, its employees, or its representatives.

10. **UNDERTAKINGS BY THE DISTRIBUTOR**

   A. Distributor agrees to be responsible for supplying or making arrangements for supplying all necessary service to products in the territory, and this includes using its best efforts to provide the best possible service for all owners of products. The Distributor shall hire an adequate number of technicians in order to provide such services promptly.

   B. Distributor shall purchase and maintain such volume and assortment of parts as may be necessary to satisfy the service needs of customers.

   C. Distributor shall use its best efforts to promote the sales of the goods in its territory as well as maintain adequate staff of salespeople to carry out such responsibility.

   D. If at any time during the continuance of this agreement, the Distributor shall become entitled to any development, improvement, or invention relating to any of the products, the Distributor shall give notice in writing to Company and grant to the Company a first option to acquire rights with respect to such invention.

   E. The Distributor shall spend a reasonable sum each year on promoting the product in the territory. The Company may make a contribution toward such costs.

   F. The Distributor shall assist the Company to produce sales literature in the language of the territory and also provide the Company any sales literature prepared by it relating to the products.

   G. The Distributor shall provide Company detailed reports of sales every ninety days, general market information in the territory, and suggestions for any improvements in December of each year.

   H. The Distributor shall refrain from purporting to act as an agent of the Company unless otherwise specified in the agreement. In addition, Distributor shall not make any contracts binding the company, warehouse, or advertise the goods outside its territory as well as get involved in the manufacture, production, sale, or advertising of competing goods in the territory.

   I. The Distributor shall not transfer or assign the benefit of this agreement to any third party without the prior written consent of the Company.

11. UNDERTAKINGS BY THE COMPANY

The Company agrees to undertake the following responsibilities:

A. Assist the Distributor in advertising the goods by providing the necessary advice and literature as it considers reasonably sufficient to promote the goods in the territory.

B. Support the Distributor in its sales and technical efforts by paying regular visits to the territory of experienced personnel. In the event that a technician is sent to assist the Distributor, the Distributor shall be responsible for traveling expenses to and from the territory, all local traveling expenses, accommodation, and reasonable subsistence costs in the territory.

C. Provide the Distributor with maintenance and servicing instructions and other documentation as well as information on technical changes that are necessary and relevant in connection with the products. The Company may provide appropriate training to suitable qualified technicians of the Distributor that is necessary to install, maintain, or service the products. The parties will determine in due course where the training will take place as well as matters pertaining to expenses.

12. TERMINATION

This agreement may be terminated by a written instrument duly executed by the parties if any of the following situations arise:

A. Either party commits any breach of contract and in the case of a breach capable of being remedied, the party does not remedy the same within sixty days after receipt of notice in writing of such breach.

B. Either party becomes insolvent or goes into liquidation or has a receiver appointed in respect of all or a substantial part of its business.

C. Payment of any sum remains unpaid to either party for a period of thirty days after the due date.

The innocent party may forthwith, by notice in writing, terminate this agreement. Any such termination shall be without prejudice to the rights of the parties accrued up to the date of termination. Neither party will be responsible, by reason of termination of this agreement, to the other for compensation or damages on account of any loss of prospective profits on anticipated sales or on account of expenditures, investments, leases, or other commitments relating to the business or goodwill of either party.

Within thirty days after the termination or expiration of this agreement, company may, at its option, repurchase from distributor, at the latter's net warehouse cost, any or all products and/or parts that are commercially usable or salable as well as any usable advertising or promotional materials. Distributor shall return any packaging or promotional materials that were provided by Company free of charge. Distributor shall cease all use of the name and trademark of Company.

13. FORCE MAJEURE

The occurrence of certain events that make the continuance of this agreement impossible, such as riots, government restrictions, or other events outside the reasonable control of the party, shall not constitute a breach of this agreement.

14. AGREEMENT AND INTERPRETATION

A. This agreement and its annexes constitute the whole of the agreement between the Company and Distributor with respect to the products. No variation, alteration, or abandonment of any of its terms shall have effect unless made in writing by the Distributor or its duly authorized representative and by the Company or its duly authorized representative.

B. This agreement shall be construed in accordance with U.S. law.

C. The illegality or invalidity of any part of this agreement shall not affect the legality or validity of the remainder thereof.

D. The headings are for reference purposes only and shall not affect the interpretation of this agreement.

LIST OF EXHIBITS

A. Products
B. Territory
C. Minimum annual purchases
D. Price list
E. Initial order
F. Intellectual property rights

Signed for ABC Company

by _____

In the presence of

_____

Signed for XYZ distributor

by _____

In the presence of

_____

Appendix C

Sample Sales Representative Agreement

MEMORANDUM OF AGREEMENT entered into in duplicate, this
_____ day of _____.

BETWEEN: duly incorporated under the laws of Canada,
_____   having its head office and principal place of
_____   business at Toronto, Province of Ontario
                            (hereinafter referred to as party of the first
                            part [PFP].

AND: a body politic and corporate, having its head
_____   office and place of business in _____ (herein-
_____   after called the Sales Representative).

WITNESSETH THAT in consideration of the premises and of the mutual
covenant and agreements hereinafter contained, the parties hereto agree
each with the other as follows:

PFP hereby engages the Sales Representative to provide services in
accordance with the terms and conditions of this Agreement for the
sale of _____ proprietary products (hereinafter called Equipment)
listed in Schedule _____ attached hereto and made an integral part
hereof to markets in _____ (hereinafter called Served Market).

1. **TERRITORY**
   The geographical area (hereinafter called Territory) in which the
Sales Representative shall undertake the responsibilities specified in
this Agreement is _____.

2. **TERMS AND SCOPE**
   The term of this Agreement shall be from _____ to _____ unless
sooner terminated as hereinafter provided. The provisions of this
Agreement shall govern all transactions between PFP and the Sales
Representative unless otherwise agreed to in writing by the duly
authorized representatives of both parties.

3. COMPANY RESPONSIBILITIES

PFP agrees that during the term of this Agreement, it will, subject to and in accordance with the terms and conditions herein expressed:

A. keep the Sales Representative advised of new products, sales plans, and objectives with respect to Equipment for Served Market Customers in the Territory;

B. support the sales efforts of the Sales Representative by furnishing printed commercial and technical data and information and other publications that PFP may have available from time to time for export distribution; and

C. pay a commission as provided in Article 5 hereof on orders for Equipment received and accepted by PFP from Served Market Customers in the Territory as a result of the effort of the Sales Representative. As used in this Agreement, the terms "order" or "orders" include contracts for Equipment with Served Market Customers in the Territory executed by PFP.

4. SALES REPRESENTATIVE RESPONSIBILITIES

The Sales Representative agrees that during the term of this Agreement, it will, subject to the terms and conditions herein expressed:

A. maintain an adequate sales organization and use its best efforts to assist PFP in the sale of Equipment to Served Market Customers in the Territory;

B. maintain active contacts with Served Market Customers in the Territory;

C. keep PFP fully informed of all governmental, commercial, and industrial activities and plans that do or could affect the sale of Equipment to Served Market Customers in the Territory;

D. provide market information to PFP on Served Market Customers' and competitors' activities;

E. recommend improvements to sales plans, assist in developing strategy, and clarify the Equipment requirements of Served Market Customers in the Territory;

F. as requested, transmit proposals and technical data to Served Market Customers in the Territory, interpret customer inquiries, requirements, and attitudes, and assist in contract negotiations. (All proposals so transmitted will contain terms and conditions of sale substantially in accordance with PFP's Standard Terms and Conditions of Sale, a copy of which is attached hereto and is subject to change by PFP from time to time. No proposal shall be transmitted to a Served Market Customer unless terms and conditions of sale are approved by PFP or the Standard Terms and Conditions of Sale are incorporated in such proposal); and

G. perform such liaison services with Served Market Customers in the Territory as PFP may from time to time direct relative to any order(s) awarded to PFP from the supply of Equipment, including assistance in the resolution of any claims or complaints of such Customers arising out of PFP's performance of said order(s).

5. COMPENSATION

A. As compensation to the Sales Representative for services rendered hereunder, PFP agrees to pay the Sales Representative a commission on the following orders for PFP's proprietary equipment from Served Market Customers in the Territory during the term of this Agreement:

(i) Orders that are forwarded by the Sales Representative.

(ii) Orders that the Sales Representative has specifically identified to PFP being forthcoming directly from a Served Market Customer in the Territory when, in the absolute judgment of PFP such commission may be warranted by the effort used by the Sales Representative resulting in said orders.

B. The commission, based on the net sale price (FOB factory), will be paid in accordance with the Schedule(s) (_____) attached hereto and made an integral part of this Agreement.

C. Said commission shall be disbursed in Canadian dollars to the Sales Representative within thirty days subsequent to the payment for the Equipment delivered to the Served Market Customer in accordance with the terms of payment established and accepted in the contract between PFP and the Served Market Customer.

D. No commissions will be paid on the value of technical, construction, installation, or similar services, nor on the value of insurance, bonds, interest, ocean freight, or other charges that may be included in the PFP's invoice to a Served Market Customer.

E. It is understood that if an order should be rescinded, revoked, or repudiated by a Served Market Customer for reasons beyond PFP's control or by PFP for breach of contract or by either party for force majeure causes, or it becomes invalid or inoperative due to any governmental regulation, the Sales Representative shall not be entitled to a commission with respect to such order, except pro rata to the extent of any amounts PFP may have received and retained as payment for Equipment delivered to a Served Market Customer.

F. It is further understood that no compensation, by way of commission or otherwise, shall be due the Sales Representative in connection with an order on which a commission would otherwise be payable, if as to such an order:

(i) any applicable governmental law, rule, or regulation prohibits or makes improper the payment of any commission, fee, or other payment to a Sales Representative;

(ii) any Served Market Customer makes it a condition that no commission, fee, or payment be made to a Sales Representative; or

(iii) any action has been taken by the Sales Representative in violation of its commitments set forth in Article 6, paragraphs C and D.

6. RELATIONSHIP OF PARTIES AND CONTROLLING LAWS

A. PFP may assign the installation and commissioning portion of its contract to the Sales Representative but, except as aforesaid, this Agreement and any rights hereunder are nonexclusive and non-assignable, and any assignment by one party without the prior written consent of the other party shall be void. The Sales Representative is an independent contractor to PFP. It is understood that the Sales Representative or its agents, subsidiaries, affiliates, and employees are in no way the legal representatives or agents of PFP for any purpose whatsoever and have no right or authority to assume or create, in writing or otherwise, any obligation of any kind, expressed or implied, in the name of or on behalf of PFP. PFP reserves the right to determine in its sole discretion the acceptability of any order, any provisions thereof, or any condition proposed by the customer and shall in no way be obligated to bid, quote to, or negotiate with any Served Market Customer.

B. This Agreement and any services hereunder are subject to and shall be governed by all the applicable laws and regulations of Canada; the rights and obligations of the Sales Representative as well as those of PFP under or in connection with this Agreement shall be governed by such laws and regulations and by the law of the Province of Ontario, Canada.

C. The Sales Representative agrees to comply with the law applicable to the performance of its obligations under the terms of this Agreement. Without limitation to the foregoing, the Sales Representative will comply fully with the export control laws and regulations of the Canadian Government with respect to the disposition of products and the printed commercial and technical data and information and other publications supplied by PFP. Further, the Sales Representative agrees that it will not pay, nor will it make any offer or commitment to pay, anything of value (either in the form of compensation, gift, contribution, or otherwise) to any employee, representative, person or organization in any way connected with any Customer, private or governmental, where such payment is contrary to applicable law, including the laws of Canada and the laws of the country in which the Sales Representative provides services under this Agreement.

D. With respect to any transaction arising under this Agreement, it is specifically understood and agreed that neither the Sales Representative nor its employees or representatives shall receive any payments in the nature of a rebate or similar benefit paid directly or indirectly by the Customer, nor shall any employee or representative of PFP receive any such payment paid directly or indirectly by the Sales Representative or by the Customer.

7. EXPIRATION, RENEWAL, TERMINATION

A. This Agreement shall automatically expire at the end of the term specified in Article 2 hereof unless specifically renewed prior thereto by mutual consent given in writing by the parties hereto.

B. This Agreement may be terminated prior to the completion of the term specified in Article 2 hereof:

(i)   by mutual consent given in writing by the parties hereto;

(ii) by either party at will, with or without cause, upon no less than sixty days notice in writing by registered mail, cable, or personal delivery to the other party; or

(iii) by PFP upon one day's similar notice in the event the Sales Representative attempts to assign this Agreement or any right hereunder without PFP's prior written consent; there is a change in the control or management of the Sales Representative that is unacceptable to PFP; the Sales Representative ceases to conduct its operations in the normal course of business; a receiver for the Sales Representative is appointed or applied for or it otherwise takes advantage of an insolvency law; the Sales Representative represents other parties whose representation, in PFP's opinion, involves a conflict with the Sales Representative's obligations hereunder; or the Sales Representative breaches this Agreement or acts in any manner deemed by PFP to be detrimental to the best interest of PFP. The foregoing events shall without limitation be deemed to be cause for termination by PFP.

8. OBLIGATIONS UPON EXPIRATION OR TERMINATION

In the event that an order from any Served Market Customer in the Territory for the supply of Equipment is accepted by PFP prior to the date of expiration or termination of this Agreement, the obligations assumed by both parties hereunder with respect to any such order shall continue in force until fully performed. In the event this Agreement expires or is terminated, and within _____ from the date of such expiration or termination an order from a Served Market Customer in the Territory for the supply of Equipment is accepted by PFP and is implemented within said _____ period by financial arrangements acceptable to PFP, the Sales Representative's rights to commission payments will be fully protected, provided such purchase order is awarded in the sole opinion of PFP as a result of services performed by the Sales Representative prior to the effective date of expiration or termination. Such acceptance of an order from, or the sale of any Equipment to, a Served Market Customer after the expiration or termination of this Agreement shall not be construed as a renewal or extension hereof, but the obligations undertaken in this Article 8 shall survive such expiration or termination.

9. **PRIVATE INFORMATION**
   A. The Sales Representative shall maintain in confidence and safeguard all business and technical information that becomes available to it in connection with this Agreement, the information being either of _____ proprietary nature or not intended for disclosure to others. This obligation shall continue for five years after expiration or termination of this Agreement.
   B. Knowledge or information of any kind disclosed by the Sales Representative to PFP shall be deemed to have been disclosed without obligation on the part of PFP to hold the same in confidence, and PFP shall have full right to use and disclose such information, subject to the approval of the Sales Representative, whose approval shall not be withheld without proper cause and without any compensation to the Sales Representative beyond that specifically provided by this Agreement.

10. **COMPANY TRADEMARKS AND TRADE NAMES**
    The Sales Representative agrees that it will comply at all times with the rules and regulations furnished to the Sales Representative by PFP with respect to the use of _____ and _____ trademarks and trade names; it will express and identify properly the "Authorized Sales Representative" relationship with PFP for Equipment; it will not publish or cause to be published any statement, nor encourage or approve any advertising or practice, that might mislead or deceive any parties or might be detrimental to the good name, trademark, goodwill, or reputation of PFP or its products. The Sales Representative further agrees

upon request to withdraw any statement and discontinue any advertising or practice deemed by PFP to have such effect.

11. **LIMITATION OF LIABILITY**

Neither party to this agreement shall have liability to the other with respect to the claims arising out of, in connection with, or resulting from this agreement, whether in contract, tort (including negligence of any degree), or otherwise except as provided under the terms of this agreement.

12. **RELEASE OF CLAIMS**

In consideration of the execution of this Agreement by PFP, the Sales Representative hereby releases PFP from all claims, demands, contracts, and liabilities, if any thereby, as of the date of execution of this Agreement by the Sales Representative, except indebtedness that may be owing founded upon a written contract.

13. **FAILURE TO ENFORCE**

The failure of either party to enforce at any time or for any period of time the provisions hereof in accordance with its terms shall not be construed to be a waiver of such provisions or of the right of such party thereafter to enforce each and every provision.

14. **NOTICES**

Any notice, request, demand, direction, or other communication required or permitted to be given or made under this agreement or in connection therewith shall be deemed to have been properly given or made if delivered to the party to whom it is addressed, or by registered mail, telegram, cable, or telex addressed as follows: _____.

15. **EXECUTION AND MODIFICATION**

A. This Agreement constitutes the entire and only agreement between the parties respecting the sales representation to the Served Market of Equipment specified herein.

B. This Agreement wholly cancels, terminates, and supersedes any and all previous negotiations, commitments, and writing between the parties with respect to Equipment. No change, modification, extension, renewal, ratification, rescission, termination, notice of termination, discharge, abandonment, or waiver of this Agreement or any of the provisions hereof; nor any representation, promise, or condition relating to this Agreement shall be binding upon PFP unless made in writing and signed by duly authorized personnel of PFP,

IN WITNESS WHEREOF, this agreement has been executed by both parties.

Appendix D

Sample Export Business Plan: Donga Michael Export Company

EXECUTIVE SUMMARY

Donga Michael is a newly created export company located in Fort Lauderdale, Florida. The company started its operation in September 1998. It exports computers and parts to the Republic of South Africa. Trade in computers between the United States and South Africa has been growing at a faster rate since the end of apartheid. The company intends to supply high-quality computers to the business sector and later to schools and universities.

South Africa is the largest computer market for the United States in Sub-Saharan Africa. Every year, it imports computer peripherals and accessories worth over $30 million dollars. With the end of apartheid and the lifting of sanctions, South Africa is open for trade and investment. The development of a black professional and business class and the building of infrastructure facilities to enable all South Africans to participate in the economic life of the country provides enormous business opportunities for U.S. exporters of information technology. Even though there is strong price competition in the computer sector, Donga Michael will focus on the upper end of the consumer market. Donga Michael's competitive advantages over existing companies include a coordinated marketing program, prompt delivery and services, as well as a professional image and expertise in the North American market.

President and founder George Hunat brings a wealth of experience to the firm. Vice President Alice Munroe also has extensive marketing experience. The estimated required investment is $200,000. Mr. Hunat will invest $40,000 of his own personal funds in the business. Ms. Munroe will invest $35,000, while $80,000 will be borrowed from a local bank. The balance of $45,000 is solicited from a venture capitalist who will acquire 37.5 percent of the corporation stock.

The company intends to become a major player in the South African market in the next five years capturing about 20 percent of the computer market. After this objective is realized, the company intends to explore export opportunities in Zimbabwe, Zambia, and Kenya.

GENERAL INDUSTRY AND COMPANY

The South African computer market is valued at close to $1 billion and is changing its focus from mainframes to personal computers (PCs) and PC-based networks. The increasing processing power coupled with decreasing prices for personal computers is also boosting demand for laptop computers and peripheral equipment, including printers and storage devices. Opportunities exist for sales of computers, peripherals, and accessories, as South African manufacturing and service companies seek to become more competitive in the domestic and global marketplaces. Presently, about four U.S. companies sell computer hardware to the South African market. Local manufacture of PCs remains negligible, and there is an increasing demand for established computer brand-name products. Donga Michael intends to bring such products into the market at competitive prices to help regain the market share lost during the sanctions period. With closer economic relations between South Africa and other African countries, the South African market will become the beachhead from which exports could be made to neighboring states, such as Zimbabwe, Zambia, Kenya, Tanzania, and Uganda. An encouraging development pertaining to the industry is the revision of U.S. controls on computer exports in 1995. The new regulations eliminate or significantly ease controls on computer exports to most countries of the world, except those which are designated as terrorist states. There are no U.S. restrictions on computer products and accessories that Donga Michael plans to export to South Africa. A problem that plagues the industry in the short term, however, is the shortage of trained manpower to manage the complex and interconnected networks proliferating everywhere.

Donga Michael is a newly created export firm that is incorporated as a Chapter S corporation in the state of Florida. The company will market digital ABD machines with central processing input-output units, parts and accessories, laptop and notebook computers, networking software, and software for computer-aided design and electronic design automation. The products need not be adapted for the South African market except for the different voltages (i.e., 100v). George Hunat and Alice Munroe comprise the two partners of the firm and also manage the company as president and vice president, respectfully.

TARGET MARKET

South Africa has a gross domestic output of $127 billion and a per capita income of $3,000 (as of 1997) and remains the largest economy in Sub-Saharan Africa. It possesses a modern infrastructure, supporting an efficient distribution of goods to major urban centers throughout the region and well-developed financial, legal, and communications sectors. Its economic growth has been in the range of 1 to 1.15 percent over the last five years. However, with favorable economic conditions and a stable political climate, it is likely to register higher rates of growth, estimated at 5 to 10 percent in the next few years and beyond. This is critical to offset high unemployment rates. Present efforts to revamp the educational system, boost economic productivity, and provide access to basic services to all South Africans present opportunities for U.S. companies to export computers and other information technology.

Total U.S. exports to South Africa in 1996 amounted to $3.1 billion. The South African information technology market is the twentieth largest in the world and constitutes one of the top ten emerging markets that are being targeted by international computer companies. The base of installed personal computers is approximately 800,000 to 900,000, and indications are that 84 percent of the top information technology users are investing in client-server systems. The U.S. market share for computer peripherals was estimated at about 25 percent in 1997, amounting to about $45 million. A couple reasons account for the continual expansion of the market for computer peripherals and accessories :

1. Because the country ended its isolation and instituted a democratic political system for all South Africans, there is a significant inflow of foreign investment. For example, between 1991 and 1994, about 184 companies set up factories or offices in South Africa. This creates business opportunities for exports of computers and information technology.
2. The black middle class has experienced faster growth since the end of the apartheid system. Hence, this emerging professional and business class will soon be a big consumer market.

In terms of market access, there are no restrictions or quotas on computer peripheral imports to South Africa. These imports are, however, subject to a 10 percent ad valorem tariff and a 14 percent value-added tax. There are no nontariff barriers such as prior deposits or foreign exchange restrictions.

There is fierce competition in the South African market. Acer Africa is the top PC assembler and distributor, followed by Mustek electronics and

IBM. Third-country suppliers from the Far East, Britain, France, Germany, and Italy are also present. Donga Michael should focus on the upper end of the consumer market for use by the business sector. Inspite of the relatively high prices compared to the competition, discerning firms know the value of quality products and would be favorably disposed to buying U.S. made computers and parts. U.S.-branded peripherals have high status in South Africa.

U.S. Equipment Exports to South Africa
(Exports of computers, peripherals, and parts
in millions of dollars)

Year	1994	1995	1996
Value of U.S. Exports	35	15	52
Import Market	197	78	294

Source: U.S. National Trade Data Bank (1996).Washington, DC: U.S. Government Printing Office, p. 15.

MARKETING PLAN AND SALES STRATEGY

Donga Michael Inc. intends to target the middle- to upper-level business firms that are in the process of using computers for various office functions, such as finance and accounting, word processing, electronic communication, and presentation. It should later begin to focus on high schools, universities, and research centers by entering into a supply agreement with the government. The company can establish retail outlets in major cities, and since it represents a well-known brand, it can have a marketing advantage.

Donga Michael can also promote sales by participating in computer trade exhibitions, advertising, and carefully managed public relations programs, such as sponsorship of special events, charitable donations to social causes, and so on.

MANAGEMENT AND ORGANIZATION

The company is managed by George Hunat, founder and president, and Alice Munroe, vice president and director of sales and marketing. George Hunat has an MSc in computer engineering from Emory University in

Atlanta, Georgia. Since graduation in 1985, he has worked as director of logistics for a multinational firm in San Diego, California (1985-1989), and later joined a successful computer export firm in Silicon Valley, California, as export manager (1989-1997). He has extensive experience in computer sales, marketing, and logistics operations. Alice Munroe received a BA in computer systems from Texas A&M in 1987 and has since worked as a marketing manager for a communications firm in New York.

Donga Michael will employ six people and a clerk. The employees will be trained to handle distribution, storage, transportation, and marketing of Donga Michael's computer products. Two of the trainees will be sent to South Africa to handle marketing and distribution. They will also recruit and train South African employees who will handle the retail outlets in major urban centers. For the first few years, the retail outlets will be located in Johannesburg, Pretoria, and Cape Town.

The employees and clerk will be paid hourly at $8.00 and $6.00 per hour, respectively. The capital structure and salary level are as follows:

Partners	Capital	Ownership Share	Salary
George Hunat	$40,000 (20 %)	33.33%	$3,500/month
Alice Munroe	$35,000 (17.5%)	29.16%	$3,000/month
Bank Loan	$80,000 (40%)	-----	
Venture capital	$45,000 (22.5%)	37.50%	

Future increases in salary will be based on sales performance.

LONG-TERM DEVELOPMENT PLAN

Donga Michael plans to show steady progress over the next five years, becoming one of the largest retailers of computers and parts in South Africa. It plans to capture 20 percent of the market by the year 2003.

The marketing staff will be increased as more sales are generated. Additional sales distribution outlets will be established in other urban areas. After five years, the company plans to expand to Zimbabwe, Zambia, and Kenya. Additional bank financing will be secured to finance the expansion.

Financial Plan: Donga Michael Export Company
Forecasted Income Statements for the Ending Year

	1998	1999	2000	2001
Sales	$120,000	$1,120,000	$3,980,000	$5,200,000
Less cost of goods sold	30,000	350,000	600,000	1,350,000
Commission	10,000	120,000	200,000	420,000
Delivery	32,000	60,000	98,000	150,000
Total variable expenses	**72,000**	**530,000**	**898,000**	**1,920,000**
Less fixed expenses				
Rent	10,000	10,000	10,000	10,000
Advertising	15,000	22,000	25,000	60,000
Travel	20,000	25,000	27,000	20,000
Utilities	7,000	7,500	7,700	8,000
Wages	25,000	38,000	45,000	45,000
Misc.	15,000	18,000	22,000	25,000
Total fixed expenses	**92,000**	**120,500**	**136,700**	**168,000**
Net Income	**(44,000)**	**549,500**	**2,945,300**	**3,112,000**

Forecasted Balance Sheet for the Ending Year

Assets	1998	1999	2000	2001
Cash	$40,000	$165,000	$600,000	$750,000
Accounts receivable	420,000	500,000	700,000	850,000
Inventory	100,000	150,000	160,000	220,000
Other	320,000	400,000	500,000	650,000
Less depreciation	15,000	25,000	30,000	45,000
Total assets	**865,000**	**1,190,000**	**1,930,000**	**2,425,000**

Liabilities	1998	1999	2000	2001
Accounts payable	$150,000	$220,000	$230,000	$150,000
Long-term debt	80,000	50,000	40,000	22,000
Retailed earnings	------	220,000	200,000	400,000
Total liabilities and capital	**230,000**	**490,000**	**470,000**	**572,000**

Appendix E

Sample Import Business Plan: Otoro Import Company

EXECUTIVE SUMMARY

Otoro Imports is a spice importing and marketing corporation established in June 1998. It is located in Los Angeles, California, and specializes in the importation and marketing of high-quality spices at competitive prices. The company also provides certain programs to educate and inform distributors, retailers, and consumers about the use and health benefits of spices.

The United States is the world's largest spice importer and consumer. With the increased ethnic diversity of the population, strong U.S. dollar, and limited domestic production, there is greater demand for and affordability of such foods. The industry is dominated by a small number of companies. Otoro intends to import three types of spices: black and white pepper, paprika, and cinnamon, products showing fast growth in domestic demand.

The management team includes Davie Lee, president, and Howard Tzu, vice-president. They both have extensive experience in the spice industry. The company has hired four full-time employees and a clerk. It will hire additional employees as the need arises. The company will market the imports through its retail outlets in California, Florida, and New York and through outside distributors in other states. Its future plan includes expansion to Canada and Mexico and maintaining a substantial presence in the U.S. market, by 2005, probably controlling about 25 percent of the market.

GENERAL DESCRIPTION OF INDUSTRY AND COMPANY

Otoro Imports intends to import spices from various countries for sale and distribution in the United States. Besides the importation and market-

430 EXPORT-IMPORT THEORY, PRACTICES, AND PROCEDURES

ing of high-quality spices, Otoro intends to provide education programs to
its distributors and retailers about the various types of spices, their uses,
and their health benefits. As sales volume increases, the company also
plans to hold free public seminars to inform and educate the North American consumer about the benefits and usage of various spices. The company aims to be known as the premier spice importing and marketing firm in
North America. Its development goals are for steady expansion, with
profitability by the second year.

The United States is the world's largest spice importer and consumer.
Per capita consumption totaled 3.3 pounds in 1998 and it is likely to grow
in the next few years. A number of factors contribute to the growing
demand for spices in the United States. First, the growth of ethnic populations has caused a surge in the use of the spices common to their different
cultures. According to the U.S. census, the Asian and Hispanic populations grew by 3.8 and 7.8 million, respectively, between 1982 and 1992.
Second, ethnic foods have become increasingly popular in the United
States. Nowadays, it is rare to see a typical shopping center without an
ethnic restaurant. There is also a trend toward the use of spices to compensate for less salt and lower fat levels in foods.

The industry is dominated by a small number of companies that process
and market imported or domestically produced spices. For example, McCor-
mick/Schilling accounts for about 37 percent of the U.S. retail market. Given
the trend toward mergers in most sectors, there is a possibility of mergers and
acquisitions in the spice industry resulting in fewer, larger firms.

Otoro intends to import high-quality spices at competitive prices. It
ensures importation of top-quality spices by maintaining constant communication with foreign producers and stationing a quality control specialist
at most export locations to determine and advise on quality before importation into the United States. Importation from Indonesia, India, and
China of seven of the most popular spices in the United States (vanilla
beans, black and white pepper, capsicums, sesame seed, cinnamon, mustard, and oregano) is planned over the next five years because of their
comparative advantages in climate, soil, and labor costs.

The seven products to be imported make up about 75 percent of U.S.
spice imports (see Table A). Otoro will import three products during the
first two years: black and white pepper, paprika, and cinnamon.

Presently, there are no restrictions on the importation of spices into the
United States. However, food safety regulations require the treatment of
spices to kill insects and microorganisms that thrive under tropical conditions.

TABLE A. U.S. Spice Imports

PRODUCT	BRIEF PROFILE
Vanilla Beans	Imports average over $60 million a year. Major suppliers include Comorus, Madagascar, and the Pacific Islands. Mainly used for ice cream.
Black and White Pepper	Imports average over $50 million a year for black pepper and about $11 million for white pepper. Major suppliers are Brazil, India, and Indonesia. Used as seasonings for food.
Capsicum and Paprika Peppers	Capsicum peppers are mainly imported from China, India, Mexico, and Palestine. Paprika is imported from Hungary, Morocco, and Spain. Total imports amount to over $60 million a year.
Mustard Seed	Import value averages at $135 million a year. There is some domestic production. Most imports come from Canada.
Cassia and Cinnamon	Widely used for doughnuts. Most imports come from Indonesia. Import value averages at about $30 million a year.
Oregano	Mostly used for pizza. Imported from Mexico and Turkey. Annual imports average about $12 million a year.
Sesame Seed	Used in the fast-food sector. Imported from Guatemala, El Salvador, and Mexico. Import value averages about $44 million a year.

Otoro will market the imported spices through its retail outlets in California, New York, and Florida. In other states, the product will be marketed through distributors.

TARGET MARKET

Otoro intends to operate retail outlets in major Metropolitan centers of California (Los Angeles, San Diego, and San Jose), Florida (Jacksonville, Miami, and Tampa), and New York (New York City, Buffalo, and Rochester). In other states, the products will be marketed through distributors. The major customers include restaurants, fast-food chains, and individual consumers.

Imports have played an important role in the American diet by providing needed spices through the year and by moderating retail prices during times of shortages or other disruptions in domestic production. The United States produces a limited supply of spices—garlic, onions, mustard, ginger, and capsicum pepper—and its average annual exports are estimated at $87 million. However, the U.S. import share of total domestic consumption stands at about 92 percent (as of 1998), and thus, there is heavy reliance on foreign suppliers. The volume of spice imports grew by about 45 percent in the past decade to an average of 550 million pounds in 1998. The major suppliers include Canada, China, India, Indonesia, and Mexico. India supplied the largest share, at 33 percent in 1990 through 1994.

A number of factors contribute to steady growth and expansion of spice imports in the United States:

- Given the current per capita consumption, total domestic use of spices is likely to increase by over $300 million over the next few years.
- The increased ethnic diversity of the U.S. population will lead to more consumption of spices.
- Because domestic production of spices is limited in volume and variety, the United States will continue to import over 90 percent of its domestic spice needs.
- The increased value of the U.S. dollar in relation to the currencies of our major exporters, such as Indonesia, as well as low U.S. tariffs for spice imports, is likely to increase the availability and affordability of such foods.
- Foreign producers have increasingly adapted new production technologies to meet the necessary safety and quality standards of U.S. consumers and have also enhanced the popularity of imported spices.

There is strong competition from established companies in the industry that sell natural as well as artificial substitutes. However, Otoro's competitive advantage will be in the supply of high-quality spices at competitive prices. Furthermore, current and future needs cannot be met by the existing competition, and Otoro wants to position itself as an important supplier of black and white pepper, paprika, and cinnamon. Industry sources also indicate that these three products will constitute the fastest growing spice import groups in the U.S. market (see Table B).

TABLE B. U.S. Spice Production and Trade (Thousands of Pounds)

Year	Imports	Domestic Production
1985	400,990	228,781
1986	438,878	217,340
1987	442,922	224,676
1988	339,974	228,875
1989	480,439	262,115
1990	505,634	296,492
1991	507,469	306,088
1992	531,080	337,700
1993	520,973	307,878
1994	582,910	303,500

Source: U.S. Department of Agriculture, Economic Reserve Society (July, 1995). Washington, DC: U.S. Government Printing Office, p. 10.

Note: Data include natural and artificial spices. Domestic production is limited to capsicums, mustard seed, dehydrated garlic and onions, and herbs used as spices.

MARKETING PLAN AND SALES STRATEGY

Otoro will invest sufficient resources to achieve improvements in quality and reliability. It is important to find a suitable manner of presentation (e.g., bags, baskets, tins, etc.) that is timesaving and attractive to customers. The product will be marketed at a low price to be competitive in the market. Promotion includes participation in food shows and advertising.

MANAGEMENT AND ORGANIZATION

The company is managed by its founder, David Lee (president), and Howard Tzu (Vice-President). They both worked as managers for a reputable spice trading firm in Las Vegas, Nevada. Four people will be hired during the first phase of operation to clear imports from customs, transport the goods, and warehouse the shipment. The employees and a clerk will be paid $10.00 and $7.00 per hour, respectively. The capital structure and salary level are as follows:

Partners	Capital	Ownership Share	Salary
David Lee	$350,000	58.33%	$4,000/month
Howard Tzu	$250,000	41.67%	$3,000/month
Bank Loan	$150,000	-----	-------

LONG-TERM DEVELOPMENT PLAN

Otoro intends to be a major retailer and distributor of natural spices, capturing about 25 percent of the U.S. market by 2005. In the next five years, expansion plans will be focused on Canada and Mexico. Additional borrowing may be required to finance expansion.

Otoro Imports: Projected Income Statement

	Year 1	Year 2	Year 3
Total net sales	$450,000	$800,000	$1,500,000
Cost of goods sold	150,000	350,000	650,000
Gross profit	300,000	450,000	850,000
Expenses			60,000
Utilities	35,000	40,000	4,500
Postage	2,000	3,000	250,000
Warehouse	86,000	100,000	100,000
Transportation	40,000	55,000	85,000
Rent	85,000	85,000	100,000
Miscellaneous	60,000	75,000	
			599,500
Total Expenses	308,000	358,000	
Net profit (loss)			250,500
before taxes	(8,000)	92,000	

Start-Up Expenses for the First Six Months

Items	Range
Supplies	$1,000 to $2,000
Insurance	400 to 600
Rent	2,000 to 2,500
Utilities	400 to 600
Insurance	500 to 700
Furniture, etc.	3,000 to 5,000
Licenses/taxes	500 to 200
Advertising	3,000 to 4,000
Professional services	5,000 to 8,000
Salaries	200,000 to 240,000
Inventory	350,000 to 500,000
Operating capital	5,000 to 8,000
Total start-up expenses	**570,800 to 771,600**

Appendix F

Tariff Rate: Selected Countries (1997-1998)

Countries	All Products (%)	Primary Products (%)	Manufactured Products (%)
Albania	15.9	14.5	16.3
Argentina	11.3	8.4	11.9
Australia	5.7	.1.2	6.8
Bangladesh	4.1	0.5	11.6
Brazil	11.9	8.7	12.6
Canada	6.0	4.0	6.5
Chile	11.0	11.0	10.9
China	17.8	17.8	17.8
Colombia	11.7	12.2	11.6
Cuba	10.7	7.6	11.6
Czech Republic	7.0	8.4	6.4
Estonia	0.1	0.1	0.1
European Union	6.0	10.4	5.6
India	30.0	25.7	31.3
Indonesia (1996)	13.2	12.3	13.5
Japan	6.0	9.0	4.8
Korea (1996)	11.1	21.2	8.2
Latvia	6.0	11.5	3.7
Lithuania	4.6	9.1	2.8
Malawi	25.3	21.1	26.5
Malaysia	9.1	4.1	12.2
Mauritius	29.1	19.7	31.7
Mexico	13.1	14.5	12.8
New Zealand	5.4	2.5	6.3
Nigeria	35.7	33.2	36.5
Norway	4.1	5.1	3.9
Peru	13.3	13.8	13.1

Appendix F *(continued)*

Countries	All Products (%)	Primary Products (%)	Manufactured Products (%)
Philippines (1995)	27.6	28.9	27.2
Poland	18.4	28.0	14.1
Russian Federation	12.7	10.8	13.5
Singapore (1989)	0.5	0.2	0.6
South Africa	8.8	8.0	9.0
Tanzania	21.6	30.6	19.6
Thailand (1993)	45.6	40.3	47.2
Trinidad and Tobago (1992)	18.7	22.9	17.4
Turkey	13.5	34.1	6.0
United States	5.0	6.0	4.9
Uruguay	10.2	8.8	10.5
Venezuela	12.0	12.3	11.9
Zambia	13.6	15.7	13.1
Zimbabwe	22.2	22.0	22.3

Source: World Bank (1999). World Development Indicators, Washington, DC: World Bank Publications, pp. 340-342.

Appendix G
Trade Profiles (1997)

Table A. Selected Developed Nations

	Merchandise Trade (US$)		Services Trade (US$)		Trade (% of GDP)	
	Exports	Imports	Exports	Imports	Exports	Imports
Australia	56,228	61,243	18,838	18,823	21.2	20.7
Austria	57,684	62,638	26,697	24,942	42.3	43.6
Belgium	165,725	151,973	34,855	31,866	74.9	70.3
Canada	211,961	195,039	30,018	36,361	40.0	38.2
Denmark	48,793	44,472	15,146	14,990	35.0	31.0
Finland	40,933	30,991	7,168	8,377	39.8	31.3
France	282,944	266,165	81,144	63,651	26.2	22.9
Germany	510,570	434,861	79,904	119,507	28.1	26.5
Greece	10,788	25,191	9,287	4,650	15.0	24.0
Ireland	53,258	39,192	6,159	15,069	84.0	70.7
Italy	238,161	204,098	72,310	70,429	27.1	22.9
Japan	420,492	337,501	69,302	123,454	11.4	10.3
Netherlands	184,295	162,155	49,774	45,197	59.2	53.0
New Zealand	13,983	14,551	3,977	4,981	59.2	53.0
Norway	48,528	35,751	14,447	14,582	41.2	34.1
Spain	101,228	118,478	43,902	24,675	27.9	26.8
Sweden	81,057	62,854	17,848	19,559	44.3	37.2
Switzerland	75,999	75,747	26,225	15,387	44.3	37.2
UK	278,784	305,074	87,239	72,032	28.5	28.9
USA	637,505	894,995	256,163	166,194	11.5	12.9

Source: World Bank (1999). World Development Indicators, Washington, DC: World Bank Publications, pp. 190-212.
Note: Data for merchandise and services trade is in millions.

Table B. Selected Developing Nations

High-income nations	Exports	Imports	Exports	Imports	Exports	Imports
Chile	16,296	18,111	3,685	4.000	27	29
Korea	135,986	144,604	26,301	29,502	38	39
Kuwait	14,122	8,102	1,764	5,238	53	41
Malaysia	77,894	79,644	15,016	17,516	94	93
Mauritius	1,600	2,211	919	684	62	65
Saudi Arabia	61,603	40,837	4,484	25,477	45	31
Singapore	124,431	131,651	30,472	19,534	187	170
Taiwan	121,850	114,400	17,020	-----	49.01	48.5
Trinidad and Tobago	2,545	3,028	343	242	49	56
Argentina	26,263	30,349	3,271	6,340	9	11
Botswana	53,000	61,400	163	344	56	38
Brazil	52,478	65,074	7,266	18,463	8	10
China	182,792	142,370	24,581	30,306	23	18
Colombia	11,455	15,379	4,180	4,375	15	18
Costa Rica	4,273	4,302	1,524	1,152	46	48
Egypt	3,908	13,095	11,241	5,048	20	25
Indonesia	53,220	41,679	6,941	16,607	28	28
Jamaica	1,837	3,183	1,478	1,175	51	64
Mexico	109,890	111,847	11,400	12,616	30	30
Peru	6,115	8,558	1,543	2,290	13	17

Table B *(continued)*

	Merchandise Trade (US$)		Services Trade (US$)		Trade (% of GDP)	
	Exports	Imports	Exports	Imports	Exports	Imports
Middle-income						
Philippines	24,988	38,576	15,137	14,122	49	59
Thailand	57,567	62,084	15,763	17,337	47	46
Turkey	26,245	48,585	19,373	8,507	25	30
Uruguay	2,713	3,716	1,475	947	23	23
Venezuela	21,658	16,214	1,415	5,350	29	20
Low-income LDCs						
Bangladesh	3,887	6,863	678	557	12	18
Ethiopia	551	1,409	413	280	16	26
Ghana	1,737	3,295	157	456	24	38
India	32,201	36,293	9,253	8,110	12	16
Kenya	1,952	3,278	944	837	29	37
Nigeria	16,028	6,734	786	4,712	41	34
Pakistan	8,632	11,182	1,761	3,259	16	21
Tanzania	716	1,958	484	797	22	36
Uganda	618	825	154	405	13	20
Vietnam	8,758	14,814	2,530	3,153	46	54
Zambia	1,178	1,070	-----	-----	33	38
Zimbabwe	2,119	3,090	-----	-----	36	43

Source: World Bank (1999). World Development Indicators, Washington, DC: World Bank Publications, pp. 190-212.
Note: Data for merchandise and services trade is in millions.

439

Table C. Selected Transition Economies

Country	Merchandise Trade (US$)		Services Trade (US$)		Trade (% of GDP)	
	Exports	Imports	Exports	Imports	Exports	Imports
Albania	210	950	64	115	12	37
Bulgaria	4,232	3,816	1,338	1,167	61	56
Czech Republic	22,723	27,176	7,132	5,389	58	63
Estonia	2,926	4,438	1,318	727	77	89
Hungary	19,093	21,232	4,874	3,695	45	46
Latvia	1,672	2,721	1,033	662	50	61
Lithuania	3,343	5,469	1,032	897	55	65
Poland	25,697	42,271	8,986	5,814	26	30
Romania	8,420	11,270	1,422	2,037	30	37
Russia	87,368	67,619	13,520	18,715	23	20
Slovakia	8,790	10,259	2,167	2,094	56	64
Ukraine	16,132	26,902	4,937	2,268	41	44

Source: World Bank (1999). World Development Indicators, Washington, DC: World Bank Publications, pp. 190-212.
Note: Data for merchandise and services trade is in millions.

References

Chapter 1

Asheghian, P. and Ibrahimi, B. (1990). *International Business*. Philadelphia, PA: HarperCollins.

Belous, R. and Wyckoff, A. (1987). Trade has job winners too. *Across the board, 24*(9) (September): 53-55.

Daniels, J. and Radebaugh, L. (1994). *International Business*. Reading, MA: Addison-Wesley.

Davis, L. (1992). Surge in U.S. exports supports economy, employment. *Business America, 113*(10) (May 18): 27.

Fong, P. and Hill, H. (1991). Technology exports from a small, very open NIC: The case of Singapore. *World Development, 19:* 553-568.

Kaynak, E. and Kothavi, V. (1984). Export behavior of small and medium-sized manufacturers: Some policy guidelines for international marketers. *Management International Review, 24:* 61-69.

Lutz, J. (1994). To import or to protect? Industrialized countries and manufactured products. *Journal of World Trade, 28*(4): 123-145.

Rostow, W. (1978). *The World Economy: History and Prospect*. Austin, TX: University of Texas Press.

Sarmand, K. (1989). The determinants of import demand in Pakistan. *World Development, 17:* 1619-1625.

U.S. Department of Commerce (1990). *A Basic Guide to Exporting from the United States*. Washington, DC: NTC Books.

U.S. Department of Commerce (1994). The economics of technology and trade. *Business America, 115*(8): 6-8.

World Bank (1999). *World Development Indicators*. Herndon, VA: World Bank Publications.

World Wide Web Sources

History of International Trade
<http://www.lsb.scu.edu/~swade/histtrad.html>. This site provides a brief history of international trade since Marco Polo.
Meccan Trade and the Rise of Islam
<http://www.fordham.edu/halsall/med/crone.html>. This is an excerpt from a book on commerce in the Middle East and the rise of Islam.

Mountain Men and the Fur Trade
<http://www.xmission.com/~drudy/amm.html>. This site is an online research center to the history, traditions, and mode of living of the trappers, explorers, and traders known as the mountain men.
World History Archives
<http://www.hartford-hwp.com/archives/25/>. Provides documents for the history of premodern world economy, world economy in general, world trade, globalization, transnational corporations, and international finance.

Chapter 2

Archer, C. and Butler, F. (1992). *The European Community.* New York: St. Martin's Press.

Breitfelder, M. (1998). The Euro currency age: Challenges and opportunities for U.S. businesses. *Business America, 119*(7) (July): 33-35.

Collins, S. and Bosworth, B. (Eds.) (1995). *The New GATT.* Washington, DC: The Brookings Institution.

Echeverri-Carroll, E. (Ed.) (1995). *NAFTA and Trade Liberalization in the Americas.* Austin, TX: Bureau of Business Research, University of Texas.

El-Agraa, A. (Ed.) (1997). *Economic Integration Worldwide.* New York: St. Martin's Press.

Hoekman, B. and Kostecki, M. (1995). *The Political Economy of the World Trading System.* New York: Oxford University Press.

Jackson, J. (1992). *The World Trading System.* Cambridge, MA: MIT Press.

Kaufmann, M. (1993). *The European Community.* New York: Stone and Quill Publishing.

Randall, S., Konrad, H., and Silverman, S. (1992). *North America Without Borders?* Calgary, Canada: University of Calgary Press.

Schott, J. and Buurman, J. (1994). *The Uruguay Round.* Washington, DC: Institute for International Economics.

World Wide Web Resources

The European Union
<http://www.eurunion.org/infores/resguide.htm>. Information on the European Union (EU), EU treaties and agreements.
<http://www.userpage.chemie.fu-berlin.de/adressen/eu.html/>. Information on EU and its institutions.
NAFTA: Economic and Commercial Information
<http://the-tech.mit.edu/Bulletins/nafta.html>. Provides the complete text of the agreement.
<http://freedonia.tpusa.com/dir07/book>. Provides a summary and analysis of NAFTA.
<http://www.-tech.mit.edu/Bulletins/Nafta.html>. This site provides the complete text of the agreement.

World Trade Organization
<http://www.wto.org>. Basic information about the WTO, its agreements, and activities.

Chapter 3

Albaum, G., Strandskov, J., Duerr, E., and Dowd, L. (1994). *International marketing and Export Management.* Wokingham, UK: Addison-Wesley.

Anderson, R. and Dunkelberg, J. (1993). *Managing Small Business.* New York: West Publishing.

August, R. (1997). *International Business Law.* Upper Saddle River, NJ: Prentice-Hall.

Barnes, M. (1997). How to select your international bank. *Business America, 118*(10) (October): 38-39.

Cheeseman, H. (1997a). *Business Law.* Upper Saddle River, NJ: Prentice-Hall.

Cheeseman, H. (1997b). *Contemporary Business Law.* Upper Saddle River, NJ: Prentice-Hall.

Cooke, R. (1995). *Doing Business Tax-Free.* New York: John Wiley and Sons.

Delphos, W. (Ed.) (1990). *The World Is Your Market.* Washigton, DC: Braddock Communications.

Friedman, R. (1993). *The Complete Small Business Legal Guide.* Dearborn, MI: Enterprise.

Harper, S. (1991). *The McGraw-Hill Guide to Starting Your Own Business.* New York: McGraw-Hill.

Internal Revenue Service (1996a). Business expenses. Department of the Treasury, Publication 535.

Internal Revenue Service (1996b). Business use of your home. Department of the Treasury, Publication 587.

Internal Revenue Service (1996c). Travel, entertainment, gift and car expenses. Department of the Treasury, Publication 463.

McDaniel, P. and Ault, H. (1981). *Introduction to United States International Taxation.* Boston, MA: Kluwer.

McGrath, K., Elias, S., and Shena, S. (1996). *Trademark: How to Name a Business or Product.* Berkeley, CA: Nolo Press.

Ogley, A. (1995). *Principles of International Tax.* London: Interfisc Publishing.

Siegal, E., Ford, B., and Bornstein, J. (1993). *The Ernest and Young Business Plan Guide.* NewYork: John Wiley and Sons.

World Wide Web Resources

Fictitious Business Names
<http://www.iesbdc.org/fictitio.htm>.
 Basic information on filing fictitious business names.
<http://www.fryberger.com/SELECTIN.html>. Provides important tips on selecting a business name.

<http://gmarketing.com/tactics/weekly_43.html>. Seven secrets of great business names.
<http://www.sos.orus/corporation/bizreg/brabn.htm>. Information on assumed business names and partnerships.
Starting a Business
<http://www.iesbdc.org/faq.htm>. Provides answers to frequently asked questions about starting a business.

Chapter 4

Ashegian, P. and Ibrahimi, B. (1990). *International Business.* Philadelphia, PA: HarperCollins.
Ball, D. and McCulloch, W. (1996). *International Business.* Chicago, IL: Irwin.
Cohen, W. (1995). *Model Business Plans for Product Business.* New York: John Wiley and Sons.
Czinkota, M., Ronkainen, I., and Moffett, M. (1996). *International Business.* Philadelphia, PA: The Dryden Press.
Silvester, J. (1995). *How to Start, Finance, and Operate Your Own Business.* New York: Birch Lane Press.
Subramanian, R., Fernandes, N., and Harper, E. (1993). Environmental scanning in U.S. companies: Their nature and their relationship to performance, *Management International Review, 33:* 271-275.
Thomas Register (1998). Thomas Register of American Manufacturers. New York: Thomas Publishing.
Tuller, L. (1994). Exporting, Importing, and Beyond. Holbrook, MA: Bob Adams.
U.S. Department of Commerce (1990). *A Basic Guide to Exporting.* Lincolnwood, Chicago, IL: NTC Books.
U.S. Department of Commerce (1992). The ABC's of exporting. *Business America, 13*(9) (July 11-15): 2-5.
U.S. Department of commerce (1998). A brief account of the ATA carnet system. *Business America, 119*(8) (August): 1.
U.S. Trade Representative (USTR) (1997). *Foreign Trade Barriers.* Washington, DC: U.S. Government Printing Office.
Vanderleest, H. (1994). Planning for international trade show participation: A practitioner's perspective. *S.A.M. Advanced Management Journal, 59*(4): 39-44.
Weiss, K. (1987). *Building an Import/Export Business.* New York: John Wiley and Sons.
Williams, E. and Manzo, S. (1983). *Business Planning for the Entrepreneur.* New York: Van Nostrand Rienhold Company

World Wide Web Resources

Agricultural Marketing Research
<http://www.agpr.com/consulting/index.html>. Agricultural marketing consulting services.

Business Plans
<http://www.bizplanit.com/>. Provides resources on business plans.
International Market Research
<http://www.sibco.se/>. Provides market research services.
Small Business
<http://www6.americanexpress.com/smallbusiness/newdefault.asp?>. Information on business opportunities, expanding internationally, and creating a business plan.
<http://www.sbaonline.sba.gov/>. SBA information on starting, financing, and expanding a small business.
U.S. Export Inc.
<http://www.us2japan.com/index.htm>. U.S. Export Inc. helps small- to medium-sized North American manufacturers export their products to Japan.

Chapter 5

Anonymous (1996). Distribution in Vietnam: Options for foreign firms. *East Asian Executive Reports, 18*(10): 25.

Anonymous (1987). Basic question: To protect yourself or to hire someone to do it for you. *Business America, 10*(9): 15.

Ball, D. and McCulloch, W. (1996). *International Business.* Chicago, IL: Irwin.

Barovick, R. and Anderson, P. (1992). EMCs/ETCs: What they are and how they work. *Business America, 113*(92): 2-5.

Bello, D. and Gilliland, D. (1997). The effect of output controls, process controls and flexibility on export channel performance. *Journal of Marketing, 61:* 22-38.

Cateora, P. (1996). *International Marketing.* Chicago, IL: Irwin.

Chan, T. (1992). Emerging trends in export channel strategy: An investigation of Hong Kong and Singaporean firms. *European Journal of Marketing, 26*(3): 18-20.

Czinkota, M., Ronkainen, I., and Moffett, M. (1998). *International Business.* New York: Dryden Press.

Czinkota, M. and Woronoff, J. (1997). Import channels in the Japanese market. *International Trade Forum, 1:* 8-13.

Kennedy, E. (1993). The Japanese distribution system. *Business America, 114*(10): 20-22.

Klein, S., Frazier, G., and Roth, V. (1990). A transaction cost analysis model of channel integration in international markets. *Journal of Marketing Research, 27:* 196-208.

Kogut, B. (1986). On designing contracts to guarantee enforceability: Theory and evidence from east-west trade. *Journal of International Business Studies, 17:* 47-61.

Meloan, T. and Graham, J. (1995). *International Global Marketing.* Chicago, IL: Irwin.

Onkvisit, S. and Shaw, J. (1997). *International Marketing.* Upper Saddle River, NJ: Prentice-Hall.

Seifert, B. and Ford, J. (1989). Export distribution channels. *Columbia Journal of World Business, 24*(2): 14-18.

Sletten, E. (1994). *How to Succeed in Exporting and Doing Business Internationally.* New York: Wiley.

U.S. Department of Commerce (1992). The ABC's of exporting. *Business America, 113*(9) (July 11-15): 2-5.

World Wide Web Resources

Channels of Distribution

<http://miep.org/tutor/chdistr.htm>. Information on overseas distributors and other channels.

<http://miep.org/tutor/quick_con.html>. This site provides an overview of distribution channels, including the selection process as well as drawing up the final agreement.

<http://www.wbenet.com/uest4.htm>. This is a web site of the World Business Exchange that covers topics such as exporting, channels of distribution, market research, service exports, pricing, documentation, and financing.

<http://www.usda.gov/agexport/channels.html>. Information on channels of distribution for U.S. agricultural exports.

International Export Guide

<http://freedonia.tpusa.com/dir01/exportgui/guide04.html>. Management, organization of exports.

Chapter 6

Anonymous (1998a). Boeing eyes commercial sector for C-17. *American Shipper, 40*(4) (April): 101.

Anonymous (1998b). Truckers back car con train technology. *American Shipper, 40*(4) (April): 104-105.

Christopher, M. (Ed.) (1992). *Logistics: The Strategic Issues.* London: Chapman and Hall.

Czinkota, M., Ronkainen, I., Moffett, M., and Moynihan, E. (1998). *Global Business.* Fort Worth, TX: The Dryden Press.

Davies, G. (1987). The international logistics concept. *International Journal of Physical Distribution and Material Management, 17*(2): 17-23.

Fabey, M. (1997). Software for shippers. *World Trade, 10*(9) (September): 54-56.

Federal Maritime Commission Regulation of Ocean Freight Forwarders. Part 510, 49 Federal Regulations (FR)36297, September 14, 1984; 46 U.S. Code app. 1702-1708.

Guelzo, M. (1986). *Introduction to Logistics Management.* Upper Saddle River, New Jersey: Prentice-Hall.

Kendall, L. (1983). *The Business of Shipping.* Centerville, MD: Cornell Maritime Press.

Murr, A. (1979). *Export/Import Traffic Management and Forwarding.* Centerville, MD: Cornell Maritime Press.

Reyes, B. and Gilles, C. (1998). Lufthansa Fights Back. *American Shipper, 40*(4) (April): 94-98.

Thuermer, K. (1998). Move 'em or wilt. *World Trade, 11*(3) (March): 61.

Ullman, G. (1995). *U.S. Regulation of Ocean Transportation, Under the Shipping Act of 1984*. Centerville, MD: Cornell Maritime Press .

Wood, D., Barone, A., Murphy, P., and Wardlow, D. (1995). *International Logistics*. New York: Chapman and Hall.

Woolley, S. (1997). Replacing inventory with information. *Forbes, 159*(6) (March 24): 2-3.

World Wide Web Sources

Logistics
<http://www.logisticsworld.com/logistics/forumsearch.asp>. Directory of logistics resources on the net. It also presents learning opportunities for logistics professionals.

<http://209.51.193.25/logtalk.asp>. International logistics discussion group. The site offers service and contact information from various companies and organizations in the logistics industry.

Outsourcing and Sites on ISO 9000
<http://www.ousourcing.com>. Web site of the Outsourcing Institute that provides information and services on outsourcing and related sourcing strategies.

<http://www.exit109.com~leebee>. A site dedicated to help organizations understand and implement the ISO 9000 and ISO 9001 models for quality assurance.

<http://www.iso.ch/infoe/intro.html>. Provides information on certification and quality for ISO, U.S. standards.

Sites on Quality
<http://quality.nist.gov/docs/99_crit/99crit.htm>. This site provides criteria for performance excellence in business, education, and health care.

<http://www.nist.gov/public_affairs/releases/g97-44.htm>. This is a site that provides the list of winners of the Baldridge quality awards.

<http://www.dbainc.com/dba2/applications/service.html>. Information on customer-focused quality for service organizations.

<http://dbainc.com>. An overview of customer-focused quality in the areas of health care, manufacturing, and service. It also provides information on ISO-9000 and QS-9000.

Chapter 7

Anonymous (1993). Price quotations and terms of sale are key to successful exporting. *Business America, 114*(20) (October 4): 12-15.

Brinton, C., Christopher, J., Wolff, R., and Winks, R. (1984). *A History of Civilization* (Volume I). Upper Saddle River, NJ: Prentice-Hall.

Dussauge, P., Hart, S., and Ramanantsoa, B. (1987). *Strategic Technology Management*. New York: John Wiley and Sons.

Herman, A. (1989). Growth in international trade law. *Financial Times* (March 30): 10.

Hiam, A. and Schewe, C. (1992). *The Portable MBA in Marketing.* New York: John Wiley and Sons.

International Chamber of Commerce (Incoterms). (1990). New York: ICC Publishing.

Martens, J., Scarpetta, S., and Pilat, D. (1996). Mark-up ratios in manufacturing industries. *OECD Working paper,* No. 162 (April): 10-12.

Oster, S. (1990). *Modern Competitive Analysis.* London: Oxford University Press.

Piercy, N. (1982). *Export Strategy: Markets and Competition.* London: Unwin Hyman.

Reich, R. (1991). *The Work of Nations.* New York: Knopf.

Silberston, A. (1970). Price behavior of firms. *Economic Journal, 80* (319): 511-570.

World Wide Web Resources

Export Pricing
<http://sominfo.syr.edu/facstaff/fgtucker/m456s98/ppt/price>. Information on export pricing and global marketing strategies.

Incoterms, 1990
<http://www.iccwbo.org>. The Web site of the International Chamber of Commerce. It provides information on important areas such as commercial crime services, court of arbitration, as well as guidelines, codes, and rules.

Pricing for Profits
<http://www.smartbiz.com/sbs/arts/ieb6.htm>. Information on pricing for an export-import business.

<http://exportsource.gc.ca/nonframe/engdoc/1b6b4.html>. Information on export pricing, developing an export plan, and other related topics.

<http://swopec.hhs.se/hastef/abs/hastef0146.htm>. A working paper prepared by the Stockholm School of Economics on pricing to market in Swedish exports.

Chapter 8

DiMatteo, L. (1997). An international contract formula: The informality of international business transactions plus the internationalization of contract law equals unexpected contractual liability. *Syracuse Journal of International Law and Commerce, 23:* 67-111.

Hornick, R. (1990). Jakarta court declares standard international sales contract illegal. *East Asian Executive Reports* (March): 6-14.

Lubman, S. (1988). Investment and exports in the People's Republic of China: Perspectives on the evolving patterns. *Brigham Young University Law Review, 3:* 543-565.

Rosett, A. (1982). Unification, harmonization, restatement, codification and reform of international commercial law. *North Carolina Journal of International and Commercial Regulation,* 7(1): 683-698.

World Wide Web Resources

General Legal Information
<www.tufts.edu/departments/fletcher/multi/trade.html>. Provides texts of important trade agreements and commercial treaties.
International Commercial Law
<http://www.jus.uio.no/lm/toc.html>. A valuable site on international commercial law and electronic commerce. It also has international trade instruments, treaties, model laws, and rules.
<http://www.spfo.unibo.it/spolfo/trade.htm>. An extensive research guide to international trade law on the Internet.
<http://www.asil.org/resource/iell.htm>. A guide to electronic resources on international economic law.
<http://www.lib.uchicago.edu/~llou/forintlaw.html>. This site provides resources on international law issues.

Chapter 9

Cheeseright, P. (1994) Maker of Reliant in receivership. *Financial Times*, (November 29): 5-6..

Day, D. and Griffin, B. (1993). *The Law of International Trade*. London: Butterworths.

European Commission (1994). *Cross-Border Payments*. Brussels: European Economic Commission.

Flint, D. and O'Keefe, P. (1997). Admiralty and maritime law. *The International Lawyer, 31:* 234-243.

Force, R. (1996). A comparison of the Hague, Hague-Visby and Hamburg rules: Much ado about nothing. *Tulane Law Review, 70*: 2051-2089.

Greene, M. and Trieschmann, J. (1984). *Risk and Insurance*. Cincinnati, OH: South-Western Publishing Company.

Luesby, J. (1994). Brussels calls time for EU late payers. *Financial Times*, (November 29): 5-6.

Mehr, R., Cammack, E., and Rose, T. (1985). *Principles of Insurance*. Homewood, IL: Irwin.

Schmitthoff, C. (1986). *Schmitthoff's Export Trade*. London: Butterworths.

Seyoum, B. and Morris, J. (1996). Economic and trade characteristics as discriminators of countries' payment behavior. *Journal of global Business, 7*(12): 59-69.

U.S. Department of Commerce (1990). *A Basic Guide to Exporting from the United States*. Lincolnwood, IL: NTC Books.

Vance, W. (1951). *Handbook of the Law of Insurance*. St. Paul, MN: West Publishing Company.

Wells, F. and Dulat, K. (1996). *Exporting from Start to Finance*. New York: McGraw-Hill.

Wood, D., Barone, A., Murphy, P., and Wardlow, D. (1995). *International Logistics.* New York: Chapman and Hall.

Yancey, B. (1983). The carriage of goods: Hague, COGSA, Visby and Hamburg. *Tulane Law Review, 57:* 1238-1259.

Zodl, J. (1995). *Export-Import.* Cincinnati, OH: Betterway Books.

World Wide Web Resources

Sites on Documentation and Shipping

<http://www.ibs-ibp.com/rp01m.htm>. Information on export documentation and shipping.

<http://www.exportproco.com/guide.htm>. An interactive guide to export documentation.

<http://wisdairyexport.org/export.htm>. Export documentation and labeling of agricultural exports.

Sites on Risks and Insurance

<http://www.internationalbusiness.com/feb/log297.htm>. Provides information on cargo theft.

<http://www.duke.edu/~charvey/Country_risk/pol/pol.htm>. Information on political, economic, and financial risk.

Chapter 10

DeRosa, D. (1991). *Managing Foreign Exchange Risk.* Chicago, IL: Probus; London, UK: Macmillan.

International Monetary Fund (IMF) (1996). *International Financial Statistics Yearbook.* Washington, DC: IMF Publications.

O'Connor, D. and Bueso, A. (1990). *International Dimensions of Financial Management.* London: Macmillan.

Taylor, A. (1995). A new boost for Japan's automakers. *Fortune, 132*(8): 30-31.

World Wide Web Resources

Exchange Rates

<http://finance.yahoo.com/m3?u>. This site provides daily exchange rates of currencies in relation to one U.S. dollar.

<http://uta.fi/~ktmatu/rates.html>. Daily foreign exchange rates, information about currencies, and currency derivatives.

Exchange Rates and Trade

<http://www.stls.frb.org/fred/data/exchange.html>. Federal Reserve data on exchange rates, balance of payments, and trade.

<http://www.clev.frb.org/research/jul97et/moning.htm#1d>. A research paper prepared by the Federal Reserve on inflation and exchange rates.

<http://www.tcb-indicators.org/articles/bci-0399/bci-0399.htm>. Articles related to international trade, exchange rates, and the U.S. economy.

Financial Information
<www.yahoo.com/Economy>. Information on the global economy and finance.
<www.euromoney.com>. Global financial news and information.
Risk Management
<http://risk.ifci.ch/135460.htm>. This site provides an introduction and guide to the most important official documents on financial risk management.

Chapter 11

Artz, R. (1991). Punitive damages for wrongful dishonor or repudiation of a letter of credit. *Uniform Commercial Code Law Journal, 24*(3): 3-48.

Barnes, J. (1994). Defining good faith letter of credit practices. *Loyola of Los Angeles Law Review 28:* 103-107.

Cheeseright, P. (1994). Maker of Reliant in receivership. *Financial Times* (November 5): 7.

Goldsmith, H. (1989). *Import/Export: A Guide to Growth, Profits and Market Share.* Upper Saddle River, NJ: Prentice-Hall.

International Chamber of Commerce (ICC) (1993). Uniform Customs and Practice for Documentary Credits, no. 500. New York: ICC Publishing Company.

International Chamber of Commerce (ICC) (1995). Uniform Rules for Collections, no. 522. New York: ICC Publishing Company.

Kelley, J. (1995). Credit management. *Financial Times,* (March) i-v.

Kozolchyk, B. (1996). The financial standby: A summary description of practice and related problems. *Uniform Commercial Code Law Journal, 28*(4): 327-374.

Macintosh, K. (1992). Letters of credit: Curbing bad-faith dishonor. *Uniform Commercial Code Law Journal, 25*(3): 3-48.

Maggiori, H. (1992). *How to Make the World Your Market.* New York: Burning Gate Press.

McLaughlin, G. (1989). Structuring commercial letters of credit transactions to safeguard the interests of the buyer. *Uniform Commercial Code Law Journal 21:* 318-325.

McMahon, A., Marsh, A., Klitzke, P., and Issenman, J. (1994). *The Basics of Exporting.* Austin, TX: Southern United States Trade Association.

Onkvisit, S. and Shaw, J. (1997). *International Marketing.* Upper Saddle River, NJ: Prentice-Hall.

Rosenblith, R. (1991). Letter of credit law. *Uniform Commercial Code Law Journal 21:* 171-175.

Rubenstein, N. (1994). The issuer's rights and obligations under a letter of credit. *Uniform Commercial Code Law Journal, 17*(2): 129-174.

Ruggiero, A. (1991). *Financing International Trade.* New York: UNZ and Company.

Ryan, R. (1990). Who should be immune from the fraud in the defense in a letter of credit transaction. *Brooklyn Law Review 56:* 119-152.

Schmitthoff, C. (1986). *Schmitthoff's Export Trade.* London: Butterworths.

Tuller, L. (1994). *Exporting, Importing, and Beyond*. Holbrook, MA: Bob Adams.
Wells, F. and Dulat, K. (1991). *Exporting from Start to Finance*. New York: McGraw-Hill.

World Wide Web Resources

Financing Exports
<http://fita.org/aotm/index.html>. This site provides articles on international trade and financing exports.
<http://ljx.com/practice/intrade/id_letter.html>. This site provides current articles on letters of credit.
<http://intbanking.org/pub.htm>. Publications of the International Financial Services Association on letters of credit.
<http://www.iiblp.org/products.htm>. Publications of the Institute of banking on financing exports and related topics.

Chapter 12

Anonymous (1997a). Dassault launches offset related aviation joint venture with Taiwan's Chenfeng. *Countertrade and Offsets, 15*(7) (April 14): 5.
Anonymous (1997b). Russian Menatep to resume Cuban oil-for-Sugar swap. *Countertrade and Offset, 15*(7) (April 14): 5.
Anonymous (1997c). Saab, Lockheed and GE pledge offset in Hungary. *Countertrade and Offset, 15*(7) (April 14): 2-3.
Anyane-Ntow K. and Harvey, C. (1995). A countertrade primer. *Management Accounting, 76*(10): 47-50.
Barter Publishing Staff (Eds.). (1992). *Barter Referral Directory*. Austin, TX: Barter Publishing
Bost, P. and Yeakel, J. (1992). Are we ignoring countrade? *Management Accounting, 76*(6): 43-47.
Brinton, C., Christopher, J., Wolff, R., and Winks, R. (1984). *A History of Civilization* (Volume I). Upper Saddle River, NJ: Prentice-Hall.
Caves, R. and Marin, D. (1992). Countertrade Transactions: Theory and Evidence. *Economic Journal, 102*(414): 1171-1183.
Cole, J. (1987). Evaluating Offset Agreements: Achieving a balance of advantages. *Law and Policy in International Business 19:* 765-811.
Egan, C. and Shipley, D. (1996). Strategic orientations toward countertrade opportunities in emerging markets. *International Marketing Review, 13:* 102-120.
Hennart, J.F. (1990). Some empirical dimensions of countertrade. *Journal of International Business Studies, 21:* 243-270.
Hennart, J. and Anderson, E. (1993). Countertrade and the minimization of transaction costs: An empirical examination. *Journal of Law, Economics and Organization, 9:* 290-314.
Liesch, P. (1991). *Government Mandated Countertrade: Deals of Arm Twisting*. Brookfield, VT: Gower Press.

McVey, T. (1984). Commercial practices, legal issues and policy dilemmas. *Law and Policy in International Business, 16:* 23-26.

Office of Management and Budget (OMB) (1986). *Second Annual Report on the Impact of Offsets in Defense-Related Exports.* Washington, DC: U.S. Government Printing Office.

Roessler, F. (1985). Countertrade and the GATT legal system. *Journal of World Trade Law, 19*(6): 604-614.

Schaffer, M. (1989). *Winning the Countertrade War: New Export Strategies for America.* New York: Wiley.

U.S. International Trade Commission (ITC) (1985). *Assessment of the Effects of Barter and Countertrade Transactions on U.S. Industries.* Washington, DC: U.S. Government Printing Office.

Verdun, V. (1985). Are governmentally imposed countertrade requirements violations of the GATT. *Yale Journal of International Law 11:*191-215.

Verzariu, P. (1985). *Countertrade, Barter and Offsets: New Strategies for Profit in International Trade.* New York: McGraw-Hill.

Verzariu, P. (1992). Trends and developments in international countertrade. *Business America, 113:* 2-6.

Welt, L. (1990). Unconventional forms of financing: Buyback/compensation/barter. *Journal of International Law and Politics 22:* 461-473.

World Wide Web Resources

Countertrade

<http://sys1.tpusa.com/inforsrc/aca/ctover.html>. Web site of the American countertrade Association. It provides an overview of forms of countertrade, legal and regulatory environment, and future of countertrade.

<http://www.access.digex.net/~cto/index.html>. Abstract of past articles of the American Countertrade Association in its newsletter.

<http://www.countrade.org/acadefin.htm>. This site provides basic definitions of Incoterms and countertrade.

<http://www.countertrade.org>. Web site of the American Countertrade Association that provides resources for countertrade activity.

Chapter 13

Anonymous (1995). Increase services to small business, survey suggests. *Bank Management, 71*(4): 9-12.

Brewer II, E., Genay, G., Jackson III, W., and Worthington, P. (1996). How are small firms financed? Evidence from small business investment companies. *Federal Reserve Bank of Chicago, 20:* 1-18.

Field, A., Korn, D., and Middleton, T. (1995). How to make them give you the money. *Money, 24*(6): 94-103.

Fraser, J. (1996). Control those credit cards. *INC., 18* (December): 128.

Gardner, L. (1994). Opportunities and pitfalls in financing during business growth. *Secured Lender, 50:* 39-42.

Grimaud, A. (1995). The evolution of small-business financing. *Canadian Bank-er, 102*(3) (June): 36-37.

Hutchinson, R. (1995). The capital structure and investment decisions of the small owner-managed firm: Some exploratory issues. *Small Business Economics, 7:* 231-239.

Ioannou, L. (1995). The trade factor. *International Business,* (May): 42-45.

Lorenz-Fife, I. (1997). *Financing Your Business.* Englewood Cliffs, NJ: Prentice-Hall.

Ring, M. (1993). Innovative export financing: Factoring and forfaiting. *Business America, 114*(1) (January): 10-12.

Schleifer, A. and Vishny, R. (1992). Liquidation values and debt capacity: A market equilibrium approach. *Journal of Finance, 47:* 1343-1366.

Silvester, J. (1995). *How to Start, Finance and Operate Your Own Business.* Seacaucus, NJ: Carol Publishing Group.

Stulz, R. (1990). Managerial discretion and optimal financing policies. *Journal of Financial Economics, 26*: 3-15.

Williamson, O. (1988). Corporate finance and corporate governance. *Journal of Finance, 43:* 567-591.

World Wide Web Resources

Small Business/Financing

<http://www.edgeonline.com>. Information for small businesses on financing, legal issues, marketing, sales, etc.

<http://www.isquare.com>. Information on how to start and operate a successful business.

<http://www.fed.org>. A Web site of the Foundation for Enterprise Development, providing information on equity compensation, and employee compensation strategies for entrepreneurs and executives.

<http://www.webcom.com/seaquest/sbrc/welcome.html>. This site provides a collection of articles and links of interest to current and prospective business owners.

Chapter 14

Eximbank (1997a). *General Information.* Washington, DC: U.S. Government Printing Office.

Eximbank (1997b). *Small Business Information.* Washington, DC: U.S. Government Printing Office.

Eximbank (1997c). *Working Capital Guarantee Program.* Washington, DC: U.S. Government Printing Office.

U.S. Department of Commerce (1990). *A Basic Guide to Exporting from the United States.* Lincolnwood, IL: NTC Books.

Wells, F. and Dulat, K. (1996). *Exporting from Start to Finance.* New York: McGraw-Hill.

World Wide Web Resources

Eximbank and Programs

<http://www.exim.gov>. Export-Import Bank of the United States—programs, projects, and other related information.

<http://www.exim.gov/mprograms.html>. A general overview of Eximbank's programs.

<http://www.exim.gov./minsprog.html>. Information on export credit insurance program.

<http://www.usda.gov:80/news/releases>. Web site of the U.S. Department of Agriculture—provides information on agricultural trade, marketing, inspection, etc.

<http://www.sbaonline.sba.gov/OIT>. Home page of the Small Business Administration—Office of International trade. It provides valuable information for small business exporters.

Chapter 15

Anonymous (1995). $24.8 million penalty paid by Lockheed. *The New York Times,* January 28, Section 1, 35.

Bernet, B. (1991). The Foreign Sales Corporation Act: Export incentive for U.S. business. *The International Lawyer, 25*(1): 223-249.

General Agreement on Tariffs and Trade (GATT) (1977). Basic Instruments and Selected documents. No. 23. Geneva: GATT(DOC L/4422).

Hall, C. (1994). Foreign Corrupt Practices Act: A competitive disadvantage, but for how long? *Tulane Journal of International and Comparative Law, 2:* 300-315.

Impert, J. (1990). A program for compliance with the Foreign Corrupt Practices Act and foreign restrictions on the use of sales agents. *The International Lawyer, 24*(4): 45-66.

Johns, R. (1988). *Colonial Trade and International Exchange.* London: Pinter Publishers.

Kramer, J., Pope T., and Phillips, L. (1997). *Federal Taxation in 1997: Corporations, Partnerships, Estates and Trusts.* Englewood Cliffs, NJ: Prentice-Hall.

Lipman, J. (1990). Young and Rubicam pleads guilty to settle Jamaica case. *The Wall Street Journal,* February 12, 5.

Mandell, M. (1995). Offshore savings. *World Trade, 8*(3): 26-32.

Marcus, S. and Hoff-Patrinas, K. (1984). Foreign sales corporations: A new form of tax relief for exporters. *Syracuse Journal of International Law and Commerce, 11:* 551-565.

Moskowitz, D. (1996). Lingering cold war legacies. *International Business, 9*(7): 40-41.

The Political Risk Services (PRS) Group (1998). *Political Risk Services.* New York: The PRS Group.

Shenefield, J. and Stelzer, I. (1993). *The Antitrust Laws.* Washington, DC: The American Enterprise Institute.

Stenger, G. (1984). The Development of American Export Control Legislation. *Wisconsin International Law Journal,* 6(1):1: 1-5.
Stein, H. and Foss, M. (1992). *An Illustrated Guide to the U.S. Economy,* Washington, DC: The American Enterprise Institute.
Wilson, C. (1989). Delaware's shared FSCs help small business exporters increase their profits. *Business America, 110*(5) (May): 9-10.

World Wide Web Resources

Antitrust/Competition
<http://www.ftc.gov/antitrust.htm>. Web site of the Federal Trade Commission on antitrust or competition matters, such as consumer fraud, misleading advertising, etc.
<http://www.ftc.gov/speeches/starek/starekda.htm>. Speeches on international aspects of antitrust enforcement.
Antitrust Law/Policy
<http://www.antitrust.org>. An online resource on antitrust policy linking economic research, policy, and cases.
<http://www.usdoj.gov/atr>. Web site of the U.S. Department of Justice Antitrust Division, providing public documents and cases.
<http://www.abanet.org/antitrust>. Web site of the American Bar Association, focusing on antitrust law.
Export Administration and Regulations
<http//:www.bxa.doc.gov>. Web site of the Bureau of Export Administration (BXA), U.S. Department of Commerce. The site provides news from the BXA as well as programs, initiatives, and regulations on U.S. exports.
<http://www.bxa.fedworld.gov>. This site provides the text of U.S. export administration regulations.
The Foreign Corrupt Practices Act (FCPA)
<http://www.abanet.org/cle/articles/turza.html>. Web site of the American Bar Association on FCPA—the knowledge standard, due diligence, defenses, etc.
<http://www.usdoj.gov/criminal/fraud/fcpa/FCPA.html>. Web site of the U.S. Department of Justice—Statutes, legislative history, and cases.
Foreign Sales Corporations (FSCs)
<http://www.corpnet.bm/corp_consult/fairway/fsc.html>. Provides basic information of FSCs.
<http://www.intltaxlaw.com/outbound/fsc/frontpage.htm>. U.S. Internal Revenue Code on FSCs and some suggested readings.
<http://teaminfinity.com/~ralph/code/t-26A-1-N111-C.html>. Rules on taxation of FSCs (Subpart C).
Hi Tech Exports to Russia
<http://www.us.net/softwar/gao128.html>. Discussion on sales of high-performance computers to Russia.

International Trade-Foreign Corrupt Practices Act
<http://www.ljx.com/practice/intrade/id_fcpa.html>. Articles on the FCPA and text of the convention on bribery of foreign public officals in international business transactions.
Rules and Treaties
<http://www.lectlaw.com/tint.htm>. Text of antibribery povisions of the FCPA.
<http://oecd.org/daf/cmis/bribery/20novle.htm>. Convention on Combating Bribery of Foreign Officials.

Chapter 16

Rossides, E. (1986). *U.S. Import Trade Regulation.* Washington, DC: The Bureau of National Affairs.

Serko, D. (1985). *Import Practice.* New York: The Practicing Law Institute.

U.S. Department of Commerce (1990). *A Basic Guide to Exporting.* Lincolnwood, IL: NTC Books.

U.S. Department of Commerce (1995). *Importing into the United States.* Rocklin, CA: Prima Publishing.

World Wide Web Resources

Foreign Trade Zones/Customs Tariffs
<http://www.imex/com/naftz/whatare.htm>. Basic information on foreign trade zones.
<http://www.ita.doc.gov/import_admin/records/ftzpage/ftzhome.htm>. This site provides information on foreign trade zones board, i.e., FTZ applications, annual reports, FTZ list.
<http://frwebgate3.access.gpo.gov/cgi-bin>. Federal regulations on customs tariffs.
<http://www.customs.ustreas.gov/index.htm>. Web site of the U.S. Customs Service: importing, exporting, NAFTA information, Harmonized Tariff Schedule, protection of intellectual property rights.
<http://www.usat.gov/reports/gsp/introduction.html>. A site on the U.S. Generalized System of Preferences.

Chapter 17

Buzzanell, P. and Lipton, K. (1995). Whether a pinch or a dash, it adds up to a growing U.S. spice market. *Food Review, 18*(3) (September/December): 1-5.

Deyak, T., Sawyer, W., and Sprinkle, R. (1993). A comparison of demand for imports and exports in Japan and the United States. *Journal of World Trade, 27:* 63-73.

Domberger, S. (1999). *The Contracting Organization: A Strategic Guide to Outsourcing.* London: Oxford University Press.

Ghymn, K. (1983). The relative importance of import decision variables. *Journal of the Academy of Marketing Science, 11:* 304-312.

Lindert, P. and Pugel, T. (1996). *International Economics.* Chicago, IL: Irwin.

Lutz, J. (1994). To import or to protect? Industrialized countries and manufactured products. *Journal of World Trade, 28*(4): 123-145.

Reinhart, C. (1995). Devaluation, relative prices, and international trade: Evidence from developing countries. *IMF Staff Papers, 42*: 290-312.

Sarmad, K. (1989). The determinants of import demand in Pakistan. *World Development, 17:* 1619-1625.

Vanderleest, H. (1994). Planning for international trade show participation: A practitioner's perspective. *SAM Advanced Management Journal, 59*(4) (Autumn): 39-44.

Warner, D. and Kreinin, M. (1983). Determinants of international trade flows. *Review of Economics and Statistics, 65*(1): 19-104.

World Wide Web Resources

Finding Your Partners
<http://www.i-trade.com/dir04/>. Information on trade opportunities and partnerships.
Learn How to Trade
<http://www.i-trade.com/dir01>. U.S. Customs guide to importation and planning for growth.
Trade Articles
<http://www.worldtrademag.com>. Articles of *World Trade* magazine online.
<http://businessweek.com>. Online articles on trade from *Business Week* magazine.
Trade Shows
<http://www.<ciber.bus.msu.edu/busres/tradeshow.htm>. Information on international trade shows and conferences.

Chapter 18

Bovard, J. (1998). Your partner: The Customs Service. *World Trade, 11*(3) (September): 48-49.

Buonafina, M. and Haar, J. (1989). *Import Marketing.* Lexington, MA: Lexington Books.

Rossides, E. (1986). *U.S. Import Trade Regulation.* Washington, DC: The Bureau of National Affairs.

Serko, D. (1985). *Import Practice.* New York: The Practicing Law Institute.

U.S. Department of Commerce (1995). *Importing into the United States.* Rocklin, CA: Prima Publishing.

World Wide Web Resources

Imports/Regulations
<http://www.i-trade.com/dir01>. Provides a guide to importation of goods into the United States.
<http://www.customs.ustreas.gov./impoexpo/impoexpo.html>. U.S. Customs rules and regulations.
<http://www.usitc.gov/tariffs.htm>. Site provides information on tariffs and related matters, including the U.S. Harmonized Tariff Schedule.
<http://www.customs.ustreas.gov/about/about.htm>. Publications of the U.S. Customs—entry of goods, classification and valuation of merchandise.

Chapter 19

U.S. International Trade Commission (USITC) (1995). The Economic effects of antidumping and countervailing duty orders and suspension agreements, Investigation No. 332-344, Publication 2900. Washington, DC: U.S. Government Printing Office.
U.S. International Trade Commission (USITC) (1996a, November). *Antidumping and Countervailing Duty Handbook.* Washington, DC: U.S. Government Printing Office.
U.S. International Trade Commission (USITC) (1996b, January). *Summary of Statutory Provisions Related to Import Relief.* Washington, DC: U.S. Government Printing Office.
U.S. International Trade Commission (1997). Annual report. Washington, DC: U.S. Government Printing Office.
U.S. Trade Representative (USTR). (1997). *Foreign Trade Barriers.* Washington, DC: U.S. Government Printing Office.
U.S. Trade Representative (USTR). (1999). *Foreign Trade Barriers.* Washington, DC: U.S. Government Printing Office.

World Wide Web Resources

Antidumping and Countervailing Duties
<http://www.usitc.gov:80/332S/pub2900D.htm>. International Trade Commission Report on the Economic Effects of Antidumping and Countervailing Duty Orders and Suspension Agreements.
<http://web4.searchbank.com/infotrac/session/621/642/19770046w3>. Judicial review of International Trade Commission determinations.
<http://www.frc.org/heritage/library/categories/trade/bgup261.html>. The Heritage Foundation antidumping laws.
<http://www.ustr.gov/reports/special/factsheets.html>. Fact sheets on Special 301 and Title VII.

Chapter 20

Ashton, T. (1988). *The Industrial Revolutionm 1760-1830.* London: Oxford University Press.

Gadbaw, M. and Richards, T. (Eds.). (1988). *Intellectual Property Rights.* Boulder, CO: Westview Press.

Kinter, E. and Lahr, J. (1983). *An Intellectual Property Law Primer.* New York: Clark Boardman.

Ladas, S. (1975). *Patents, Trademarks and Related Rights: National and International Protection.* Cambridge, MA: Harvard University Press.

Seyoum, B. (1993). Property rights versus public welfare in the protection of trade secrets in developing countries. *The International Trade Journal, 3:* 341-359.

U.S. Congress (1995). Intellectual Property Rights Protection Under Special 301. 102nd Congress Second session.

U.S. Trade Representative (USTR) (1997). *Foreign Trade Barriers,* Washington, DC: U.S. Government Printing Office.

U.S. Trade Representative (USTR) (1999). *Foreign Trade Barriers.* Washington, DC. U.S. Government Printing Office.

Williams, L. (1983). Transfer of technology to developing countries. *Federal Bar News and Journal, 30:* 266-267.

Wolfhard, E. (1991). International trade in intellectual property: The emerging GATT regime. *University of Toronto Faculty of Law Review, 49:* 106-151.

World Wide Web Resources

Intellectual Property: Copyrights, Trademarks, and Patents
<http://www.brint.com/IntellP.htm>. The site includes articles, reports, and other information on intellectual property.

Intellectual Property Mall
 <http://www.ipmall.fplc.edu>. Gives a unique collection of intellectual property resources.

News on Patent, Trademark, Design, and Copyright from Japan
<http://www.okuyama.com/index-2.html>. Information on intellectual property in Japan.

Patents and Intellectual Property
<http://members.tripod.com/~patents2>. Provides important background information on intellectual property and the protection of intellectual property rights outside the United States.

U.S. Intellectual Property for Nonlawyers
<http://www.fplc.edu/tfield/ipbasics.htm>. Information on intellectual property for artists, craftspeople, inventors, and small business owners.

Index

Page numbers followed by the letter "b" indicate boxed material; those followed by the letter "i" indicate illustrations; those followed by the letter "t" indicate tables.